James De Mille

The Living Link

A Novel

James De Mille

The Living Link
A Novel

ISBN/EAN: 9783337029609

Printed in Europe, USA, Canada, Australia, Japan

Cover: Foto ©Thomas Meinert / pixelio.de

More available books at **www.hansebooks.com**

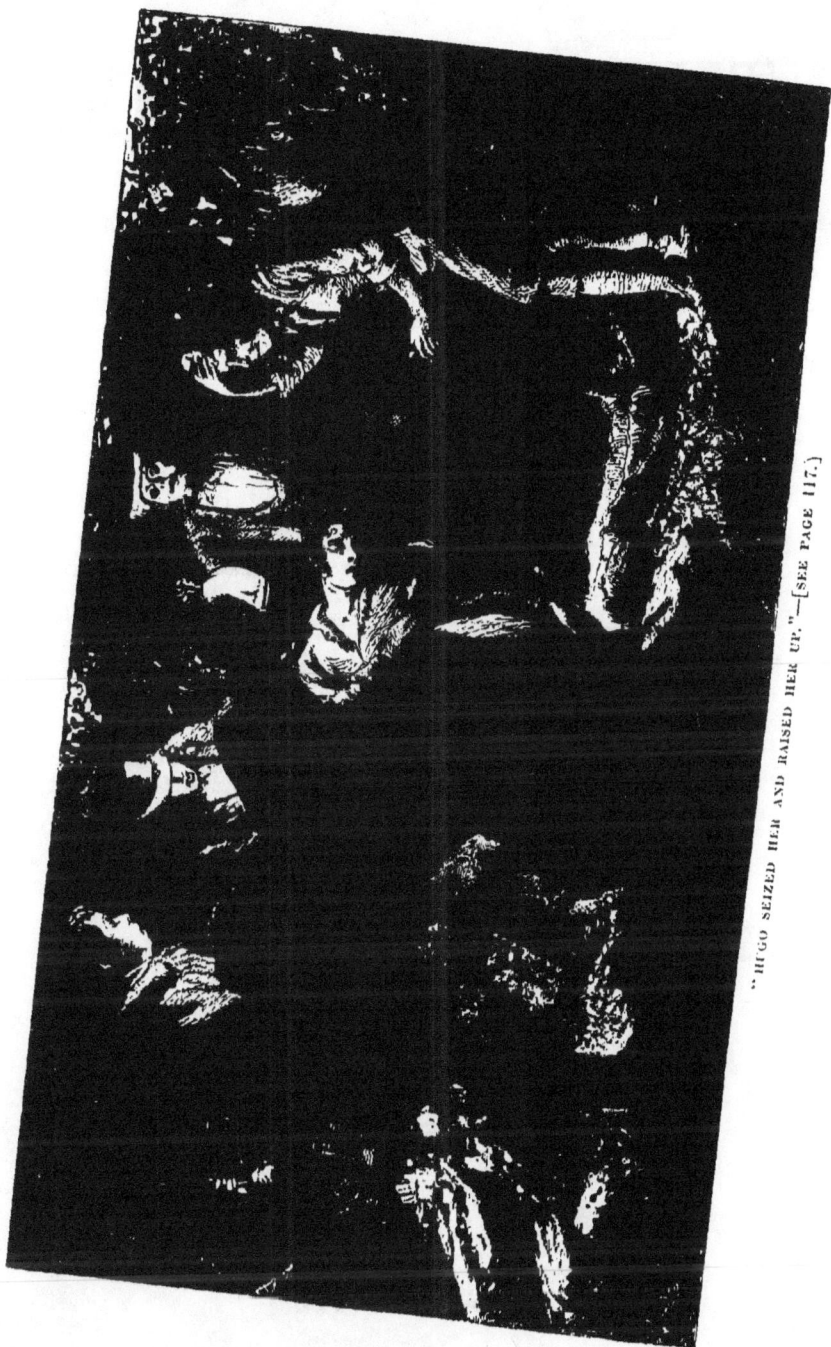

"HUGO SEIZED HER AND RAISED HER UP."—[SEE PAGE 117.]

THE LIVING LINK.

A Novel.

By JAMES DE MILLE,

AUTHOR OF

"THE DODGE CLUB," "CORD AND CREESE," "THE CRYPTOGRAM," "THE AMERICAN
BARON," &c., &c.

ILLUSTRATED BY W. L. SHEPPARD.

NEW YORK:

HARPER & BROTHERS, PUBLISHERS,

FRANKLIN SQUARE.

1874.

By Prof. JAMES DE MILLE.

THE DODGE CLUB; or, Italy in 1859. Illustrated. 8vo, Paper, 75 cents; Cloth, $1 25.

CORD AND CREESE. A Novel. Illustrated. 8vo, Paper, 75 cents; Cloth, $1 25.

THE CRYPTOGRAM. A Novel. Illustrated. 8vo, Paper, $1 50; Cloth, $2 00.

THE AMERICAN BARON. A Novel. Illustrated. 8vo, Paper, $1 00; Cloth, $1 50.

THE LIVING LINK. A Novel. Illustrated. 8vo, Paper, $1 00; Cloth, $1 50.

Published by HARPER & BROTHERS, New York.

☞ *Sent by mail, postage prepaid, to any part of the United States, on receipt of the price.*

THE LIVING LINK.

on a spirited bay came at full speed toward the portico. Arriving there, she stopped abruptly; then leaping lightly down, she flung the reins over the horse's neck, who forthwith galloped away to his stall.

The rider who thus dismounted was a young girl of about eighteen, and of very striking appearance. Her complexion was dark, her hair black, with its rich voluminous folds gathered in great glossy plaits behind. Her eyes were of a deep hazel color, radiant, and full of energetic life. In those eyes there was a certain earnestness of expression, however, deepening down into something that seemed like melancholy, which showed that even in her young life she had experienced sorrow. Her figure was slender and graceful, being well displayed by her close-fitting riding-habit, while a plumed hat completed her equipment, and served to heighten the effect of her beauty.

At her approach a sudden silence had fallen over the company, and they all stood motionless, looking at her as she dismounted.

"Why, what makes you all look at me so strangely?" she asked, in a tone of surprise, throwing a hasty glance over them. "Has any thing happened?"

To this question no answer was given, but each seemed waiting for the other to speak. At length a little thing of about twelve came up, and encircling the new-comer's waist with her arm, looked up with a sorrowful expression, and whispered,

"Edith dearest, Miss Plympton wants to see you."

The silence and ominous looks of the others, and the whispered words of the little girl, together with her mournful face, increased the surprise and anxiety of Edith. She looked with a strange air of apprehension over the company.

"What is it?" she asked, hurriedly. "Something has happened. Do any of you know? What is it?"

She spoke breathlessly, and her eyes once more wandered with anxious inquiry over all of them. But no one spoke, for, whatever it was, they felt the news to be serious —something, in fact, which could not well be communicated by themselves. Once more Edith repeated her question, and finding that

CHAPTER I.
A TERRIBLE SECRET.

On a pleasant evening in the month of May, 1840, a group of young ladies might have been seen on the portico of Plympton Terrace, a fashionable boarding-school near Derwentwater. They all moved about with those effusive demonstrations so characteristic of young girls; but on this occasion there was a general hush among them, which evidently arose from some unusual cause. As they walked up and down arm in arm, or with arms entwined, or with clasped hands, as young girls will, they talked in low earnest tones over some one engrossing subject, or occasionally gathered in little knots to debate some point, in which, while each offered a different opinion, all were oppressed by one common sadness

While they were thus engaged there arose in the distance the sound of a rapidly galloping horse. At once all the murmur of conversation died out, and the company stood in silence awaiting the new-comer. They did not have to wait long. Out from a place where the avenue wound amidst groves and thickets a young girl mounted no answer was forth-coming, her impatience allowed her to wait no longer; and so, gathering up her long skirts in one hand and holding her whip in the other, she hurried into the house to see Miss Plympton.

Miss Plympton's room was on the second floor, and that lady herself was seated by the window as Edith entered. In the young girl's face there was now a deeper anxiety, and seating herself near the centre-table, she looked inquiringly at Miss Plympton.

The latter regarded her for some moments in silence.

"Did you wish to see me, auntie dear?" said Edith.

Miss Plympton sighed.

"Yes," she said, slowly; "but, my poor darling Edie, I hardly know how to say to you what I have to say. I—I—do you think you can bear to hear it, dear?"

At this Edith looked more disturbed than ever; and placing her elbow on the centre-table, she leaned her cheek upon her hand, and fixed her melancholy eyes upon Miss Plympton. Her heart throbbed painfully, and the hand against which her head leaned trembled visibly. But these signs of agitation did not serve to lessen the emotion of the other; on the contrary, she seemed more distressed, and quite at a loss how to proceed.

"Edith," said she at last, "my child, you know how tenderly I love you. I have always tried to be a mother to you, and to save you from all sorrow; but now my love and care are all useless, for the sorrow has come, and I do not know any way by which I can break bad news to—to—a—a bereaved heart."

She spoke in a tremulous voice and with frequent pauses.

"Bereaved!" exclaimed Edith, with white lips. "Oh, auntie! Bereaved! Is it that? Oh, tell me all. Don't keep me in suspense. Let me know the worst."

Miss Plympton looked still more troubled. "I—I—don't know what to say," she faltered.

"You mean *death!*" cried Edith, in an excited voice; "and oh! I needn't ask who. There's only one—only one. I had only one—only one—and now—he is—gone!"

"Gone," repeated Miss Plympton, mechanically, and she said no more; for in the presence of Edith's grief, and of other facts which had yet to be disclosed—facts which would reveal to this innocent girl something worse than even bereavement—words were useless, and she could find nothing to say. Her hand wandered through the folds of her dress, and at length she drew forth a black-edged letter, at which she gazed in an abstracted way.

"Let me see it," cried Edith, hurriedly and eagerly; and before Miss Plympton could prevent her, or even imagine what she was about, she darted forward and snatched the letter from her hand. Then she tore it open and read it breathlessly. The letter was very short, and was written in a stiff, constrained hand. It was as follows:

"DALTON HALL, *May* 6, 1840.

"MADAME,—It is my painful duty to communicate to you the death of Frederick Dalton, Esq., of Dalton Hall, who died at Hobart Town, Van Diemen's Land, on the 2d of December, 1839. I beg that you will impart this intelligence to Miss Dalton, for as she is now of age, she may wish to return to Dalton Hall.

"I remain, madame,
"Your most obedient servant,
"JOHN WIGGINS.
"MISS PLYMPTON, *Plympton Terrace.*"

Of this letter Edith took in the meaning of the first three lines only. Then it dropped from her trembling hands, and sinking into a chair, she burst into a torrent of tears. Miss Plympton regarded her with a face full of anxiety, and for some moments Edith wept without restraint; but at length, when the first outburst of grief was past, she picked up the letter once more and read it over and over.

Deep as Edith's grief evidently was, this bereavement was not, after all, so sore a blow as it might have been under other circumstances. For this father whom she had lost was virtually a stranger. Losing her mother at the age of eight, she had lived ever since with Miss Plympton, and during this time her father had never seen her, nor even written to her. Once or twice she had written to him a pretty childish letter, but he had never deigned any reply. If in that unknown nature there had been any thing of a father's love, no possible hint had ever been given of it. Of her strange isolation she was never forgetful, and she felt it most keenly during the summer holidays, when all her companions had gone to their homes. At such times she brooded much over her loneliness, and out of this feeling there arose a hope, which she never ceased to cherish, that the time would come when she might join her father, and live with him wherever he might be, and set herself to the task of winning his affections.

She had always understood that her father had been living in the East since her mother's death. The only communication which she had with him was indirect, and consisted of business letters which his English agent wrote to Miss Plympton. These were never any thing more than short, formal notes. Such neglect was keenly felt, and Edith, unwilling to blame her father altogether, tried to make some one else responsible for it. As she knew of no other human being who had any connection with her father except this agent, she brought herself gradually to look upon him as the cause of her father's coldness, and so at length came to regard him with a hatred that was unreasoning and intense. She considered him her father's evil genius, and believed him to be somehow at the bottom of the troubles of her life. Thus every year this man, John Wiggins, grew more hateful, and she accustomed herself to think of him as an evil fiend, a Mephistopheles, by whose crafty wiles her father's heart had been estranged from her. Such, then, was the nature of Edith's bereavement; and as she mourned over it she did not mourn so much over the reality as over her vanished hope. He was gone, and with him was gone the expectation of meeting him and winning his affection. She would never see him—never be able to tell how she loved him, and hear him say with a father's voice that he loved his child!

These thoughts and feelings overwhelmed Edith even as she held the letter in her hand for a new perusal, and she read it over and over without attaching any meaning to the words. At length her attention was arrested by one statement in that short letter which had hitherto escaped her notice. This was the name of the place where her father's death had occurred—Van Diemen's Land.

"I don't understand this," said she. "What is the meaning of this—Van Diemen's Land? I did not know that poor papa had ever left India."

Miss Plympton made no reply to this for some time, but looked more troubled than ever.

"What does it mean," asked Edith again —"this Hobart Town, Van Diemen's Land? What does it mean?"

"Well, dear," said Miss Plympton, in a strangely gentle and mournful voice, "you have never known much about your poor father, and you have never known exactly where he has been living. He did not live in India, dear; he never lived in India. He lived in—in—Van Diemen's Land."

Miss Plympton's tone and look affected Edith very unpleasantly. The mystery about her father seemed to grow darker, and to assume something of an ill-omened character. The name also—Van Diemen's Land—served to heighten her dark apprehensions; and this discovery that she had known even less than she supposed about her father made it seem as though the knowledge that had thus been hidden could not but be painful.

"What do you mean?" she asked again; and her voice died down to a whisper through the vague fears that had been awakened. "I thought that poor papa lived in India— that he held some office under government."

"I know that you believed so," said Miss Plympton, regarding Edith with a look that was full of pity and mournful sympathy.

"That was what I gave out. None of the girls have ever suspected the truth. No one knows whose daughter you really are. They do not suspect that your father was Dalton of Dalton Hall. They think that he was an Indian resident in the Company's service. Yes, I have kept the secret well, dear—the secret that I promised your dear mother on her death-bed to keep from all the world, and from you, darling, till the time should come for you to know. And often and often, dear, have I thought of this moment, and tried to prepare for it; but now, since it has come, I am worse than unprepared. But preparations are of no use, for oh, my darling, my own Edith, I must speak, if I speak at all, from my heart."

These words were spoken by Miss Plympton in a broken, disconnected, and almost incoherent manner. She stopped abruptly, and seemed overcome by strong agitation. Edith, on her part, looked at her in equal agitation, wondering at her display of emotion, and terrified at the dark significance of her words. For from those words she learned this much already—that her father had been living in Van Diemen's Land, a penal colony; that around him had been a dark secret which had been kept from her most carefully; that her parentage had been concealed most scrupulously from the knowledge of her school-mates; and that this secret which had been so guarded was even now overwhelming Miss Plympton so that she shrunk from communicating it. All this served to fill the mind of Edith with terrible presentiments, and the mystery which had hitherto surrounded her father seemed now about to result in a revelation more terrible than the mystery itself.

After some time Miss Plympton rose, and drawing her chair nearer, sat down in front of Edith, and took both her hands.

"My poor darling Edith," said she, in pitying tones, "I am anxious for you. You are not strong enough for this. Your hands are damp and cold. You are trembling. I would not have brought up this subject now, but I have been thinking that the time has come for telling you all. But I'm afraid it will be too much for you. You have already enough to bear without having this in addition. You are too weak."

Edith shook her head.

"Can you bear it?" asked Miss Plympton, anxiously, "this that I wish to tell you? Perhaps I had better defer it."

"No," said Edith, in a forced voice. "No —now—now—tell me now. I can bear whatever it is better than any horrible suspense."

Miss Plympton sighed, and leaning forward, she kissed the pale forehead of the young girl. Then, after a little further delay, during which she seemed to be collecting her thoughts, she began:

"I was governess once, Edith dearest, in your dear mamma's family. She was quite a little thing then. All the rest were harsh, and treated me like a slave; but she was like an angel, and made me feel the only real happiness I knew in all those dreary days. I loved her dearly for her gentle and noble nature. I loved her always, and I still love her memory; and I love you as I loved her, and for her sake. And when she gave you to me, on her death-bed, I promised her that I would be a mother to you, dear. You have never known how much I love you—for I am not demonstrative—but I do love you, my own Edith, most dearly, and I would spare you this if I could. But, after all, it is a thing which you must know some time, and before very long—the sooner the better."

"I wish to know it now," said Edith, as Miss Plympton hesitated, speaking in a constrained voice, the result of the strong pressure which she was putting on her feelings —"now," she repeated. "I can not wait. I must know all to-day. What was it? Was it—crime?"

"The charge that was against him," said Miss Plympton, "involved crime. But, my darling, you must remember always that an accusation is not the same as a fact, even though men believe it; yes, even though the law may condemn the accused, and the innocent may suffer. Edith Dalton," she continued, with solemn earnestness, "I believe that your father was as innocent as you are. Remember that! Cling to that! Never give up that belief, no matter what you may hear. There was too much haste and blind passion and prejudice in that court where he was tried, and appearances were dark, and there was foul treachery somewhere; and so it was that Frederick Dalton was done to ruin and his wife done to death. And now, my darling, you have to make yourself acquainted not with a father's crimes, but with a father's sufferings. You are old enough now to hear that story, and you have sufficient independence of character to judge for yourself, dear. There is no reason why you should be overwhelmed when you hear it—unless, indeed, you are overcome by pity for the innocent and indignation against his judges. Even if society considers your father's name a stained and dishonored one, there is no reason why his daughter should feel shame, for you may take your stand on his own declaration of innocence, and hold up your head proudly before the world."

Miss Plympton spoke this with vehement emotion, and her words brought some consolation to Edith. The horrible thought that had at first come was that her father had been a convict in some penal settlement, but this solemn assurance of his innocence mitigated the horror of the thought, and changed it into pity. She said not a

word, however, for her feelings were still too strong, nor could she find voice for any words. She sat, therefore, in silence, and waited for Miss Plympton to tell the whole story.

Miss Plympton surveyed Edith anxiously for a few moments, and then rising, went over to an escritoire. This she unlocked, and taking from it a parcel, she returned to her seat.

"I am not going to tell you the story," said she. "I can not bear to recall it. It is all here, and you may read it for yourself. It was all public ten years ago, and in this package are the reports of the trial. I have read them over so often that I almost know them by heart; and I know, too, the haste of that trial, and the looseness of that evidence. I have marked it in places—for your eyes only, dearest—for I prepared it for you, to be handed to you in case of my death. My life, however, has been preserved, and I now give this into your own hands. You must take it to your own room, and read it all over by yourself. You will learn there all that the world believes about your father, and will see in his own words what he says about himself. And for my part, even if the testimony were far stronger, I would still take the word of Frederick Dalton!"

Miss Plympton held out the parcel, and Edith took it, though she was scarce conscious of the act. An awful foreboding of calamity, the mysterious shadow of her father's fate, descended over her soul. She was unconscious of the kiss which Miss Plympton gave her; nor was she conscious of any thing till she found herself seated at a table in her own room, with the door locked, and the package lying on the table before her. She let it lie there for a few moments, for her agitation was excessive, and she dreaded to open it; but at length she mastered her feelings, and began to undo the strings.

The contents of the parcel consisted of sheets of paper, upon which were pasted columns of printed matter cut from some newspaper. It was the report of the trial of Frederick Dalton, upon charges which ten years before had filled the public mind with horror and curiosity. In those days the most cursory reader who took up the report came to the work with a mind full of vivid interest and breathless suspense; but that report now lay before the eyes of a far different reader—one who was animated by feelings far more intense, since it was the daughter of the accused herself. That daughter also was one who hitherto had lived in an atmosphere of innocence, purity, and love, one who shrank in abhorrence from all that was base or vile; and this was the one before whose eyes was now placed the horrible record that had been made up before the world against her father's name.

The printed columns were pasted in such

a way that a wide margin was left, which was covered with notes in Miss Plympton's writing. To give any thing like a detailed account of this report, with the annotations, is out of the question, nor will any thing be necessary beyond a general summary of the facts therein stated.

CHAPTER II.
THE CONTENTS OF THE MANUSCRIPT.

ON the date indicated in the report, then, the city of Liverpool and the whole country were agitated by the news of a terrible murder. On the road-side near Everton the dead body of a Mr. Henderson, an eminent banker, had been found, not far from his own residence. The discovery had been made at about eleven o'clock in the evening by some passers-by. Upon examination a wound was found in the back of the head which had been caused by a bullet. His watch and purse were still in their places, but his pocket-book was gone. Clasped in one of the hands was a newspaper, on the blank margin of which were some red letters, rudely traced, and looking as though they had been written with blood. The letters were these:

"DALTON SHOT ME BEC—"

It was evident that the writer intended to write the word "because," and give the reason why he had been shot, but that his strength had failed in the middle of the word.

A closer search revealed some other things. One was a small stick, the point of which was reddened with a substance which microscopic examination afterward showed to be blood. The other was a scarf-pin made of gold, the head of which consisted of a Maltese cross, of very rich and elegant design. In the middle was black enamel inclosed by a richly chased gold border, and at the intersection of the bars was a small diamond of great splendor. If this cross belonged to the murderer it had doubtless become loosened, and fallen out while he was stooping over his victim, and the loss had not been noticed in the excitement of the occasion.

At the coroner's inquest various important circumstances were brought to light. The fact that his watch and purse remained made it plain that it was not a case of common highway robbery, and the loss of the pocket-book showed that the deed was prompted by a desire for something more than ordinary plunder. Proceeding from this, various circumstances arose which, in addition to the terrible accusation traced in blood, tended to throw suspicion upon Frederick Dalton.

It came out that on the morning of that very day Mr. Henderson had discovered a check for two thousand pounds that had been forged in his name. Being a very choleric man, he felt more than the anger which is natural under such circumstances, and vowed vengeance to the uttermost upon the forger. That same morning Mr. Frederick Dalton came to see him, and was shown into his private office. He had just arrived in the city, and had come on purpose to pay this visit. The interview was a protracted one, and the clerks outside heard the voice of Mr. Henderson in a very high key, and in a strain of what sounded like angry menace and denunciations of vengeance, though they could not make out any words. At last the office door opened, and Dalton came out. He was very pale, and much agitated. One of the clerks heard him say, in a low voice, "Only one day—till this time to-morrow." Whereupon Mr. Henderson roared out in a loud voice, which all the clerks heard, "No, Sir! Not one day, not one hour, if I die for it!"

Upon this Dalton walked away, looking paler and more agitated than ever.

In the course of the day Mr. Henderson told his confidential clerk that the check had just been used by Dalton, who, however, denied that he was the forger; that the visit of Dalton professed to be on behalf of the guilty party, whom he wished to screen. Dalton had refused to give the culprit's name, and offered to pay the amount of the check, or any additional sum whatever, if no proceedings were taken. This, however, Mr. Henderson refused, and in his indignation charged Dalton himself with the crime. Under these circumstances the interview had terminated.

Thus the evidence against Dalton was the forged check, the clerks' reports concerning the exciting interview with Mr. Henderson, the awful accusation of the deceased himself, written in his own blood, together with the Maltese cross, which was believed to belong to Dalton. The arrest of Dalton had been made at the earliest possible moment; and at the trial these were the things which were made use of against him by the prosecution. By energetic efforts discovery was made of a jeweler who recognized the Maltese cross as his own work, and swore that he had made it for Frederick Dalton, in accordance with a special design furnished him by that gentleman. The design had been kept in his order-book ever since, and was produced by him in court. Thus the testimony of the jeweler and the order-book served to fix the ownership of the Maltese cross upon Dalton in such a way that it corroborated and confirmed all the other testimony.

On the other hand, the defense of Dalton took up all these points. In the first place, it was shown that in his case there was no conceivable temptation that could have led to the commission of such a crime. He was a man of great wealth, possessed of a fine estate, and free from all pecuniary embarrassments. He was not what was called a sporting man, and therefore could not have secretly accumulated debts while appearing rich. It was shown, also, that his character was stainless; that he was essentially a domestic man, living quietly at Dalton Hall with his wife and child, and therefore, from his worldly means as well as from his personal character and surroundings, it was morally impossible for him to have forged the check.

With reference to the interview with Mr. Henderson, it was maintained that it arose, as he himself said, from a desire to shield the real culprit, whom he knew, and for whom he felt a strong and unusual regard. Who this culprit was the defense did not assert, nor could they imagine, though they tried every possible way of finding him out. Whoever he was, he appeared to be the only one who could have had a motive strong enough for the murder of Mr. Henderson. The unknown assassin had evidently done the deed so as to obtain possession of the forged check, and prevent its being used against him. In this he was unsuccessful, since the check had already been intrusted to the hands of others; but the aim of the assassin was sufficiently evident.

Again, as to the writing in blood, a vigorous effort was made to show that this was a conspiracy against an innocent man. It was argued that Mr. Henderson did not write it at all; and efforts were made to prove that the wound in his head must have caused instantaneous death. He himself, therefore, could not have written it, but it must have been the work either of some one who was plotting against Dalton, or who was eager to divert suspicion from himself.

The testimony of the Maltese cross was met by counter-testimony to the effect that Dalton had never worn such an ornament. His servants all swore that they had never seen it before. Mr. Henderson's clerks also swore that Mr. Dalton wore no pin at all on that morning of the interview.

And, finally, an effort was made to prove an *alibi*. It was shown that Dalton's occupation of his time during that evening could be accounted for with the exception of one hour. Witnesses were produced from the hotel where he put up who swore that he had been there until eight o'clock in the evening, when he left, returning at nine. An hour, therefore, remained to be accounted for. As to this hour—on the one hand, it seemed hardly sufficient for the deed, but yet it was certainly possible for him to have done it within that time; and thus it remained for the defense to account for that hour. For this purpose a note was produced,

which was scribbled in pencil and addressed to John Wiggins, Esq.

It was as follows:

"DEAR WIGGINS,—I have been here ever since eight, and am tired of waiting. Come to my room as soon as you get back. I'll be there. Yours, F. DALTON."

Mr. John Wiggins testified that he had made an appointment to meet Dalton at the hour mentioned in the note, but had been detained on business until late. He had found this on his return thrust under the office door. On going to see him the following morning he had learned of his arrest.

This note and the testimony of Wiggins were felt to bear strongly in Dalton's favor. If the accused had really been waiting at the office, as the note stated, then clearly he could not have followed on Mr. Henderson's track to Everton. The force of this weighed more than any thing else with the court; the summing up of the judge also bore strongly toward an acquittal; and, consequently, Dalton was declared not guilty.

But the acquittal on this first charge did not at all secure the escape of Dalton from danger. Another charge, which had been interwoven with the first, still impended over him, and no sooner was he declared free of murder than he was arrested on the charge of forgery, and remanded to prison to await his trial on that accusation.

Now during the whole course of the trial the public mind had been intensely excited; all men were eager that vengeance should fall on some one, and at the outset had made up their minds that Dalton was guilty. The verdict of acquittal created deep and widespread dissatisfaction, for it seemed as though justice had been cheated of a victim. When, therefore, the trial for forgery came on, there weighed against Dalton all the infamy that had been accumulating against him during the trial for murder. Had this trial stood alone, the prisoner's counsel might have successfully pleaded his high character, as well as his wealth, against this charge, and shown that it was false because it was morally impossible. But this was no longer of avail, and in the public mind Frederick Dalton was deemed only a desperate murderer, whose good reputation was merely the result of life-long hypocrisy, and whose character was but an empty name.

And so in this trial it was shown that Dalton had first put forth the forged check, and afterward learning that it was discovered prematurely, had hurried to Liverpool so as to get it back from Mr. Henderson. His asserted wealth was not believed in. Efforts were made to show that he had been connected with men of desperate fortunes, and had himself been perhaps betting heavily;

THE LIVING LINK.

and all the arts which are usually employed by unscrupulous or excited advocates to crush an accused man were freely put forth. Experts were brought from London to examine Dalton's handwriting, and compare it with that of the forged check; and these men, yielding to the common prejudice, gave it as their opinion that he was, or *might have been* (!), the author of the forgery.

But all this was as nothing when compared with the injury which Dalton himself did to his own cause by the course which he chose to adopt. Contenting himself with the simple assertion of his innocence, he refused to give the name of the guilty man, or to say any thing that might lead to his discovery. Actuated by a lofty sense of honor, a chivalrous sentiment of loyalty and friendship, he kept the secret with obstinate fidelity; and the almost frantic appeals of his counsel, who saw in the discovery of the real offender the only chance for the escape of the accused, and who used every possible argument to shake his resolve, availed not in the slightest degree to shake his firmness. They employed detectives, and instituted inquiries in all directions in the endeavor to find out who might be this friend for whom Dalton was willing to risk honor and life; but their search was completely baffled. Dalton's silence was therefore taken as an evidence of guilt, and his refusal to confess on a friend was regarded as a silly attempt to excite public sympathy. When the counsel ventured to bring this forward to the jury, and tried to portray Dalton as a man who chose rather to suffer than to say that which might bring a friend to destruction, it was regarded as a wild, Quixotic, and maudlin piece of sentimentalism on the part of said counsel, and was treated by the prosecution with unspeakable scorn and ridicule. Under such circumstances the result was inevitable: Frederick Dalton was declared guilty, and sentenced to transportation for life.

Among the notes which had been written by Miss Plympton, Edith was very forcibly struck by some which referred to John Wiggins.

"Who is this J. W.?" was written in one place. "How did F. D. become acquainted with him?"

In another place, where Wiggins gave his testimony about the note, was written: "Where was J. W. during that hour? Had he gone to Everton himself?"

And again: "J. W. was the friend of F. D., and wished to save him. Might he not have done more?"

Again: "Mark well! J. W. is a Liverpool man. H. was a Liverpool man. Had F. D. ever heard of even the name of H. before the forgery? What was the nature of the dealings between F. D. and J. W.?"

Again, when Dalton's silence was so sharp-

ly commented on and urged as a proof of his guilt, there occurred the following: "If F. D. was silent, why did not J. W. open his mouth? Must he not have known at least something? Could he not have set the authorities upon the track of the real criminal, and thus have saved F. D.?"

Again: "The Maltese cross did not belong to Dalton. He had ordered it to be made. For whom? Was it not for this same friend for whom he was now suffering? Was not this friend the murderer? Has he not thrown suspicion upon F. D. by that writing in blood? The same one who committed the murder wrote the false charge, and left the Maltese cross."

Other notes of a similar character occurred in various places, but those which impressed Edith most were the following:

"F. D. was evidently betrayed by his false friend. Was not that false friend the real murderer? Did he not contrive to throw on F. D. the suspicion of the murder? Might not the forgery itself from the very beginning have been part of a plan to ruin F. D.? But why ruin him? Evidently to gain some benefit. Now who has been most benefited by the ruin of F. D.? Whoever he is, must not he be the murderer and the false friend?"

Again, a little further on: "Has any one gained any thing from the ruin of F. D. but J. W.? Has not J. W. ever since had control of the Dalton property? Is he not rich now? Has not the ruin of F. D. made the fortune of J. W.?"

Such was the substance of the papers which Edith perused. They were voluminous, and she continued at her task all through that night, her heart all the time filled with a thousand contending emotions.

Before her mind all the time there was the image of her father in the judgment-hall. There he stood, the innocent man, betrayed by his friend, and yet standing there in his simple faith and truth to save that friend, obstinate in his self-sacrificing fidelity, true to faith when the other had proved himself worthless, suffering what can only be suffered by a generous nature as the hours and the days passed and the end approached, and still the traitor allowed him to suffer. And there was the hate and scorn of man, the clamor for vengeance from society, the condemnation of the jury who had prejudged his case, the sneer of the paid advocate, the scoff of the gaping crowd, to whom the plea of *noblesse oblige* and stainless honor and perfect truth seemed only maudlin sentimentality and Quixotic extravagance.

All these thoughts were in Edith's mind as she read, and these feelings swelled within her indignant heart as all the facts in that dread tragedy were slowly revealed one by one. Coming to this task with a mind convinced at the outset of her father's innoeence, she met with not one circumstance that could shake that conviction for a moment. In her own strong feeling she was incapable of understanding how any one could honestly think otherwise. The testimony of adverse witnesses seemed to her perjury, the arguments of the lawyers fiendish malignity, the last summing up of the judge bitter prejudice, and the verdict of the jury a mockery of justice.

CHAPTER III.

THE MOMENTOUS RESOLVE.

EARLY on the following morning Miss Plympton called on Edith, and was shocked to see the changes that had been made in her by that one night. She did not regard so much the pallor of her face, the languor of her manner, and her unelastic step, but rather the new expression that appeared upon her countenance, the thoughtfulness of her brow, the deep and earnest abstraction of her gaze. In that one night she seemed to have stepped from girlhood to maturity. It was as though she had lived through the intervening experience. Years had been crowded into hours. She was no longer a school-girl—she was a woman.

Miss Plympton soon retired, with the promise to come again when Edith should feel stronger. Breakfast was sent up, and taken away untasted, and at noon Miss Plympton once more made her appearance.

"I have been thinking about many things," said Edith, after some preliminary remarks, "and have been trying to recall what I can of my own remembrance of papa. I was only eight years old, but I have a pretty distinct recollection of him, and it has been strengthened by his portrait, which I always have had. Of my mother I have a most vivid remembrance, and I have never forgotten one single circumstance connected with her last illness. I remember your arrival, and my departure from home after all was over. But there is one thing which I should like very much to ask you about. Did none of my mother's relatives come to see her during this time?"

"Your mother's relatives acted very badly indeed, dear. From the first they were carried away by the common belief in your dear father's guilt. Some of them came flying to your mother. She was very ill at the time, and these relatives brought her the first news which she received. It was a severe blow. They were hard-hearted or thoughtless enough to denounce your father to her, and she in her weak state tried to defend him. All this produced so deplorable an effect that she sank rapidly. Her relatives left her in this condition. She tried to be carried to your dear father in his prison,

but could not bear the journey. They took her as far as the gates, but she fainted there, and had to be taken back to the house. So then she gave up. She knew that she was going to die, and wrote to me imploring me to come to her. She wished to intrust you to me. I took you from her arms—"

Miss Plympton paused, and Edith was silent for some time.

"So," said she, in a scarce audible voice, "darling mamma died of a broken heart?"

Miss Plympton said nothing. A long silence followed.

"Had my father no friends," asked Edith, "or no relatives?"

"He had no relatives," said Miss Plympton, "but an only sister. She married a Captain Dudleigh, now Sir Lionel Dudleigh. But it was a very unhappy marriage, for they separated. I never knew the cause; and Captain Dudleigh took it so much to heart that he went abroad. He could not have heard of your father's misfortunes till all was over and it was too late. But in any case I do not see what he could have done, unless he had contrived to shake your father's resolve. As to his wife, I have never heard of her movements, and I think she must have died long ago. Neither she nor her husband is mentioned at the trial. If they had been in England, it seems to me that they would have come forward as witnesses in some way; so I think they were both out of the country. Sir Lionel is alive yet, I think, but he has always lived out of the world. I believe his family troubles destroyed his happiness, and made him somewhat misanthropical. I have sometimes thought in former years that he might make inquiries about you, but he has never done so to my knowledge, though perhaps he has tried without being able to hear where you were. After all, he would scarcely know where to look. On the whole, I consider Sir Lionel the only friend you have, Edith darling, besides myself, and if any trouble should ever arise, he would be the one to whom I should apply for assistance, or at least advice."

Edith listened to this, and made no comment, but after another thoughtful pause she said,

"About this Wiggins—have you ever heard any thing of him since the—the trial?"

Miss Plympton shook her head.

"No," said she, "except from those formal business notes. You have seen them all, and know what they are."

"Have you ever formed any opinion of him more favorable than what you wrote in those notes?"

"I do not think that I wrote any thing more than suspicions or surmises," said Miss Plympton; "and as far as suspicions are concerned, I certainly have not changed my mind. The position which he occupied during the trial, and ever since, excites my suspicions against him. All others suffered; he alone was benefited. And now, too, when all is over, he seems still in his old position—perhaps a better one than ever—the agent of the estates, and assuming to some extent a guardianship over you. At least he gives directions about you, for he says you are to go back to Dalton Hall. But in that he shall find himself mistaken, for I will never allow you to put yourself in his power."

"Have you ever seen him ?" asked Edith.

"No."

She bent down her head, and leaned her forehead on her hand.

"Well," said she, in a low voice, half to herself, "it don't matter; I shall see him soon myself."

"See him yourself!" said Miss Plympton, anxiously. "What do you mean ?"

"Oh, I shall see him soon—when I get to Dalton Hall."

"Dalton Hall!"

"Yes," said Edith, simply, raising her head and looking calmly at Miss Plympton.

"But you are not going to Dalton Hall."

"There is no other place for me," said Edith, sadly. "I am going—I am going as soon as possible."

"Oh no—oh no, darling; you are going to do nothing of the kind," said Miss Plympton. "I can not let you go. We all love you too dearly. This is your home, and I now stand in the place of those whom you have lost. You are never to leave me, Edith dearest."

Edith sighed heavily, and shook her head.

"No," she said, speaking in a low, melancholy voice—"no, I can not stay. I can not meet my friends here again. I am not what I was yesterday. I am changed. It seems as though some heavy weight has come upon me. I must go away, and I have only one place to go to, and that is my father's home."

"My darling," said Miss Plympton, drawing her chair close to Edith, and twining her arms about her, "you must not talk so ; you can not imagine how you distress me. I can not let you go. Do not think of these things. We all love you. Do not imagine that your secret will be discovered. No one shall ever know it. In a few days you yourself will feel different. The consciousness of your father's innocence will make you feel more patient, and the love of all your friends will make your life as happy as ever."

"No," said Edith, "I can not—I can not. You can not imagine how I dread to see the face of any one of them. I shall imagine that they know all; and I can not tell them. They will tease me to tell them my troubles, and it will only worry me. No, for me to stay here is impossible. I would go any where first."

She spoke so firmly and decisively that Miss Plympton forbore to press her further just then.

"At any rate, my darling," said she, "you need not think of Dalton Hall. I can find you other places which will be far more suitable to you in every way. If it distresses you to stay here, I can find a happy home for you, where you can stay till you feel able to return us again."

"There is no place," said Edith, "where I can stay. I do not want to go among strangers, or to strange places. I have a home, and that is the only place that I can go to now. That home is familiar to me. I remember it well. It is where I was born. Dear mamma's room is there, where I used to sit with her and hear her voice. My dear papa and mamma were happy there; and she died there. It has its own associations ; and now since this great sorrow has come, I long to go there. It seems the fittest place for me."

"But, my child," said Miss Plympton, anxiously, "there is one thing that you do not consider. Far be it from me to stand in the way of any of your wishes, especially at a time like this, but it seems to me that a return to Dalton Hall just now is hardly safe."

"Safe !"

Edith spoke in a tone of surprise, and looked inquiringly at Miss Plympton.

"I don't like this John Wiggins," said Miss Plympton, uneasily ; "I am afraid of him."

"But what possible cause can there be of fear ?" asked Edith.

"Oh, I don't know," said Miss Plympton, with a sigh ; "no one can tell. If my suspicions are at all correct, he is a man who might be very dangerous. He has control of all the estates, and—"

"But for that very reason I would go home," said Edith, "if there were no stronger inducement, to do what I can to put an end to his management."

"How could you do any thing with him ?" asked Miss Plympton ; "you so young and inexperienced."

"I don't know," said Edith, simply ; "but the estates are mine, and not his ; and Dalton Hall is mine ; and if I am the owner, surely I ought to have some power. There are other agents in the world, and other lawyers. They can help me, if I wish help. We are not living in the Middle Ages, when some one could seize one's property by the strong hand and keep it. There is law in the country, and Wiggins is subject to it."

"Oh, my child," said Miss Plympton, anxiously, "I am terrified at the very thought of your being in that man's power. You can not tell what things are possible ; and though there is law, as you say, yet it does not always happen that one can get justice."

"That I know, or ought to know," said

Edith, iu a mournful voice; "I have learned that this past night only too well."

"It seems to me," said Miss Plympton, with the same anxiety in her voice, "that to return to Dalton Hall will be to put yourself in some way into his power. If he is really the unscrupulous, crafty, and scheming man that I have suspected him to be, he will not find it difficult to weave some plot around you which may endanger your whole life. There is no safety in being near that man. Be mistress of Dalton Hall, but do not go there till you have driven him away. It seems by his last letters as though he is living there now, and if you go there you will find yourself in some sense under his control."

"Well," said Edith, "I do not doubt his willingness to injure me if he can, or to weave a plot which shall ruin me; but, after all, such a thing takes time. He can not ruin me in one day, or in one week, and so I think I can return to Dalton Hall in safety, and be secure for a few days at least."

Miss Plympton made some further objections, but the vague fears to which she gave expression met with no response from Edith, who looked upon her journey home in a very sober and commonplace light, and refused to let her imagination terrify her. Her argument that Wiggins would require time to injure her was not easy to answer, and gradually Miss Plympton found herself forced to yield to Edith's determination. In fact, there was much in that resolve which was highly natural. Edith, in the first place, could not bear to resume her intimacy with her school-mates, for reasons which she had stated already; and, in addition to this, she had a strong and irresistible longing to go to the only place that was now her home. There she hoped to find peace, and gain consolation in the midst of the scenes of her childhood and the memories of her parents. These were her chief motives for action now; but in addition to these she had others. The chief was a strong desire to dismiss Wiggins from his post of agent.

The detestation which she had already conceived for this man has been noticed in a previous chapter. It had grown during past years out of a habit of her mind to associate with him the apparent alienation of her father. But now, since her father's past life was explained, this John Wiggins appeared in a new light. The dark suggestions of Miss Plympton, her suspicions as to his character and motives, had sunk deep into the soul of Edith, and taken root there. She had not yet been able to bring herself to think that this John Wiggins was himself the treacherous friend, but she was on the high-road to that belief, and already had advanced far enough to feel convinced that Wiggins could have at least saved her father if he had chosen. One thing, however, was evident to all the

world, and that was what Miss Plympton laid so much stress on, the fact that he had profited by her father's ruin, and had won gold and influence and position out of her father's tears and agonies and death. And so, while she longed to go home for her own consolation, there also arose within her another motive to draw her there—the desire to see this Wiggius, to confront him, to talk to him face to face, to drive him out from the Dalton estates, and if she could not vindicate her father's memory, at least put an end to the triumph of one of his false friends.

The result of this interview was, then, that Edith should return to Dalton Hall; and as she was unwilling to wait, she decided to leave in two days. Miss Plympton was to go with her.

"And now," said Miss Plympton, "we must write at once and give notice of your coming."

"Write?" said Edith, coldly, "to whom?"

"Why, to—to Wiggins, I suppose," said Miss Plympton, with some hesitation.

"I refuse to recognize Wiggins," said Edith. "I will not communicate with him in any way. My first act shall be to dismiss him."

"But you must send some notice to some one; you must have some preparations made."

"Oh, I shall not need any elaborate preparations; a room will be sufficient. I should not wish to encounter the greetings of this man, or see him complacently take credit to himself for his attentions to me—and his preparations. No; I shall go and take things as I find them, and I should prefer to go without notice."

At this Miss Plympton seemed a little more uneasy than before, and made further efforts to change Edith's decision, but in vain. She was, in fact, more perplexed at Edith herself than at any other thing; for this one who but a day before had been a gentle, tractable, docile, gay, light-hearted girl had suddenly started up into a stern, self-willed woman, with a dauntless spirit and inflexible resolve.

"There is only one more thing that I have to mention," said Edith, as Miss Plympton rose to go. "It is a favor that I have to ask of you. It is this;" and she laid her hand on the papers of the report, which were lying rolled up in a parcel on the table. "Have you any further use for this? Will you let me keep it?"

"The need that I had for it," said Miss Plympton, "was over when I gave it to you. I prepared it for you, and preserved it for you, and now that you have it, its work is accomplished. It is yours, dearest, for you to do as you choose with it."

To this Edith murmured some words of thanks, and taking up the parcel, proceeded to tie it up more carefully.

CHAPTER IV.

THE WELCOME HOME.

DALTON HALL was one of the most magnificent country-seats in Somersetshire. The village of Dalton, which bears the same name as the old family seat, is situated on the banks of a little river which winds through a pleasant plain on its course to the Bristol Channel, and at this place is crossed by a fine old rustic bridge with two arches. The village church, a heavy edifice, with an enormous ivy-grown tower, stands on the further side; and beyond that the gables and chimneys of Dalton Hall may be seen rising, about a mile away, out of the midst of a sea of foliage. The porter's lodge is about half a mile distant from the church, and the massive wall which incloses Dalton Park runs along the road for some miles.

There was a railway station about four miles away from the village, and it was at this station that Edith arrived on her way home. Miss Plympton had come with her, with the intention of remaining long enough to see Edith comfortably installed in her new abode, and with the hope of persuading her to go back if circumstances did not seem favorable. A footman and a maid also accompanied them.

On reaching the station they found themselves at first at a loss how to proceed, for there were no carriages in waiting. Of course, as no notice had been sent of her journey, Edith could not expect to find any carriage from Dalton Hall; nor did she think much about this circumstance. Dressed in deep mourning, with her pale face and dark, thoughtful eyes, she seemed to be given up to her own mournful reflections; and on finding that they would have to wait, she seated herself on a bench, and looked with an abstracted gaze upon the surrounding scene. Miss Plympton gave some directions to the footman, who at once went off to seek a carriage; after which she seated herself near Edith, while the maid sat on a trunk at a little distance. They had traveled all day long, and felt very much fatigued; so that nothing was said by any of them as they sat there waiting for the footman's return. At length, after about half an hour, a hackney-coach drove up, which the footman had procured from an inn not far away, and in this undignified manner they prepared to complete their journey. A long drive of four or five miles now remained; and when at length they reached the park gate none of them had much strength left. Here the coach stopped, and the footman rang the bell loudly and impatiently.

There was no immediate answer to this summons, and the footman rang again and again; and finally, as the delay still continued, he gave the bell a dozen tremendous pulls in quick succession. This brought an answer, at any rate; for a man appeared, emerging from a neighboring grove, who walked toward the gate with a rapid pace. He was a short, bull-necked, thickset, broad-shouldered man, with coarse black hair and heavy, matted beard. His nose was flat on his face, his chin was square, and he looked exactly like a prize-fighter. He had a red shirt, with a yellow spotted handkerchief flung about his neck, and his corduroy trowsers were tucked into a pair of muddy boots.

The moment he reached the gate he roared out a volley of the most fearful oaths: Who were they? What did they mean, dash them? What the dash dash did they mean by making such a dash dash noise?

"You'll get your ugly head broken, you scoundrel!" roared the footman, who was beside himself with rage at this insult to his mistress, coming as it did at the close of so long and irritating a delay. "Hold your infernal tongue, and open the gate at once. Is this the way you dare to talk before your mistress?"

"Mistress! You dashed fool," was the response, "what the dash do I know about mistresses? And if it comes to breaking heads, I'll make a beginning with you, you sleek, fat powder-monkey, with your shiny beaver and stuffed calves!"

Edith heard all this, and her amazement was so great that it drove away all fatigue. Her heart beat high and her spirit rose at this insult. Opening the carriage door, she sprang out, and, walking up to the gate, she confronted the porter as a goddess might confront a satyr. The calm, cold gaze which she gave him was one which the brute could not encounter. He could face any one of his own order; but the eye that now rested on him gave him pain, and his glance fell sulkily before that of his mistress.

"I am your mistress—Miss Dalton," said Edith. "Open that gate immediately."

"I don't know any thing about mistresses," said the fellow. "My orders are not to open them gates to nobody."

At this rebuff Edith was for a moment perplexed, but soon rallied. She reflected that this man was a servant under orders, and that it would be useless to talk to him. She must see the principal.

"Who gave those orders?" she asked.

"Mr. Wiggins," said the man, gruffly.

"Is that man here now?" asked Edith.

The man looked up suspiciously and in evident surprise, but his eyes fell again.

"Mr. Wiggins? He is here; he lives here."

"Then do you go at once," said Edith, loftily, "and say to that man that Miss Dalton is here."

The fellow glanced furtively at the carriage, where he saw the pale face of Miss Plympton and the paler face of the maid, and then with a grunt he turned and walked up the avenue. Edith went back to the carriage and resumed her seat.

This scene had produced a profound effect upon her two companions. Miss Plympton's worst apprehensions seemed justified by this rude repulse at the gates, and the moment that Edith came back she began to entreat her to return.

"Come back," she said, "to the inn. Do, darling, at least for the night, till we can send word to Wiggins."

"No," said Edith, firmly; "I will not recognize Wiggins at all. I am going to dismiss him the moment that I enter the Hall. I can wait patiently just now."

"But at least come back for this night. You may be sure that they will not be ready for you. You will have to come back after all."

"Well," said Edith, "I shall at least take formal possession of Dalton Hall first, and let Wiggins see that I am mistress there."

Miss Plympton sighed. Every hour only showed in a stronger manner how hopeless was any attempt of hers to move Edith from any resolve that she might make. Already she recognized in that slender young girl the stubborn spirit of her father—a spirit which would meet death and destruction rather than swerve from its set purpose.

Nothing more was said, but they all waited patiently for the porter's return. It seemed a very long time. The footman fussed and fumed, and at length beguiled the time by smoking and chatting with the coachman, whom he questioned about Mr. Wiggins. The coachman, however, could give him no information on the subject. "I on'y know," said he, "as how that this yer Wiggins is a Liverpool gent, an' latterly he seems inclined to live here. But he don't never see no company, an' keeps hisself shut up close."

At length, after waiting for more than half an hour, the noise of carriage wheels was heard, and a brougham appeared driven by the porter. He turned the brougham inside the gate, and then getting down, he unlocked the small gate and advanced to the carriage. The fellow seemed now to try to be more respectful, for he had a hat on his head which he took off, and made a clumsy attempt at a bow.

"Beg pardon, miss," said he, "for keepin' you waitin'; but I had to put the hosses in. Mr. Wiggins says as how you're to come up in the brougham, an' your trunks an' things 'll be took up afterward."

"But I want to drive up in this coach. I can't remove the luggage," said Edith.

"I don't know about that, miss," said the porter. "I've got to do as I'm told."

At this Edith was silent; but her flashing eyes and a flush that swept over her pale face showed her indignation.

"So this is the way he dares to treat me," said she, after some silence. "Well," she

continued, "for the present I must yield and submit to this insolence. But it only shows more clearly the character of the man. I suppose we must go," she continued, looking at Miss Plympton, and once more opening the coach door herself.

Miss Plympton had been more agitated than ever at this last message, and as Edith opened the door she asked her, breathlessly, "What do you mean? What are you going to do, dear?"

"I am going to Dalton Hall," said Edith, quietly. "We must go in the brougham, and we must quit this."

Miss Plympton hesitated, and the maid, who was still more terrified, clasped her hands in silent despair. But the porter, who had heard all, now spoke.

"Beg pardon, miss," said he, "but that lady needn't trouble about it. It's Mr. Wiggins's orders, miss, that on'y you are to go to the Hall."

"What insufferable insolence!" exclaimed Miss Plympton. "What shocking and abominable arrogance!"

"I do not regard it in the slightest," said Edith, serenely. "It is only assumption on his part. You are to come with me. If I pass through that gate you are to come also. Come."

"Oh, my dearest, my own dearest Edith, do not!—wait!—come back and let us talk over what we ought to do. Let us see a lawyer. Let us wait till to-morrow, and see if a stranger like Wiggins can refuse admission to the mistress of Dalton Hall."

"Beg pardon, mum," said the porter, "but Mr. Wiggins ain't refusin' admission to Miss Dalton—it's others that he don't want, that's all. The lawyers can't do any thin' agin that."

"My child," said Miss Plympton, "do you hear that? You shall not go. This man knows well what he can do. He understands all the worst injustice that can be done in the name of law. His whole life has been lived in the practice of all those iniquities that the law winks at. You see now at the outset what his purpose is. He will admit you, but not your friends. He wishes to get you alone in his power. And why does he not come himself? Why does he use such an agent as this?"

Miss Plympton spoke rapidly, and in excited tones, but her excitement did not affect Edith in the slightest degree.

"I think you are altogether too imaginative," said she. "His orders are absurd. If I go through that gate, you shall go too. Come."

"Edith! Edith! I implore you, my darling," cried Miss Plympton, "do not go. Come back. It will not be long to wait. Come to the village till to-morrow. Let us at least get the advice of a lawyer. The law can surely give an entrance to the rightful owner."

"HE DREW FROM HIS BREAST A LARGE CLASP-KNIFE."

"But he doesn't deny an entrance to me," said Edith, "and if I go, you shall come also. Come."

Miss Plympton hesitated. She saw that Edith was fully determined to go to Dalton Hall, and she could not bear to part with her. But at the same time she was so terrified at the thought of forcing a way in spite of the opposition of so formidable a villain as Wiggins that she shrank from it. Love at length triumphed over fear, and she followed Edith out of the coach, together with the maid.

Meanwhile the porter had stood in deep perplexity watching this scene, but at length when Miss Plympton had reached the ground and prepared to follow Edith he put himself in front of them.

"Beg pardon, miss," said he, "but its agin orders for them others to go. It's on'y you that Mr. Wiggins 'll let in."

"Mr. Wiggins has nothing to say about the matter," said Edith, coldly.

"But I've got to obey orders," said the man.

"Will you please stand aside and let me pass?" said Edith.

"I can't let them others in," said the porter, doggedly. "You may go."

"John," said Edith, quietly, "I'm sorry to trouble you, but you must watch this man; and, driver, do you stand at the gate and keep it open."

At this John flung down his hat upon the road, tore off his coat and tossed it after the hat, and, with a chuckle of something like exultation, prepared to obey his mistress by putting himself in a "scientific" attitude. He saw well enough that the porter was a formidable foe, and his face was a diploma in itself that fully testified to the skill and science of that foe; but John was plucky, and in his prime, and very confident in his own powers. So John stood off and prepared for the fray. On the other hand, the porter was by no means at a loss. As John prepared he backed slowly toward the gate, glaring like a wild beast at his assailant. But John was suddenly interrupted in his movements by the driver.

"See here, young man," said the latter, who had sprung from the box at Edith's order, "do you stand by the gate, an' I'll tickle that feller with this whip, an' see how he likes it."

The driver was a stout, solid, muscular fellow, with broad shoulders and bull-dog aspect. In his hand he flourished a heavy whip, and as he spoke his eyes sought out some part of the porter's person at which he might take aim. As he spoke the porter became aware of this second assailant, and a dark and malignant frown lowered over his evil face. He slowly drew from his breast a large clasp-knife which was as formidable as a dagger, and opening this, he held it significantly before him.

But now a new turn was given to the progress of affairs. Had the porter said nothing,

Miss Plympton might have overcome her fears far enough to accompany Edith; but his menacing looks and words, and these preparations for a struggle, were too much.

"Edith, my child, my dearest, do not! do not! I can not go; I will not. See these men; they will kill one another. John, come away. Driver, go back to the box. Come away at once. Do you hear, John?"

John did hear, and after some hesitation concluded to obey. He stepped back from the gate, and stood awaiting the progress of events. The driver also stood, waiting further orders.

"Edith dearest," said Miss Plympton, "nothing would induce me to go through those gates. You must not go."

"I'm sure," said Edith, "I shall be very sorry if you will not come; but, for my own part, I am quite resolved to go. Don't be afraid. Come."

Miss Plympton shuddered and shook her head.

"Well," said Edith, "perhaps it will be as well for you to wait, since you are so agitated; and if you really will not come, you can drive back to the village. At any rate, I can see you to-morrow, and I will drive down for you the first thing."

Miss Plympton looked mournfully at Edith.

"And you, Richards," said Edith, looking at her maid, "I suppose it is no use for me to ask you. I see how it is. Well, never mind. I dare say she needs you more than I do; and to-morrow will make all right. I see it only distresses you for me to press you, so I will say no more. Good-by for the present."

Edith held out her hand. Miss Plympton took it, let it go, and folding Edith in her arms, she burst into tears.

"I'm afraid—I'm afraid," said she.

"What of?" said Edith.

"About you," moaned Miss Plympton.

"Nonsense," said Edith. "I shall call on you to-morrow as soon as you are up."

Miss Plympton sighed.

Edith held out her hand to her maid, Richards, and kindly bade her good-by. The girl wept bitterly, and could not speak. It was an unusual thing for Edith to do, and was rather too solemn a proceeding in view of a short separation for one night, and this struck Edith herself. But who knows what one night may bring forth?

Edith now left them, and, passing through the gate, she stood and waved her hand at them. The porter followed and shut the gate. Miss Plympton, the maid, the driver, and John all stood looking after Edith with uneasy faces. Seeing that, she forced a smile, and finding that they would not go till she had gone, she waved a last adieu and entered the brougham. As she did so she heard the bolt turn in the lock as the porter fastened the gate, and an ominous dread arose within

her. Was this a presentiment? Did she have a dim foreshadowing of the future? Did she conjecture how long it would be before she passed through that gate again, and how and wherefore? It matters not. Other thoughts soon came, and the porter jumping into the seat, drove rapidly off.

Edith found herself carried along through lordly avenues, with giant trees, the growth of centuries, rising grandly on either side and overarching above, and between which long vistas opened, where the eye could take in wide glades and sloping meadows. Sometimes she caught sight of eminences rising in the distance covered with groves, and along the slopes herds of deer sometimes came bounding. Finally there came to view a broad lawn, with a pond in the centre, beyond which arose a stately edifice which Edith recognized as the home of her childhood.

It needed only one glance, however, to show Edith that a great change had taken place since those well-remembered days of childhood. Every where the old order and neatness had disappeared, and now in all directions there were the signs of carelessness and neglect. The once smooth lawn was now overgrown with tall grass; the margin of the pond was filled with rushes, and its surface with slime; some of the windows of the Hall were out, and some of the chimney-pots were broken; while over the road grass had been allowed to grow in many places. Edith recognized all this, and an involuntary sigh escaped her. The carriage at length stopped, and she got out and ascended the steps to the door of the house.

The door was open, and an ungainly-looking negro servant was standing in the hall.

"Who has charge of this house?" asked Edith. "Is there a housekeeper?"

The servant grinned.

"Housekeepa, miss? Yes, miss, dar's Missa Dunbar."

"Call the housekeeper, then," said Edith, "and tell her that I am waiting for her in the drawing-room."

The servant went off, and Edith then entered the drawing-room.

CHAPTER V.

THE STRANGE INMATES OF DALTON HALL.

IN that well-remembered drawing-room there was much that renewed the long past grief of childhood, and nothing whatever to soothe the sorrow of the present. Looking around, Edith found many things the same as she once remembered them; but still there were great changes — changes, too, which were of the same nature as those which she had noticed outside. Every thing showed traces of carelessness and long neglect. The seats of many of the handsome, richly carved chairs were ruined. Costly vases had disappeared. Dust covered every thing. Books and ornaments which lay around were soiled and spoiled. In that apparently deserted house there seemed to have been no one for years who cared to preserve the original grace and elegance of its decorations. But Edith did not have a very long time to give to her survey of this room, for in a few minutes she heard the rustle of a dress, and, turning, she saw a woman approaching who was evidently the housekeeper.

Edith was prepared to see some woman who might be in keeping with these desolate surroundings and with the ruffian porter at the gate—some coarse, insolent female; and she had also prepared herself to encounter any rudeness with fortitude. But the first sight of Mrs. Dunbar was enough to show her that her anticipations were completely unfounded.

She was a woman who might have been about fifty, and even older. The outline of her features showed marks of former beauty, and the general air of her face was altogether above the rank of a household domestic. The expression was one of calm, strong self-control, of dignity, and of resolution; at the same time there was in her dark, earnest eyes a certain vigilant outlook, as of one who is on guard at all times; and her gaze as she fixed it upon Edith was one of searching, eager, yet most cautious and wary examination. On the whole, this woman excited some surprise in Edith; and while she was gratified at finding in her one who was not out of the reach of respect, she yet was perplexed at the calm and searching scrutiny of which she was the object. But she did not now take any time to think about this. A vague idea occurred to her that Mrs. Dunbar, like many other housekeepers, was one of that numerous class who "have seen better days;" so, after the first look, she felt sufficiently satisfied, and advancing a step or two to meet her, she frankly held out her hand.

The housekeeper took it, and said, simply, "Welcome to Dalton Hall."

"Thank you," said Edith. "If I had met you before, I might have been spared some humiliation. But I need not talk of that. I am very tired and very faint. I have traveled all day, and have met with gross insult at my own gate. I want food and rest. Will you have the kindness, then, to take me to my own room at once, and then get me a cup of tea?"

Mrs. Dunbar had not removed her earnest eyes from Edith; and even after she had ceased speaking she still looked at her for a few moments in the same way without answering.

"We did not know that you were coming

so soon," said she at length; "and I can not tell you how I regret what has happened. It was too hard for you. But we were taken by surprise. I entreat you not to suppose that any thing but kindness was intended."

Edith looked now at Mrs. Dunbar with an earnest scrutiny that was fully equal to the searching gaze of the former. Mrs. Dunbar's tone was cordial and lady-like, but Edith felt repugnance at her use of the word "we." By that little word she at once identified herself with Wiggins, and made herself in part responsible for the scene at the gate.

"Kindness," said she, "is a strange word to use in connection with that scene, when I found myself forced to part with the only mother that I have known since my own mamma died."

Mrs. Dunbar looked at her in silence, and there came over her face a strange, patient expression that at any other time would have excited Edith's sympathy and pity. Some reply seemed to rise to her lips, but if it was so, it was instantly checked; and after a moment's hesitation she said, in a low voice,

"It is cheerless in this room. If you will come with me I will take you where you can be more comfortable."

Saying this, she led the way out, and Edith followed, feeling a little perplexed at Mrs. Dunbar's manner, and trying to understand how it was that she was so identified with Wiggins. She thought she could see an evident kindliness toward herself, but how that could coexist with the treatment which she had received at the gates was rather a puzzle.

Mrs. Dunbar led the way up to the second story, and along a corridor toward the right wing. Here she came to a room in the front of the house which looked out upon the park, and commanded an extensive view. There was a well-furnished bedroom off this room, to which Mrs. Dunbar at once led her.

"If we had only received notice that you were coming," said she, "you would have met with a better reception."

Edith said nothing, for once more the word "we" jarred unpleasantly upon her.

"Shall you have any objection to occupy this room for to-night?" asked Mrs. Dunbar.

"Thank you," said Edith, "none whatever; but I should like very much to have my luggage. It was taken back to Dalton."

"Taken back?"

"Yes. Miss Plympton was not admitted, and my luggage was on the coach."

Mrs. Dunbar made no reply for some moments.

"I should feel much obliged if you would send one of the servants to fetch it," said Edith.

"I don't see why not," said Mrs. Dunbar, in a hesitating voice.

"And have you any writing materials?" asked Edith. "I should like to send a few lines to Miss Plympton."

Mrs. Dunbar looked at her with one of those strange, searching glances peculiar to her, and after some hesitation said, "I will look."

"Thank you," said Edith, and turned away. Mrs. Dunbar then left her, and did not return for some time. At length she made her appearance, followed by the black servant, who carried a tray. A table was laid in the outer room, and a bountiful repast spread there. Edith did not eat much, however. She sat sipping a cup of tea, and thinking profoundly, while Mrs. Dunbar took a seat a little on one side, so as to be unobserved, from which position she watched Edith most closely. It was as though she was studying the character of this young girl so as to see what its promise might be. And if Mrs. Dunbar had any knowledge of the world, one thing must have been plainly manifest to her in that examination, and that was that this young girl was not to be managed or controlled after the fashion of most of her kind, but would require very difficult and very peculiar treatment if she were to be bent to the will of others. Mrs. Dunbar seemed to recognize this, and the discovery seemed to create distress, for a heavy sigh escaped her.

The sigh roused Edith. She at once rose from her seat and turned round.

"And now, Mrs. Dunbar," said she, "if you will let me have the writing materials I will send a few lines to poor Miss Plympton."

Mrs. Dunbar at once arose, and going out of the room, returned in a few minutes with a desk, which she laid upon another table. Edith at once seated herself to write, and while the black servant was removing the things she hurriedly wrote the following:

"DALTON HALL.

"MY DARLING AUNTIE,—I write at once because I know you will be devoured with anxiety, and will not sleep to-night unless you hear from me. You will be delighted to learn, then, that I am safe and unharmed. The man Wiggins has not yet made his appearance, but I hope to see him this evening. The Hall looks familiar, but desolate, except in the room where I now am writing, where I find sufficient comfort to satisfy me. I am too much fatigued to write any more, nor is it necessary, as I intend to call on you as early as possible to-morrow morning. Until then good-by, and don't be foolishly anxious about your own EDITH."

This note Edith folded and directed to "Miss Plympton, Dalton." After which she handed it to Mrs. Dunbar, who took it in silence and left the room.

For some time Edith sat involved in thought. She had written cheerfully enough to Miss Plympton, but that was from a kindly desire to reassure her. In reality, she was overwhelmed with loneliness and melancholy. The aspect of the grounds below and of the drawing-room had struck a chill to her heart. This great drear house oppressed her, and the melancholy with which she had left Plympton Terrace now became intensified. The gloom that had overwhelmed her father seemed to rest upon her father's house, and descended thence upon her own spirit, strong and brave though it was.

In the midst of her melancholy thoughts she was startled at the sound of a low sigh immediately behind her. She turned hastily, and saw a man standing there, who had entered the room so silently that, in her abstraction, she had not heard him. He was now standing about half-way between her and the door, and his eyes were fixed upon her with something of that same earnest scrutiny which she had already observed in the gaze of Mrs. Dunbar. One glance at this man was sufficient to show her that it was no servant, and that it could be no other than Wiggins himself. He was not a man, however, who could be dismissed with a glance. There was something in him which compelled a further survey, and Edith found herself filled with a certain indefinable wonder as she looked at him. His eyes were fixed on her; her eyes were fixed on him; and they both looked upon each other in silence.

He was a man who might once have been tall, but now was stooping so that his original height was concealed. He was plainly dressed, and his coat of some thin black stuff hung loosely about him. He wore slippers, which served to account for his noiseless entrance. Yet it was not things like these that Edith noticed at that time, but rather the face that now appeared before her.

It was a face which is only met with once in a lifetime—a face which had such an expression that the beholder could only feel baffled. It was the face of one who might be the oldest of men, so snow-white was the hair, so deep were the lines that were graven upon it. His cheek-bones were prominent, his mouth was concealed by a huge gray mustache, and his cheeks were sunken, while his forehead projected, and was fringed with heavy eyebrows, from behind which his dark eyes glowed with a sort of gloomy lustre from cavernous depths. Over his whole face there was one pervading expression that was more than despondency, and near akin to despair. It was the expression of a man whose life had been a series of disheartening failures, or of one who had sinned deeply, or of one who had suffered unusual and protracted anguish of soul, or of one who has been long a prey to that form of madness which takes the form of melancholy. So this might mean

"AND THIS WAS WIGGINS!"

a ruined life, or it might mean madness, or it might be the stamp of sorrow, or it might be the handwriting of remorse. Whatever it was could not certainly be gathered from one survey, or from many, nor, indeed, could it be known for certain at all without this man's confession.

For in addition to this mysterious expression there was another, which was combined with it so closely that it seemed to throw conjecture still further off the track and bewilder the gazer. This was a certain air of patient and incessant vigilance, a look-out upon the world as from behind an outpost of danger, the hunted look of the criminal who fears detection, or the never-ending watchfulness of the uneasy conscience.

All this Edith could not help seeing, and she gathered this general result from her survey of that face, though at that time she could not put her conclusion in words. It seemed to her to be remorse which she saw there, and the manifestations of a stricken conscience. It was the criminal who feared detection, the wrong-doer on the constant look-out for discovery—a criminal most venerable, a wrong-doer who must have suffered; but if a criminal, one of dark and bitter memories, and one whose thoughts, reaching over the years, must have been as gloomy as death.

And this was Wiggins!

Not the Mephistopheles which she had imagined; not the evil mocking fiend; but one rather who originally had not been without good instincts, and who might have become a virtuous man had fate not prevented. It was not the leering, sneering tempter that she saw, but rather some representation of that archangel ruined, for it was as though "his brow deep scars of thunder had intrenched, and care sat on his faded cheek."

At first the woman's heart of Edith made itself felt, and she pitied him; but quickly the daughter's heart spoke, and it denounced him. If this man felt remorse, it could only be for one great crime, and what crime was so great as that of the betrayal of Frederick Dalton? Was it this that had crushed the traitor? Thoughts like these flashed through her mind, and her glance, which at first had softened from commiseration, now grew stern and cold and hard; and the fixed, eager look which came to her from those gloomy and mournful eyes was returned by one which was hard and pitiless and repellent. Back to her heart came that feeling which for a moment had faltered: the old hate, nourished through her lifetime, and magnified during the last few days to all-absorbing proportions: the strongest feeling of her nature, the hate of the enemy of herself and the destroyer of her father.

Wiggins, on his part, with his quick, vigilant eyes, did not fail to mark at once the change that had come over Edith. He saw the first glance of pity, and then the transition to coldness deepening into hate. Until then there had seemed a spell upon him which fixed his gaze on Edith, but now the spell was suddenly broken. He removed his gaze, and then, taking a chair, he sat upon it, and for a few moments remained with his eyes fixed on the floor.

At last he raised his head, and, looking fixedly at Edith, began to speak, and spoke in a strange, low, measured tone, with frequent hesitations; in a way also that gave the idea of one who, for some cause or other, was putting a strong constraint upon himself, and only speaking by an effort.

"I regret, very deeply," said he, "that you were treated with rudeness. Had I known that you would come so soon, I should have notified the—the porter. But he—he meant no harm. He is very faithful—to orders."

"I am sorry to say," said Edith, "that it was not the rudeness of the porter that was offensive, but rather the rudeness of yourself."

Wiggins started.

"Of myself?" he repeated.

"Certainly," said Edith; "in refusing to admit one who is my dearest friend on earth."

Wiggins drew a long breath, and looked troubled.

"It was distressing to me," said he at length; "but it could not be."

At this, Edith felt inexpressibly galled, but for the time restrained herself.

"Perhaps you would have been pleased," said she, "if I had gone away with her."

"Oh no," said Wiggins, dreamily—"oh no."

"I thought for a time of doing so," said Edith; "and in that case I should have come to-morrow, or as soon as possible, with the officers of the law, to reply to your orders."

At this Wiggins looked at her with a strange and solemn glance, which puzzled Edith.

"You would have regretted it," said he, "eventually."

"Few would have done as I did," said Edith, "in coming here alone."

"You did right," said Wiggins.

"At the same time," said Edith, firmly, "if I have forborne once, I assure you I shall not do so again. You are in a wrong course altogether. I shall put an end to this at once. And I tell you now that this place must be made ready for Miss Plympton to-morrow. I will have that brutal porter dismissed at once. As to yourself and the housekeeper, I need say nothing just now."

If it had been possible for that gray face to have turned grayer or paler, it would have done so as Edith uttered these words. Wiggins fixed his solemn eyes on her, and their glance had something in it which was almost awful. After a moment he slowly passed his thin hand over his brow, frowned, and looked away. Then he murmured, in a low voice, as if to himself,

"The girl's mad!"

Edith heard these words, and for a moment thought that Wiggins himself must be mad; but his calmness and cold constraint looked too much like sober sense. She herself had her own dark and gloomy feelings, and these glowed in her heart with a fervid fire—too fervid, indeed, to admit of utterance. She too had to put upon herself a constraint to keep back the words, glowing with hot wrath and fervid indignation, which she could have flung upon her father's betrayer. But because words were weak, and because such deeds as his had to be repaid by act and in kind, she forbore.

"It is necessary," said Wiggins at length, "to live here in seclusion for a time. You will gradually become accustomed to it, and it will be all for the best. It may not be for so very long, after all—perhaps not more than one year. Perhaps you may eventually be admitted to—to our purposes."

"This," said Edith, "is childish. What you mean I do not know, nor do I care to. You seem to hint at seclusion. I do not feel inclined for society, but a seclusion of your making is not to my taste. You must yourself go elsewhere to seek this seclusion. This is mine, and here I intend to bring the friends whom I wish to have with me. I can only regard your present course as the act of a thoroughly infatuated man. You have had things all your own way thus far, and seem to have come to regard this place as yours, and never to have counted upon any thing but acquiescence on my part in your plans."

Wiggins fastened his solemn eyes upon her, and murmured,

"True."

"It is useless, therefore," said Edith, loftily, "for you to make any opposition. It will only be foolish, and you will ultimately be ruined by it."

Wiggins rose to his feet.

"It is only a waste of time," said he. "I confess you are different from what I anticipated. You do not know. You can not understand. You are too rash and self-confident. I can not tell you what my plans are;· I can only tell you my wishes."

Edith rose to her feet, and stood opposite, with her large eyes flaming from her white face.

"This insolence," said she, "has lasted too long. It is you who must obey me—not I you. You speak as though there were no such thing as law."

"I said nothing about obedience," said Wiggins, in a mournful voice, which, in spite of herself, affected Edith very strangely. "I spoke of plans which could not be communicated to you yet, and of my wishes."

"But I," said Edith, mildly, "wish you to understand that I have my own wishes. You make use of a tone which I can not tolerate for a moment. I have only one thing more to say, and that is to repeat my former direction. I *must* have Miss Plympton here tomorrow, and preparations for her *must* be made. Once for all, you must understand that between you and me there is absolutely nothing in common; and I tell you now that it is my intention to dispense with your services at the earliest possible date. I will not detain you any longer."

Saying this, she waved her hand toward the door, and then resumed her seat.

As for Wiggins, he looked at her with his usual solemn gaze during these remarks. His bowed form seemed to be bent more as he listened to her words. When she ceased and sat down he stood listening still, as though he heard some echo to her words. Edith did not look up, but turned her eyes in another direction, and so did not see the face that was still turned toward her. But if she had looked there she would have seen a face which bore a deeper impress than ever of utter woe.

In a few moments he turned and left the room, as silently as he came.

Before retiring that night Edith called Mrs. Dunbar, and gave her some directions about preparing another bedroom and the drawing-room. To her orders, which were somewhat positive, Mrs. Dunbar listened in silence, and merely bowed in reply.

After which Edith retired, weary and worn out, and troubled in many ways.

CHAPTER VI.

WALLED IN.

VERY early on the following day Edith arose, and found Mrs. Dunbar already moving about. She remarked that she had heard Edith dressing herself, and had prepared a breakfast for her. This little mark of attention was very grateful to Edith, who thanked Mrs. Dunbar quite earnestly, and

"SHE SAW THE BLACK SERVANT, HUGO."

found the repast a refreshing one. After this, as it was yet too early to think of calling on Miss Plympton, she wandered about the house. The old nooks and corners dear to memory were visited once more. Familiar scenes came back before her. Here was the nursery, there her mother's room, in another place the library. There, too, was the great hall up stairs, with pictures on each side of ancestors who went back to the days of the Plantagenets. There were effigies in armor of knights who had fought in the Crusades and in the Wars of the Roses; of cavaliers who had fought for King Charles; of gallant gentlemen who had followed their country's flag under the burning sun of India, over the sierras of Spain, and in the wilderness of America. And of all these she was the last, and all that ancestral glory was bound up in her, a weak and fragile girl. Deeply she regretted at that moment that she was not a man, so that she might confer new lustre upon so exalted a lineage.

As she wandered through the rooms and galleries all her childhood came back before her. She recalled her mother, her fond love, and her early death. That mother's picture hung in the great hall, and she gazed at it long and pensively, recalling that noble face, which in her remembrance was always softened by the sweet expression of tenderest love. But it was here that something met her eyes which in a moment chased away every regretful thought and softer feeling, and brought back in fresh vehemence the strong glow of her grief and indignation. Turning away from her mother's portrait by a natural impulse to look for that of her father, she was at first unable to find it. At length, at the end of the line of Dalton portraits, she noticed what at first she had supposed to be part of the wall out of repair. Another glance, however, showed that it was the back of a picture. In a moment she understood it. It was her father's portrait, and the face had been turned to the wall.

Stung by a sense of intolerable insult, her face flushed crimson, and she remained for a few moments rooted to the spot glaring at the picture. Who had dared to do this—to heap insult upon that innocent and suffering head, to wrong so foully the memory of the dead? Her first impulse was to tear it down with her own hands, and replace it in its proper position; her next to seek out Wiggins at once and denounce him to his face for all his perfidy, of which this was the fitting climax. But a more sober thought followed—the thought of her own weakness. What could her words avail against a man like that? Better far would it be for her to wait until she could expel the usurper, and take her own place as acknowledged mistress in Dalton Hall. This thought made her calmer, and she reflected that she need not wait very long. This day would decide it all, and this very night her father's portrait should be placed in its right position.

This incident destroyed all relish for further wandering about the house, and though it was yet early, she determined to set out at once for the village and find Miss Plympton. With this design she descended to the lower hall, and saw there the same black servant whom she had seen the day before.

"What is your name?" she asked.

"Hugo," said the black, with his usual grin.

"Well, Hugo," said she, "I want the brougham. Go to the stables, have the horses put in, and come back as soon as you can. And here is something for your trouble."

Saying this, she proffered him a sovereign. But the black did not appear to see it. He simply said, "Yes, miss," and turned away. Edith was surprised; but thinking that it was merely his stupidity, she went up stairs and waited patiently for a long time. But, in spite of her waiting, there were no signs of any carriage; and at length, growing impatient, she determined to go to the stables herself. She knew the way there perfectly well, and soon reached the place. To her surprise and vexation, the doors were locked, and there were no signs whatever of Hugo.

"The stupid black must have misunderstood me," thought she.

She now returned to the house, and wandered all about in search of some servants. But she saw none. She began to think that Hugo was the only servant in the place; and if so, as he had disappeared, her chance of getting the brougham was small indeed. As for Wiggins, she did not think of asking him, and Mrs. Dunbar was too much under the influence of Wiggins for her to apply there. She was therefore left to herself.

Time passed thus, and Edith's impatience grew intolerable. At length, as she could not obtain a carriage, she determined to set out on foot and walk to Dalton. She began now to think that Wiggins had seen Hugo, found out what she wanted, and had forbidden the servant to obey. This seemed the only way in which she could account for it all. If this were so, it showed that there was some unpleasant meaning in the language which Wiggins had used to her on the previous evening about a secluded life, and in that case any delay made her situation more unpleasant. She had already lost too much time, and therefore could wait no longer. On the instant, therefore, she set out, and walked down the great avenue toward the gates. It was a longer distance than she had supposed: so long, indeed, did it seem that once or twice she feared that she had taken the wrong road; but at last her fears were driven away by the sight of the porter's lodge.

On reaching the gates she found them locked. For this she had not been prepared; but a moment's reflection showed her that this need not excite surprise. She looked up at them with a faint idea of climbing over. One glance, however, showed that to be impossible; they were high, and spiked at the top, and over them was a stone arch which left no room for any one to climb over. She looked at the wall, but that also was beyond her powers. Only one thing now remained, and that was to apply to the porter. After this fellow's rudeness on the previous day, she felt an excessive repugnance toward making any application to him now; but her necessity was urgent, and time pressed. So she quieted her scruples, and going to the door of the porter's house, knocked impatiently.

The porter came at once to the door, and bowed as respectfully as possible. His demeanor, in fact, was totally different from what it had been on the previous day, and evinced every desire to show respect, though perhaps he might manifest it rather awkwardly. Edith noticed this, and was encouraged by it.

"I want you to let me out," said Edith. "I'm going to Dalton."

The man looked at her, and then at the ground, and then fumbled his fingers together; after which he plunged his hands in his pockets.

"Do you hear what I say?" said Edith, sharply. "I want you to unlock the gate."

"Well, miss, as to that—I humbly beg your pardon, miss, but I've got my orders not to."

"Nonsense," said Edith. "No one here gives orders but me. I am mistress here."

"Beg pardon, miss, but I don't know any master but Master Wiggins."

"Wiggins!" said Edith.

"Yes, miss, an' hopin' it's no offense. I have to obey orders."

"But he couldn't have given you orders about me," said Edith, haughtily.

"He said all persons, miss, comin' or goin', all the same. No offense bein' intended, miss, an' beggin' your pardon."

"But this is absurd," said Edith. "He knows that I am going to Dalton. You have misunderstood him."

"I'm sorry, miss. I'd do any thin' to oblige, miss; but I've got to do as I'm bid."

"Who employs you?"

"Master, miss—Master Wiggins."

"Do you want to keep this situation?"

"Keep this situation?"

"Yes. You don't want to be turned out, do you?"

"Oh no, miss."

"Well, obey me now, and you shall remain. I am the mistress of Dalton Hall, and the owner of these estates. Wiggins is the agent, and seems disinclined to do what I wish. He will have to leave. If you don't want to leave also, obey me now."

All this seemed to puzzle the porter, but certainly made no impression upon his resolve. He looked at Edith, then at the ground, then at the trees, and finally, as Edith concluded, he said:

"Beg pardon, miss, but orders is orders, an' I've got to obey mine."

Edith now began to feel discouraged. Yet there was one resource left, and this she now tried. Drawing forth her purse, she took out some pieces of gold.

"Come," said she, "you do very well to obey orders in ordinary cases; but in my case you are violating the law, and exposing yourself to punishment. Now I will pay you well if you do me this little service, and will give you this now, and much more afterward. Here, take this, and let me out quick."

The porter kept his eyes fixed on the ground, and did not even look at the gold.

"See!" said Edith, excitedly and hurriedly—"see!"

The porter would not look. But at last he spoke, and then came the old monotonous sentence,

"Beggin' your pardon, miss, an' hopin' there's no offense, I can't do it. I've got to obey orders, miss."

At this Edith gave up the effort, and turning away, walked slowly and sadly from the gates.

This was certainly more than she had anticipated. By this she saw plainly that Wiggins was determined to play a bold game. The possibility of such restraint as this had never entered into her mind. Now she recalled Miss Plympton's fears, and regretted when too late that she had trusted herself within these gates. And now what the porter had told her showed her in one instant the full depth of his design. He evidently intended to keep her away from all communication with the outside world. And she—what could she do? How could she let Miss Plympton know? How could she get out? No doubt Wiggins would contrive to keep all avenues of escape closed to her as this one was. Even the walls would be watched, so that she should not clamber over.

Among the most disheartening of her discoveries was the incorruptible fidelity of the servants of Wiggins. Twice already had she tried to bribe them, but on each occasion she had failed utterly. The black servant and the porter were each alike beyond the reach of her gold.

Her mind was now agitated and distressed. In her excitement she could not yet return to the Hall, but still hoped that she might escape, though the hope was growing faint indeed. She felt humiliated by the defeat of her attempts upon the honesty of the servants. She was troubled by the thought of her isolation, and did not know what might be best to do.

One thing now seemed evident, and this was that she had a better chance of escaping at this time than she would have afterward. If she was to be watched, the outlook could not yet be as perfect or as well organized as it would afterward be. And among the ways of escape she could think of nothing else than the wall. That wall, she thought, must certainly afford some places which she might scale. She might find some gate in a remote place which could afford egress. To this she now determined to devote herself. With this purpose on her mind, she sought to find her way through the trees to the wall. This she was able to do without much difficulty, for though the trees grew thick, there was no underbrush, but she was able to walk along without any very great trouble. Penetrating in this way through the trees, she at length came to the wall. But, to her great disappointment, she found its height here quite as great as it had been near the gate, and though in one or two places trees grew up which threw their branches out over it, yet those trees were altogether inaccessible to her.

Still she would not give up too quickly, but followed the wall for a long distance. The further she went, however, the more hopeless did her search seem to grow. The ground was unequal, sometimes rising into hills, and at other times sinking into valleys; but in all places, whether hill or valley, the wall arose high, formidable, not to be scaled by one like her. As she looked at it the thought came to her that it had been arranged for that very purpose, so that it should not be easily climbed, and so it was not surprising that a barrier which might baffle the active poacher or trespasser should prove insuperable to a slender girl like her.

She wandered on, however, in spite of discouragement, in the hope of finding a gate. But this search was as vain as the other. After walking for hours, till her feeble limbs could scarcely support her any longer, she sank down exhausted, and burst into tears.

For a long time she wept, overwhelmed by accumulated sorrow and despondency and disappointment. At length she roused herself, and drying her eyes, looked up and began to think of returning to the Hall.

To her amazement she saw the black servant, Hugo, standing not far away. As she raised her eyes he took off his cap, and grinned as usual. The sight of him gave Edith a great shock, and excited new suspicions and fears within her.

Had she been followed?

She must have been. She had been watched and tracked. All her desperate efforts had been noted down to be reported to Wiggins—all her long and fruitless search, her baffled endeavors, her frustrated hopes! It was too much.

CHAPTER VII.

A PARLEY WITH THE JAILERS.

COMING as it did close upon her baffled efforts to escape, this discovery of Hugo proclaimed to Edith at once most unmistakably the fact that she was a prisoner. She was walled in. She was under guard and under surveillance. She could not escape without the consent of Wiggins, nor could she move about without being tracked by the spy of Wiggins. It was evident also that both the porter and the black servant Hugo were devoted to their master, and were beyond the reach both of persuasion and of bribery.

The discovery for a moment almost overwhelmed her once more; but the presence of another forced her to put a restraint upon her feelings. She tried to look unconcerned, and turning away her eyes, she sat in the same position for some time longer. But beneath the calm which her pride forced her to assume her heart throbbed painfully, and her thoughts dwelt with something almost like despair upon her present situation.

But Edith had a strong and resolute soul in spite of her slender and fragile frame; she had also an elastic disposition, which rose up swiftly from any prostration, and refused to be cast down utterly. So now this strength of her nature asserted itself; and triumphing over her momentary weakness, she resolved to go at once and see Wiggins himself. With these subordinates she had nothing to do. Her business was with Wiggins, and with Wiggins alone.

Yet the thought of an interview had something in it which was strangely repugnant to Edith. The aspect of her two jailers seemed to her to be repellent in the extreme. That white old man, with the solemn mystery of his eyes, that weird old woman, with her keen, vigilant outlook—these were the ones who now held her in restraint, and with these she had to come in conflict. In both of them there seemed something uncanny, and Edith could not help feeling that in the lives of both of these there was some mystery that passed her comprehension.

Still, uncanny or not, whatever might be the mystery of her jailers, they remained her jailers and nothing less. It was against this thought that the proud soul of Edith chafed and fretted. It was a thought which was intolerable. It roused her to the intensest indignation. She was the lady of Dalton Hall; these who thus dared to restrain her were her subordinates. This Wiggins was not only her inferior, but he had been the enemy of her life. Could she submit to fresh indignities or wrongs at the hands of one who had already done so much evil to her and hers? She could not.

That white old man with his mystery, his awful eyes, his venerable face, his unfathomable expression, and the weird old woman, his associate, with her indescribable look and her air of watchfulness, were both partners in this crime of unlawful imprisonment. They dared to put restrictions upon the movements of their mistress, the lady of Dalton Hall. Such an attempt could only be the sign of a desperate mind, and the villainy of their plan was of itself enough to sink them deep in Edith's thoughts down to an abyss of contempt and indignation. This indignation roused her, and her eagerness to see Miss Plympton impelled her to action. Animated by such feelings and motives, she delayed no longer, but at once returned to the Hall to see Wiggins himself.

On her way back she was conscious of the fact that Hugo was following; but she took no notice of it, as it was but the sequel to the preceding events of the day. She entered the Hall, and finding Mrs. Dunbar, told her to tell Wiggins that she wished to see him. After this she went down to the dreary drawing-room, where she awaited the coming of her jailer.

The room was unchanged from what it had been on the preceding day. By this time also Edith had noticed that there were no servants about except Hugo. The drear desolation of the vast Hall seemed drearier from the few inmates who dwelt there, and the solitude of the place made it still more intolerable.

After some time Wiggins made his appearance. He came in slowly, with his eyes fixed upon Edith, and the same expression upon his face which she had noticed before. A most singular man he was, whoever or whatever he might be. That hoary head and that venerable face might have awed her under other circumstances, and the unfathomable mystery of its expression might have awakened intense interest and sympathy; but as it was, Edith had no place for any other feelings than suspicion, indignation, and scorn.

"What do you mean by this treatment?" said Edith, abruptly. "It seems as though you are trying to imprison me. I have told you that I wish to call on Miss Plympton. I can not get a carriage, and I am not allowed to leave this place on foot. You are responsible for this, and I tell you now that I must go, and at once."

At this peremptory address Wiggins stood looking at her with his usual expression, and for some moments made no reply.

"I did not know," said he at length, in a slow and hesitating voice, "that you wished to leave so soon."

"But I told you so. You drove away Miss Plympton yesterday from my gates. I promised to call on her this morning. She is anxiously expecting me. I must go to her."

Wiggins again waited for a few moments before replying, and at length said, in an abstracted tone:

"No, no; it can not be—it can not be!"

"Can not be!" repeated Edith. "It seems to me that you are trying to carry out a most extraordinary course of action toward me. This looks like restraint or imprisonment."

Wiggins looked at her with an expression of earnest entreaty on his face, with which there was also mingled an air of indescribable sadness.

"It is necessary," said he, in a mournful voice. "Can you not bring yourself to bear with it? You do not know what is at stake. Some day all will be explained."

"This is silly," exclaimed Edith. "No explanation is possible. I insist on leaving this place at once. If you refuse to let me go, it will be worse for you than for me."

"You do not know what you ask," said Wiggins.

"I ask you," said Edith, sternly and proudly, "to open those gates to your mistress."

Wiggins shook his head.

"I ask you to open those gates," continued Edith. "If you let me go now, I promise not to prosecute you—at least for this. I will forget to-day and yesterday."

Saying this, she looked at him inquiringly. But Wiggins shook his head as before.

"It can not be," said he.

"You decide, then, to refuse my demand?" said Edith, impatiently.

"I must," said Wiggins, with a heavy sigh. "It is necessary. All is at stake. You do not know what you are doing."

"It is evident to me," said Edith, mastering herself by a strong effort, "that you are playing a desperate game, but at the same time you are trusting much to chance. Why did you wish me to come here? It was by the merest chance that I decided to come. It was also by another chance that I entered those gates which you now shut against my departure. Few would have done it."

"Your presence seemed necessary to my plans," said Wiggins, slowly. "What those plans are I can not yet confide to you. You are concerned in them as much as I am. Opposition will be of no avail, and will only injure you. But I hope you will not try to oppose me. I entreat you to bear with me. I entreat you to try to put a little confidence in me. I was your father's friend; and I now implore you, that daughter whom he loved so dearly, for your father's sake—yes, and for the sake of your sainted mother—not to—"

"This is mere hypocrisy," interrupted Edith. "My father was one with whom one like you can have nothing in common. You add to your crimes by this treatment of his daughter. What you have already been guilty of toward him you alone know. If you hope for mercy hereafter, do not add to your guilt."

"Guilt!" cried Wiggins, in an awful voice. He started back, and regarded her with eyes of utter horror. "Guilt!" he repeated, in a voice so low that it was scarcely above a whisper—"and she says that word!"

Edith looked at him with unchanged severity.

"You made a great mistake," said she, coldly and sternly, "when you drove Miss Plympton away. If you hope to keep me imprisoned here, you will only destroy yourself. I have a friend who knows you, and who will know before evening that I am here under restraint. She will never rest until she effects my deliverance. Have you counted on that?"

Wiggins listened attentively, as usual, to every word. The effort seemed to give him pain, and the suggestion of her friend was undoubtedly most unpleasant.

"No, I have not," said he. He spoke as though to himself. The candor of this confession stimulated Edith to dwell to a greater extent upon this subject.

"She was not willing for me to come in," said she. "She wished me not to enter without a lawyer or the sheriff. If she finds that I am detained, she will enter here in that way herself. She will deliver me in spite of you. If she does not see me to-day, she will at once use every effort to come to me. Your porters and your spies will be of no use against the officers of the law."

At this Wiggins looked at the floor, and was evidently in a state of perplexity. He stood in silence for some time, and Edith waited impatiently for his answer, so as to learn what effect these last hints had produced. At length Wiggins looked up. He spoke slowly and mournfully.

"I am very sorry," said he. "I hope it will not come to that. I'm afraid that I shall have to take you elsewhere."

These words fell upon Edith's ears ominously and threateningly. They conveyed to her mind a menace dark and gloomy, and showed the full determination of Wiggins to maintain at all hazards the control that he had gained over her. Edith therefore was silent, and apprehensive of evil. She was afraid that she had said too much. It might have been better not to threaten, or to show her hand prematurely. It might be the best plan to wait in silence and in patience for Miss Plympton. Wiggins was desperate. He might take her away, as he darkly hinted, from this place to some other where Miss Plympton could never find her.

She stood for some time in silence, with her mind full of such thoughts as these. Wiggins waited for a few moments, and then turned and slowly left the room. Edith said nothing, and made no effort to recall him, for she now felt that her situation was growing serious, and that it would be better for her to think it all over seriously, and not speak to Wiggins again until she had decided upon some definite plan of action. She therefore allowed him to take his departure, and soon afterward she went to her own room, where she remained for hours in deep thought.

At length Mrs. Dunbar brought in dinner. After laying the table she stood for a few moments in silence looking at Edith; but at length, yielding to some sudden impulse, she came forward, and as Edith looked up in surprise, she exclaimed, with startling abruptness,

"Oh, how unfortunate! and oh, what a wretched mistake you are under! If you had not come home so suddenly, all might have been well. We hoped that you would be content and patient. Mr. Wiggins has plans of immense importance; they require great quiet and seclusion. Oh, if you could only have some faith in us!"

She stopped as abruptly as she had begun. This style of address from a housekeeper seemed to Edith to be altogether too familiar, and she resented it deeply. Besides, the identification of herself with Wiggins put Mrs. Dunbar in an odious position in Edith's eyes.

"Mr. Wiggins's plans are of no consequence to me whatever," said she, coldly.

"They are; they are of immense importance," cried Mrs. Dunbar.

Edith looked at her for a few moments with a cold stare of wonder, for this volunteered advice seemed something like insolence, coming thus from a subordinate. But she contented herself with answering in a quiet tone:

"You are mistaken. Nothing is of importance to me but my liberty. It will be very dangerous to deprive me of that. My friends will never allow it. In Wiggins this attempt to put me under restraint is nothing less than desperation. Think yourself how frantic he must be to hope to be able to confine me here, when I have friends outside who will move heaven and earth to come to me."

At this a look of uneasiness came over Mrs. Dunbar's face. It seemed to Edith that this hint at friends without was the only thing that in any way affected either of her jailers.

"The punishment for such a crime as unlawful imprisonment," continued Edith, "is a severe one. If Wiggins has ever committed any crimes before, this will only aggravate his guilt, and make his punishment the worse."

At this Mrs. Dunbar stared at Edith with the same horror in her eyes which Wiggins had lately shown.

"Crime?" she repeated. "Guilt? Punishment? Oh, Heavens! Has it come to this? This is terrible. Girl," she continued, with a frown, "you don't know the dreadful nature of those words. You are a marplot. You have come home to ruin every thing. But I thought so," she murmured to herself. "I told him so. I said it would be ruin, but he would have his way. And now—" The remainder of her remarks was inaudible. Suddenly her manner changed. Her anger gave way once more to entreaty.

"Oh!" she said, "can nothing persuade you that we are your friends? Trust us—oh, trust us! You will soon learn how we love you. He only thinks of you. You are the final aim of all his plans."

Edith gave a light laugh. That she was the final aim of Wiggins's plans she did not doubt. She saw now that plan clearly, as she thought. It was to gain control of her for purposes of his own in connection with the estate. Under such circumstances Mrs. Dunbar's entreaties seemed silly, and to make any answer was absurd. She turned away and sat down at the table. As for Mrs. Dunbar, she left the room.

Night came. Edith did not sleep; she could not. The day had been the most eventful one of her life. The thought that she was a prisoner was terrible. She could only sustain herself by the hope that Miss Plympton would save her. But this hope was confronted by a dark fear which greatly distressed her. It might take time for Miss Plympton to do any thing toward releasing her. She knew that the law worked slowly: she did not feel at all certain that it worked surely. Her father's fate rose before her as a warning of the law's

"CRIME! GUILT!"

uncertainty and injustice. Could she hope to be more fortunate than he had been? Wiggins had passed his life in the study of the law, and knew how to work it for his own private ends. He had once succeeded in his dark plot against her father. Might not his present "plan," about which he and his associate talked, be equally successful? Mrs. Dunbar had called her a "marplot." To mar the plot of this man, and avenge upon him the wrongs of her father, would be sweet indeed; but could it be possible for her to do it? That was the question.

The next morning came, and Edith rose full of a new purpose. She thought of her efforts on the preceding day, and concluded that she had made one great mistake. She saw now that Miss Plympton had most probably called, and had not been admitted. If she had only remained by the gate, she could have seen her friend, and told her all. That she had not thought of this before was now a matter of the deepest regret, and she could only hope that it might not yet be too late. She determined to go to the gates at once and watch.

She therefore hurried down to the gates as soon as she could. No efforts were made to prevent her. She had feared that she might be locked up in the Hall; but, to her surprise and relief, she was not. Such forbearance made her situation still more perplexing. It was evident that Wiggins hesitated about proceeding to extremities with

her, and did not venture as yet to exercise more than a general restraint.

Arriving at the gate, Edith sat down close by it on a seat in front of the porter's lodge, and waited and watched. The gates were of iron bars, so that it was easy to see through them, and the road ran in front. The road was not much frequented, however. An occasional farmer's wagon or solitary pedestrian formed the only life that was visible outside. The porter watched her for some time in surprise, but said nothing. Hugo came up after about half an hour and talked with the porter, after which he loitered about within sight of Edith. Of all this, however, Edith took no notice whatever; it was what she expected.

The hours of the day passed by, but there were no signs of Miss Plympton. As hour after hour passed, Edith's hopes grew fainter and fainter. She longed to ask the porter whether she had called or not, but could not bring herself to do so—first, because she did not like to destroy all hope; and secondly, because she did not wish to hold any further communication with him.

She sat there all day long. Miss Plympton did not come. The hours passed by. Evening came. She had eaten nothing all day. She was faint and weary, and almost in despair. But to wait longer was useless now; so she rose from her seat, and with feeble footsteps returned to the house.

Early the next morning she returned to

C

the gates to take up her station as before and watch. She did not hope to see Miss Plympton now; for she concluded that she had called already, had been turned back, and was now perhaps engaged in arranging for her rescue. But Edith could not wait for that. She determined to do something herself. She resolved to accost all passers-by and tell them her situation. In this way she thought she might excite the world outside, and lead to some interposition in her behalf.

Full of this purpose, she went down to the gates. As she drew near, the first sight of them sent a feeling of dismay to her heart. A change had taken place. Something had been done during the night.

She drew nearer.

In a few moments she saw it all.

The gates had been boarded up during the night so that it was impossible to see the road.

One look was enough. This last hope was destroyed. There was nothing to be done here; and so, sick at heart, Edith turned back toward the Hall.

CHAPTER VIII.

MISS PLYMPTON BAFFLED.

MEANWHILE Miss Plympton had been undergoing various phases of feeling, alternating between anxiety and hope, and terminating in a resolution which brought forth important results. On the departure of Edith she had watched her till her carriage was out of sight, and then sadly and reluctantly had given orders to drive back to Dalton. On arriving there she put up at the inn, and though full of anxiety, she tried to wait as patiently as possible for the following day.

Accustomed to move among the great, and to regard them with a certain reverence that pervades the middle classes in England, she tried first of all to prevent any village gossip about Edith, and so she endeavored, by warning and by bribery, to induce the maid, the footman, and the driver to say nothing about the scene at the gates. Another day, she hoped, would make it all right, and idle gossip should never be allowed to meddle with the name of Edith in any way.

That evening Edith's note was brought to her. On receiving it she read it hurriedly, and then went down to see who had brought it. She saw the porter, who told her that he had come for Miss Dalton's baggage. The porter treated her with an effort to be respectful, which appeared to Miss Plympton to be a good omen. She offered him a piece of gold to propitiate him still further, but, to her amazement, it was declined.

"Thank ye kindly, mum," said he, touch-

ing his hat, "an' hope it's no offense; but we beant allowed to take nothin' savin' an' except what he gives us hisself."

A moment's surprise was succeeded by the thought that even this was of good omen, since it seemed to indicate a sort of rough, bluff, sterling honesty, which could not co-exist with a nature that was altogether bad.

Returning to her room, she once more read Edith's note. Its tone encouraged her greatly. It seemed to show that all her fears had been vain, and that, whatever the character of Wiggins might be, there could be no immediate danger to Edith. So great, indeed, was the encouragement which she received from this note that she began to think her fears foolish, and to believe that in England no possible harm could befall one in Edith's position. It was with such thoughts, and the hope of seeing Edith on the following day, that she retired for the night.

Her sleep was refreshing, and she did not awake till it was quite late. On awaking and finding what time it was, she rose and dressed hastily. Breakfast was served, and she began to look out for Edith.

Time passed, however, and Edith did not make her appearance. Miss Plympton tried to account for the delay in every possible way, and consoled herself as long as she could by the thought that she had been very much fatigued, and had not risen until very late. But the hours passed, and at length noon came without bringing any signs of her, and Miss Plympton was unable any longer to repress her uneasiness. This inaction grew intolerable, and she determined to set forth and see for herself. Accordingly she had the carriage made ready, and in a short time reached the park gate.

She had to ring for a long time before any one appeared; but at length, after fully an hour's delay, the porter came. He touched his hat on seeing her, but stood on the other side of the iron gateway without opening it.

"Is Miss Dalton at the Hall?" asked Miss Plympton.

"Yes, mum."

"I wish to see her."

"Beg yer pardon, mum, but there be no callers allowed in."

"Oh, it's different with me. Miss Dalton wrote that she would come to see me this morning, and I'm afraid she's ill, so I have come to see her."

"She beant ill, then," said the other.

Miss Plympton reflected that it was of no use to talk to this man, and thought of Wiggins himself.

"Is your master in?" she asked.

"He is, mum."

"Tell him I wish to see him."

"Beggin' yer pardon, mum, he never sees nobody."

"But I wish to see him on business of a very important kind."

"Can't help it, mum—beggin' yer pardon; but I've got to obey orders, mum."

"My good fellow, can't you take my message, or let me in to see him?"

"Sorry, mum, but I can't; I've got my orders."

"But he can't know. This business is so important that it will be very bad for him if he does not see me now. Tell him that. Go, now; you can't know what his business is. Tell him that—"

"Well, mum, if you insist, I don't mind goin'," said the porter. "I'll tell him."

"Say that I wish to see him at once, and that the business I have is of the utmost importance."

The porter touched his hat, and walked off. Now followed another period of waiting. It was fully half an hour before he returned. Miss Plympton saw that he was alone, and her heart sank within her.

"Mr. Wiggins presents his respects, mum," said he, "and says he's sorry he can't see you."

"Did you tell him that my business was of the most important kind?"

"Yes, mum."

"And he refuses to come?"

"He says he's sorry he can't see you, mum."

At this Miss Plympton was silent for a little while.

"Come," said she at last, "my good fellow, if I could only see him, and mention one or two things, he would be very glad. It will be very much to his injury if he does not see me. You appear to be a faithful servant, and to care for your master's interests, so do you let me pass through, and I'll engage to keep you from all harm or punishment of any kind."

"Sorry, mum, to refuse; but orders is orders, mum," said the man, stolidly.

"If I am not allowed to go in," said Miss Plympton, "surely Miss Dalton will come here to see me—here at the gates."

"I don't know, mum."

"Well, you go and tell her that I am here."

"Sorry to refuse, mum; but it's agin orders. No callers allowed, mum."

"But Miss Dalton can come as far as the gates."

The man looked puzzled, and then muttered,

"Mr. Wiggins's orders, mum, is to have no communication."

"Ah!" said Miss Plympton; "so she is shut up here."

"Beggin' your pardon, mum, she beant shut up at all nowheres: she goes about."

"Then why can't I see her here?"

"Agin orders, mum."

By this Miss Plympton understood the worst, and fully believed that Edith was under strict restraint.

"My good man," said she, solemnly, "you and your master are committing a great crime in daring to keep any one here in imprisonment, especially the one who owns these estates. I warn him now to beware, for Miss Dalton has powerful friends. As to you, you may not know that you are breaking the law now, and are liable to transportation for life. Come, don't break the laws, and incur such danger. If I choose I can bring here to-morrow the officers of the law, release Miss Dalton, and have you and your master arrested."

At this the man looked troubled. He scratched his head, drew a long breath, and looked at the ground with a frown.

Miss Plympton, seeing that this shot had told, followed it up.

"Refuse me admittance," said she, "and I will bring back those who will come here in the name of the law; but if you let me in, I promise to say nothing about this matter."

The porter now seemed to have recovered himself. He raised his head, and the old monotonous reply came:

"Sorry, mum, but it's agin orders."

Miss Plympton made one further attempt. She drew forth her purse, and displayed its contents.

"See," said she, "you will be doing a kindness to your master, and you shall have all this."

But the man did not look at the purse at all. His eyes were fixed on Miss Plympton, and he merely replied as before:

"Sorry, mum, but it's agin orders."

"Very well," said Miss Plympton. "There is only one thing left for me to do. I wish you to take one final message from me to your master. Tell him this: It is my intention to procure help for Miss Dalton at once. Tell him that her uncle, Sir Lionel Dudleigh, is now in England, and that this very day I shall set out for Dudleigh Manor. I shall tell Sir Lionel how his niece is situated, and bring him here. He will come with his own claims and the officers of the law. Wiggins shall be arrested, together with all who have aided and abetted him. If he refuses to admit me now, I shall quit this place and go at once without delay. Go, now, and make haste, for this matter is of too great importance to be decided by you."

The porter seemed to think so too, for, touching his hat, he at once withdrew. This time he was gone longer than before, and Miss Plympton waited for his return with great impatience. At length he came back.

"Mr. Wiggins presents his respects, mum," said the man, "and says he is not breakin' any law at all, and that if you choose to go for Sir Lionel, he is willin' to have you do so. He says if you fetch Sir Lionel here he will let both of you in. He says he'll be very happy indeed to see Sir Lionel."

This singular way of taking what was

meant to be a most formidable threat took away Miss Plympton's last hope, and reduced her to a state of dejection and bewilderment; for when she sent that threatening message, it was not because she had really any fixed design of carrying it into execution, but rather because the name of Sir Lionel Dudleigh seemed to her to be one which might overawe the mind of Wiggins. She thought that by reminding Wiggins of the existence of this powerful relative, and by threatening an instant appeal to him, she would be able to terrify him into releasing Edith. But his cool answer destroyed this hope. She felt puzzled at his assertion that he was not breaking any law, when he himself must know well that such a thing as the imprisonment of a free subject is a crime of the most serious character; but she felt even more puzzled at his reference to Sir Lionel. Her own connection and association with the aristocracy had never destroyed that deep unswerving reverence for them with which she had set out in life; and to find Wiggins treating the mention of Sir Lionel with such cool indifference was to her an incomprehensible thing. But there was nothing more for her to do at this place, and feeling the necessity of immediate action, she at once drove back to the inn.

Arriving here, she hoped that her prompt departure might frighten Wiggins, and lead to a change in his decision, and she concluded to remain that evening and that night, so as to give him time for repentance.

Nothing was left now but to devise some plan of action. First of all, she made inquiries of the landlord about Wiggins. That personage could tell her very little about him. According to him, Mr. Wiggins was a lawyer from Liverpool, who had been intrusted with the management of the Dalton estate for the past ten years. He was a very quiet man, devoted to his business, and until latterly had never been at Dalton oftener or longer than was absolutely necessary. Of late, however, he had been living here for some months, and it was believed that he intended to stay here the greater part of his time.

This was all that Miss Plympton was able to learn about Wiggins.

CHAPTER IX.

SIR LIONEL DUDLEIGH.

ALTHOUGH Miss Plympton had indulged the hope that Wiggins might relent, the time passed without bringing any message from him, and every hour as it passed made a more pressing necessity for her to decide on some plan. The more she thought over the matter, the more she thought that her best plan of action lay in that very threat

which she had made to Wiggins. True, it had been made as a mere threat, but on thinking it over it seemed the best policy.

The only other course lay in action of her own. She might find some lawyer and get him to interpose. But this involved a responsibility on her part from which she shrank so long as there was any other who had a better right to incur such responsibility. Now Sir Lionel was Edith's uncle by marriage; and though there had been trouble between husband and wife, she yet felt sure that one in Edith's position would excite the sympathy of every generous heart, and rouse Sir Lionel to action. One thing might, indeed, prevent, and that was the disgrace that had fallen upon the Dalton name. This might prevent Sir Lionel from taking any part; but Miss Plympton was sanguine, and hoped that Sir Lionel's opinion of the condemned man might be like her own, in which case he would be willing, nay, eager, to save the daughter.

The first thing for her to do was to find out where Sir Lionel Dudleigh lived. About this there was no difficulty. Burke's *Peerage and Baronetage* is a book which in most English homes lies beside the Bible in the most honored place, and this inn, humble though it might be, was not without a copy of this great Bible of society. This Miss Plympton procured, and at once set herself to the study of its pages. It was not without a feeling of self-abasement that she did this, for she prided herself upon her extensive knowledge of the aristocracy, but here she was deplorably ignorant. She comforted herself, however, by the thought that her ignorance was the fault of Sir Lionel, who had lived a somewhat quiet life, and had never thrust very much of his personality before the world, and no one but Sir Bernard Burke could be expected to find out his abode. That great authority, of course, gave her all the information that she wanted, and she found that Dudleigh Manor was situated not very far distant from Cheltenham. This would require a detour which would involve time and trouble; but, under the circumstances, she would have been willing to do far more, even though Plympton Terrace should be without its tutelary genius in the mean time.

On the next morning Miss Plympton left Dalton on her way to Dudleigh Manor. She was still full of anxiety about Edith, but the thought that she was doing something, and the sanguine anticipations in which she indulged with reference to Sir Lionel, did much to lessen her cares. In due time she reached her destination, and after a drive from the station at which she got out, of a mile or two, she found herself within Sir Lionel's grounds. These were extensive and well kept, while the manor-house itself was one of the noblest of its class.

After she had waited for some time in an elegant drawing-room a servant came with Sir Lionel's apologies for not coming to see her, on account of a severe attack of gout, and asking her to come up stairs to the library. Miss Plympton followed the servant to that quarter, and soon found herself in Sir Lionel's presence.

He was seated in an arm-chair, with his right foot wrapped in flannels and resting upon a stool in front of him, in orthodox gout style. He was a man apparently of about fifty years of age, in a state of excellent preservation. His head was partially bald, his brow smooth, his cheeks rounded and a little florid, with whiskers on each side of his face, and smooth-shaven chin. There was a pleasant smile on his face, which seemed natural to that smooth and rosy countenance; and this, together with a general tendency to corpulency, which was rather becoming to the man, and the gouty foot, all served to suggest high living and self-indulgence.

"I really feel ashamed of myself, Miss—ah—Plympton," said Sir Lionel, "for giving you so much trouble; but gout, you know, my dear madam, is not to be trifled with; and I assure you if it had been any one else I should have declined seeing them. But of course I could not refuse to see you, and the only way I could have that pleasure was by begging you to come here. The mountain could not come to Mohammed, and so Mohammed, you know—eh? Ha, ha, ha!"

The baronet had a cheery voice, rich and mellow, and his laugh was ringing and musical. His courtesy, his pleasant smile, his genial air, and his hearty voice and laugh, all filled Miss Plympton with sincere delight, and she felt that this man could do nothing else than take up Edith's cause with the utmost ardor.

After a few apologies for troubling him, which Sir Lionel turned aside by protesting that apologies were only due from himself to her, Miss Plympton began to state the object of her visit.

"In the first place, Sir Lionel," said she, "I take it for granted that you have heard of the death of Frederick Dalton, Esquire, in Van Diemen's Land."

The smile on the baronet's face died out at this, and his eyes fixed themselves upon Miss Plympton's face with quick and eager curiosity. Then he turned his face aside. A table stood on his right, with some wine and glasses within reach.

"Excuse me," said he; "I beg ten thousand pardons; but won't you take a glass of wine? No?" he continued, as Miss Plympton politely declined; "really I think you had better." And then, pouring out a glass, he sipped it, and looked at her once more. "Poor Dalton!" said he, with a sigh. "Yes, of course, I saw it in the papers. A most

melancholy affair. Poor Dalton! Let me inform you, madam, that he was more sinned against than sinning." Sir Lionel sighed.

"Oh, Sir Lionel," exclaimed Miss Plympton, earnestly, "how it rejoices my heart to hear you say that! For my part, I never, never had one single doubt of his perfect innocence."

"Nor had I," said Sir Lionel, firmly, pouring out another glass of wine. "It was excessively unfortunate. Had I not myself been in—in—ah—affliction at the time, I might have done something to help him."

"Oh, Sir Lionel, I'm sure you would!"

"Yes, madam," said Sir Lionel; "but domestic circumstances to which I am not at liberty to allude, of a painful character, put it out of my power to—to—ah—to interpose. I was away when the arrest took place, and when I returned it was too late."

"So I have understood," said Miss Plympton; "and it is because I have felt so sure of your goodness of heart that I have come now on this visit."

"I hope that you will give me the chance of showing you that your confidence in me is well founded," said Sir Lionel, cordially.

"You may have heard, Sir Lionel," began Miss Plympton, "that about the time of the trial Mrs. Dalton died. She died of a broken heart. It was very, very sudden."

Sir Lionel sighed heavily.

"She thought enough of me to consider me her friend; and as she did not think her own relatives had shown her sufficient sympathy, she intrusted her child to me when dying. I have had that child ever since. She is now eighteen, and of age."

"A girl! God bless my soul!" said Sir Lionel, thoughtfully. "And does she know about this—this—melancholy business?"

"I deemed it my duty to tell her, Sir Lionel," said Miss Plympton, gravely.

"I don't know about that. I don't—know—about—that," said Sir Lionel, pursing up his lips and frowning. "Best wait a while; but too late now, and the mischief's done. Well, and how did she take it?"

"Nobly, Sir Lionel. At first she was quite crushed, but afterward rallied under it. But she could not remain with me any longer, and insisted on going home—as she called it—to Dalton Hall."

"Dalton Hall! Yes—well? Poor girl! poor little girl!—an orphan. Dalton Hall! Well?"

"And now I come to the real purpose of my visit," said Miss Plympton; and thereupon she went on to give him a minute and detailed account of their arrival at Dalton and the reception there, together with the subsequent events.

To all this Sir Lionel listened without one word of any kind, and at length Miss Plympton ended.

"Well, madam," said he, "it may surprise

you that I have not made any comments on your astonishing story. If it had been less serious I might have done so. I might even have indulged in profane language—a habit, madam, which, I am sorry to say, I have acquired from not frequenting more the society of ladies. But this business, madam, is beyond comment, and I can only say that I rejoice and feel grateful that you decided as you did, and have come at once to me."

"Oh, I am so glad, and such a load is taken off my mind!" exclaimed Miss Plympton, fervently.

"Why, madam, I am utterly astounded at this man's audacity," cried Sir Lionel—"utterly astounded! To think that any man should ever venture upon such a course! It's positively almost inconceivable. And so you tell me that she is there now?"

"Yes."

"Under the lock and key, so to speak, of this fellow?"

"Yes."

"And she isn't allowed even to go to the gate?"

"No."

"The man's mad," cried Sir Lionel—"mad, raving mad. Did you see him?"

"No. He wouldn't consent to see me."

"Why, I tell you, he's a madman," said Sir Lionel. "He must be. No sane man could think of such a thing. Why, this is England, and the nineteenth century. The days of private imprisonment are over. He's mad! The man's mad!"

"But what is to be done, Sir Lionel?" asked Miss Plympton, impatiently.

"Done?" cried Sir Lionel—"every thing! First, we must get Miss Dalton out of that rascal's clutches; then we must hand that fellow and his confederates over to the law. And if it don't end in Botany Bay and hard labor for life, then there's no law in the land. Why, who is he? A pettifogger—a miserable low-born, low-bred, Liverpool pettifogger!"

"Do you know him?"

"Know him, madam? I know all about him—that is, as much as I want to know."

"Do you know any thing about the relations that formerly existed between him and Mr. Frederick Dalton?"

"Relations?" said Sir Lionel, pouring out another glass of wine—"relations, madam—that is—ah—to say—ah—business relations, madam? Well, they were those of patron and client, I believe—nothing more. I believe that this Wiggins was one to whom poor Dalton behaved very kindly—made him what he is, in fact—and this is his reward! A pettifogger, by Heaven!—a pettifogger! Seizing the Dalton estates, the scoundrel, and then putting Miss Dalton under lock and key! Why, the man's mad—mad! yes, a raving maniac! He is, by Heaven!"

"And now, Sir Lionel, when shall we be able to effect her release?"

"Leave it all to me. Leave it all to me, madam. This infernal gout of mine ties me up, but I'll take measures this very day; I'll send off to Dalton an agent that will free Miss Dalton and bring her here. Leave it to me. If I don't go, I'll send—yes, by Heaven, I'll send my son. But give yourself no trouble, madam. Miss Dalton is as good as free at this moment, and Wiggins is as good as in jail."

Miss Plympton now asked Sir Lionel if he knew what Wiggins meant by his answer to her threat, and she repeated the message. Sir Lionel listened with compressed lips and a frowning brow. After Miss Plympton had told it he sat for some minutes in silent thought.

"So that is what he said, is it?" exclaimed Sir Lionel at last. "Well, madam, we shall see about that. But don't give yourself a moment's uneasiness. I take the matter in hand from this moment. The insolence of this fellow, Wiggins, is unparalleled, madam; but be assured all this shall surely recoil on his own head with terrible effect."

Some further conversation followed to the same effect, and at length Miss Plympton took her leave, full of hope and without a care. Sir Lionel had hinted that she was not needed any more in the matter; and as she felt a natural delicacy about obtruding her services, she decided to go back to Plympton Terrace and wait.

Accordingly Miss Plympton, on leaving Dudleigh Manor, went back to Plympton Terrace.

CHAPTER X.

LEON.

FOR some time after Miss Plympton's departure Sir Lionel remained buried in thought. At length he rang the bell.

A servant appeared.

"Is Captain Dudleigh here yet?" asked Sir Lionel.

"Yes, Sir Lionel."

"Tell him that I want to see him."

The servant departed, and in a short time the door opened and a young man entered. He was tall, muscular, well-formed, and with sufficient resemblance to Sir Lionel to indicate that he was his son. For some time Sir Lionel took no notice of him, and Captain Dudleigh, throwing himself in a lounging attitude upon a chair, leaned his head back, and stared at the ceiling. At length he grew tired of this, and sitting erect, he looked at Sir Lionel, who was leaning forward, with his elbow on the arm of his chair, supporting his head in his hand, and evidently quite oblivious of the presence of any one.

"Did you wish to see me, Sir?" said Captain Dudleigh at length.

Sir Lionel started and raised his head.

"By Jove!" he exclaimed. "Is that you, Leon? I believe I must have been asleep. Have you been waiting long? Why didn't you wake me? I sent for you, didn't I? Oh yes. Let me see. It is a business of the greatest importance, and I'm deuced glad that you are here, for any delay would be bad for all concerned."

Sir Lionel paused for a few moments, and then began:

"You know about that—that melancholy story of—of poor Dalton."

Leon nodded.

"Did you hear that he is dead?"

"Well, some paragraphs have been going the rounds of the papers to that effect, though why they should drag the poor devil from his seclusion, even to announce his death, is somewhat strange to me."

"Well, he is dead, poor Dalton!" said Sir Lionel, "and—and so there's an end of him and that melancholy business. By-the-way, I suppose you haven't heard any particulars as to his death?"

"No," said Leon, "nothing beyond the bare fact. Besides, what does it matter? When a man's dead, under such circumstances, too, no one cares whether he died of fever or gunshot."

"True," said Sir Lionel, with a sigh. "It isn't likely that any one would trouble himself to find out how poor Dalton died. Well, that is the first thing that I had to mention. And now there is another thing. You know, of course, that he left a daughter, who has been growing up all these years, and is now of age. She has been living under the care of a Miss Plympton, from whom I had the pleasure of a call this morning, and who appears to be a remarkably sensible and right-minded person."

"A daughter?" said Leon. "Oh yes! Of course I remember. And of age! Well, I never thought of that. Why, she must be heiress to the immense Dalton property. Of age, and still at school! What's her name? I really forget it, and it's odd too, for, after all, she's my own cousin, in spite of the short-comings of her father and—and other people."

"Yes, Leon," said Sir Lionel, "you're right. She is your own cousin. As to her father, you must remember how I have always said that he was innocent, and sinned against rather than sinning. Heaven forbid that we should visit on this poor child the disgrace of her father, when he was not guilty at all. I feel confident, Leon, that you will espouse her cause as eagerly as I do; and since I am prevented from doing any thing by this infernal gout, I look to you to represent me in this business, and bring that infernal scoundrel to justice."

"Infernal scoundrel! What infernal scoundrel?"

"Why, this Wiggins."

"Wiggins?"

"Yes. The madman that is trying to shut up Edith, and keep her under lock and key."

"Edith! Who's Edith? What, Dalton's daughter? Oh, is that her name? But what do you mean? What madman? what lock and key?"

"You know Wiggins, don't you?" asked Sir Lionel.

"Which Wiggins? There are several that I know—Wiggins the sausage man, Wiggins the rat-catcher, Wig—"

"I mean John Wiggins, of John Wiggins and Company, solicitors, Liverpool. You know them perfectly well. I sent you there once."

"Yes," said Leon, slowly, "I remember."

"What sort of a man was this John Wiggins himself when you saw him?"

"Oh, an ordinary-looking person—grave, quiet, sensible, cool as a clock, and very reticent. I told you all about him."

"Yes, but I didn't know but that you might remember something that would throw light on his present actions. You went there to ask some questions in my name with reference to poor Dalton, and the disposal of his property."

"Yes, and got about as little satisfaction as one could get."

"He was not communicative."

"Not at all. Every answer was an evasion. What little I did get out of him had to be dragged out. The most important questions he positively refused to answer."

"Of course. I remember all that, for I was the one who wished to know, and consequently his refusal to answer affected me most of all. I wondered at the time, and thought that it might be some quiet plan of his, but I really had no idea of the audacity of his plans."

"How is that?"

"Wait a moment. Did you see any thing in this man that could excite the suspicion that he was at all flighty or insane?"

"Insane! Certainly not. He was, on the contrary, the sanest person I ever met with."

"Well, then, he must have become insane since. I've no doubt that he has for years been planning to get control of the Dalton property; and now, when he has become insane, he is still animated by this ruling passion, and has gone to work to gratify it in this mad way."

"Mad way? What mad way? I don't understand."

"Well, I'll tell you all about it. I merely wished to get your unbiased opinion of the man first;" and upon this Sir Lionel told him the whole story which Miss Plympton had narrated to him. To all this Leon listened with the deepest interest and the most profound astonishment, interrupting his father by frequent questions and exclamations.

"What can be his design?" said Leon. "He must have some plan in his head."

"Plan! a mad plan enough!" exclaimed Sir Lionel. "It is clearly nothing else than an attempt to get control of the property by a *coup de main.*"

"Well, the opinion that I formed of Wiggins is that he is altogether too shrewd and deep a man to undertake any thing without seeing his way clear to success."

"The man's mad!" cried Sir Lionel. "How can any sane man hope to succeed in this? Why, no one can set up a private prison-house in that style. If the law allowed that, I know of one person who could set up a private jail, and keep it pretty well filled, too."

"An idea strikes me," said Leon, "which may explain this on other grounds than madness, and which is quite in accordance with Wiggins's character. He has been the agent of the estates for these ten years, and though he was very close and uncommunicative about the extent of his powers and the nature of his connection with Dalton, yet it is evident that he has had Dalton's confidence to the highest degree; and I think that before Dalton's unfortunate business he must have had some influence over him. Perhaps he has persuaded Dalton to make him the guardian of his daughter."

"Well, what good would that do?" asked Sir Lionel.

"Do you know any thing about the law of guardianship?"

"Not much."

"Well, it seems to me, from what I have heard, that a guardian has a great many very peculiar rights. He stands in a father's place. He can choose such society for his ward as he likes, and can shut her up, just as a father might. In this instance Wiggins may be standing on his rights, and the knowledge of this may be the reason why he defied you so insolently."

Sir Lionel looked annoyed, and was silent for a few moments.

"I don't believe it," said he; "I don't believe any thing of the kind. I don't believe any law will allow a man to exercise such control over another just because he or she is a minor. Besides, even if it were so, Edith is of age, and this restraint can not be kept up. What good would it do, then, for him to imprison her for three or four months? At the end of that time she must escape from his control. Besides, even on the ground that he is *in loco parentis*, you must remember that there are limits even to a father's authority. I doubt whether even a father would be allowed to imprison a daughter without cause."

"But this imprisonment may only be a restriction within the grounds. The law can not prevent that. Oh, the fact is, this guardianship law is a very queer thing, and we shall find that Wiggins has as much right over her as if he were her father. So we must go to work carefully; and my idea is that it would be best to see him first of all, before we do any thing, so as to see how it is."

"At any rate," said Sir Lionel, "we can force him to show by what right he controls her liberty. The law of guardianship can not override the *habeas corpus* act, and the liberty of the subject is provided for, after all. If we once get Edith out of his control, it will be difficult for him to get her back again, even if the law did decide in his favor. Still I think there is a good deal in what you say, and it certainly is best not to be too hasty about it. An interview with him, first of all, will be decidedly the best thing. I think, before going there, you had better see my solicitors in London. You see I intrust the management of this affair to you, Leon, for this infernal gout ties me up here closer than poor Edith at Dalton Hall. You had better set about it at once. Go first to London, see my solicitors, find out about the law of guardianship, and also see what we had better do. Then, if they approve of it, go to Dalton Hall and see Wiggins. I don't think that you are the sort of man who can be turned back at the gates by that ruffian porter. You must also write me what the solicitors say, for I think I had better keep Miss Plympton informed about the progress of affairs, partly to satisfy her anxiety, and partly to prevent her from taking any independent action which may embarrass our course of conduct."

CHAPTER XI.

LUCY.

ABOUT a week after the conversation detailed in the last chapter, the train stopped at the little station near Dalton village, and Leon Dudleigh stepped out. At the same time a woman got out of another carriage in the train. She was dressed in black, and a crape veil concealed her face. Leon Dudleigh stood and looked about for a few moments in search of some vehicle in which to complete his journey, and as the train went on he walked into the little station-house to make inquiries. The woman followed slowly. After exchanging a few words with the ticket clerk, Leon found out that no vehicle was to be had in the neighborhood, and with an exclamation of impatience he told the clerk that he supposed he would have to walk, and at the same time asked him some questions about getting his luggage forwarded to the inn at Dalton. Hav-

"AT THAT MOMENT THE WOMAN RAISED HER VEIL."

ing received a satisfactory answer, he turned to the door and walked toward the village.

The woman who had followed him into the station-house had already left it, and was walking along the road ahead of him. She was walking at a slow pace, and before long Leon came up with her. He had not noticed her particularly, and was now about passing her, when at that very moment the woman raised her veil, and turned about so as to face him.

At the sight of her face Leon uttered an exclamation of amazement and started back.

"Lucy!" he exclaimed, in a tone of deep and bitter vexation.

"Aha, Leon!" said the woman, with a smile. "You thought you would give me the slip. You didn't know what a watch I was keeping over you."

At this Leon regarded her in gloomy silence, while the expression of deep vexation remained unchanged on his face.

The woman who had thus followed him was certainly not one who ought to inspire any thing like vexation. Her face was beau-tiful in outline and expression. Her eyes were dark and animated, her tone and manner indicated good-breeding and refinement, though these were somewhat more vivacious than is common with English ladies.

"I don't see what brought you here," said Leon at last.

"I might say the same of you, mon cher," replied the lady; "but I have a faint idea, and I have no desire to give you too much liberty."

"It's some more of your confounded jealousy," said Leon, angrily. "My business here is a very delicate one indeed. I may have to do it incognito, and it may ruin all if I have any one here who knows me."

"Incognito?" said the lady. "That will be charming; and if so, who can help you better than I? I can be your mother, or your grandmother, or your business partner, or any thing. You ought to have insisted on my accompanying you."

The light tone of raillery in which this was spoken did not in any way mollify the chagrin of the other, who still looked at her with a frown, and as she ended, growled out,

"I don't see how you got on my track, confound it!"

"Nothing easier," said the lady. "You didn't take any pains to hide your tracks."

"But I told you I was going back to Dudleigh."

"I know you did, *mon cher;* but do you think I believed you?"

"I don't see how you followed me," said Leon again.

"Well, I don't intend to let you know all my resources," said the lady, with a smile, "for fear you will baffle me some other time. But now come, don't let yourself get into a passion. Look at me, and see how good-natured and sweet-tempered I am. Your reception of me is really quite heart-rending, and I have a great mind to go back again at once and leave you."

"I wish you would," said Leon, rudely.

"But I won't," said the lady. "So come, be yourself again, for you can be sweet-tempered if you only try hard, you know."

"Now see here, Lucy," said Leon, sternly, "you don't know what you're doing. It's all very well to pass it off as a frolic, but it won't do. This business of mine is too serious to admit of trifling. If it were my own affair, I wouldn't care; and even if I didn't want you, I should submit with a good grace. But this is a matter of extreme delicacy, and my father has sent me here because he was unable to come himself. It is a—a law matter. I went to London merely to see the solicitors. I didn't tell a soul about my business, and I thought that no one knew I was coming here except my father and the solicitors."

"Well, but I'm always an exception, you know," said the lady, pleasantly.

"Oh, see here, now," said the other, "it's all very well for you to meddle with my own affairs; but you are now forcing yourself into the midst of the concerns of others—the business affairs of two great estates. I must attend to this alone."

"*Mon cher,*" said the lady, with unalterable placidity, "business is not one of your strong points. You really are not fit to manage any important matter alone. At Dudleigh you have your papa to advise with, at London your papa's solicitors, and here at Dalton you need a sound adviser too. Now is there any one in whom you could put greater confidence, or who could give you better advice on innumerable matters, than the unworthy being who now addresses you? Come, don't keep up the sulks any longer. They are not becoming to your style of beauty. For my part, I never sulk. If you will reflect for a moment, you will see that it is really a great advantage for you to have with you one so sagacious and shrewd as I am; and now that the first mo-

ment of irritation has passed, I trust you will look upon my humble offer of service with more propitious eyes."

Something in these words seemed to strike Leon favorably, for the vexation passed away from his face, and he stood looking thoughtfully at the ground, which he was mechanically smoothing over with his foot. The lady said no more, but watched him attentively, in silence, waiting to see the result of his present meditations.

"Well," said he at last, "I don't know but that something may arise in this business, Lucy, in which you may be able to do something—though what it may be I can not tell just now."

"Certainly," said the lady, "if you really are thinking of an incognito, my services may be of the utmost importance."

"There's something in that," said Leon.

"But whether the incognito is advisable or not should first be seen. Now if you would honor me with your confidence to ever so small an extent, I could offer an opinion on that point which might be worth having. And I will set you a good example by giving you my confidence. Frankly, then, the only reason why I followed you was because I found out that there was a lady in the case."

"So that's it, is it?" said Leon, looking at her curiously.

"Yes," said the lady. "And I heard that your father sent you, and that you had been talking with his solicitors. Now as you are not in the habit of doing business with your father, or talking with his solicitors, the thing struck me very forcibly; and as there was a lady—in fact, a rich heiress—in the case, and as you are frightfully in debt, I concluded that it would be well for me to see how the business proceeded; for I sometimes do not have that confidence in you, Leon, which I should like to have."

This was spoken in a serious and mournful voice which was totally different from the tone of raillery in which she had at first indulged. As she concluded she fixed her eyes sadly on Leon, and he saw that they were suffused with tears.

"You preposterous little goose!" said Leon. "There never was a wilder, a sillier, and at the same time a more utterly groundless fancy than this. Why, to begin with, the lady is my cousin."

"I know," said the lady, sadly.

"It seems to me you found out every thing, though how the deuce you contrived it is more than I can tell," said Leon.

"Our faculties are very much sharpened where our interests are concerned," said the lady, sententiously.

"Now, see here," said Leon. "It is true that this lady is my cousin, and that she is an heiress, and that I am infernally hard up, and that my father sent me here, and that I have been talking with the solicitors; but I swear to you the subject of marriage has not once been mentioned."

"But only thought of," suggested the other.

"Well, I don't know any thing about people's thoughts," said Leon. "If you go into that style of thing, I give up. By-the-way, you know so much, that I suppose you know the lady's name."

"Oh yes: Miss Dalton—Edith Dalton."

"The devil!" exclaimed Leon. "Well, I confess I'm mystified. How you could have found out all this is utterly beyond me."

"So you have no idea of matrimony, *mon cher?*" said the lady, attempting to use a sprightly tone, but looking at him with a glance so earnest that it showed what importance she attached to his reply.

Leon was silent for a moment, and looked at the ground. At last he burst forth impatiently:

"Oh, confound it all! what's the use of harping forever on one string, and putting a fellow in a corner all the time? You insist on holding an inquisition about thoughts and intentions. How do I know any thing about that? You may examine me about facts if you choose, but you haven't any business to ask any thing more."

"Well, I suppose it *is* rather unfair," said the lady in a sweet voice, "to force one to explain all one's thoughts and intentions; so, *mon cher,* let's cry quits. At any rate, you receive me for your ally, your adviser, your guide, philosopher, and friend. If you want incognitos or disguises, come to me."

"Well, I suppose I must," said Leon, "since you are here, and won't go; and perhaps you may yet be really useful, but—"

"But at first I ought to know what the present condition is of this 'business' of yours."

"Oh, I've no objection to tell you now, since you know so much; in fact, I believe you know all, as it is."

"Well, not quite all."

"It seems to me," said Leon, "if we're going to talk over this matter any further, we might find some better place than the middle of a public road. Let me see," he continued, looking all around—"where shall we go?"

As he looked around his eyes caught sight of the little river that flowed near, on its course through Dalton to the Bristol Channel. Some trees grew on the margin, and beneath them was some grass. It was not more than twenty yards away.

"Suppose we sit there by the river," said Leon, "and we can talk it over."

The lady nodded, and the two walked to the river margin.

"SHE WAS SEATED NEAR THE WINDOW."

CHAPTER XII.

A SOLEMN APPEAL.

A FEW days passed away in Dalton Hall, and Edith began to understand perfectly the nature of the restraint to which she was subjected. That restraint involved nothing of the nature of violence. No rude or uncivil word was spoken to her. Wiggins and Mrs. Dunbar had professed even affection for her, and the two servants never failed to be as respectful as they could. Her restraint was a certain environment, so as to prevent her from leaving the park grounds. She felt walled in by a barrier which she could not pass, but within this barrier liberty of movement was allowed. At the same time, she knew that she was watched; and since her first discovery of Hugo on her track, she felt sure that if she ever went any where he would stealthily follow, and not allow her to go out of sight. Whether he would lift his hand to prevent actual escape, if the chance should present itself, was a thing which she could not answer, nor did she feel inclined to try it as yet.

During the few days that followed her first memorable experience she made no further attempt to escape, or even to search out a way of escape. What had become of Miss Plympton she did not know, and could only imagine. She still indulged the hope, however, that Miss Plympton was at Dalton, and looked forward with confidence to see her coming to Dalton Hall, accompanied by the officers of the law, to effect her deliverance. It was this hope that now sustained her, and prevented her from sinking into despair.

Of Wiggins during those few days she saw nothing more than a distant glimpse. She remained in the room which she first occupied during the greater part of the time. Nor did she see much of Mrs. Dunbar. From an occasional remark she gathered that she was cleaning the drawing-room or dusting it; but in this Edith now took no interest whatever. The Hall was now a prison-house, and the few plans which she had been making at first were now thrown aside and forgotten. Mrs. Dunbar brought her her meals at regular intervals, but Edith never took the slightest notice of her. She could not help observing at times in Mrs. Dunbar's manner, and especially in her look, a whole world of sorrowful sympathy, but after her unmistakable championship of Wiggins, she could not feel the slightest confidence in her.

At length one morning Wiggins once more called upon her. She was seated near the window when she heard a knock. The door was already open, and turning, she saw Wiggins. She bowed slightly, but said nothing, and Wiggins bowed in return, after which he entered and seated himself, fixing his solemn eyes upon her in his usual way.

"It is a matter of great regret," said he, "that I am forced to give pain to one for whom I entertain so much kindness, and even, let me add, affection. Had you made your return to this place a little less abruptly, you would have found, I am sure, a different reception, and your position would have been less unpleasant."

"Would you have allowed me my liberty," asked Edith, "and the society of my friends, if I had delayed longer before my return? If so, let me go back now, and I will give you notice before coming here again."

Wiggins shook his head mournfully.

"I am one," said he, "who has had deeper sorrows than usually fall to the lot of man; yet none, I assure you—no, not one—has ever caused me more pain than my present false position toward you. Can you not place some confidence in me, and think that this is all for—for your good?"

"You speak so plaintively," said Edith, "that I should be touched, if your words were not belied by your acts. What do you think can compensate for the loss of liberty? Were you ever imprisoned? Did you ever have a jailer over you? Did you ever know what it was to be shut in with walls over which you could not pass, and to know that the jailer's eyes were always upon you? Wait till you have felt all this, and then you will understand how empty and idle all your present words must be."

While she said these words Wiggins sat as if he had been turned to stone. His eyes were fixed on her with a look of utter horror. His hands trembled. As she stopped he shuddered, and hastily looked behind him. Then another shudder passed through him. At last, with a violent effort, he recovered something of his former calm.

"God grant," said he, "that you may never know what I have known of all that which you now mention!"

His voice trembled as he spoke these words, and when he had said them he relapsed into silence.

"Since you have invoked the name of the Deity," said Edith, solemnly, "if you have any reverence for your Maker, I ask you now, in His name, by what right you keep me here."

"I am your—guardian," said Wiggins, slowly; "your—guardian; yes," he added, thoughtfully, "that is the word."

"My guardian! Who made you my guardian? Who had the right to put you over me?"

Wiggins paused, and raised his head, which had been bent forward for a few moments past, looked at Edith with a softer light in his solemn eyes, and said, in a low voice, which had a wonderful sweetness in its intonation,

"Your father."

Edith looked at him earnestly for a moment, affected in spite of herself by his look and by his voice; but suddenly the remembrance of her wrongs drove off completely her momentary emotion.

"Do you think my father would have made you my guardian," said she, "if he had suspected what you were going to do with me?"

"I solemnly assure you that he did know, and that he did approve."

At this Edith smiled. Wiggins now seemed too methodical for a madman, and she began to understand that he was assuming these solemn airs, so as to make an impression upon her. Having made up her mind to this, she determined to question him further, so as to see what more he proposed to do.

"Your father," said Wiggins, "was my friend; and I will do for you whatever I would have done for him."

"I have no doubt of that," said Edith. "Indeed, you are doing for me now precisely what I have reason to understand you did for him."

"I do not comprehend you," said Wiggins.

"It is of no consequence," said Edith. "We will let it pass. Let us return to the subject. You assert that you are my guardian. Does that give you the right to be my jailer—to confine me here, to cut me off from all my friends?"

"You use harsh words," said Wiggins; "but nevertheless it is a fact that the law does allow the guardian this power. It regards him in the place of a parent. All that a father can do, a guardian can do. As a father can restrain a child, so can a guardian, if he deems such restraint necessary.

Moreover, if the ward should escape, the law will hand him back to his guardian, just as it would hand back a child to its father." Not one word of this did Edith believe, and so it made no impression. Having already got the idea in her mind that Wiggins was melodramatic, and playing a part, she had no doubt that his words would be regulated by the same desire that governed his acts, and would be spoken exclusively with the view of producing an impression upon herself. She therefore looked at him with unchanged feelings, and instantly replied:

"It would be very fortunate for you if it were so, but for my part I think better of the law. At the same time, since you claim all this authority over me, I should like to know how long you think this power will last. You do not seem to think that I am of age."

"That matters not," said Wiggins. "My control over the estates and my guardianship over you are of such a nature that they can not cease till your marriage."

"Oh, then," said Edith, "according to that, I ought to try to get married as soon as possible. And this, I suppose, is your sole reason for shutting me up?"

Wiggins said nothing, but sat looking gloomily at her.

By his last words Edith now found what appeared to her a clew to his whole plan. He was, or pretended to be, her guardian; he had been appointed, or pretended to have been appointed, by her father. It might have been so. Edith could well imagine how in previous years he had made this false friend his executor and the guardian of his child; and then, in the anguish of the trial and of the punishment, forgotten to annul the deed; or Wiggins may have forged the document himself. If he really was the false friend who had betrayed her father, and who had committed that forgery for which her father innocently suffered, then he might easily forge such a document as this in her father's name.

Such was her conclusion from his words, though she did not think fit to say as much to him. What she did say, however, seemed to have affected him, for he did not speak for some time.

"You have no conception," said he at length, "of the torment that some of your careless words cause. You do not know what you do, or what you say. There is something that I can not tell, whatever be the price of silence—something that concerns you and me, and your father, and two great houses—and it is this that makes me dumb, and forces me to stand in this false position. You look upon me as the crafty, scheming steward—one who is your pitiless jailer—and I have to bear it. But there is something which I can say—and I warn you, or rather I implore you, not to disbe-

lieve me; I entreat you to let my words have some weight. I declare to you, then, by all that is most sacred among men, that this restraint which I ask you to undergo is out of no selfish desire, no avarice, no lack of honor for you, and—affection, but because of a plan which I have, the success of which concerns all of us, and you not the least."

Edith listened to this without emotion, though at another time the solemnity of such an appeal could not have failed to enforce belief. But now Wiggins seemed only melodramatic, and every word seemed false.

"What plan?" she asked.

"It is this," said Wiggins, looking all around with his usual cautious vigilance, and drawing nearer to her. "Your father's name is a dishonored one—the name you bear is covered with the stain of infamy. What would you not give if his memory could be redeemed from wrong; if even at this late hour his character could be vindicated? You have, I am sure, a noble and a devoted heart. You would be willing to do much for this. But what I ask of you is very little. I ask only silence and seclusion. If you should consent to this, my work may be done before very long; and then, whatever may be your feelings toward me, I shall feel that I have done my work, and nothing further that this world may do, whether of good or evil, shall be able to affect me. I ask this—more, I entreat it of you, I implore you, in the sacred name of an injured father, by all his unmerited wrongs and sufferings, to unite with me in this holy purpose, and help me to accomplish it. Do not be deceived by appearances. Believe me, I entreat you, for your father's sake."

Never were words spoken with greater apparent earnestness than these; and never was any voice or manner more solemn and impressive. Yet upon Edith no more effect was produced than before. When she had asked him what his plan was, she had been prepared for this, or something like it. She saw now that the mode by which he tried to work upon her was by adopting the solemn and the pathetic style. The consequence was that every gesture, every intonation, every look, seemed artificial, hollow, and insincere. For never could she forget the one fatal fact that this was her jailer, and that she was a helpless prisoner. More than this, he had as good as asserted his intention of keeping her a prisoner till her marriage, which, under such circumstances, meant simply till her death. Not for one instant could he be brought to consent to relax the strictness of his control over her. For such a man to make such an appeal as this was idle; and she found herself wondering, before he had got half through, why he should take the trouble to try to deceive her. When he had finished she did not care to answer him, or to tell him what was on her mind. She was averse to quarrels, scenes, or any thing approaching to scolding or empty threats. What she did say, therefore, was perfectly commonplace, but for that reason perhaps all the more disappointing to the man who had made such an appeal to her.

"What you say," said she, "does not require any answer. It is as though I should ask you to submit to imprisonment for an indefinite period, or for life, for instance, for the sake of a friend. And you would not think such a request very reasonable. What I require of you is, not idle words, but liberty. When you ask me to believe you, you must first gain my confidence by treating me with common justice. Or if you will not release me, let me at least see my friends. That is not much. I have only one friend—Miss Plympton."

"You appear to think more of this Miss Plympton than you do of your own father," said Wiggins, gloomily.

"What I think of my father is of no consequence to you," said Edith; "but as to Miss Plympton, she took me as a dying gift from my dear mamma, and has loved me with a mother's love ever since, and is the only mother I have known since childhood. When you turned her away from my gates you did an injury to both of us which makes all your protestations of honesty useless. But she is not under your control, and you may be sure that she will exert herself on my behalf. It seems to me that you have not considered what the result will be if she comes back in the name of the law."

"I have considered every thing," said Wiggins. Then, after a pause, he added, "So you love Miss Plympton very dearly?"

"Very, very dearly!"

"And her words would have great weight with you?"

"Very great weight."

"If, now, she should tell you that you might put confidence in me, you would feel more inclined to do so?"

Edith hesitated at this; but the thought occurred to her of Miss Plympton's detestation of Wiggins, and the utter impossibility of a change of opinion on her part.

"If Miss Plympton should put confidence in you," said she, "I should indeed feel my own opinions changed."

Upon this Wiggins sat meditating profoundly for a short time.

"Suppose, now," said he at length, "that you should receive a note from Miss Plympton in which she should give you a more favorable opinion of me, would you accept it from her?"

"I certainly should be happy to get any thing of that kind from her," said Edith.

"Well," said Wiggins, "I had not intended to take any one into my confidence, certainly not any stranger, and that stranger a

woman; but I am so unable to tell you all, and at the same time I long so to have your confidence, that I may possibly decide to see Miss Plympton myself. If I do, rest assured her opinion of me will change. This will endanger the success of my plan; but I must run the risk—yes, whatever it is; for if this goes on, I must even give up the plan itself, and with it all my hopes for myself—and for you."

These last words Wiggins spoke in a low voice, half to himself, and with his eyes turned to the ground. Edith heard the words, but thought nothing of the meaning of them. To her, every thing was done for effect, nothing was sincere. If she did not understand the meaning of some of his words, she did not trouble herself to try to, but dismissed them from her thoughts as merely affectations. As to his allusion to Miss Plympton, and his idea of visiting her, Edith did not for a moment imagine that he meant it. She thought that this was of a piece with the rest.

With these last words Wiggins arose from his chair, and with a slight bow to Edith, took his departure. The interview had been a singular one, and the manner of entreaty which Wiggins had adopted toward her served to perplex her still more. It was part of the system which he had originated, by which she was never treated in any other way than with the utmost apparent respect and consideration, but in reality guarded as a prisoner with the most sleepless vigilance.

CHAPTER XIII.

A WONDERFUL ACTOR.

A FEW more days passed, and Edith remained in the same state as before. Occasionally she would walk up and down the terrace in front of the house, but her dislike to being tracked and watched and followed prevented her from going any distance. She saw that she could not hope to escape by her unassisted efforts, and that her only hope lay in assistance from the outside world. Miss Plympton, she felt sure, could never forget her, and would do all that possibly could be done to effect her release as soon as possible. But day after day passed, and still no deliverer appeared.

She saw nothing of Wiggins during those days, but Mrs. Dunbar attended on her as usual. To her, however, Edith now paid no attention whatever. In her opinion she was the associate of her jailer, and a willing partner in the wrong that was being done to her. Under these circumstances she could not show to her any of that gentle courtesy and kindly consideration which her nature impelled her to exhibit to all with whom she was brought in contact. On the contrary, she never even looked at her; but often, when she was conscious that Mrs. Dunbar was gazing upon her with that strange, wistful look that characterized her, she refused to respond in any way. And so the time passed on, Edith in a state of drear solitude, and waiting, and waiting.

At length she received another visit from Wiggins. He came to her room as before, and knocked in his usual style. He looked at her with his usual solemn earnestness, and advanced toward her at once.

"You will remember," said he, "that when I was last here, a few days ago, I said that I might possibly decide to see Miss Plympton myself. It was solely for your sake; and to do so I have made a great sacrifice of feeling and of judgment."

"Miss Plympton?" interrupted Edith, eagerly. "Have you seen Miss Plympton?"

"I have."

"Where? At Dalton? Is she at Dalton still?"

"She is not."

Edith's countenance, which had flushed with hope, now fell at this. It looked as though Miss Plympton had gone away too hastily.

"Where did you see her?" she asked, in a low voice, trying to conceal her agitation.

"At Plympton Terrace," said Wiggins.

"Plympton Terrace," repeated Edith, in a dull monotone, while her breast heaved with irrepressible emotion. Her heart sank within her. This indeed looked like a desertion of her on the part of her only friend. But after a moment's despondency she rallied once more, as the thought came to her that this was all a fiction, and that Wiggins had not seen her at all.

"Yes," said Wiggins, "I have seen her, and had a long interview, in which I explained many things to her. It was all for your sake, for had you not been concerned, I should never have thought of telling her what I did. But I was anxious to get you to confide in me, and you said that if Miss Plympton should put confidence in me, you yourself would feel inclined to do so. It is because I want your confidence, your trust —because I can't tell you all yet, and because without your trust I am weak—that I have done this. Your misery breaks up all my plans, and I wish to put an end to it. Now I have seen Miss Plympton at Plympton Terrace, and she has written you a letter, which I have brought."

With these words he drew from his pocket a letter, and handed it to Edith. With a flushed face and a rapidly throbbing heart Edith took the letter. It seemed like that for which she had been so long waiting, but at the same time there was a certain ill-defined apprehension on her mind of disappointment. Had that letter come through any other channel, it would have excited

nothing but unmingled joy; but the channel was suspicious, and Edith did not yet believe that he had really been to Plympton Terrace. She suspected some new piece of acting, some new kind of deceit or attempt to deceive, and the fact that she was still a prisoner was enough to fortify all her obstinate disbelief in the protestations of this man.

But on the letter she saw her own name in the well-known and unmistakable handwriting of Miss Plympton. She was quite familiar with that writing, so much so that she could not be deceived. This letter, then, was from her own hand, and as she read it she began to think that after all Wiggins was true in his statement that he had seen her. Then, seeing this, with deep agitation, and with a thousand conflicting emotions, she tore it open. She read the following:

"PLYMPTON TERRACE.

"MY DARLING EDITH,—I can not tell you, my own sweet love, how I have suffered from anxiety since I parted from you at the gates of Dalton Hall. I went back, and received your dear note that night, which consoled me. On the following day I looked for you, but you did not come. Full of impatience, I went to the gate, but was not admitted, though I tried every inducement to make the porter open to me. Turning away, I determined to go at once in search of some means by which I could gain access to you, or free you from your position. After much thought I went to visit Sir Lionel Dudleigh, who heard my story, and promised to act at once on my behalf. He advised me to return to Plympton Terrace, and wait here till he should take the necessary steps, which I accordingly did. I have been here ever since, and I can truly say, my darling, that you have not once been out of my thoughts, nor have I till this day been free from anxiety about you. My worst fear has been about your own endurance of this restraint; for, knowing your impatient disposition, I have feared that you might fret yourself into illness if you were not soon released from your unpleasant situation.

"But, my dearest, this day has brought me a most wonderful and unexpected deliverance from all my fear. This morning a caller came who refused to send up his name. On going to the parlor I found a venerable man, who introduced himself as Mr. Wiggins. I confess when I saw him I was surprised, as I had imagined a very different kind of man. But you know what a bitter prejudice I have always had against this man, and so you may imagine how I received him. In a few words he explained his errand, and stated that it was exclusively with reference to you.

"And now, my own darling Edith, I come to that about which I scarce know how to speak. Let me hasten to say that both you and I have totally misunderstood Mr. Wiggins. Oh, Edith, how can I speak of him, or what can I say? He has told me such a wonderful and such a piteous story! It can not be told to you, for reasons which I respect, though I do not approve altogether of them. I think it would be better to tell you all, for then your situation would be far different, and he would not stand in so fearfully false a position. But his reasons are all-powerful with himself, and so I shall say nothing. But oh, my dearest, let me implore you, let me entreat you, to give to this man your reverence and your trust! Be patient, and wait. Perhaps he may overcome his high and delicate scruples, and let you know what his purposes are. For my part, my only grief now is that I have done something toward giving you that fear and hate and distrust of him which now animate you. I entreat you to dismiss all these feelings, and bear with your present lot till brighter days come. The purpose of Mr. Wiggins is a high and holy one, and this he will work out successfully, I hope and believe. Do not, dearest, by your impatience give any additional pang to that noble heart. Beware of what you say or do now, for fear lest hereafter it may cause the deepest remorse. Spare him, for he has suffered much. The name of your family, the memory of your injured father, are all at stake now; and I pray you, dearest, to restrain yourself, and try to bear with the present state of things. If you can only believe me or be influenced by me, you will give him all your trust, and even your affection. But if you can not do this at once, at least spare him any further pain. Alas, how that noble heart has suffered! When I think of his mournful story, I almost lose all faith in humanity, and would lose it altogether were it not for the spectacle which is afforded by himself—a spectacle of purest and loftiest virtue, and stainless honor, and endless self-devotion. But I must say no more, for fear that I may say too much, so I will stop.

"Mamma unites with me in kindest love, and believe me, my dearest Edith,

"Ever affectionately yours,
"PAMELA PLYMPTON.

"P.S.—I have not referred to that noblest of women, Mrs. Dunbar. Oh, dearest Edith, I hope that ere this she has won your whole heart, and that you have already divined something of that exalted spirit and that meek self-sacrifice which make her life so sublime. I can say no more. P. P."

Now it will be evident to the reader that if Miss Plympton had really written the above, and had meant to incite Edith to give her affectionate reverence to her two jailers, she could not have gone about it in a worse way. Edith read it through, and at the beginning thought that it might be authentic, but when she came to the latter half, that idea began to depart. As she read on further and further, it appeared more and more unlike Miss Plympton. The sudden transition from hate to admiration, the extravagant terms that were made use of, the exhortations to herself to change her feelings toward one like Wiggins, the stilted phraseology, the incoherencies, all seemed so unlike the manner of Miss Plympton as to be only fit for derision. But the postscript seemed worst of all. Here the writer had overdone herself, or himself, and by dragging in the housekeeper, Mrs. Dunbar, and holding her up for the same extravagant admiration, a climax of utter absurdity had been attained.

On reading this singular letter Edith's thoughts came quick and vehement through her mind. If this letter were indeed the work of Miss Plympton, then all hope for her interference was utterly gone. If Miss Plympton wrote that, then she was evidently either mad, or else she had undergone a change of mind so incomprehensible that it was equivalent to madness. But Miss Plympton could never have written it. Of that she felt as sure as she was of her own existence.

If she did not, who did write it? The handwriting was exactly like that of her revered friend. There was not the slightest difference between this and that with which she was so familiar. It was her handwriting indeed, but it was not Miss Plympton who spoke there. The hand was the hand of Miss Plympton, but the voice was the voice of Wiggins.

He had written all this, she felt sure. These allusions to his sufferings, these hints about a plan, these references to her father, these entreaties to her to give him her affection and trust—all these were familiar. Wiggins had already made use of them all. It was, then, the work of Wiggins beyond a doubt.

And how? Could she doubt for a moment how? By imitating the writing of Miss Plympton. Perhaps he had sent a messenger there, and obtained a letter, part of which he had copied. The first half might have been copied verbatim, while the last must certainly be his own work. As to his power to imitate her writing, need she hesitate about that? Was not her father condemned for a forgery which another had done? Had she not already suspected that this false friend was no other than John Wiggins himself? Forgery! that was only too easy for a man like him. And she now saw in that letter an effort to accomplish her ruin by the same weapon with which her father's had been wrought.

All these thoughts rushed through her mind as she read and as she stood looking over the pages and thinking about what

"STEADYING HIMSELF, HE STOOD THERE TREMBLING."

had been done. All the hate that she had ever felt for her father's betrayer, which had increased when he had become her own oppressor, now glowed hot within her heart, and could not be repressed.

Meanwhile Wiggins had stood before her on the same spot where he had stopped when he handed her the letter. He had stood there with his eyes fixed upon her, and on his face an expression of solemn suspense—a suspense so anxious that one might have supposed his whole life depended upon Edith's decision. So he stood, rigid, mute, with all his soul centring itself in that gaze which he fixed on her, in an attitude which seemed almost that of a suppliant, for his reverend head was bowed, and his aged form bent, and his thin hands folded over one another, before him.

Such were the face and figure and look and attitude that Edith saw as she raised her head. Had her anger been less fervid and her indignation less intense, she would surely have been affected by that venerable suppliant form; but as it was, there was no place for any softer emotion.

She rose from her chair, and as her white face showed itself opposite to his, her eyes looked upon him, as once before, hard, stern, pitiless; but this time their glance was even more cruel and implacable. She held out the letter to him, and said, quietly,

"Take it."

Wiggins looked at her, and spoke in a voice that was scarcely audible.

"What—do—you—mean?"

Carried beyond herself now by this attempt to prolong what seemed so stupid and transparent a deceit, Edith spoke her whole mind plainly:

"This is a close imitation of Miss Plympton's handwriting, but she could never write such words—never! You have not visited her; you have not seen her. This is a forgery. Once you were successful in forging, but now you can not be. By that crime you once destroyed the father, but if you destroy the daughter, you must—"

But what Edith was going to say remained unsaid, for at this point she was interrupted.

Wiggins had listened to her with a stunned

D

expression, as though not able to comprehend her. But as the fullness of the meaning of her words reached his ears he shuddered from head to foot. A low moan escaped him. He started back, and regarded Edith with eyes that stared in utter horror.

"Stop! stop!" he cried, in a low, harsh voice. "No more, no more! This is madness. Girl, you will some day weep tears of blood for this! You will one day repent of this, and every word that you have spoken will pierce your own heart as they now pierce mine. You are mad: you do not know what you are saying. O Heavens! how mad you are in your ignorance! And I need only utter one word to reduce you to despair. If I were dying now I could say that which would give you life-long remorse, and make you carry a broken heart to your grave!"

He stopped abruptly, and staggered back, but caught at a chair, and, steadying himself, stood there trembling, with his head bowed, and heavy sighs escaping him. Soon hasty footsteps were heard, and Mrs. Dunbar hurried into the room, with a frightened face, looking first at Edith and then at Wiggins. She said not a word, however, but approaching Wiggins, drew his arm in hers, and led him out of the room.

Edith stood for some time looking after them.

"What a wonderful actor he is!" she thought; "and Mrs. Dunbar was waiting behind the scenes to appear when her turn should come. They went out just like people on the stage."

CHAPTER XIV.
TWO CALLERS.

TIME passed slowly with the prisoner, but the freedom for which she longed seemed as distant as ever. Miss Plympton's apparent desertion of her was the worst blow that she had yet received, and even if the letter that Wiggins had shown her was a forgery, it still remained evident that but little was to be hoped for now in that quarter. It seemed to her now as if she was cut off from all the world. Her relatives were indifferent; Sir Lionel Dudleigh was inaccessible; Miss Plympton appeared to have given her up; the county families who, under ordinary circumstances, might have tried to call on her, would probably view with indifference, if not prejudice, the daughter of a convict. All these circumstances, therefore, reduced her to deep dejection, and made her feel as though she was indeed at the mercy of her jailer.

While thus conscious of her helplessness, however, she did not fear any thing worse than imprisonment. The idea had occurred to her of further injury, but had been at once

dismissed. She did not think it possible that her life could be in danger. It seemed to her that Wiggins owed all his power to the very fact of her life. He was her guardian, as he had said, and if she were to die, he would be no more than any one else. The nearest heirs would then come forward, and he would have to retire. Those nearest heirs would undoubtedly be those relatives of whom Miss Plympton had told her, or perhaps Sir Lionel Dudleigh, of whom she now thought frequently, and who began to be her last hope.

The fact that Wiggins was her guardian till her marriage showed her plainly that he would endeavor to postpone any such a thing as marriage for an indefinite period. In order to do this he would, no doubt, keep her secluded as long as he could. He would feel it to be for his interest that her health should be taken care of, for any sickness of hers would necessarily alarm him. The thought of this made her wish for illness, so that she might have a doctor, and thus find some one who was not in his employ. But then, on the other hand, she feared that the doctor whom he might send would be some one in his pay, or in his confidence, like all the rest, and so her desire for illness faded out.

At last a day came when the monotony of her life was interrupted. She was looking out of her window when she was startled by the sound of a carriage coming up the main avenue. The sound filled her with excitement. It could not be Wiggins. It must be some one for her, some friend— Miss Plympton herself. Her heart beat fast at the thought. Yes, it must be Miss Plympton. She had not given her up. She had been laboring for her deliverance, and now she was coming, armed with the authority of the law, to effect her release. Edith's first impulse was to hurry down and meet the carriage, but long and frequent disappointment had taught her the need of restraint, and so she remained at the window till the carriage came into view.

Well was it for her that she had tried to repress her hopes, and had forborne to rush down at her first impulse. One glance showed her that the new-comers were strangers. It was a handsome baronche that she saw, and in it were a lady and a gentleman, neither of whom she had seen before. But even in the midst of her disappointment hope still found a place, and the thought occurred to her that though these might not be familiar to her, they yet might be friends, and might even have been sent by Miss Plympton. But, if so, how came they here? Did they have any trouble at the gate? How was it that Wiggins relaxed his regulations in their favor? Could they be friends of his own, after all? Yes, it must be so. Filled with thoughts like these, which thus alternated between hope and fear, Edith watched the new-comers, as the carriage rolled up to the Hall, with something of the same emotions that fill the shipwrecked sailor as he watches the progress of a lifeboat that comes to save him. Even now it was with difficulty that she prevented herself from rushing down and meeting them, and imploring their help at once. But she restrained her impatience with a great effort, and summing up all her self-control, she waited.

She heard the great bell resounding through the long halls; she heard the footsteps of Mrs. Dunbar as she went down. Then there was a long delay, after which Mrs. Dunbar returned and entered the room. She appeared troubled, and there was on her face a larger share than usual of that anxious, fearful watchfulness which made its wonted expression. There was also something more—something that seemed like utter consternation and bewilderment; she was as white as ashes; her hands clutched one another convulsively; her eyes were fixed in an abstracted gaze on vacancy; and when she spoke it was in a low voice like a whisper, and in scarcely articulate words.

"Some one—to see you."

That was all that Mrs. Dunbar said.

"To see me!" repeated Edith, starting from her chair, and too excited to notice Mrs. Dunbar's manner. Hope arose once more, eager and unrestrained, and without stopping a moment to ask any thing about them, or to make any preparations to see them, she hurried down, fearing lest the smallest delay might be dangerous.

On entering the room the visitors introduced themselves as Captain and Mrs. Mowbray; but as the captain was young, and Mrs. Mowbray apparently about fifty, they appeared to Edith to be mother and son.

Mrs. Mowbray's features showed that in her youth she might have been beautiful; yet there was an expression on them which was not attractive to Edith, being a compound of primness and inanity, which made her look like a superannuated fashion plate. She was elaborately dressed: a rich robe of very thick silk, a frisette with showy curls, a bonnet with many ornaments of ribbons and flowers, and a heavy Cashmere shawl—such was her costume. Her eyes were undeniably fine, and a white veil covered her face, which to Edith looked as though it was painted or powdered.

The gentleman at first sight seemed like a remarkably handsome man. He was tall and well formed; chestnut hair curled short over his wide brow; square chin, whiskers of the intensely fashionable sort, and heavy mustache. His eyes were gray, and his features were regular and finely chiseled.

In spite of Edith's longing for friends, there was something in the appearance of these two which excited a feeling akin to aversion in her mind; and this was more particularly the case with regard to Captain Mowbray. As he looked at her there was a cold, hard light in his eyes which gave her the idea of a cruel and pitiless nature; and there was a kind of cynicism in his tone when he spoke which repelled her at once. He had all the air of a roué, yet even roués have often a savor of jolly recklessness about them which conciliates. About this man, however, there was nothing of this; there was nothing but cold, cynical self-regard, and Edith saw in him one who might be as hateful as even Wiggins, and far more to be dreaded.

"I'm afraid," said Mrs. Mowbray, "that we are intruders on your seclusion; but we waited some time, and at last concluded to break in upon you in spite of your rigid restrictions. But others have anticipated us, I presume, and so perhaps you will pardon us."

"My seclusion is not my own choice," said Edith, mournfully. "You are the first whom I have seen."

"Then, my dear Miss Dalton, since we are not unwelcome, I feel very glad that we have ventured. May I hope that we will see a great deal of one another?"

Mrs. Mowbray's manner of speaking was essentially in keeping with her appearance. It may be called a fashion-plate style. It was both fluent and insincere. She spoke in what is sometimes called a "made voice"—that is to say, a voice not her own, made up for company—a florid falsetto: a tone that Edith detested.

Could she throw herself upon the sympathies of these? Who were they? Might they not be in league with Wiggins for some purpose unknown to her? It was curious that these strangers were able to pass the gates which were shut to all the rest of the world. These were her thoughts, and she determined to find out from these Mowbrays, if possible, how it was that they got in.

"Had you any difficulty at the gates with the porter?" asked Edith.

"Oh no," said Captain Mowbray, "not the least."

"Did he offer no resistance?"

"Certainly not. Why should he?"

"Because he has been in the habit of turning back all visitors."

"Ah," said Mowbray, listlessly, "that is a thing you ought not to allow."

"I was afraid," said Edith, "that he had tried to keep you back."

"Me?" said Mowbray, with strong emphasis. "He knows better than that, I fancy."

"And yet he is capable of any amount of insolence."

"Indeed!" said Mowbray, languidly.

"Then why don't you turn him off, and get a civil man?"

"Because—because," said Edith, in a tremulous voice, "there is one here who—who countermands all my orders."

"Ah!" said Mowbray, in a listless tone, which seemed to say that he took no interest whatever in these matters.

"Dear me!" said Mrs. Mowbray, in a querulous voice. "Servants are such dreadful plagues. Worry? why, it's nothing else but worry! And they're so shockingly impertinent. They really have no sense of respect. I don't know for my part what the world's coming to. I suppose it's all these dreadful radicals and newspapers and working-men's clubs and things. When I was young it was not so."

"You have not been in Dalton Hall since you were a young girl, Miss Dalton?" said Mowbray, inquiringly.

"No; not for ten years."

"Do you find it much changed?"

"Very much—and for the worse. I have had great difficulties to contend with."

"Indeed?" said Mowbray, indifferently. "Well, at any rate, you have a noble old place, with every thing around you to make you enjoy life."

"Yes—all but one thing."

"Ah?"

"I am a prisoner here, Captain Mowbray," said Edith, with an appealing glance and a mournful tone.

"Ah, really?" said Mowbray; and taking up a book he began to turn over the leaves in a careless way.

"A prisoner?" put in Mrs. Mowbray. "Yes, and so you are. It's like imprisonment, this dreadful mourning. But one has to act in accordance with public sentiment. And I suppose you grieve very much, my dear, for your poor dear papa. Poor man! I remember seeing him once in London. It was my first season. There were Lord Rutland and the Marquis of Abercorn and the young Duke of Severn—all the rage. Do you know, my dear, I was quite a belle then."

From this beginning Mrs. Mowbray went on to chatter about the gayeties of her youth—and Lord A, how handsome he was; and Sir John B, how rich he was; and Colonel C, how extravagant he was. Then she wandered off to the subject of state balls, described the dress she wore at her first presentation at court, and the appearance of his Gracious Majesty King George, and how he was dressed, and who were with him, and what he said—while all the time poor Edith, who was longing for an opportunity to tell them about herself, sat quivering with impatience and agitation.

During all this time Captain Mowbray looked bored, and sat examining the furniture and Edith alternately. He made no effort to take part in the conversation, but seemed anxious to bring the visit to a close. This Edith saw with a sinking heart. These, then, were the ones from whom she had hoped assistance. But unpromising as these were, they formed just now her only hope, and so, as they at length rose to go, Edith grew desperate, and burst forth in a low but quick and excited tone.

"Wait one moment," said she, "and excuse me if I give you trouble; but the position I am in forces me to appeal to you for help, though you are only strangers. I am actually imprisoned in this place. A man here—Wiggins, the late steward—confines me within these grounds, and will not let me go out, nor will he allow any of my friends to come and see me. He keeps me a prisoner under strict watch. Wherever I go about the grounds I am followed. He will not even allow my friends to write to me. I am the owner, but he is the master. Captain Mowbray, I appeal to you. You are an officer and a gentleman. Save me from this cruel imprisonment! I want nothing but liberty. I want to join my friends, and gain my rights. I entreat you to help me, or if you can not help me yourself, let others know, or send me a lawyer, or take a letter for me to some friends."

And with these words poor Edith sank back into the chair from which she had risen, and sobbed aloud. She had spoken in feverish, eager tones, and her whole frame quivered with agitation.

Mrs. Mowbray listened to her with a complacent smile, and when Edith sank back in her chair she sat down too, and taking out her handkerchief and a bottle of salts, began to apply the one to her eyes and the other to her nose alternately. As for Captain Mowbray, he coolly resumed his seat, yawned, and then sat quietly looking first at Edith and then at Mrs. Mowbray. At length Edith by a violent effort regained her self-control, and looking at the captain, she said, indignantly,

"You say nothing, Sir. Am I to think that you refuse this request?"

"By no means," said Captain Mowbray, dryly. "Silence is said usually to signify consent."

"You will help me, then, after all?" cried Edith, earnestly.

"Wait a moment," said Captain Mowbray, a little abruptly. "Who is this man, Miss Dalton, of whom you complain?"

"Wiggins."

"Wiggins?" said Mowbray. "Ah! was he not the steward of your late father?"

"Yes."

"I have heard somewhere that he was appointed your guardian. Is that so?"

"I don't know," said Edith. "He claims to be my guardian; but I am of age, and I don't see how he can be."

"The law of guardianship is very peculiar," said Mowbray. "Perhaps he has right on his side."

"Right!" cried Edith, warmly. "How can he have the right to restrict my liberty, and make me a prisoner on my own estate? I am of age. The estate is absolutely mine. He is only a servant. Have I no rights whatever?"

"I should say you had," said Mowbray, languidly stroking his mustache. "I should say you had, of course. But this guardian business is a troublesome thing, and Wiggins, as your guardian, may have a certain amount of power."

Edith turned away impatiently.

"I hoped," said she, "that the mere mention of my situation would be enough to excite your sympathy. I see that I was mistaken, and am sorry that I have troubled you."

"You are too hasty," said Mowbray. "You see, I look at your position merely from a legal point of view."

"A legal point!" exclaimed Mrs. Mowbray, who had now dried her eyes and restored the handkerchief and the salts bottle to their proper places. "A legal point! Ah, Miss Dalton, my son is great on legal points. He is quite a lawyer. If he had embraced the law as a profession, which I once thought of getting him to do, though that was when he was quite a child, and something or other put it quite out of my head—if he had embraced the law as a profession, my dear, he might have aspired to the bench."

Edith rested her brow on her hand and bit her lips, reproaching herself for having confided her troubles to these people. Wiggins himself was more endurable.

"Your case," said Captain Mowbray, tapping his boot with his cane in a careless manner, "is one which requires a very great amount of careful consideration."

Edith said nothing. She had become hopeless.

"If there is a will, and Wiggins has powers given him in that instrument, he can give you a great deal of trouble without your being able to prevent it."

This scene was becoming intolerable, and Edith could bear it no longer.

"I want to make one final request," said she, with difficulty controlling the scorn and indignation which she felt. "It is this—will you give me a seat in your carriage as far as the village inn?"

"The village inn?" repeated Mowbray, and then he was silent for some time. His mother looked at him inquiringly and curiously.

"I have friends," said Edith, "and I will go to them. All that I ask of you is the drive of a few rods to the village inn. You can leave me there, and I will never trouble you again."

"Well, really, Miss Dalton," said Mowbray, after another pause, in which Edith suffered frightful suspense—"really, your request is a singular one. I would do any thing for you—but this is different. You see, you are a sort of ward, and to carry you away from the control of your guardian might be a very dangerous offense."

"In fact, you are afraid, I see," said Edith, bitterly. "Well, you need say no more. I will trouble you no further."

Saying this, she rose and stood in all her stately beauty before them—cold, haughty, and without a trace of emotion left. They were struck by the change. Thus far she had appeared a timid, agitated, frightened girl; they now saw in her something of that indomitable spirit which had already baffled and perplexed her jailers.

"We hope to see more of you," said Mrs. Mowbray. "We shall call again soon."

To this Edith made no reply, but saw them to the drawing-room door. Then they descended the stairs and entered the carriage, and she heard them drive off. Then she went up to her room, and sat looking out of the window.

"He is worse than Wiggins," she muttered. "He is a gentleman, but a villain—and a ruined one too—perhaps in the pay of Wiggins. Wiggins sent him here."

CHAPTER XV.

A PANIC AMONG THE JAILERS.

THE arrival of these visitors had produced an extraordinary effect upon Mrs. Dunbar. So great was her agitation that she could scarcely announce them to Edith. So great was it that, though she was Edith's jailer, she did not dream of denying them the privilege of seeing her, but summoned Edith at once, as though she was free mistress of the house.

After Edith had gone down the agitation of Mrs. Dunbar continued, and grew even greater. She sank into a chair, and buried her face in her hands. In that position she remained motionless for a long time, and was at length aroused by the return of Edith from her interview with her visitors. At her entrance Mrs. Dunbar started up suddenly, and with downcast face left the room, without exciting any attention from Edith, who was too much taken up with her own thoughts about her visitors to notice any thing unusual about the appearance of her housekeeper.

Leaving Edith's room, Mrs. Dunbar walked along the hall with a slow and uncertain step, and at length reached a room at the west end. The door was closed. She knocked. A voice cried, "Come in," and she entered.

It was a large room, and it looked out upon the grounds in front of the house. A desk was in the middle, which was covered with papers. All around were shelves filled with books. It seemed to be a mixture of library and office. At the desk sat Wiggins, who looked up, as Mrs. Dunbar entered, with his usual solemn face.

Into this room Mrs. Dunbar entered without further ceremony, and after walking a few paces found a chair, into which she sank with something like a groan. Wiggins looked at her in silence, and regarding her with that earnest glance which was usual with him. Mrs. Dunbar sat for a few moments without saying a word, with her face buried in her hands, as it had been in Edith's room; but at length she raised her head, and looked at Wiggins. Her face was still deathly pale, her hands twitched the folds of her dress convulsively, and her eyes had a glassy stare that was almost terrible. It could be no common thing that had caused such deep emotion in one who was usually so self-contained.

At last she spoke.

"I have seen him!" said she, in a low tone, which was hardly raised above a whisper.

Wiggins looked at her in silence for some time, and at length said, in a low voice,

"He is here, then?"

"He is here," said Mrs. Dunbar. "But have you seen him? Why did you not tell me that he was here? The shock was terrible. You ought to have told me."

Wiggins sighed.

"I intended to do so," said he; "but I did not know that he would come so soon."

"When did you see him?" asked Mrs. Dunbar, abruptly.

"Yesterday—only yesterday."

"You knew him at once, of course, from his extraordinary likeness to—to the other one. I wish you had told me. Oh, how I wish you had told me! The shock was terrible."

And saying this, Mrs. Dunbar gave a deep sigh that was like a groan.

"The fact is," said Wiggins, "I have been trying to conjecture how he came here, and as I did not think he would come to the Hall—at least, not just yet—I thought I would spare you. Forgive me if I have made a mistake. I had no idea that he was coming to the Hall."

"How could he have come here?" said Mrs. Dunbar. "What possible thing could have sent him?"

"Well," said Wiggins, "I can understand that easily enough. This Miss Plympton, you know, as I told you, threatened that she would go to see Lionel. I forgot to ask her about that when I saw her, but it seems now that she must have carried out her threat. She has undoubtedly gone to see Lionel, and Lionel has sent his boy instead of coming

himself. Had he only come himself, all would have been well. That is the chief thing that I hoped for. But he has not chosen to come, and so here is the son instead of the father. It is unfortunate; it delays matters most painfully; but we must bear it."

"Do you think Lionel can suspect?" asked Mrs. Dunbar, anxiously.

"Suspect? Not he. I think that he objected to come himself for a very good reason. He has good grounds for declining to revisit Dalton Hall. He has sent his son to investigate, and how this enterprise will end remains to be seen."

"I don't see how he managed to get into the place at all," said Mrs. Dunbar. "Wilkins is usually very particular."

"Well," said Wiggins, "I can understand that only too well. Unfortunately he recognized Wilkins. My porter is unknown here, but any one from Lionel's place whose memory reaches back ten years will easily know him—the desperate poacher and almost murderer, whose affair with the gamekeeper of Dudleigh Manor cost him a sentence of transportation for twenty years. His face is one that does not change much, and so he was recognized at once. He came to me in a terrible way, frightened to death for fear of a fresh arrest; but I calmed him. I went to the lodge myself, and yesterday I saw him. I knew him at once, of course."

"But did he recognize you?" cried Mrs. Dunbar, in a voice full of fresh agitation.

"I fear so," said Wiggins.

At this Mrs. Dunbar started to her feet, and stared at Wiggins with a face full of terror. Then gradually her strength failed, and she sank back again, but her face still retained the same look.

"He did not recognize me at first," said Wiggins. "He seemed puzzled; but as I talked with him, and heard his threats about Wilkins, and about what he called Edith's imprisonment, he seemed gradually to find out all, or to surmise it. It could not have been my face; it must have been my voice, for that unfortunately has not changed, and he once knew that well, in the old days when he was visiting here. At any rate, he made it out, and from that moment tried to impress upon me that I was in his power."

"And did you tell him—all?"

"I—I told him nothing. I let him think what he chose. I was not going to break through my plans for his sake, nor for the sake of his foolish threats. But in thus forbearing I had to tolerate him, and hence this visit. He thinks that I am in his power. He does not understand. But I shall have to let him come here, or else make every thing known, and for that I am not at all prepared as yet. But oh, if it had only been Lionel!—if it had only been Lionel!"

"And so," said Mrs. Dunbar, after a long silence, "he knows all."

"He knows nothing," said Wiggins. "It is his ignorance and my own patient waiting that make him bold. But tell me this—did he recognize you?"

At this question Mrs. Dunbar looked with a fixed, rigid stare at Wiggins. Her lips quivered. For a moment she could not speak.

"He—he looked at me," said she, in a faltering voice—"he looked at me, but I was so overcome at the sight of him that my brain whirled. I was scarcely conscious of any thing. I heard him ask for Edith, and I hurried away. But oh, how hard—how hard it is! Oh, was ever any one in such a situation? To see him here—to see that face and hear that voice! Oh, what can I do—what can I do?"

And with these words Mrs. Dunbar broke down. Once more her head sank, and burying her face in her hands, she wept and sobbed convulsively. Wiggins looked at her, and as he looked there came over his face an expression of unutterable pity and sympathy, but he said not a word. As he looked at her he leaned his head on his hand, and a low, deep, prolonged sigh escaped him, that seemed to come from the depths of his being.

They sat in silence for a long time. Mrs. Dunbar was the first to break that silence. She roused herself by a great effort, and said,

"Have you any idea what his object may be in coming here, or what Lionel's object may be in sending him?"

"Well," said Wiggins, "I don't know. I thought at first when I saw him that Lionel had some idea of looking after the estate, to see if he could get control of it in any way; but this call seems to show that Edith enters into their design in some way. Perhaps he thinks of paying attentions to her," he added, in a tone of bitterness.

"And would that be a thing to be dreaded?" asked Mrs. Dunbar, anxiously.

"Most certainly," said Wiggins.

"Would you blame the son for the misdeeds of the father?" she asked, in the same tone.

"No," said Wiggins; "but when the son is so evidently a counterpart of the father, I should say that Edith ought to be preserved from him."

"I don't know," said Mrs. Dunbar. "I'm afraid you judge too hastily. It may be for the best. Who knows?"

"It can only be for the worst," said Wiggins, with solemn emphasis.

"There is a woman with him," said Mrs. Dunbar, suddenly changing the conversation. "Who can she be?"

"A woman? What kind of a woman?"

"Elderly. I never saw her before. He calls himself Mowbray, and she is Mrs. Mow-

bray. What can be the meaning of that? The woman seems old enough to be his mother."

"Old?" said Wiggins. "Ah—Mowbray—h'm! It must be some design of his on Edith. He brings this woman, so as to make a formal call. He will not tell her who he is. I don't like the look of this, and, what is worse, I don't know what to do. I could prohibit his visits, but that would be to give up my plans, and I can not do that yet. I must run the risk. As for Edith, she is mad. She is beyond my control. She drives me to despair."

"I do not see what danger there is for Edith in his visits," said Mrs. Dunbar, in a mournful voice.

"Danger!" said Wiggins. "A man like that!"

"You are judging him too hastily," said Mrs. Dunbar.

Wiggins looked at her in silence for a moment, and then said,

"I hope I am, I'm sure, for your sake; but I'm afraid that I am right and that you are wrong."

After some further conversation Mrs. Dunbar retired, carrying with her in her face and in her heart that deep concern and that strong agitation which had been excited by the visit of Mowbray. Edith, when she next saw her, noticed this, and for a long time afterward wondered to herself why it was that such a change had come over the housekeeper.

CHAPTER XVI.
ANOTHER VISIT.

ABOUT two weeks afterward the Mowbrays called again. Edith was a little surprised at this, for she had not expected another visit; but on the whole she felt glad, and could not help indulging in some vague hope that this call would be for her good.

"I am sorry," said she to Mrs. Mowbray, that I have not been able to return your call. But I have already explained how I am imprisoned here."

"Oh, my dear," said Mrs. Mowbray, "pray don't speak of that. We feel for you, I assure you. Nothing is more unpleasant than a bereavement. It makes such a change in all one's life, you know. And then black does not become some people; they persist in visiting, too; but then, do you know, they really look to me like perfect frights. Not that you look otherwise than well, dear Miss Dalton. In fact, I should think that in any dress you would look perfectly charming; but that is because you are a brunette. Some complexions are positively out of all keeping with black. Have you ever noticed that? Oh yes, dear Miss Dalton," continued Mrs. Mowbray, after a short pause. "Bru-

"IT WAS A CHILD."

nettes are best in black—mark my words, now; and blondes are never effective in that color. They do better in bright colors. It is singular, isn't it? You, now, my dear, may wear black with impunity; and since you are called on in the mysterious dispensation of Providence to mourn, you ought at least to be grateful that you are a brunette. If you were a blonde, I really do not know what would ever become of you. Now, I am a blonde—but in spite of that I have been called on to mourn. It—it was a child."

As Mrs. Mowbray said this she applied the handkerchief and smelling-bottle for a few minutes.

"A child!" said Edith, in wonder.

"Yes, dear—a sweet son, aged twelve, leaving me to mourn over him. And as I was saying, my mourning did not become my complexion at all. That was what troubled me so. Really, a blonde ought never to lose friends—it is so unbecoming. Positively, Providence ought to arrange things differently."

"It would be indeed well if blondes or any other people could be saved from sorrow," said Edith.

"It would be charming, would it not?" said Mrs. Mowbray. "Now, when my child died, I mourned for him most deeply—indeed, as deep as that," she said, stretching out her hands so as to measure a space of about eighteen inches—"most deeply: a border around the skirt of solid crape half a yard wide; bonnet smothered in crape; and really and positively I myself was literally all crape, I do believe; and with my light complexion, what people could have thought, I'm sure I do not know."

"There is not much to choose between mother and son," thought Edith. "They are capable of any baseness, they are so heartless. There is no hope here." Yet in spite of such thoughts she did not shun them. Why not? How could an honorable nature like hers associate with such people? Between them and herself was a deep gulf, and no sympathy between them was possible. The reason why she did not shun them lay solely in her own loneliness. Any thing in the shape of a human being was welcome rather than otherwise, and even people whom she despised served to mitigate the gloom of her situation. They made the time pass by, and that of itself was something.

"I went into half-mourning as soon as I could," continued Mrs. Mowbray; "but even half-mourning was very disagreeable. You may depend upon it, no shade of black ought ever to be brought near a blonde. Half-mourning is quite as bad as deep mourning."

"You must have had very much to bear," said Edith, absently.

"I should think I had. I really could not go into society, except, of course, to make calls, for that one *must* do, and even then I felt like a guy—for how absurd I must have looked with such an inharmonious adjustment of colors! But you, my dear Miss Dalton, seem made by nature to go in mourning."

"Yes," said Edith, with a sigh which she could not suppress; "nature has been lavish to me in that way—of late."

"You really ought always to mourn," said Mrs. Mowbray, in a sprightly tone.

"I'm afraid I shall always have to, whether I wish it or not," said Edith, with another sigh.

"You are such a remarkable brunette— quite an Italian; your complexion is almost olive, and your hair is the blackest I ever saw. It is all dark with you."

"Yes, it is indeed all dark with me," said Edith, sadly.

"The child that I lost," said Mrs. Mowbray, after a pause, "was a very nice child, but he was not at all like my son here. You often find great differences in families. I suppose he resembled one side of the family, and the captain the other."

"You have lived here for a good many years?" said Edith, abruptly changing the conversation.

"Oh yes," said Mrs. Mowbray. "It's a very nice county—don't you think so?"

"I really have not had an opportunity of judging."

"No? Of course not; you are mourning. But when you are done mourning, and go into society, you will find many very nice people. There are the Congreves, the Wiltons, the Symbolts, and Lord Connomore, and the Earl of Frontington, and a thousand delightful people whom one likes to know."

"You do not belong to the county, do you?"

"N—no; my family belongs to Berks," said Mrs. Mowbray. "You don't know any thing about Berks, I suppose? I'm a Fydill."

"A fiddle?" said Edith, somewhat bewildered, for Mrs. Mowbray pronounced her family name in that way, and appeared to take great pride in it.

"Yes," said she, "a Fydill—one of the oldest families there. Every one has heard of the Fydills of Berks. I suppose you have never been there, and so have not had the opportunity of hearing about them."

"No," said Edith; "I have passed most of my life at school."

"Of course. You are so deliciously young. And oh, Miss Dalton, what a delightful thing it is to be young! One is so admired, and has so many advantages! It is a sad, sad thing that one grows old so soon. I'm so gray, I'm sure I look like eighty. But, after all, I'm not so very old. There's Lady Poyntz, twice my age, who goes into society most energetically; and old Miss De Frissure, who, by-the-way, is enormously rich, actually rides on horseback, and she is old enough to be my mother; and Mrs. Rannie, the rich widow—you must have heard about her—positively does nothing but dance; and

old Mrs. Scott, the brewer's wife, who has recently come here, whenever she gives balls for her daughters, always dances more than any one. All these people are very much older than I am; and so I say to myself, 'Helen, my dear, you are quite a girl; why shouldn't you enjoy yourself?' And so I do enjoy myself."

"I suppose, then, that you like dancing?" said Edith, who, in spite of her sadness, found a mournful amusement in the idea of this woman dancing.

"I'm par-tic-u-lar-ly fond of dancing," said Mrs. Mowbray, with strong emphasis. "Only the young men are so rude! They fly about after young chits of girls, and don't notice me. And so I don't often have an opportunity, you know. But there is a German gentleman here—a baron, my dear —and he is very polite. He sometimes asks me to dance, and I enjoy it very much, only he is so short and fat and bald that I fear he looks very ridiculous. But the young men, Miss Dalton, are very, very neglectful."

"That is a pity," said Edith.

"Oh, they are so, I do assure you. Now that is the very thing that I have tried to impress upon the captain. 'My dearest boy,' I have always said, 'mind the ladies. That is the first and highest duty of a true gentleman. Particularly those ladies who are mature. Don't confine your attentions to giddy and thoughtless girls. There are many ladies at every ball of estimable character, and sometimes even of considerable wealth, who deserve your attentions far more than those poor young creatures who have nothing more to recommend them than their childish good looks.' And I trust my son has not failed to profit by my advice. At balls he does not often seek out the young, but rather the old. Indeed, so marked is his preference for married ladies that all the younger ones notice it and resent it, so that they have formed really quite an aversion to him; and now, whether he will or not, he has to dance exclusively with the elder ones. Once he danced with me, and it was a proud moment for me, I assure you."

"I should think so," said Edith, with a look at Mowbray. "But still, is it not strange that young ladies should refuse to dance with one who is an officer and a gentleman?"

During the whole of this conversation the captain had said nothing, but had been sitting turning over the leaves of a book, and furtively watching Edith's face and manner. When the conversation turned upon him, however, his face flushed, and he looked angrily at Mrs. Mowbray. At last, as Edith spoke, he started, and said:

"See here, now! I don't think it's altogether the correct thing to make remarks about a gentleman in his presence. I'm aware that ladies are given to gossip, but they generally do it behind a fellow's back. I've done nothing to deserve this just now."

"There was nothing offensive in my remark," said Edith, quietly.

"Oh," said Mrs. Mowbray, "my son is very quick and very sensitive, and very nice on a point of honor. He is the most punc-til-i-ous man you ever saw;" and Mrs. Mowbray held up her hands, lost in amazement at the conception which was in her mind of the punctiliousness of her son. "But, my dear Miss Dalton," she continued, "he is quick to forgive. He don't bear malice."

"Haven't I said," growled Mowbray, "that I don't like this? Talk of me behind my back, if you choose. You can't imagine that it's particularly pleasant for a fellow to sit here and listen to all that rot."

"But, my son," said Mrs. Mowbray, fondly, "it's all love."

"Oh, bother your love!" muttered this affectionate son.

"Well, then, you naughty, sensitive boy," said Mrs. Mowbray, "I will come here by myself, and tell dear Miss Dalton all about you behind your back. I will tell her about some of your adventures in London, and she will see what a naughty, wicked, rakish fellow you have been. He is sadly like me, dear Miss Dalton—so sensitive, and so fond of society."

Edith gave a polite smile, but said nothing.

Then the conversation lagged for a little while. At length Edith, full of the idea that Wiggins had sent them for some purpose, and desirous of finding out whether her suspicions were correct or not, said, in a careless tone,

"I suppose you know this Wiggins very well?"

"Mr. Wiggins?" said Mrs. Mowbray, quickly. "Oh yes; my son and he often meet, though for my part I know little or nothing about the man."

"Pooh!" cried Mowbray, interrupting her. "Miss Dalton, Mrs. Mowbray is so talkative that she often says things that she does not mean, or, at least, things that are liable to mislead others. I have met Wiggins, it is true, but do not imagine that he is a friend of mine. On the contrary, he has reason to hate me quite as much as he hates you. Your idea of any connection between him and me, which I plainly see you hint at, is altogether wrong, and you would not have even suspected this if you know me better."

"You came here so easily," said Edith, "that I very naturally supposed that you were on friendly terms."

"I come here easily," said Mowbray, "not because he is my friend, but because he is so afraid of me that he does not dare to keep me back."

"You understand, then," said Edith, "that he keeps others back. If you have such

power over him, how is it that you can calmly stand by and see him imprison a free-born and a high-born English lady?"

"Oh," muttered Mowbray, "I don't know any thing about that. He is your guardian, and you are his ward, and the law is a curious thing that I do not understand."

"Yet Mrs. Mowbray says that you are distinguished for your knowledge of legal points," said Edith.

Mowbray made no reply, and in a few moments Mrs. Mowbray rose to go.

"Positively," said she, "my dear Miss Dalton, we must see more of one another; and since your mourning confines you here, I must come often, and I know very well that we shall all be great friends."

"BECAUSE I BEAT HIM."

CHAPTER XVII.
A STROKE FOR LIBERTY.

THE Mowbrays came occasionally, but no others ever managed to get through the gates. Edith could not help feeling a sort of resentment against these people, who thus were able to do what no others could do, and came to her so easily whenever they wished. Still she did not think it worth while to refuse to see them. They beguiled the monotony of her life, and she still had a half hope that something might result from their visits. Even if they were in the pay of Wiggins, as she believed, they yet might feel inclined to assist her, from the hope of larger pay, and she hoped that the occasion might arise in which she might be able to hint at such a thing. As yet they met her on an equal footing, and in spite of her contempt for them, she did not quite like the idea of regularly offering them a bribe to assist her. Yet she thought that the time might come when she could do so, and this thought sustained her.

In her visits Mrs. Mowbray still prattled and chattered in her usual manner about her usual themes. Dress, society, and the incivility of young men seemed to be her favorite topics. The captain usually came with her, and seemed desirous to do the agreeable to Edith, but either from a natural lack of gallantry, or from the discouraging treatment which he received from her, he was somewhat unsuccessful.

About two months after his first call the captain came alone. He was on horseback, and was accompanied by a magnificent Newfoundland dog, which Edith had noticed once or twice before. On seeing Edith he showed more animation than was usual with him, and evidently was endeavoring, to the best of his power, to make himself agreeable.

"I have come, Miss Dalton," said he, after the usual greetings, "to see if you would do me the honor of going out riding with me."

"Riding?" said Edith; "you are very kind, I am sure; but will you pardon me if I first ask you where you propose to take me?"

"Oh, about the park," said Mowbray, somewhat meekly.

"The park?" said Edith, in a tone of disappointment. "Is that all? Why, Captain Mowbray, this park is only my jail yard, and to go about it can not be very pleasant to a prisoner, either on horseback or on foot. But surely I do not understand you. I must be too hasty. Of course you mean to do as every gentleman would do, and let the lady select the place where she wishes to go?"

"I assure you, Miss Dalton," said Mowbray, "I should be most happy to do so if I were able; but you are not allowed to go out of the park, you know."

"Who prohibits me, pray?"

"Wiggins."

"Wiggins! And why should you care for any of his regulations? Do you not know who he is, and what he is, and in what position he stands toward me?"

"Oh, well," said Mowbray, in a hesitating voice, "he is your guardian, you know."

"But I am of age," said Edith. "Guardians can not imprison their wards as he imprisons me. I am of age. I own this place. It is mine. He may have some right to attend to its business for the present, but he has no right over me. The law protects me. You know that as well as I do."

"Yes, true; but—ah—you know—ah— you are really so very *peculiarly* situated, Miss Dalton, that I should not like to do any

thing which might compromise your—ah— position."

"Surely, Captain Mowbray, you must now be speaking without thinking. In what way, pray, can it compromise my position to ride with you through the village streets, rather than over the roads of the park?"

"Well—ah—you are in mourning, you know."

"Really I do not see what that has to do with it. If I have the sorrow of bereavement, that is no reason why I should have the additional sorrow of imprisonment."

"Oh, you know, Wiggins would make a fuss about it, and put you to no end of trouble."

Mowbray's unwillingness to help her, and hesitation, had once before roused Edith's indignation; but now she believed him to be in Wiggins's employ, and therefore felt calm, and talked with him chiefly for the sake of seeing what she could get out of him, either in the way of explanation or concession.

"When you speak of trouble," said she, "I think it is I who will give trouble to him rather than undergo it from him."

"Oh, well—either way," said Mowbray, "there would be trouble, and that is what I wish to avoid."

"Gentlemen are not usually so timid about encountering trouble on behalf of a lady," said Edith, coldly.

"Oh, well, you know, if it were ordinary trouble I wouldn't mind it, but this is legal trouble. Why, before I knew where I was I might be imprisoned, and how would I like that?"

"Not very well, as I can testify," said Edith.

"Believe me, Miss Dalton," said Mowbray, with a desperate effort to appear earnest and devoted, "there is nothing that I would not do for you, and I feel exceedingly pained that you are not content with your present position; but you see I do not want to put myself in the clutches of the law if I can help it. Wiggins is an enemy of mine, as I told you, and only tolerates me here because he dare not prevent me—neither he nor his man; but—ah—you know—that is—I mean —he—ah—he watches me very closely, you know, and if I were to do any thing that he could lay hold of, he would be very glad to do so, and put me to trouble and expense —no end."

Here Edith understood once more a profession of enmity against Wiggins, but whether it was real or not she could not tell. She believed, rather, that it was pretended.

"Oh, I beg of you to make no more excuses," said she. "Your explanations are quite satisfactory."

"I have had trouble enough from lawyers," continued Mowbray, "and don't want to have any more."

"That is quite prudent in you, and careful."

"The first thing that a man of the world learns, Miss Dalton," said the captain, in a confidential tone, "is to take care of himself. That is a lesson that I have learned by bitter experience, and I have resolved, among other things, and above all, never, under any circumstances, to put myself within the grasp of the lawyers; and if you only knew what bother I've had, you wouldn't blame me."

"I fear that I must have given you great pain, then," said Edith, "by even hinting at such a thing as taking my part and helping me. You feel so strongly about your personal safety that you must have been deeply agitated at such a proposal from me."

"Oh, well," said the captain, not choosing to notice the sarcasm of Edith's tone, "one grows wiser from experience, you know, and mine has been a bitter one. I would gladly open your gates for you, I assure you, if I could do it without danger, and if Wiggins had no authority; but as it is, I really do not see how I can possibly interfere."

"Well, for that matter," said Edith, "if it were not for Wiggins, I suppose I could open the gates for myself, and so I could save you even that trouble."

Mowbray made no reply to this, but merely stroked his mustache.

"After all," said he at last, "I don't see why you should be so discontented here. There are many who would be glad to live as you do, in so magnificent a house, with such noble grounds. You have every thing that you want. Why you should be so discontented I can not imagine. If you did get out, and live in the village, you would not like it. It's not a pleasant place. For my part I would much rather live where you do than where I do. If you would confine your attention to this place, and give up all ideas of getting away, you might be as happy as the day is long."

Saying this, the captain looked at Edith to see the effect of his words. Edith was looking at him with a very strange expression, something like what may appear in the face of the naturalist at discovering an animal of some new species—an expression of interest and surprise and curiosity.

"So those are your sentiments?" she said; and that was all.

"Yes," said the captain.

"Well," said Edith, "it may be my misfortune, but I think differently."

"At any rate," said the captain, in a more animated tone, "since we can not agree in this discussion, why not drop it? Will you not ride with me about the park? I'm sure I like the park very well. I have not become so tired of it as you have. I have a very nice lady's horse, which is quite at your disposal."

At this request Edith was silent for a few moments. The man himself grew more abhorrent to her, if possible, every moment; but her desire to find out what his purposes were, and her hope of making use of him still, in spite of present appearances, made her think that it might be best to accept his offer.

"Oh, well," said she, "I have no objection, since you choose to subject me to such limitations, and I suppose I must add that I thank you."

"Don't speak of thanks, Miss Dalton," said Mowbray. "Let me say rather that I thank you from the bottom of my heart."

Two days after this Mowbray again called on Edith. This time, in addition to his own horse, he brought another with a lady's saddle, and was followed by the Newfoundland dog. Edith was soon dressed for the ride, and joined Mowbray in the drawing-room. As they went out the dog was sitting on the portico, and leaped forward joyfully at the sight of his master, but suddenly retreated in fear.

"It's all very well, Miss Dalton," said Mowbray, "for them to talk about cruelty to animals, but the only way you can make them fond of you is by fear. See how that dog loves me. And why? Because I beat him."

There was something in these words, and in the tone in which they were spoken, that afforded Edith a new view of Mowbray's character. There were a ferocity and a cruelty there which were quite in keeping with the paltriness and meanness which he had already evinced. But Edith kept silence. In a few moments they were mounted, and rode away side by side.

As they turned the corner of the Hall Edith saw a face among the trees—white, solemn, watchful, stern—and the sight gave her a strange shock, for it was the face of Wiggins. It seemed to her at that moment that this man must hate Mowbray, for the glance which he gave was by no means that of a friend or confederate. Mowbray might, therefore, have spoken the truth when he said that Wiggins hated him, and if so, he might now be dreading the presence of this unwelcome guest. This thought was not unpleasant, for though Mowbray could not be a friend, she thought it not a bad substitute that he was at least an enemy of Wiggins.

The consequence was that she really enjoyed the ride; and Mowbray, seeing her in good spirits, thought that it arose from more favorable inclinations toward himself, and exerted himself to please. They rode at a rapid pace through the long avenues, under magnificent overarching trees, and over fields and meadows. Mowbray was a fine horseman, and Edith had been accustomed to riding from childhood, and liked nothing better than to rush along at headlong speed. She felt exhilaration and enthusiasm such as she had not known for a long time. As she looked at Mowbray's splendid figure she could not help regretting that a man with such rare physical advantages should have, after all, but a craven spirit. Was it, then, she thought, altogether fear that prevented him from assisting her to escape? The idea seemed absurd. There must be some reason of a different kind. She felt certain that he was an unprincipled villain, and that he had some designs of his own upon her. What they were she could not imagine. If he wished to gain her hand, he had certainly taken a singular way to make himself agreeable. He was cruel, cynical, mean, and sordid, and took no pains to conceal this. He had advised her to submit to imprisonment, and had refused to help her in any way. What his designs could possibly be she could not conjecture.

During the ride but little was said. Mowbray was not talkative at any time, and on the present occasion he confined himself to remarks which he intended to be amiable and agreeable. To these Edith made civil replies. At last they rode back to the Hall, and Mowbray prepared to dismount.

"Are you going?" said Edith. "For my part I should rather not dismount just yet. It is too dull in the house. I would rather ride a little distance with you, and walk back."

At this Mowbray looked at her in silence, and with a perplexed expression on his countenance.

Edith calmly waited for him to start.

"Miss Dalton," said he at length, "I really do not know—" And then he paused.

"I beg your pardon," said Edith.

"You see," said Mowbray, "I don't know about your riding any more."

"Why, surely," said Edith, "you are not going to refuse your horse for a few minutes longer?"

Mowbray looked gloomily at her, and then started off. Edith rode by his side, and they both kept silence until they reached the park gate.

The porter came out, but on seeing Edith he stopped.

"It's all right," said Edith. "You see I am with Captain Mowbray."

Mowbray looked deeply perplexed, and as he said nothing, the porter began to open the gate.

"Stop," said Mowbray.

"What!" cried Edith. "Captain Mowbray, what do you mean?"

"You must not go out," said Mowbray. "I thought you were only going as far as the gate, and would walk back. You must not try to follow me."

"Must not!" cried Edith, whom the hope of escape had roused to intense excitement. "Do you say that to me?"

"Yes," said Mowbray.

"What right have you?" said Edith, haughtily. And then turning to the porter, she said, imperatively, "Open that gate at once."

But the obdurate porter did not obey her now any more than before.

"Captain Mowbray," said she, "order that man to open the gate."

"I will not," said Mowbray, rudely.

"Then I shall ride by your side till you go out."

"You shall not."

"Is that the way that a gentleman speaks to a lady?"

"You won't get me into trouble, anyway."

"I don't intend to," said Edith, scornfully. "It is my own act. You will not take me out, but I go out of my own accord."

The porter meanwhile stood bewildered, with the gate only partly open, holding it in this way, and waiting for the end of this singular scene.

"Miss Dalton," cried Mowbray, fiercely, "you will make me resort to extreme measures."

"You dare not!" cried Edith, who by this time was fearfully excited. She had a horse beneath her now. That horse seemed part of herself. In that horse's strength and speed she lost her own weakness, and so she was now resolved to stake every thing on one effort for liberty.

"Don't force me to it," said Mowbray, "or you will make me do something that I shall be sorry for."

"You dare not!" cried Edith again. "Do you dare to threaten me—me, the mistress of Dalton Hall?"

"Catch hold of her reins, captain," cried the porter, "and make her go back."

"Hold your bloody tongue!" roared Mowbray.—"Miss Dalton, you must go back."

"Never!" said Edith. "I will go out when you do."

"Then I will not go out at all. I will go back to the Hall."

"You shall not enter it," said Edith, as firmly as though she possessed the keys of Dalton Hall.

"Miss Dalton, you force me to use violence."

"You dare not use violence," said Edith, with a look that overawed the craven soul of Mowbray. For Edith now was resolved to do any thing, however desperate, and even the threat of violence, though she felt that he was capable of it, did not deter her. The two faced one another in silence for a few moments, the one strong, muscular, masculine, the other slight, fragile, delicate; yet in that girlish form there was an intrepid spirit which Mowbray recognized, defiant, haughty, tameless, the spirit of all her fathers, strengthened and intensified by a ve-

"IN HER FRENZY EDITH STRUCK THAT HAND AGAIN AND AGAIN."

hement desire for that liberty that lay outside the gates.

"Well," said the porter, "I'd better be a-shuttin' the gates till you two settle yer business. She'll dash through if I don't. I see it in her eye."

"No, she won't," said Mowbray. "Don't shut the gates; wait a moment." Then turning to Edith, he said,

"Miss Dalton, for the last time, I say go back, or you'll be sorry."

Edith looked steadfastly and sternly at the captain, but said not one word. The captain looked away.

"Porter," said he.

"Sir."

"Hold her horse."

"But she'll rush through the gates. Shall I fasten them?"

"No; I'll hold the reins till you get them. And, porter, I leave this horse with Miss Dalton, since she won't dismount. You see that he's well taken care of."

"Yes, Sir."

The captain, while speaking, had reached out his arm to take Edith's reins, but she turned her horse's head, and he missed them. The porter saw this movement, and sprang forward. Edith pulled the reins. Her horse reared. Wild with excitement, and seeing the gates open before her, and the road beyond, Edith struck at the porter with her whip over his face, and then drove her horse at the open gates. The horse sprang through like the wind. The porter shrieked after her. She was on the road. She was free!

No—not free!

Not free, for after her there came the thundering tramp of another horse. It was Mowbray in pursuit.

His horse was far better than hers. He gained on her step by step. Nearer and nearer he came. He was behind her; he was abreast of her before she had ridden a quarter of a mile. The tower of the village church was already in sight, when suddenly a strong hand was laid on her reins.

In her frenzy Edith struck that hand again and again with the heavy butt of her riding-whip, but it did not loosen its grasp. Her horse stopped.

"Curse you!" roared Mowbray to Edith, while his face was livid with passion and pain, "I'll kill you!" and seizing her whip hand, he wrenched the whip out of it.

Edith was silent.

Mowbray said no more. He turned her horse and led it back. Edith looked around wildly. Suddenly, as they came near the gates, the intolerable thought of her renewed imprisonment maddened her, and the liberty which she had so nearly gained roused her to one more effort; and so, with a start, she disengaged herself and leaped to the ground. Mowbray saw it, and, with a terrible oath, in an instant leaped down and gave chase. The horses ran forward and entered the gates.

Edith held up her long skirts and ran toward the village. But again Mowbray was too much for her. He overtook her, and seizing her by the wrist, dragged her back. Edith shrieked for help at the top of her voice. Mowbray looked fiercely around, and seeing no one, he took his handkerchief and bound it tightly around her mouth. Then, overcome by despair, Edith's strength gave way. She sank down. She made no more resistance. She fainted.

Mowbray raised her in his arms, and carried her into the porter's lodge. The gates were then locked.

CHAPTER XVIII.

A STRANGE CONFESSION.

EDITH came to herself in the porter's lodge. Her re-awakened eyes, in looking up confusedly, saw the hateful face of Mowbray bending over her. At once she realized the horror of her position, and all the incidents of her late adventure came vividly before her mind. Starting up as quickly as her feeble limbs would allow, she indignantly motioned him away.

Mowbray, without a word, stepped back and looked down.

Edith staggered to her feet.

"Miss Dalton," said Mowbray, in a low voice, "your carriage has been sent for. It is here, and will take you to the Hall."

Edith made no reply, but looked absently toward the door.

"Miss Dalton," said Mowbray, coming a little nearer, "I implore you to hear me. I would kneel at your feet if you would let me. But you are so imbittered against me now that it would be useless. Miss Dalton, it was not hate that made me raise my hand against you. Miss Dalton, I swear that you are more dear to me than life itself. A few moments ago I was mad, and did not know what I was doing. I did not want you to go away from this place, for I saw that you would be lost to me forever. I saw that you hated me, and that if you went away just then I should lose you. And I was almost out of my senses. I had no time to think of any thing but the bitter loss that was before me, and as you fled I seized you, not in anger, but in excitement and fear, just as I would have seized you if you had been drowning."

"Captain Mowbray," said Edith, sternly, "the violence you have offered me is enough to satisfy even you, without such insult as this."

"Will you not even listen to me?"

"Listen!" exclaimed Edith, in an indescribable tone.

"Then I must be heard. I love you. I—"

"Love!" interrupted Edith, in a tone of unutterable contempt.

"Yes, love," repeated Mowbray, vehemently, "from the first time that I saw you, when you implored my help."

"And why did you not give me your help?" asked Edith, looking at him in cold and haughty indignation.

"I will tell you," said Mowbray. "Before I saw you I knew how you were situated. Wiggins would have kept me away, but dared not. I know that about him which makes me his master. When I saw you, I loved you with all my soul. When you appealed to me, I would have responded at once, but could not. The fact is, Mrs. Mowbray was present. Mrs. Mowbray is not what she appears to be. Before her I had to pretend an indifference that I did not feel. In short, I had to make myself appear a base coward. In fact, I had to be on my guard, so as not to excite her suspicions of my feelings. Afterward, when I might have redeemed my character in your eyes, I did not know how to begin. Then, too, I was afraid to help you to escape, for I saw that you hated me, and my only hope was to keep you here till you might know me better."

"Captain Mowbray," said Edith, "if you are a captain, which I doubt, such explanations as these are paltry. After what you have done, the only thing left is silence."

"Oh, Miss Dalton, will nothing lead you to listen to me? I would lay down my life to serve you."

"You still wish to serve me, then?" asked Edith.

"Most fervently," cried Mowbray.

"Then open that gate," said Edith.

Mowbray hesitated.

"Open that gate," said Edith, "and prove your sincerity. Open it, and efface these marks," she cried, as she indignantly held up her right hand, and showed her wrist, all black from the fierce grasp in which Mowbray had seized it. "Open it, and I promise you I will listen patiently to all that you may have to say."

"Miss Dalton," said Mowbray, " if I opened that gate I should never see you again."

"You will never see me again if you do not."

"At least I shall be near you."

"Near me? Yes, and hated and despised. I will call on Wiggins himself to help me. He was right ; he said the time would come when I would be willing to trust him."

"Trust him? What, that man? You don't know what he is."

"And what are you, Captain Mowbray?"

"I! I am a gentleman."

"Oh no," said Edith, quietly, "not that—any thing rather than that."

At this Mowbray's face flushed crimson, but with a violent effort he repressed his passion.

"Miss Dalton," said he, "it is a thing that you might understand. The fear of losing you made me desperate. I saw in your flight the loss of all my hopes."

"And where are those hopes now?"

"Well, at any rate, I have not altogether lost you. Let me hope that I may have an opportunity to explain hereafter, and to retrieve my character. Miss Dalton, a woman will sometimes forgive offenses even against herself, when she knows that they are prompted by love."

"You seem to me," said Edith, "to seek the affections of women as you do those of dogs—by beating them soundly." The sight of Mowbray's dog, who was in the room, reminded Edith of the master's maxim which he had uttered before this memorable ride.

"Miss Dalton, you do me such wrong that you crush me. Can you not have some mercy?"

"Open the gate," said Edith. "Do that one thing, and then you may make all the explanations that you wish. I will listen to any thing and every thing. Open the gate, and I will promise to forgive, and even to forget, the unparalleled outrage that I have suffered."

"But you will leave me forever."

"Open that gate, Captain Mowbray. Prove yourself to be what you say—do something to atone for your base conduct—and then you will have claims on my gratitude which I shall always acknowledge."

Mowbray shook his head.

"Can I let you go?" he said. "Do you ask it of me?"

"No," said Edith, impatiently, "I don't ask it. I neither hope nor ask for any thing from you. Wiggins himself is more promising. At any rate, he has not as yet used absolute violence, and, what is better, he does not intrude his society where it is not wanted."

"Then I have no hope," said Mowbray, in what was intended to be a plaintive tone.

"I'm sure I don't know," said Edith; "but I know this—that the time will surely come, after all, when I shall get my freedom, and then, Captain Mowbray, you will rue the day when you dared to lay hands on me. Yes, I could get my freedom now, I suppose, if I were to parley with Wiggins, to bribe him heavily enough; and I assure you I am tempted now to give up the half of my estate, so as to get free and have you punished."

Mowbray turned pale.

"There were no witnesses," said he, hastily.

"You forget that the porter saw it all. But this is useless," she added ; and passing by Mowbray, she went to the door. Outside was a carriage, which the porter had brought down from the Hall, into which she got, and then drove away, while Mowbray stood looking at her till she drove out of sight.

The effects of this adventure were felt for some time. Excitement, fatigue, pain, and grief, all affected Edith, so that she could not leave her room for weeks. Mrs. Dunbar was assiduous in her attentions, and Edith supposed that both she and Wiggins knew all about it, as the porter would undoubtedly have informed them; but her communications with her were limited only to a few words, and she regarded her with nothing but distrust. In Mrs. Dunbar's manner, also, she saw something which indicated a fresh trouble, something which had been manifested by her ever since Mowbray's first appearance, and which Edith now suspected to be the result of Mowbray's violence. This led to vain speculations on her part as to the mysterious connection that existed between her jailers. Mowbray professed to be the enemy and the master of Wiggins. Her remembrance of Wiggins's look of hate made her think that this was true. But Mrs. Dunbar she did not believe to be an enemy of Mowbray's; and the porter, who was the incorruptible servant of Wiggins, seemed equally devoted to Mowbray.

She recalled also Mowbray's words to herself in explanation of his own course. He had asserted that he had the power over Wiggins from some knowledge which he possessed, and also that Mrs. Mowbray was not what she appeared to be. He had spoken as though he was afraid of Mrs. Mowbray's finding out what he called his love for Edith. Was this his mother, then, at all? What did it all mean? For Edith, at any rate, it was not possible to understand it, and the character, motives, and mutual relationship of all those with whom she had come in contact remained an impenetrable mystery.

To the surprise of Edith, the Mowbrays called several times to make inquiries about her, and after her recovery they still visited her. At first she refused to see them, but one day Mrs. Mowbray came alone, and Edith determined to see her, and get rid of her effectually.

Mrs. Mowbray rose as she entered, and advancing to greet her, held out her hand with a cordial smile. Edith did not take it, yet Mrs. Mowbray took no offense, but, on the contrary, met her in the most effusive manner.

"Oh, my dear Miss Dalton," said she, "what an age it has been since we met! It seems like years! And when I wanted to see you so par-tic-u-lar-ly! And are you quite well? Have you quite recovered? Are you sure? How glad I am!"

"Mrs. Mowbray," said Edith, as soon as she could make herself heard, "I have sent word to you several times that I do not wish to see you again. You know the reason why as well as I do. I can only say that I am surprised at this persistence, and shall in future be under the necessity of shutting my doors against you."

Thus Edith, in spite of her severe afflictions, could still speak of the place as hers, and under her orders.

"Oh, my dear Miss Dalton," burst forth Mrs. Mowbray, "that is the very reason why I have so in-sist-ed on seeing you. To explain, you know—for there is nothing like an explanation."

"You may spare yourself the trouble," said Edith. "I do not want any more explanations."

"Oh, but you positively must, you know," said Mrs. Mowbray, in her most airy manner.

"Pardon me. I wish to hear nothing whatever about it."

"It's that sad, sad boy," said Mrs. Mowbray, coolly ignoring Edith's words, "and deeply has he repented. But do you know, dear, it was only his fondness for you. Pos-i-tive-ly nothing else, dear, but his fondness for you. Oh, how he has talked about it! He says he is willing to give up his right eye, or hand—I really forget which—to recall the past. My poor dear boy is very impetuous."

"Mrs. Mowbray, I do not wish to be unkind or rude, but you really force me to it."

"He's impetuons," said Mrs. Mowbray, without noticing Edith, "but he's warm-hearted. He's a most affectionate son, and he is so affectionate toward you. It's all his fondness for you."

"Mrs. Mowbray, this is intolerable."

"Oh, Miss Dalton, you don't know—you really don't know. He has loved you ever since he first saw you—and so true! Why, he dotes on you. He was afraid that he would lose you. You know, that was the reason why he interfered. But he says now most distinctly that he thinks his interference was quite un-war-rant-a-ble—quite, I assure you, my dear Miss Dalton."

Edith sat looking at this insolent woman with a clouded brow, not knowing whether to order her out of the house or not. But

E

Mrs. Mowbray seemed beautifully unconscious of any offense.

"The only thing that he has been talking about ever since it happened," she continued, "is his sorrow. Oh, his sorrow! And it is deep, Miss Dalton. I never saw such deep sorrow. He really swears about it in a shocking manner; and that with him is a sign that his feelings are concerned very strongly. He always swears whenever he is deeply moved."

Edith at this started to her feet with a look in her eyes which showed Mrs. Mowbray that she would not be trifled with any longer.

"Mrs. Mowbray," said she, "I came down for the sole purpose of telling you that in future I shall dispense with the pleasure of your calls."

Mrs. Mowbray rose from her chair.

"What?" she exclaimed, with a gesture of consternation; "and live in complete seclusion? Not receive calls? No, no; you really must not think of such a thing. We are your friends, you know, and you must not deny us an occasional sight of you. My poor boy will positively die if he doesn't see you. He's pining now. And it's all for you. All."

"Mrs. Mowbray," said Edith, in a severe tone, "I do not know whether you give offense intentionally or not. You seem unable to take a hint, however strongly expressed, and you force me to speak plainly, although I dislike to do so. You must not, and you shall not, come here any more."

"Oh, my dear Miss Dalton, you really are quite excited," said Mrs. Mowbray, with a pleasant smile.

"I mean what I say," said Edith, coldly. "You are not to come here again."

Mrs. Mowbray laughed lightly.

"Oh, you really can't keep us away. We positively must come. My son insists. These lovers, you know, dear, are so pertinacious. Well," she added, looking hastily at Edith, "I suppose I must say good-morning; but, Miss Dalton, think of my boy. Good-morning, my dear Miss Dalton."

And so Mrs. Mowbray retired.

She called again four times, twice alone, and twice in company with the captain, but Edith refused to see her.

Yet, after all, in spite of her scorn for these people, and her conviction that they were in league with Wiggins—in spite of the captain's brutality—it was not without sorrow that Edith dismissed Mrs. Mowbray; for she looked upon her as a kind of tie that bound her to the outer world, and until the last she had hoped that some means might arise through these, if not of escape, at least of communication with friends.

But she was cut off from these now more than ever; and what remained? What? A prison-house!

CHAPTER XIX.

A NEW-COMER.

It seemed now to Edith that her isolation was complete. She found herself in a position which she had thought impossible in free England—a prisoner in the hands of an adventurer, who usurped an authority over her to which he had no right. His claim to exercise this authority in his office of guardian she did not admit for a moment. She, the mistress of Dalton Hall, was nothing more than a captive on her own estates. She did not know how this could end or when it could end. Her hopes had one by one given way. The greatest blow of all was that which had been administered through the so-called letter of Miss Plympton. That letter she believed to be a forgery, yet the undeniable fact remained that Miss Plympton had done nothing. That Miss Plympton should write that letter, however, and that she should leave her helpless at the mercy of Wiggins, seemed equally improbable, and Edith, in her vain effort to comprehend it, could only conclude that some accident had happened to her dear friend; that she was ill, or worse. And if this was so, it would be to her the worst blow of all.

Other hopes which she had formed had also been doomed to destruction. She had expected something from the spontaneous sympathy of the outside world, who, whatever their opinion about her father, would stir themselves to prevent such an outrage upon justice as that which Wiggins was perpetrating. But these hopes gradually died out. That world, she thought, was perhaps ignorant not only of her situation, but even of her very existence. The last hopes that she had formed had been in the Mowbrays, and these had gone the way of all the others.

Nothing appeared before her in the way of hope, and her despondency was often hard to endure. Still her strong spirit and hightoned nature rendered it impossible for her to be miserable always. Added to this was her perfect health, which, with one interruption, had sustained her amidst the distresses of her situation. By her very disposition she was forced to hope for the best. It must not be supposed that she was at all like "Mariana in the moated grange." She did not pine away. On the contrary, she often felt a kind of triumph in the thought that she had thus far shown the spirit of a Dalton.

There was an old legend in the Dalton family upon which great stress had been laid for many generations, and this one stood out prominently among all the stories of ancestral exploits which she had heard in her childhood. One of the first Daltons, whose grim figure looked down upon her now in the armor of a Crusader, had taken part in the great expedition under Richard Cœur de Lion. It happened that he had the ill luck to fall into the hands of the infidel, but as there were a number of other prisoners, there was some confusion, and early one morning he managed to seize a horse and escape. Soon he was pursued. He dashed over a wide plain toward some hills that arose in the distance, where he managed to elude his pursuers for a time, until he found refuge upon a cliff, where there was a small place which afforded room for one or two. After some search his pursuers discovered him, and ordered him to come down. He refused. They then began an attack, shooting arrows from a distance, and trying to scale the cliff. But Dalton's defense was so vigorous that by the end of that day's fight he had killed eight of his assailants. Then the contest continued. For two days, under a burning sun, without food or drink, the stern old Crusader defended himself. When summoned to surrender he had only one word, and that was, "Never!" It happened that a band of Crusaders who were scouring the country caught sight of the Saracens, and made an attack upon them, putting them to flight. They then sought for the object of this extraordinary siege, and, climbing up, they saw a sight which thrilled them as they gazed. For there lay stout old Michael Dalton, with many wounds, holding a broken sword, and looking at them with delirious eyes. He recognized no one, but tried to defend himself against his own friends. It was with difficulty that they restrained him. They could not remove him, nor was it necessary, for death was near; but till the last his hand clutched the broken sword, and the only word he said was, "Never!" The Crusaders waited till he was dead, and then took his remains to the camp. The story of his defense, which was gathered from their prisoners, rang through the whole camp, and always afterward the crest of the Daltons was a bloody hand holding a broken sword, with the motto, "Never!"

And so Edith took to her heart this story and this motto, and whenever she looked at the grim old Crusader, she clinched her own little hand and said, "Never!"

She determined to use what liberty she had; and since Wiggins watched all her movements, to show him how unconcerned she was, she began to go about the grounds, to take long walks in all directions, and whenever she returned to the house, to play for hours upon the piano. Her determination to keep up her courage had the effect of keeping down her despondency, and her vigorous exercise was an unmixed benefit, so that there was a radiant beauty in her face, and a haughty dignity that made her look like the absolute mistress of the place.

What Wiggins felt or thought she did not know. He never came across her path by any chance. Occasional glimpses of the ever-watchful Hugo showed her that she was tracked with as jealous a vigilance as ever. She hoped, however, that by her incessant activity something might result to her advantage.

One day while she was strolling down the grand avenue she saw a stranger walking up, and saw, to her surprise, that he was a gentleman. The face was altogether unknown to her, and, full of hope, she waited for him to come up.

"Have I the honor of addressing Miss Dalton?" said the stranger, as he reached her. He spoke in a very pleasant but somewhat effeminate voice, lifting his hat, and bowing with profound courtesy.

"I am Miss Dalton," said Edith, wondering who the stranger might be.

He was quite a small, slight man, evidently young; his cheeks were beardless; he had a thick dark mustache; and his small hands and feet gave to Edith the idea of a delicate, fastidious sort of a man, which was heightened by his very neat and careful dress. On the whole, however, he seemed to be a gentleman, and his deep courtesy was grateful in the extreme to one who had known so much rudeness from others.

His complexion was quite dark, his eyes were very brilliant and expressive, and his appearance was decidedly effeminate. Edith felt a half contempt for him, but in a moment she reflected how appearances may mislead, for was not the magnificent Mowbray a villain and a coward?

"Allow me, Miss Dalton," said he, "to introduce myself. I am Lieutenant Dudleigh, of —— ——."

"Dudleigh!" cried Edith, in great excitement. "Are you any relation to Sir Lionel?"

"Well, not very close. I belong to the same family, it is true; but Sir Lionel is more to me than a relation. He is my best friend and benefactor."

"And do you know any thing about him?" cried Edith, in irrepressible eagerness. "Can you tell me any thing?"

"Oh yes," said Dudleigh, with a smile. "I certainly ought to be able to do that. I suppose I know as much about him as any one. But what is the meaning of all this that I find here," he continued, suddenly changing the conversation—"that ruffian of a porter—the gates boarded up and barred so jealously? It seems to me as if your friends should bring pistols whenever they come to make a call."

Dudleigh had a gay, open, careless tone. His voice was round and full, yet still it was effeminate. In spite of this, however, Edith was, on the whole, pleased with him. The remote relationship which he professed to bear to Sir Lionel, his claim that Sir Lionel was his friend, and the name that he gave himself, all made him seem to Edith like a

true friend. Of Sir Lionel and his family she knew nothing whatever; she knew not whether he had ever had any children or not; nor did she ever know his disposition; but she had always accustomed herself to think of him as her only relative, and her last resort, so that this man's acquaintance with him made him doubly welcome.

"What you mention," said she, in answer to his last remark, "is a thing over which I have not the smallest control. There is a man here who has contrived to place me in so painful a position that I am a prisoner in my own grounds."

"A prisoner?" said Dudleigh, in a tone of the deepest surprise. "I do not understand you."

"He keeps the gates locked," said Edith, "refuses to let me out, and watches every thing that I do."

"What do you mean? I really can not understand you. No one has any right to do that. How does he dare to do it? He couldn't treat you worse if he were your husband."

"Well, he pretends that he is my guardian, and declares that he has the same right over me as if he were my father."

"But, Miss Dalton, what nonsense this is! You can not be in earnest—and yet you must be."

"In earnest!" repeated Edith, with vehemence. "Oh, Lieutenant Dudleigh, this is the sorrow of my life—so much so that I throw myself upon the sympathy of a perfect stranger. I am desperate, and ready to do any thing to escape—"

"Miss Dalton," said Dudleigh, solemnly, "your wrongs must be great indeed if this is so. Your guardian! But what then? Does that give him the right to be your jailer?"

"He takes the right."

"Who is this man?"

"His name is Wiggins."

"Wiggins? Wiggins? Why, it must be the steward. Wiggins? Why, I saw him yesterday. Wiggins? What! That scoundrel? that blackleg? that villain who was horsewhipped at Epsom? Why, the man is almost an outlaw. It seemed to me incredible when I heard he was steward here; but when you tell me that he is your guardian it really is too much. It must be some scoundrelly trick of his—some forgery of documents."

"So I believe," said Edith, "and so I told him to his own face. But how did you get in here? Wiggins never allows any one to come here but his own friends."

"Well," said Dudleigh, "I did have a little difficulty, but not much—it was rather of a preliminary character. The fact is, I came here more than a week ago on a kind of tour. I heard of Dalton Hall, and understood enough of Sir Lionel's affairs to know that you were his niece; and as there had been an old difficulty, I thought I couldn't do better than call and see what sort of a person you were, so as to judge whether a reconciliation might not be brought about. I came here three days ago, and that beggar of a porter wouldn't let me in. The next day I came back, and found Wiggins, and had some talk with him. He said something or other about your grief and seclusion and so forth; but I knew the scoundrel was lying, so I just said to him, 'See here now, Wiggins, I know you of old, and there is one little affair of yours that I know all about—you understand what I mean. You think you are all safe here; but there are some people who could put you to no end of trouble if they chose. I'm going in through those gates, and you must open them.' That's what I told him, and when I came to-day the gates were opened for me. But do you really mean to say that this villain prevents your going out?"

"Yes," said Edith, mournfully.

"Surely you have not tried. You should assert your rights. But I suppose your timidity would naturally prevent you."

"It is not timidity that prevents me. I have been desperate enough to do any thing. I have tried. Indeed, I don't know what more I could possibly do than what I have done." She paused. She was not going to tell every thing to a stranger.

"Miss Dalton," said Dudleigh, fervently, "I can not express my joy at the happy accident that has brought me here. For it was only by chance that I came to Dalton, though after I came I naturally thought of you, as I said, and came here."

"I fear," said Edith, "that it may seem strange to you for me to take you into my confidence, after we have only interchanged a few words. But I must do so. I have no alternative. I am desperate. I am the Dalton of Dalton Hall, and I find myself in the power of a base adventurer. He imprisons me. He sets spies to watch over me. He directs that ruffian at the gates to turn away my friends, and tell them some story about my grief and seclusion. I have not seen any visitors since I came."

"Is it possible?"

"Well, there was one family—the Mowbrays, of whom I need say nothing."

"The Mowbrays?" said Dudleigh, with a strange glance.

"Do you know any thing about them?" asked Edith.

"Pardon me, Miss Dalton; I prefer to say nothing about them."

"By all means, I prefer to say nothing about them myself."

"But, Miss Dalton, I feel confounded and bewildered. I can not understand you even yet. Do you really mean to say that you, the mistress of these estates, the heiress, the lady of Dalton Hall—that you are restricted in this way and by him?"

"It is all most painfully true," said Edith. "It almost breaks my heart to think of such a humiliation, but it is true. I have been here for months, literally a prisoner. I have absolutely no communication with my friends, or with the outside world. This man Wiggins declares that he is my guardian, and can do as he chooses. He says that a guardian has as much authority over his ward as a father over his child."

"Oh! I think I understand. He may be partly right, after all. You are young yet, you know. You are not of age."

"I am of age," said Edith, mournfully, "and that is what makes it so intolerable. If I were under age I might bear it for a time. There might then appear to be, at least, the show of right on his side. But as it is, there is nothing but might. He has imprisoned me. He has put me under surveillance. I am watched at this moment."

"Who? where?" exclaimed Dudleigh, looking hastily around.

"Oh, in the woods—a black named Hugo. He tracks me like a blood-hound, and never loses sight of me when I am out. He may not hear what we are saying, but he will tell his master that I have spoken with you."

"Are there spies in the Hall?"

"Oh yes; his housekeeper watches me always."

"Is there no place where we can talk without being seen or heard? Believe me, Miss Dalton, your situation fills me with grief and pity. All this is so unexpected, so strange, so incredible!"

"We may, perhaps, be more free from observation in the Hall—at least I think so. The drawing-room is better than this. Will you allow me to do the honors of Dalton Hall?"

Dudleigh bowed, and the two walked toward the Hall, and entering, proceeded to the drawing-room.

"We are undoubtedly watched, even here," said Edith, with a melancholy smile, "but the watcher can not observe us very well, and has to stand too far off to hear us easily, so that this room is perhaps better than out-of-doors; at any rate, it is more convenient."

"Miss Dalton," said Dudleigh, "I am glad beyond all that words can say that I managed to get through your gates. My vague threats terrified Wiggins, though in reality I have no knowledge about him sufficiently definite to give me any actual power over him. I have only heard general scandal, in which he was mixed up. But he has given me credit for knowing something important. At any rate, now that I am here, let me do something for you at once. Command me, and I will obey."

"I want but one thing," said Edith, "and that is to get out."

"Well?"

"Will you lead the way and let me follow? That is all I ask of you."

"Certainly, and if you could only go out over my dead body, that price should be paid, and you should go,"

Dudleigh spoke quickly, but with no particular earnestness. Indeed, in all his tones there was a lack of earnestness. The words were excellent, but they lacked depth and warmth. Edith, however, was too much excited by the prospect of help to notice this.

"There is no need of that," said she; "there is no real danger."

"I rather think from the look of that ruffian at the gate that there will be some such price," said Dudleigh, carelessly. "If I had only brought my pistols, all would be easy. Can it be managed? How shall we do it? Do you think that you have nerve enough, Miss Dalton, to witness a fight?"

"Yes," said Edith, calmly.

"If I had my pistols," said Dudleigh, thoughtfully, "I might— But as it is, if they see you accompanying me, they will assemble in force."

"Yes," said Edith, sadly, for she began to see difficulties.

"Now do you think that if you are with me the porter will open the gates?"

"He will not."

"Well, we must get out in some other way. Can you climb the wall? I might climb and help you over."

"Yes, but they would follow and prevent us."

Dudleigh looked at the floor. Then he put his small gloved hand on his forehead, and appeared for a few moments to be lost in thought.

"Miss Dalton," said he at last, "I am at your service. Can you tell me what I can do?—for to save my life I can think of nothing just now. Give me my orders."

Edith looked perplexed. She knew that this man could not force his way unarmed through the gates. She did not feel inclined just yet to tell him to arm himself and shoot any one dead who opposed him. She could not bear to think of that. But here was Dudleigh, ready.

"Have you any fire-arms in the house?" he asked.

"No," said Edith, "and, besides, I can not bear just yet to cause any thing like bloodshed."

"If not, then you can not get free at once. Can you wait one day, or two days?"

"One or two days!" said Edith. "Oh yes; one or two weeks, or even months. Only let me have hope, and I can wait."

"You have this to comfort you, at any rate," said Dudleigh, "that outside the gates you have a friend. And now I will not intrude any longer. I must go. But if you will allow me I will come back to-morrow. Meanwhile I will try to think over what is best to be done."

"You will promise," said Edith, imploringly, "not to desert me?"

"Desert you? Never! On the honor of a gentleman!" cried Dudleigh; and as he bowed his head there came over his face a very singular smile, which Edith, however, did not see.

He then took his leave.

———————

CHAPTER XX.

FAITHFUL UNTO DEATH.

EDITH slept but little that night. The prospect of escape agitated her whole being, and the new friend who had so unexpectedly appeared took up all her thoughts.

He was a little man most certainly, and Edith already caught herself thinking of him as "Little Dudleigh." He had nothing whatever of the hero about him. Mowbray, as far as appearances went, far surpassed her new acquaintance in that respect. Still Edith felt bound to overlook or to excuse his slight frame, and in the effort to do this she recalled all the little men of history. She thought of a saying which she had once heard, that "all great men are small men." This sentiment included under the head of little men Alexander the Great, Julius Cæsar, Napoleon, with others of the same class, for the list had evidently been made up by one who was himself a little man, and was anxious to enter a forcible protest against the scorn of his bigger brethren. On the present occasion the list of little heroes was so formidable that Edith was prepared to find in "Little Dudleigh" all she wished. Still, in spite of his generous offers, and his chivalrous proposal to put down his dead body for her to march over, she did not feel for him that admiration which such heroism deserved; and she even reproached herself for her lack of common gratitude, for in her high spirits at the prospect of escape, she caught herself more than once smiling at the recollection of "Little Dudleigh's" little ways, his primness, and effeminacy.

At about ten o'clock on the following day "Little Dudleigh" came back.

"That beggar at the gate," said he, after the usual greetings, "looks very hard at me, but he doesn't pretend to hinder me from coming or going just yet, though what he may do in time remains to be seen."

"Oh," said Edith, "you must manage to get me out before Wiggins has a chance to prevent you from coming in."

"I hope so," said Dudleigh. "Of course, Miss Dalton, as you may suppose, I have been

"I MUST USE THESE, THEN."

thinking of you ever since I left you, and planning a thousand schemes. But I have made up my mind to this, and you must make up yours to the same. I am sorry, but it can not be avoided. I mean *bloodshed.*"

"Bloodshed!" said Edith, sadly.

"Of course it is terrible to a lady to be the cause of bloodshed," said Dudleigh, quietly, "and if there were any other way I would find it out, or you would know about it. But from what I have seen and heard, and from what I know of Wiggins, I see that there is nothing left but to force our way out, for the place is thoroughly guarded day and night."

"So it is," said Edith, mournfully.

"If I take you out, I must— Are we overheard?" he asked, looking cautiously around.

"I think not; at least not if you speak low."

"I must use these, then," said he, drawing a brace of pistols in a careless way from his coat pocket, and showing them to Edith.

Edith recoiled involuntarily. Bloodshed, and perhaps death, the scandal that would arise, arrest perhaps, or examination before magistrates—all these thoughts came before her. She was brave, but things like these could not be lightly faced. She was brave, but she could not decide just yet that any man's life should be taken for the sake of her liberty.

"I can not bear that," said she.

"You will get used to them," said Dudleigh, cheerfully. "They are easy to handle."

"Put them back."

"But what else is there to do?"

"I'm sure I don't know," said Edith, in a dejected tone.

"Well," said Dudleigh, after a pause, "I thought of this. It is natural. I anticipated some such objection as this on your part. I know very well what it is that you fear, and I don't know but that you are right. Still, I have other plans, which may not appear so objectionable. But in the first place, let me know finally, do you positively and absolutely reject this?" and he tapped the pistols significantly.

"I can not yet consent to risk any life," said Edith.

"Very well; this may remain over until every thing else fails."

"But couldn't you use these pistols to terrify them? The sight might make them open the gates."

"But it might not, and what then? Are you prepared to answer that?" And "Little Dudleigh," who had been speaking about these things as lightly and as carelessly as a lady would speak about a dress or the trimmings of a bonnet, paused, and looked at her inquiringly. "The fact is," he continued, as Edith did not answer, "you must be willing to run the risk of *killing a man.* Your liberty is worth this price. If you say to me, 'Open those gates,' that is what you must encounter. Will you face it? Say the word, and now, *now*, at this very moment, I will lead you there."

The offer of immediate escape was thus presented, and for a moment Edith hesitated, but the cost was too great.

"Oh," she cried, "this is terrible! But I will not consent. No, I will suffer longer rather than pay so frightful a price as human life."

"Well," said Dudleigh, "after all, since you have decided this way, I think you are about right. After all, there is really no necessity for so desperate a course. But I have a high idea of what a lady has a right to demand of a gentleman, and I am ready to do what you say."

"But you have other plans, have you not?"

"Yes, but slow ones—safe but slow. The question is, can you wait? Can you endure your present life? and how long?"

"Rather than cause the loss of life," said Edith, "I would endure this very much longer."

"Oh, you will not have to endure it so very long. If you are not too impatient, the time may pass quickly too. But before I make any further proposals, will you allow me to ask you one question? It is this: Suppose you were to escape to-day, where would you go?"

"I have thought about that," said Edith. "My dearest friend is Miss Plympton. She is the head of the school where I have spent the greater part of my life. She is the one to whom I should naturally go, but she keeps a boarding-school, and I do not wish to go there and meet my old school-mates and see so many. I wish to be secluded. I have sometimes thought of going to that neighborhood, and finding a home where I could occasionally see Miss Plympton, and at other times I have thought of going to my uncle, Sir Lionel Dudleigh."

At this last remark Dudleigh opened his eyes.

"Who?" he asked. "I don't understand."

"He is my uncle, you know," said Edith —"that is, by marriage—and therefore he is naturally the one to whom I should look for defense against Wiggins. In that case Sir Lionel will be far better than poor dear Auntie Plympton: I'm afraid that Wiggins has already frightened her away from me."

"But how would you get to Sir Lionel?" asked Dudleigh, with a puzzled expression.

"Well, that is what I want to find out. I have no idea where he lives. But you can tell me all about him. I should have asked before, but other things interfered. I will go to him. I feel confident that he will not cast me off."

"Cast you off! I should think not," said

Dudleigh; "but the difficulty is how to find him. You can get to Dudleigh Manor easily enough—every body knows where that is. But what then? Nobody is there."

"What! Is not Sir Lionel there?"

"Sir Lionel there! I only wish he was. Why, is it possible that you do not know that Sir Lionel is positively not in England? He travels all the time, and only comes home occasionally. Perhaps you know the cause—his family troubles ten years ago. He had a row with his wife then, and it has blighted his life. Sir Lionel? Why, at this moment I dare say he is somewhere among the Ural Mountains, or Patagonia, or some other equally remote country. But who told you that he was in England?"

Edith was silent. She had taken it for granted that Sir Lionel lived in his own home.

"Can I not write to him?" she asked.

"Of course, if you can only secure his address; and that I will do my utmost to find out for you. But to do this will be a work of time."

"Yes," sighed Edith.

"And what can you do in the mean time? Where can you go?"

"There is Miss Plympton."

"Yes, your teacher. And you don't wish to go to the school, but to some private place near it. Now what sort of a woman is Miss Plympton? Bold and courageous?"

"I'm afraid not," said Edith, after a thoughtful pause. "I know that she loves me like a mother, and when I first came here I should have relied on her to the utmost. But now I don't know. At any rate, I think she can be easily terrified." And Edith went on to tell about Miss Plympton's letter to her, and subsequent silence.

"I think with you," said Dudleigh, after Edith had ended, "that the letter is a forgery. But what is difficult to understand is this apparent desertion of you. This may be accounted for, however, in one of two ways. First, Wiggins may actually have seen her, and frightened her in some way. You say she is timid. The other explanation of her silence is that she may be ill."

"Ill!" exclaimed Edith, mournfully.

"It may be so."

"May she not all this time have been trying to rescue me, and been baffled?"

Dudleigh smiled.

"Oh no. If she had tried at all you would have heard something about it before this; something would certainly have been done. The claim of Wiggins would have been contested in a court of law. Oh no; she has evidently done nothing. In fact, I think that, and as it may seem to you, there can be no doubt about her illness. You say she left you here. No doubt she felt terrible anxiety. Her love for you, and her anxiety, would, perhaps, be too much for her. She may have been taken home ill."

Edith sighed. The picture of Miss Plympton's grief was too much for her.

"At any rate," said she, "if I can't find any friends—if Sir Lionel is gone, and poor dear auntie is ill, I can be free. I can help nurse her. Any life is better than this; and I can put my case in the hands of the lawyers."

"You are, of course, well supplied with money," said Dudleigh, carelessly.

"Money?"

"Yes; so as to travel, you know, and live, and pay your lawyers."

"I have no money," said Edith, helplessly; "that is, not more than a few sovereigns. I did not think of that."

"No money?"

"No—only a little."

"No money? Why, how is that? No money? Why, what can you do?"

"Wiggins manages every thing, and has all the money."

"You have never obtained any from him as yet, then?"

"I have never needed any."

"He spends your own money in paying these spies and jailers. But if you have no money, how can you manage to live, even if you do escape?"

Edith looked down in despair. The idea of money had never entered her mind. Yet now, since it was mentioned, she felt its importance. Yes, money was the chief thing; without that flight was useless, and liberty impossible. But how could she get it? Wiggins would not give her any. And where could she go? Could she go to Miss Plympton's, to be a dependent upon her at the school? That thought was intolerable. Much as she loved Miss Plympton, she could not descend to that.

"You are certainly not very practical," said Dudleigh, "or your first thought would have been about this. But you have none, you say, and so it can not be remedied. Is there any thing else? You see you can escape; but what then?"

Dudleigh was silent, and Edith looked at him in deep suspense.

"You say you never see Wiggins now?"

"No."

"You are not subject to insults?"

"No—to none."

"Have you the Hall to yourself?"

"Oh yes; I am not interfered with. As long as I stay inside the Hall I am left to myself—only I am watched, of course, as I told you."

"Of course; but, at any rate, it seems a sort of honorable captivity. You are not like a captive in a dungeon, for instance."

"Oh no."

"Would you rather be here, as you are, or at Miss Plympton's school as a sort of dependent?"

"Here, of course. I could not go back there, and face them all."

"Would you rather live here or in some mean lodging, without money to pay your board?"

"Here," said Edith, after a pause.

"There are worse situations in the world than this, then?"

"It seems so," said Edith, slowly.

"By leaving this just now you would be doing worse, then?"

"It looks like it."

"Well, then, may it not be better for you to remain here, for the present at least, until you hear something from Sir Lionel Dudleigh?"

"But how long will that be?"

"I can not tell."

"Is there nothing else?"

"Certainly the first thing for you to do is to see a lawyer."

"But how can I?"

"I can find one."

"But will you?"

"Of course. I shall be most happy. Only answer me this: If a lawyer takes up your case, shall you be willing to live here, or shall you insist on leaving?"

"I should prefer leaving," said Edith; "but at the same time, if a lawyer has my case, and I can feel that something is being done, I can be content here, at least for a time, until I hear from Sir Lionel—or Miss Plympton."

"Well, then, for the present at least, you give up the idea of fighting your way out?"

"Yes—I suppose so."

"Then all that I have to do is to get a lawyer for you, and write to Sir Lionel, wherever he is."

"You will not let Wiggins keep my lawyer away?" said Edith, in an imploring voice.

"Oh, I fancy he has such a wholesome dread of lawyers that he won't try to keep one out. At any rate, these lawyers have all kinds of ways, you know, of getting into places."

"And of getting people out of places, too, I hope."

"I should be sorry not to hope that."

So Edith found herself compelled to face the difficulties of her present situation a little longer, and endure as best she could the restraint of her imprisonment.

CHAPTER XXI.

A WARNING.

THE barriers which Wiggins had raised between Edith and the outer world had thus been surmounted by two persons—first, Mowbray, and second, Little Dudleigh. Mowbray had come and gone without any sign of objection or remonstrance from her jail-

THE LIVING LINK. 73

or; and now Edith could not help wondering
at the facility with which the new-comer,
Dudleigh, passed and repassed those jealously guarded limits. Dudleigh's power arose
from some knowledge of the past history of
Wiggins, but the knowledge did not seem
very definite, and she could not help wondering how long his visits would be tolerated.

She was not left to wonder long. On the
evening of the day on which Dudleigh had
made his last visit Wiggins came to see her.
She had not seen him since that time when
he had brought her the so-called letter of
Miss Plympton, except once when she had
caught a glimpse of him when riding with
Mowbray. He now entered in his usual
manner, with his solemn face, his formal
bow, his abstracted gaze. He sat down,
and for a few moments said nothing.

"I do not often inflict my presence on
you, Miss Dalton," said he at length. "I
have too much regard for you to intrude
upon you. Some day you will understand
me, and will appreciate my present course.
It is only for your own sake that I now
come, because I see that you are thoughtless and reckless, and are living under a
delusion. You are almost beyond my control, yet I still hope that I may have some
faint influence over you—or at least I can
try."

His tone was gentle and affectionate. It
was, in fact, paternal in its character; but
this tone, instead of softening Edith, only
seemed to her a fresh instance of his arrogant
assumption, and, as such, excited her contempt and indignation. These feelings,
however, she repressed for the moment, and
looked at him with a cold and austere face.

"You have been receiving visitors," he
continued, "visitors whom I could have kept
away if I had—chosen. But to do so would
have interfered with my plans, and so I have
tolerated them. You, however, have been
all along under such a—mistake—about me
—and my intentions—that you have thrown
yourself upon these strangers, and have,
I grieve to say, endangered your own future, and mine, more than you can possibly imagine. Your first visitor was objectionable, but I tolerated him for reasons that
I need not explain; but this last visitor is
one who ought not to be tolerated either by
you or by me. And now I come to you to
give you—a—an affectionate warning—to
ask of you not to be so reckless, so careless of your best interests, so blind to the
great issues that are at stake in—a—my—
present plans."

"You appear to me," said Edith, coldly,
"to have some reference to Lieutenant Dudleigh."

"That is what he calls himself."

"Calls himself?"

"Yes. This name Dudleigh is an assumed

one. He took that so as to gain your confidence."

"You appear to know him very well."

"I do not."

"How do you know, then, that this name
is assumed?"

"Because I happen to know the Dudleigh family, and this man does not belong
to it. I never saw him before."

"There are more Dudleighs in the world
than the family you speak of."

"He is an adventurer," said Wiggins.
"You know nothing about him. I believe
his name is false, as he himself is false.
Does he not pretend to be the son of Sir
Lionel?"

"No; he says that he is only a distant
relation to Sir Lionel."

"He is no relation whatever," said Wiggins. "You are allowing yourself to be
led astray by a man of whom you know
nothing—a designing villain, an adventurer."

"It is strange that you should apply such
terms to a man of whom you yourself acknowledge that you know nothing. But,
at any rate," continued Edith, with strong
emphasis, "he knows you. It is this knowledge that gives him the power of passing
through those gates which you shut against
me; what that knowledge may be you yourself know best."

"He does not know me," said Wiggins.

"He must," said Edith, "for the simple
reason that you dare not keep him out."

Wiggins looked at her in silence for some
time.

"It is a terrible ordeal for me," said he at
last, in a slow, measured tone, "to talk with
you. You seem to me like one who is mad;
but it is the madness of utter ignorance.
You do not know. Oh, how you tempt me
to tell you all! But I can not, I can not.
My lips are sealed as yet. But I will say no
more on that. I will ask you one question
only. It is this: Can you not see with your
own eyes that this man is nothing more than
a mere adventurer?"

"An adventurer!" repeated Edith, indignantly. "It ill becomes one like you to use
such a word as that. For what are you
yourself? Lieutenant Dudleigh is a gentleman; and though I have only known him
for a short time, I am happy in calling him
my friend. I will tolerate no abuse of him.
Why do you not say this to his face? If he
is what you say, why do you allow him to
come here? An adventurer? Why, that is
the very name I apply in all my thoughts to
you!"

A look of anguish came over the face of
Wiggins. He trembled violently, but with
an effort mastered his feelings. Evidently
what he said was true, and to him it was a
severe ordeal to carry on a conversation with
Edith. Her scorn, her anger, and her hate

all flamed forth so vehemently that it was hard to endure.

"If you could only refrain from these bitter insults!" said he, in a mournful voice. "If you could only put a check upon yourself when you talk with me! I wish to speak calmly, but you hurl taunts at me that inflict exquisite pain. The remembrance of them will one day give you no less anguish to you, believe me—oh, believe me! Spare me these taunts and insults, I entreat you, for the sake of both of us!"

"Both of us?" repeated Edith, without being in the slightest degree affected by the words of Wiggins. "Both of us? You seem to me to be including yourself and me in the same class, as though there could be any thing in common between me and one like you. That is impossible. Our interests are forever separate."

"You do not know," said Wiggins, with a great effort to be calm. "This man—this Lieutenant Dudleigh, as he calls himself—is an enemy to both of us."

"You use that expression with strange pertinacity. I must tell you again that there can not possibly be any thing in common between you and me. For my part, I consider you as my natural enemy. You are my jailer. I am your prisoner. That is all. I am at war with you. I would give half of my possessions to escape from your hands, and the other half to punish you for what you have done. I live in the hope of some day meting out to you the punishment which your crimes deserve. If any one is an enemy of yours, that one thing is a sufficient recommendation to make him a friend of mine."

At these words Wiggins seemed to endure a keener anguish, and his face bore upon it the same pallid horror which she had seen there before upon a similar provocation. He stared at her for a few moments, and then bowing down, he leaned his head upon his hand and looked at the floor in silence. At last he raised his head and looked at her with a calm face.

"Is there no possible way," said he, "in which I can speak to you without receiving wounds that sting like the fangs of a serpent? Be patient with me. If I offend, try to be a little forbearing just now, for the sake of yourself, if for nothing else. See, I am humbling myself. I ask your forbearance. I wish to speak for your own good. For, as it is, you are doing you know not what. You are ruining yourself; you are blighting and blasting your own future; you are risking your reputation; you are exposing the family name to the sneers of the world, once again. Think of your frantic adventure at the gates with that—that Mowbray!"

Now if Wiggins had wished to mollify Edith, or to persuade her to fall in with his own wishes, he was certainly most unfortunate in his way of going about it; and especially in such an allusion as this. For no sooner did he mention the name of Mowbray than Edith was roused to a fresh excitement.

"What!" she exclaimed. "Do you throw that up to me—you of all men? Who, I ask you, was the cause of all the shame and misery and violence that I suffered there? Who was the one that made it necessary? Who was the one that brought me to such a pitch of desperation that I was ready to do any thing, however wild or frantic? Who? Why, you yourself—you, who come to me now, and with a solemn voice ask me to calm myself. Is it not possible for you to see what a horrible mockery all this must be to me? But I will do what you ask. I will be calm in spite of all. Come, now, I will meet you on your own ground. I will ask you one thing. How much money will you take to let me go free?"

At this request Wiggins stared at her with the expression of one who, while already reeling under a stroke, has received some new blow. He started from his chair to his feet, and stood for a moment regarding her with an indescribable look. But again he mastered his emotions, and finally resumed his seat.

"I don't know what to say to you!" he exclaimed. "I came to advise you, and to warn you. I have done every thing. There is one thing which would put an end to all this misery which you inflict on me, but that one thing I wish on no account to say just now. I can not just yet give up the hope that has cheered me for so long a time; still, I must warn you. Rash girl, you have already suffered from this Mowbray, as he calls himself. Do you not see that this new visitor, this so-called Dudleigh, is nothing else than the ally, the associate, the partner, the emissary of Mowbray?"

"The associate of Mowbray," said Edith, quietly, "is yourself. You sent him to me, I have no doubt. You have your own schemes. What they are I do not know, nor do I care to know. As for Lieutenant Dudleigh, he is, I feel sure, an honorable gentleman, and his associates are far, very far different from such as you and Mowbray. He is the friend of one whom I also regard now as my only friend—one whom I never cease to pray to reach—one whom I hope yet to find, and by his help escape from your infamous control, and punish you for all your villainy toward me and mine."

"What is this? What do you mean? A friend?"

Wiggins uttered these words in a bewildered way.

"The friend whom I hope to reach," said Edith, "the one to whom I look for vengeance on you, is Sir Lionel Dudleigh."

"Sir Lionel Dudleigh!" repeated Wiggins, with a groan. "You!"

"Yes, Sir Lionel Dudleigh!" said Edith. "I see that you are agitated at the mention of that name—the name of an honorable man—a man of stainless name, who has nothing in common with such as you. Let me tell you that the time will yet come when you shall have to meet Sir Lionel Dudleigh face to face, and then you will have reason to tremble!"

At this Wiggins rose. He did not look at Edith. He did not say a word. He seemed overwhelmed. His head was bowed down on his breast; his eyes were fixed on the floor; and he walked with a slow and weary pace out of the room.

"It was the threat of Sir Lionel Dudleigh," thought Edith, "that terrified him. He knows that the time is coming when he will have to give an account; and he fears Sir Lionel Dudleigh more than any other living man."

"DEAR LITTLE DUDLEIGH."

CHAPTER XXII.

LITTLE DUDLEIGH.

LITTLE Dudleigh now came to the Hall nearly every day, and devoted himself to Edith. In spite of his devotion, however, her admiration for him never rose to a very high pitch. There was something about the little man which was too prim and precise —an indescribable something which made her feel a half contempt, against which it was difficult to struggle even by keeping her mind fixed on his valuable services. His lit-

tle particular ways were more appropriate to a woman than to a man, and excited her impatience. Still she felt that he must have plenty of courage, for had he not offered to risk his life, and had he not come armed and prepared to force a way for her out of the park?

Edith, like all generous natures, was frank and confiding. She was warm-hearted, impulsive, and quick to show gratitude. After the society of the Mowbrays, she found that of Little Dudleigh an inexpressible relief. What struck her most about him was his unvarying calmness. He must have some personal regard for her, she was sure, for on what other grounds would he come to see her so incessantly, and spend so much time with her? Yet he never showed much of this in his manner. He frequently paid compliments, and alluded to his willingness to do any thing to serve her; but he seldom indulged in sentiment. He never showed any approach to the tenderness of love. On the whole Edith was immensely relieved at this, for the little man was one whom she could cordially appreciate as a disinterested friend, but whose approach toward gallantry or sentiment would have been repugnant in the extreme.

Little Dudleigh certainly exerted all his powers to make himself agreeable, and not without success. For Edith, who was naturally of a radiant temper, was now in high spirits at her brightening prospects, and it was easy to amuse her. Dudleigh had innumerable stories to tell of London life, and these stories referred almost exclusively to the theatre. He appeared to be intimately acquainted with all the "professional" world, and more particularly with the actresses. His stories about them were generally of a light, gossiping character, referring to their petty failings, jealousies, and weaknesses, and seemed like the malicious tales which actresses tell about one another. Still none of them were at all unfit for a lady's ear, and in all of them there was some absurdity which compensated for their maliciousness. Little Dudleigh seemed to understand most thoroughly the female nature, its excellences and its defects, its strength and its weaknesses. In his anecdotes about men he was never so successful. His familiarity with women's ways was quite remarkable, and extended even to the smallest details of dress and ornament. His whole manner put Edith singularly at her ease, and she sometimes caught herself speaking to him almost as she used to speak to her fellow school-girls.

Little Dudleigh's society thus became quite agreeable, and Edith looked forward each day to his appearance with something like impatience. There was, after all, every reason why she should enjoy it. She had no other associate, and this one upon whom she was thrown exerted all his powers for the sole purpose of pleasing her.

There was very little of any thing like enthusiasm about Little Dudleigh, and in this respect he differed very widely from Edith. She would go into raptures over every beautiful scene. A brilliant sky, a rich landscape, a quiet woodland view, all served to excite her admiring comments. Little Dudleigh, however, showed no such feeling. He confessed himself indifferent to natural scenery, and partial only to city life; and while he acknowledged the beauty of the place, he yet declared that he found more to admire in a drawing-room or a theatre.

Meanwhile the little man had not been idle. On his first visit after the conversation last detailed he informed Edith that he had written to London, making inquiries about Sir Lionel. A few days afterward he showed Edith a letter which he said he had received from Sir Lionel's London solicitors. The writer stated that he did not know where Sir Lionel was, but that he would write to a firm in Marseilles, who were his bankers and agents. The opinion of the writer was that the baronet was somewhere about the Mediterranean. This intelligence was rather distressing to Edith, but she had been prepared for something of the kind; and as Little Dudleigh encouraged her, and pointed out many reasons for hope, she took heart and hoped for the best.

According to Little Dudleigh, Sir Lionel was always traveling. During ten or twelve years he said that he had not been in England more than three or four times. It was on one of these occasions that he had met with him, and had received from him certain acts of kindness which made him grateful to his benefactor. Sir Lionel, he said, had been a great traveler, having been through every part of Europe and America, and most of Asia. He was constantly roving about to different places, sometimes by land, at other times in his own yacht. This, he thought, must be the reason why Edith had never heard from him. Personally he was most kind-hearted and generous, and if he only knew the situation in which she was, he would fly to her assistance.

Little Dudleigh also alluded in a general way to Sir Lionel's family troubles. The quarrel with his wife, he said, had broken up the baronet's life, and made him a wanderer. He knew nothing about the cause, but had heard that Lady Dudleigh had been very much to blame, and had deserted her husband under very painful circumstances. It was this that had made the unhappy husband a wanderer. Lady Dudleigh, he thought, had died years ago.

Such was the state of things, according to Little Dudleigh, and Edith had only to make up her mind to wait until something more definite was known. In the mean time,

however, Little Dudleigh had not been unmindful of Miss Plympton, but wrote a letter to her, which he showed to Edith. Edith also wrote one, which was inclosed in his. Several weeks passed away, but no reply was received, and this silence distressed Edith greatly. At length, when she had lost all hope of hearing from her dear friend, a reply came. It was written from Italy, and Edith read it with feelings of mingled amazement and anxiety.

It was written in a strange hand, and informed Lieutenant Dudleigh that his letter and inclosure had been forwarded from Plympton Terrace, where it had been first sent, to Miss Plympton's present abode at Nice; and went on to say that Miss Plympton had come back from Dalton care-worn by anxiety and fatigue, that a severe illness had been the result, and that she had been sent to the south of France. The writer stated that she was still too feeble to undergo any excitement, and therefore that Lieutenant Dudleigh's letter and inclosure had not been shown her. As soon as Miss Plympton's health would admit of it the letters would be given to her. It was uncertain how long she would remain at Nice. They were thinking now of taking her to Germany or Switzerland. The school had been broken up for the present. This letter was signed by "Adèle Swinburne," who said that she was Miss Plympton's "attendant." It was a name that Edith had never heard of before.

It never occurred to Edith to question for one moment the authenticity of this letter. She accepted it all as truth, and was filled with grief. Miss Plympton, then, had not been forgetful. She had done what she could, and this illness was the result. It seemed now to Edith that the climax of her sorrows had been reached in the sufferings and exile of her only friend.

"And now, Miss Dalton," said Little Dudleigh, after a long silence, in which he had watched her with respectful sympathy, "what do you wish to do?"

"I'm afraid that I shall have to rely upon you altogether," said Edith.

"You want something to be done as soon as possible, of course."

"Of course—most earnestly."

"You see, then, that both Sir Lionel and Miss Plympton are quite out of our reach. If you wish for deliverance you must try something else."

"What else can I try?"

"Well, the law."

"The law? Of course, that is just what I wish."

"It is tedious, remember."

"Oh, if I can only make a beginning, I can wait. It isn't my life here, or even my imprisonment, that is intolerable so much as my helplessness, and the thought that I am doing nothing, and the impunity with which this wretched Wiggins carries out his purposes. If I could only know that the affair was in the hands of a lawyer, I should feel content."

"Yes, women have a great faith in lawyers."

"At any rate, there must be something in the law, although it is often baffled."

"There ought to be, certainly; but of course you must be prepared to have your suit resisted. Wiggins will also have lawyers, and the ablest ones that he can find."

"Then I must get better ones."

"Of course."

"And immediately, too, without waiting any longer," said Edith, impatiently.

"Well, I will get you one as soon as possible, if you say so."

"Lieutenant Dudleigh," said Edith, with deep emotion, "you have claims on my gratitude which I can never repay."

"It is the happiest moment of my life," said Little Dudleigh, with greater animation than usual, "since I have heard you say that. But don't speak of gratitude. Say, at the most, friendship. If you will only accept my humble services, they are all yours, and my life too, if necessary."

"Oh," said Edith, with a smile, "there will be no danger to your life now, you know, if I put my case in the hands of lawyers."

"Well, now, talking of lawyers," said Little Dudleigh, "since you have made up your mind to this, it will be necessary to be very cautious in choosing one."

"I must have the best counsel in England."

"Certainly, for Wiggins will be on the alert. With him every thing is at stake. If he loses, it will be absolute ruin. In the course of the trial his whole past life must come up."

"And it ought to come up," said Edith, indignantly.

"We must, as you say, have the best counsel in England. An ordinary man might ruin all. You must get the best lawyer in London. And now I would not advise you to choose the most eminent one there, for fear lest the multitude of his engagements might prevent him from giving to your case the attention which it requires. You want some one who will give his whole soul to the case—some shrewd, deep, wily, crafty man, who understands thoroughly all the ins and outs of law, and can circumvent Wiggins in every way."

"But I don't like these wily lawyers," said Edith, doubtfully. "I prefer honorable men."

"Yes, certainly, as friends, no doubt you do; but you are not now seeking for a friend. You are on the look-out for a servant, or, rather, for one who can fight your battle best, and deal the best and surest blows upon Wiggins."

"Well, I'm sure I don't know," said Edith, doubtfully.

"Now I'll tell you what I'll do, if you'll consent," said Little Dudleigh. "I'll go to London and seek out the right man myself. There is no use in writing letters. I must go and explain the thing personally."

"Lieutenant Dudleigh," said Edith, in deep emotion, "I do not know what to say. You really overwhelm me with kindnesses. I can only say that you have earned my life-long gratitude."

Little Dudleigh shook his head deprecatingly.

"Miss Dalton," said he, in a tone of respectful devotion, "the favor is all yours, and the pleasure is all mine. Believe me, I feel happy beyond expression at being able to do any thing for you."

And after some further conversation, Little Dudleigh took his leave.

"How noble and generous he is!" thought Edith, as she watched him walk down the avenue. "Dear Little Dudleigh, what a pity it is that he is not a few inches taller!"

CHAPTER XXIII.

THE MAN OF LAW.

THE departure of Dudleigh left Edith to the monotony of her solitary life. If Dudleigh had desired to win her affections, he could certainly have chosen no better way of doing so, for by this course he made himself greatly missed, and caused Edith to count the days in her impatience for his return. In her loneliness she could not help recalling the hours she had passed with her agreeable visitor, and thus was forced to give him a large portion of her thoughts. His connection with Sir Lionel seemed of itself a recommendation of the strongest kind, and all that he had done for her, and was still doing, filled her generous soul with gratitude.

Thinking thus about him, she recalled his whole manner and appearance. The worst that could be said against him was that he was effeminate. But at any rate that was better than being brutal. Otherwise he was frank and engaging and clever and gentlemanly. He had evidently a high sense of honor. He was devoted to her. From the first time when he had heard her story down to the present moment he had not ceased to think for her and to work for her. Even now he had gone to London to obtain for her what she most wanted—the assistance of the law.

All these things made him appear in a more favorable light than ever. She recalled his heroism and devotion. She considered that he had done as much as if he had laid down his life for her, since he had offered to do so, and had only been prevented by her prohibition. Little Dudleigh, then, she thought, with his slight frame and small hands, had more real manhood than a hundred such big brutes as Mowbray. If he is not a true man, who is? Could she ever hope again to find so devoted a friend? Impossible. He had come to her in her very darkest hour; he had eagerly espoused her cause, and had devoted himself with all his soul to her interests. What more could she wish than this?

For several weeks Dudleigh remained away, and Edith grew excessively impatient. She began to fear for his safety. In her anxiety she sometimes imagined that Wiggins might have caused some harm to fall on him in London. She recalled all the dangers of the London streets, of which she had read in various works of fiction, and imagined Wiggins hiring some cut-throat to follow him, assassinate him at the first opportunity, and throw his body into the river. She imagined that some ruffian, hired of course by Wiggins, might tempt him to take a friendly glass, drug his liquor, and then dispose of his victim in the same convenient river. Then her mood changed, and she laughed at the absurdity of such fears, for she well knew that he must be perfectly familiar with London life and the London streets, so that any thing of this kind was nonsensical. Then she thought that perhaps no lawyer would undertake her case without money being paid at once. In fact, all the fears that could be suggested by an uneasy mind and a very vivid imagination came crowding before her as the time passed by and Dudleigh did not return.

But at last all her fears came to an end. One morning, at the usual hour, she saw his well-known figure approaching the house. In her eager joy she hurried at once down stairs, and could scarcely prevent herself from running down the avenue to meet him. It was with difficulty that she controlled herself, and waited for him in the drawing-room.

Little Dudleigh entered with his usual calmness and self-possession. Edith greeted him with the warmest welcome.

"But you come alone," said she, in a tone of disappointment. "You have not been successful."

"In one sense," said he, "I have been most successful, for I have found the very man I wanted. I had to wait for him, though. He was in Lyons when I reached London, and I went over for him and brought him here."

"Lyons!" exclaimed Edith. "Why, that's in France. Did you really go over to France?"

"Why not?" said Dudleigh, calmly. "I set forth on a certain purpose, and I am not in the habit of giving up what I undertake to do. Besides, you forget for whom that

business was undertaken, and the impulse that drove me forward."

Edith looked at the floor and said nothing. She felt under such obligations to him that she hardly knew what to say.

"I should like to have brought the lawyer here at once," he continued, "but did not. He is now in this neighborhood, however. The reason why I did not bring him now was because I wished first to see Wiggins myself. He must be prepared, or he may make trouble. I wish to frighten him into allowing him to pass. I shall have to make up some plausible story, however, to account for his visiting you. I have not yet decided on what it shall be. I think, however, that the lawyer had better come here alone. You will, of course, know that he is to be trusted. You may say to him, in fact, whatever you like."

"But wouldn't it be better for you to be present also?" said Edith. "I may require your advice."

"Thank you, Miss Dalton. I assure you I value most highly every expression of your confidence. But I think it will be better for you to see him alone. He will give you his card. His name is Barber. If I were to come with him, Wiggins might suspect. At the same time, I don't know, after all, but that I may change my mind and come with him. But in any case you may talk to him freely. He has not been idle, for he has already mastered your whole situation. You may trust him just as much as you trust me. You may, in fact, regard him the same as me."

"And he will be here to-morrow?" said Edith.

"Yes."

"I know you hate expressions of gratitude," said Edith, after a pause; "but I can only say that my own gratitude is beyond expression. You have given me hope—"

"Say nothing about it," said Dudleigh, interrupting her. "That will be the best thanks, though really I have done nothing to merit thanks. Duty and honor both impelled me to serve you, without mentioning —any—a—deeper and stronger feeling."

Edith again looked at the floor. She suspected the existence of this stronger feeling, and did not altogether like to think of it. Her own feelings toward him were singularly cool, and she did not wish him to be otherwise. His general calmness of demeanor was very pleasant to her, and his occasional allusions to any deeper sentiment than common, few though they were, troubled her greatly. What if he should seek as his reward that which he surely had a right to hope for—her hand? Could she give it? On the other hand, could she have the heart to refuse it? The alternative was not pleasant.

On the following day, while Edith was

waiting in great impatience, a stranger came to the Hall to call upon her.

The stranger was a small-sized man, with round shoulders, gray hair, bushy eyebrows, and sallow skin. He wore spectacles, his clothes were of good material, but rather loose fit, betokening one who was indifferent to dress. His boots were loose, his gloves also, and an umbrella which he carried, being without a band, had a baggy appearance, which was quite in keeping with the general style of this man's costume. He looked to Edith so much like a lawyer that she could not help wondering at the completeness with which one's profession stamps itself upon the exterior.

"I am sent," said the stranger, after a brief, stiff salutation, "by Lieutenant Dudleigh, to communicate with you about your present position. I take it for granted that we shall not be overheard, and propose to carry on this conversation in as low a tone as possible."

Saying this, the stranger took a quick, sharp glance through his spectacles around the room.

His voice was dry and thin, his manner abrupt and stiff and business-like. Evidently he was a dried-up lawyer, whose whole life had been passed among parchments.

Edith assured him that from where they were sitting they could not be overheard if they spoke in a moderately low voice. This appeared to satisfy the stranger, and after another survey of the room, he drew forth from his breast pocket a wallet filled with papers — a well-worn, fat, business-like wallet — and taking from this a card, he rose stiffly and held this toward Edith. She took it, and glancing over it read the address :

HENRY BARBER,
SOLICITOR,
Inner Temple, London.

Edith bowed. "Lieutenant Dudleigh told me your name," said she.

"And now," said he, "let us proceed to business, for my time is limited.

"Lieutenant Dudleigh," he began, "has already explained to me, in a general way, the state of your affairs. He found me at Lyons, where I was engaged in some important business, and made me come to England at once. He directed me verbally, though not formally or in proper order, to investigate as much as I could about your affairs before coming here, and requested me to consider myself as your solicitor. That, I suppose, is quite correct, is it not ?"

"It is," said Edith.

"Under these circumstances," continued Barber, "I at once went to the proper quarter, and investigated the will of your late father; for your whole position, as you must be aware, depends upon that. Of course no

will can deprive you of your lawful inheritance in real estate, which the law of the country secures to you and yours forever ; but yet it may surround you with certain restrictions more or less binding. Now it was my object to see about the nature of these restrictions, and so understand your peculiar position."

Here Barber paused, and taking out his wallet, drew from it a slip of paper on which he had penciled some memoranda.

"In the multiplicity of my legal cares, Miss Dalton," he continued, "I find it necessary to jot down notes with reference to each individual case. It prevents confusion and saves time, both of which are, to a lawyer, considerations of the utmost moment.

"And now, with reference to your case, first of all, the will and the business of the guardianship—let us see about that. According to this will, you, the heir, are left under the care of two guardians for a certain time. One of these guardians is on the spot. The other is not. Each of these men has equal powers. Each one of these is trustee for you, and guardian of you. But one has no power superior to the other. This is what the will distinctly lays down. Of course, Miss Dalton, you will perceive that the first necessary thing is to know this, What are the powers of a guardian ? Is it not ?"

Edith bowed. The mention of two guardians had filled her with eager curiosity, but she repressed this feeling for the present, so as not to interrupt the lawyer in his speech.

"What, then, are the powers of a guardian ? To express this in the simplest way, so that you can understand those powers perfectly, a guardian stands, as the law has it, in loco parentis—which means that he is the same as a father. The father dies ; he perpetuates his authority by handing it over to another. He is not dead, then. The man dies, but the father lives in the person of the guardian whom he may have appointed. Such," said Mr. Barber, with indescribable emphasis—"such, Miss Dalton, is the LAW. You must know," he continued, "that the law is very explicit on the subject of guardianship. Once make a man a guardian and, as I have remarked, he forthwith stands in loco parentis, and the ward is his child in the eye of the LAW. Do you understand ?"

"Yes," said Edith, in a despondent tone. She felt disappointment and discouragement at hearing all this, and could only hope that there would be something yet which would open better prospects.

"Such, then, are the powers of a guardian," continued Barber. "They are very strong, and that will, by giving you guardians, has tied you up."

"But I am of age," said Edith, meekly. Barber waved his hand slightly. "That," said he, "is a point which I shall consider presently. Just now I will say this—that the framer of that will considered all these points, and arranged that the guardianship should continue until such time as you might obtain another guardian of another kind, before whom all others are powerless."

"But who are my guardians?" asked Edith, in great excitement, unable any longer to repress her curiosity. "One is Wiggins, I know. Who is the other?"

"One," said Barber, "is, as you say, John Wiggins; the other is Sir Lionel Dudleigh."

"Sir Lionel Dudleigh!" exclaimed Edith, while a feeling of profound satisfaction came to her. "Oh, how glad I am!"

"It is indeed a good thing that it is so," said Barber; "but, unfortunately, he can not at present be of service. For where is he? He is in parts unknown. He is out of the country. He is, for the present, the same as though he were dead. It is not probable that he has heard of your father's death, or of the existence of this will, unless, indeed, Mr. Wiggins has taken the trouble to find out where he is, and send him the information. That, however, is not likely. How, then, is it with you? You have, in point of fact, at the present time virtually but *one* guardian. He is here on the spot. He is exerting his authority, and you assert, I think, that he subjects you to a sort of imprisonment. Miss Dalton, he has a right to do this."

Saying this, Barber was silent for a moment, and looked at Edith, and then at the floor. On the other hand, she looked steadfastly at him; but her hand trembled, and an expression of utter hopelessness came over her face.

"Is that all that you have to tell me?" she said at last, in a despairing voice.

"Certainly not, Miss Dalton," said Barber —"certainly not. I have much more to say. But first it was necessary to explain your position, and lay down the LAW. There is only one reason why you sent for me, and why I came. You wish, by some means or other, to get free from the control of this guardian, John Wiggins."

"Yes," said Edith, earnestly.

"Very well," said Barber. "I know all about that. I have been informed by Lieutenant Dudleigh. You wish in some way or other to gain your freedom. Now in order to do this there are two different ways, Miss Dalton, and only two. The first is to find your other guardian, and obtain his assistance. Who is he? Sir Lionel Dudleigh. Where is he? No one knows. What then? He must be found. You must send out emissaries, messengers, detectives, in short; you must send off some one who will find him wherever he is, and make him acquainted with your position. But suppose that you can not find him, or that he is indifferent to your interests—a thing which is certainly possible—what then? What are you to do? You are then under the control of John Wiggins, your remaining guardian; and it remains to be seen whether, by the provisions of the will, there is any other way in which you may escape from that control. Now the will has made provisions, and here is the other of those two ways of escape of which I spoke. This is marriage. If you were to marry, that moment you would be free from the control of John Wiggins; and not only so, but he would at once be compelled to quit the premises, and hand in his accounts. Of course his object is to prevent any thing of that kind, which would be so ruinous to him, and therefore he will keep you shut up, if possible, as long as he lives; but if you should adopt this way of escape, Miss Dalton, you would turn the tables at once; and if, as I have understood is the case, he has made any misappropriations of money, or defalcations of any kind, he will be bound to make them good, to the uttermost farthing. Such, Miss Dalton, is the LAW."

"And I have no better prospect than this?" exclaimed Edith, in deep dejection.

"Those, Miss Dalton, are the only two courses possible."

"And if Sir Lionel can not be found?"

"Then you will have to fall back on the other alternative."

"But that is out of the question."

"Such, unfortunately, are the only provisions of the will."

"Then there is no hope," sighed Edith.

"Hope? Oh yes! There is plenty of hope. In the first place, I would urge you to lose no time in searching after your uncle."

"I shall do so. Will you see to it?"

"I will do all that I can. You wish me, of course, to act in connection with Lieutenant Dudleigh."

"Of course."

"I will begin at once. And now I must go."

The lawyer put his memoranda back in the wallet, restoring the latter to his pocket, and took his hat.

"But must I remain a prisoner here?" cried Edith. "Is there no law to free me—none whatever? After all, I am a British subject, and I have always understood that in England no one can be imprisoned without a trial."

"You are a ward, Miss Dalton, and guardians can control their wards, as parents control children."

"But parents can not control children who are of age."

"A ward is under age till the time specified in the legal instrument that appoints

"SUCH, MISS DALTON, IS THE LAW!"

the guardian. You, until marriage, are what the law calls an 'infant.' But do not be discouraged, Miss Dalton. We will hunt up Sir Lionel, and if he can be found we will bring him back to England."

Saying this, in the same dry, business-like tone that he had used all along, Barber bowed himself out.

CHAPTER XXIV.

NEW OBLIGATIONS.

THAT interview with the lawyer left Edith in a state of the deepest dejection. She had certainly not anticipated any thing like this. She expected that measures would at once be taken to carry on a contest with Wiggins, and give her her lawful rights, and above all her freedom. It never for a moment entered her mind to question the truth of a single statement that Barber had made. His whole communication with her was of the most business-like character, as it seemed to her, and she thought he must be eminent in his profession, or else Dudleigh would not have employed him. And this was the end of all that hope in which she had been indulging! Her freedom now seemed farther removed than ever. How could Sir Lionel ever be found? According to Dudleigh, he lived the life of a wanderer, and left no trace behind him. It was hard for her to think that her only hope depended upon finding him.

F

On the following day Dudleigh came, looking as calm and as unruffled as usual.

"Barber has gone back," said he. "I knew before what he was going to tell you. I had not the heart to tell you myself, or even to be here when he was telling you."

"It might have saved me some disappointment if you had told me."

"But the disappointment would have been as great, and I had not the heart to inflict sorrow myself upon you! I know, after Barber had explained it to me, how I felt; and I can form some idea of the nature of your feelings."

"So there is nothing to be done," said Edith, with a sigh.

"Pardon me, there is very much indeed to be done, though whether it will result in any thing remains to be seen."

"What can I do?"

"Do! Why, as Barber said, hunt up Sir Lionel."

"I'll never find him."

"Yes, you can."

"How?"

"By searching, of course. And that is what I have come about now."

"Have you thought of any thing new?"

"No, nothing. I merely came to make a proposal."

"What is it?" asked Edith, languidly; for now there seemed no chance for any thing.

"It is this," said Dudleigh. "I propose, if you will allow me, to go myself."

"You!" exclaimed Edith, in great surprise.

" Yes."

" But can you obtain leave to go? You will have to go abroad, won't you?"

" Yes, of course."

" But can you leave your regiment?"

" Oh yes. I can get leave of absence for as long a time as will be needed for that, I think, without difficulty. In fact, before leaving London, as soon as I heard Barber's opinion, I put in my request at once for two months' leave, and I have every reason to believe that they will allow it. I have one or two influential friends, you know."

" And will you really go?" asked Edith, in tones of deep feeling, with all her gratitude evident in her tone and expression.

" Yes, if you will allow me."

" If—allow you? I am only too glad to have a friend who is willing to undertake such a thing for me in my distress."

" There is nothing, Miss Dalton, which I would not undertake for you."

" You are overwhelming me with obligations," said Edith. " What you have already done is more than I can ever repay."

" Do not speak of obligations," said Dudleigh, earnestly. " My best reward is the thought that I may have given you even a temporary relief."

" You have given me much happiness," said Edith, earnestly; " and if it proves to be only temporary it will not be your fault. You overwhelm me with a sense of obligation."

" Now really, Miss Dalton, if you talk in that way, you will make me feel ashamed. After all, what have I done? Nothing more than any gentleman would do. But do not say a word about it again. Let it be taken for granted that I do this from a selfish motive—simply to please myself, you know; simply because I love—to do it."

Dudleigh spoke in his usual quiet way, without any particular ardor, although once or twice his voice grew more earnest than usual. Edith said nothing. She felt a little embarrassed, but the self-possession of Dudley was perfect; he hinted strongly at love, but seemed not at all like an ardent lover. He looked and acted simply like a friend; and as Edith needed a friend above all things, she was glad to accept his services.

" My present plan," said he, " can be easily explained. Sir Lionel seems to be somewhere about the Mediterranean. Any letters that are sent to him have to be directed to Messrs. Chatellon, Comeaux, and Co., Marseilles, who forward them to him. I have already written to these gentlemen, asking where he is; but when they sent their reply they did not know. They stated, however, that on hearing from him they would let me know. But to wait for an answer from these gentlemen would be too great a trial for your patience. You can not be satisfied, nor could I, unless something is being done. It would simply kill you to wait here, day after day, week after week, month after month, for letters that would never come. Nothing is so terrible. You must send some one. Now I think that the best one you can send is myself, and I hope I speak without vanity. No mere hireling can go on this service. The one who goes should have different motives, and for my part I should feel the search to have a personal interest, and should work for you as I would for myself."

" Oh, Lieutenant Dudleigh," said Edith, " there is no need for me to say how I should feel about a search made by you. I refrain from expressions of gratitude, since you forbid them; and so I do not know what to say."

" Say nothing, then, and—I do not like to say it, but I must—hope for nothing. If you hope, you may be disappointed. If you do not hope, you can not be. But in any case, whether you are disappointed or not, remember this—that in spite of these musty lawyers, if the worst comes to the worst you have one steadfast friend, and that if you say the word I will force a way for you through those gates. If you ever feel discouraged, remember that. It is a great preventive against despair to know that you have an alternative of some kind. And now I will take my departure, for the train will leave soon, and I must go at once."

———◆———

CHAPTER XXV.

THE SOURCES OF THE NILE.

At length, after an absence of four or five weeks, Dudleigh returned. Edith had tried hard not to hope, so as to be prepared for a disappointment; but after all, in spite of her efforts, she could not help hoping. She put great confidence in Dudleigh's energy and perseverance, and thought that he would be able not only to find out where Sir Lionel might be, but even to see him, and make him acquainted with her situation. He had already done so much for her that it seemed quite possible for him to do this. As the days passed by she found herself looking forward to his return as the time of her certain deliverance, until at length hope grew into confidence, and the idea of disappointment was completely driven away.

At last he came, and his first appearance put to flight all her hopes, and filled her with a nameless terror. He looked dejected and weary. He asked after her health, and whether she had been in any way molested; after which Edith entreated him to tell her the worst.

" For you bring bad news," said she—" I see it in your face. Tell me the worst."

Dudleigh mournfully shook his head.

"You have not found him, then?"

"No."

"But you must have heard something about him. He is at least alive, is he not?"

"I don't know even that."

"What! has any thing happened to him?"

"Not that I know of. But he has started on a long and perilous excursion; and whether he will ever return or not is more than I can say."

"Then there is no hope," said Edith, in a voice of despair.

Dudleigh was silent for a time.

"I will tell you all," he replied at length. "When I left you I went at once to Marseilles. I called on Sir Lionel's agents there, but found that they had heard nothing from him whatever. They said that when he last left that city he had gone to Turkey. I then set off for Constantinople, and spent a week there, trying to find some traces of him. At the British Embassy they said that he had only remained one day in the city, and had then gone in his yacht, which he had brought with him, on a cruise in the Black Sea. But whether he had returned or not no one knew. At last I met with a merchant who knew him, and he told me that he had returned and gone to Athens. I went to Athens, and found that he had been there at one of the hotels, the landlord of which informed me that he had spent three days there and had left for parts unknown. I left letters at each of these places, and sent others to Smyrna, Beyrout, Jaffa, and Alexandria. Then I returned to Marseilles. There, to my surprise, I learned that, a few days after I left, they had heard from Sir Lionel, who was in Alexandria, and about to start on the maddest expedition that was ever heard of—a journey up the Nile, into the inaccessible regions of Central Africa—to try to discover the sources of that river. He simply announced to his agents that all his preparations were completed, and that he would leave immediately. What could I do then? I did the only thing there was to be done, and hurried to Alexandria. Of course he had left the place before my letter reached it; and I learned that from the rapid way in which he set out he must already be far out of reach. Even then I would have gone after him, and tracked him to the sources of the Nile themselves, if I had been able. But I had no experience in travel of that kind. I couldn't manage a band of Arabs, for I didn't know a word of their language, and of course I could not stop to study it. That idea would have been absurd. Besides, other reasons had weight with me, and so I came reluctantly back."

"Africa! the sources of the Nile!" exclaimed Edith, dolefully. "I can't understand why he should have chosen those places."

"Well, it is no new idea. It is a thing that he has had in his mind for years. I have heard him talk of it long ago. I remember hearing him once say that the only chance now remaining by which a man could gain brilliant distinction was the discovery of the sources of the Nile. Every other part of the world, he said, is known."

"How long should you think he might be absent on such a journey?" asked Edith, anxiously.

"How long? Ah! Miss Dalton, so long that it should not be thought of. Years must elapse before he returns."

"Years!"

"Yes—if he ever does return," said Dudleigh, in a mournful voice. "With him now the question is not, When will he return? but rather, Will he ever return? It is, as you must know, a most desperate and hopeless undertaking. For thousands of years men have tried that journey, and failed."

"But may he not be baffled and turn back? There is some hope in that. He will find out that it is impossible." And Edith for a moment grasped at that thought.

"You will think me one of Job's comforters," said Dudleigh, with a melancholy smile. "But I think it is a poor mark of friendship to hide the truth. It is better for you to know all now. The fact is, there would be some hope of his return if he were any other than Sir Lionel Dudleigh. But being what he is, he will follow his purpose to the end. He is a man of unflinching courage and inflexible determination. More than this, he announced to his friends before he left that he would either bring back the truth about the sources of the Nile, or else he would not come back at all. So now he has not only his resolution to impel him, but his pride also."

"This hope, then, fails me utterly," said Edith, after a long pause.

"I fear so."

"He is, in fact, the same as dead."

"Yes, as far as you are concerned, and your present needs."

"This is terrible!"

"Miss Dalton, I do not know what to say. I can only say that my heart aches for you. I delayed on the road, because I could not bear to bring this news to you. Then I wrote a letter, and thought of sending that, but I feared you might not get it. I could not bear to see you in sorrow."

"You, at least, Lieutenant Dudleigh," said Edith, earnestly, "have acted toward me like a true friend and a true gentleman. No one could have done more. It is some consolation to know that every thing which was possible has been done."

There was now a long pause. Each one was lost in thought. Edith's sad face was turned toward Dudleigh, but she did not notice him. She was wrapped in her own thoughts, and wondering how long she could endure the life that now lay before her.

"Miss Dalton," said Dudleigh at length, in a mournful voice, "I have to leave at once to join my regiment, for my leave is up, and it may be some time before I see you again."

He paused.

Edith looked at him earnestly, fearful of what she thought might be coming. Would it be a confession of love? How strong that love must be which had prompted him to such devotion! And yet she could not return it? Yet if he said any thing about it, what could she say? Could she refuse one who had done so much, one who loved her so deeply, one who was the only friend now left her?

"It is heart-breaking to leave you here, Miss Dalton," he continued, "among unscrupulous enemies. When I am away I shall be distracted by a thousand fears about you. How can you endure this life? And yet I might do something to save you from it. My own life is at your disposal. Do you wish to be free now? Will you have that gate opened, and fly?"

Edith said not a word. She was filled with extreme agitation. Fly! Did that mean to fly with him? to escape with a lover? and then—what?

"If you wish to escape now, at this moment, Miss Dalton, all that you have to do is to go out with me. I am armed. If there is any resistance, I can force a way through. The first man that dares to bar the way dies. As for me, if I fall, I shall ask nothing more."

And saying this, Dudleigh looked at Edith inquiringly.

But Edith faltered. Her horror of bloodshed was great. Was her situation so desperate that she could sacrifice a human life to gain her freedom? Perhaps that life might be Dudleigh's. Could she risk the life of the man who had done so much for her? She could not. No, after all, she shrank from gaining her freedom at such a risk.

Then, again, if she were free, where could she go? She knew now how utterly forlorn she was. Miss Plympton was gone, and Sir Lionel was gone. There were none left. She could not live without money, and all her vast property was under the control of another. Dudleigh had said nothing about this. He had said nothing about love either; and she was grateful for his delicacy. Did he intend in his deep devotion to support her himself, or what did he intend?

"You hesitate, Miss Dalton," said he at last. "Have you your old fear about bloodshed?"

"I can not bear to risk such a sacrifice," said Edith.

"But one has a right to fly from slavery, and to destroy any one who tries to prevent his escape."

"I can not," said Edith. "The blood that might be shed would stain all my life. Better to endure my misery as best I can. It must become far worse before I can consent to any thing so terrible as the death of a fellow-being."

"You may yet consent even to that, may you not?"

"I don't know."

"Well, if you do, you have one on whom you can rely. At any rate, I do not think there is any reason for you to fear downright cruelty here. The law protects you from that, just as it protects a child. You are not a captive in the hands of one of those old feudal barons whom we read about. You are simply a ward under the control of a guardian—a thing most odious to one like you, yet one which does not make you liable to any physical evil. But this is poor comfort. I know that your position will become more intolerable as time goes on; and, Miss Dalton, whenever you can bear it no longer, remember that I am ready. Your only danger would be if I should happen to be ordered out of England. But even then I would order Barber to watch over you."

Edith sighed. Her future seemed dark indeed. The chance that Dudleigh might be ordered to America or India filled her with new alarm.

Dudleigh rose to go.

"In six or eight weeks," said he, "I hope to come again. I shall never forget you, but day and night I shall be planning for your happiness."

He took her hand as he said this. Edith noticed that the hand which held hers was as cold as ice. He raised her hand and pressed it to his lips.

Soon after he left.

CHAPTER XXVI.

A THREATENING LETTER.

On the day after the departure of Dudleigh, Edith found a letter lying on her table. It was addressed to her in that stiff, constrained hand which she knew so well as belonging to that enemy of her life and of her race—John Wiggins. With some curiosity as to the motive which he might have in thus writing to her, she opened the letter, and read the following:

"DEAR MISS DALTON,—I feel myself incapable of sustaining another interview with you, and I am therefore reduced to the necessity of writing.

"I have been deeply pained for a long time at the recklessness with which you receive total strangers as visitors, and admit them to your confidence. I have already warned you, but my warnings were received by you in such a manner as to prevent my encountering another interview.

"I write now to inform you that for your own sake, your own future, and your own good name, it is my fixed intention to put a stop to these interviews. This must be done, whatever may be the cost. You must understand from this that there is nothing left for you but to obey.

"If after this you allow these adventurers one single interview more, I shall be under the unpleasant necessity of limiting your freedom to an extent that may be painful to you, and even still more so to myself.

"Yours,   JOHN WIGGINS."

Edith read this letter over and over again, with many mingled feelings. Wiggins had left her so much to herself of late that she had begun to count upon his continued inaction, and supposed that he was too much afraid of Dudleigh to interfere, or to make any opposition whatever to his visits. Now, however, she saw that he had made up his mind to action, and she fully believed that he was not the man who would make any idle menace.

The thing that offended Edith most in this letter was what she considered its insolence. Its tone was that of a superior addressing an inferior—a patron speaking to a dependent. At this all the stubborn pride of Edith's nature was outraged, and rose in rebellion; but above all was that pride stimulated by the word "obey."

She also saw in that letter the indications of an unpleasant development of the policy of Wiggins, which would make her future darker than her present was. Hitherto he had simply surrounded her with a barrier over which she could not pass, admitting to her only those whom he wished, or whom he could not keep away. But now she saw some approach made to a more positive tyranny. There was a threat of limiting her freedom. What that meant she could easily conjecture. Wiggins was evidently dissatisfied with the liberty which she still had of walking over the grounds. He now intended to confine her within the Hall—perhaps in her own room.

This showed her what she had to expect in the future. The steps of her tyrant's progress would be gradual, but terrible. First, perhaps she would be confined to the Hall, then to her own rooms, and finally perhaps to some small chamber—some cell—where she would live a living death as long as her jailer might allow her.

In addition to this open show of tyranny, she also saw what seemed to her the secret craft by which Wiggins had contrived an excuse for further restraint. She considered Mowbray and Mrs. Mowbray as direct agents of his. As for Dudleigh, she now thought that Wiggins had not been so much afraid of him as he had appeared to be, but had allowed him to come so as to gain an excuse for further coercion. It was evident to Edith that Dudleigh's transparent integrity of character and his ardent espousal of her cause must be well known to Wiggins, and that he only tolerated this visitor so as to gain a plausible pretext for putting her under restraint.

That letter threw an additional gloom over Edith's life, and lent a fresh misery to her situation. The prospect before her now was dark indeed. She was in a prison-house, where her imprisonment seemed destined to grow closer and closer. There was no reason why Wiggins should spare her at all. Having so successfully shut her within the grounds for so long a time, he would now be able to carry out any mode of confinement which might be desirable to him. She had heard of people being confined in private mad-houses, through the conspiracy of relatives who coveted their property. Thus far she had believed these stories to be wholly imaginary, but now she began to believe them true. Her own case had shown her the possibility of unjust and illegal imprisonment, and she had not yet been able to find out any mode of escape. This place seemed now to be her future prison-house, where her imprisonment would grow from bad to worse, and where she herself, under the terrible struggle of feeling to which she would be subject, might finally sink into a state of madness.

Such a prospect was terrible beyond words. It filled her with horror, and she regarded her future with the most gloomy forebodings. In the face of all this she had a sense of the most utter helplessness, and the disappointments which she had thus far encountered only served to deepen her dejection.

In the midst of all this there was one hope for her, and one only.

That solitary hope rested altogether on her friend Dudleigh. When he last left her he had promised to come to her again in six or eight weeks. This, then, was the only thing left, and to his return she looked forward incessantly, with the most eager and impatient hope.

To her it now seemed a matter of secondary importance what might be her own feelings toward Dudleigh. She felt confident of his love toward her, and in the abhorrence with which she recoiled from the terrible future which Wiggins was planning for her she was able to contemplate Dudleigh's passion with complacency. She did not love the little man, but if he could save her from the horror that rose before her, she resolved to shrink from no sacrifice of feeling, but grant him whatever reward he might claim.

Time passed. Six weeks were over, but

there were no signs of Dudleigh. The suspense of Edith now became terrible. She began to fear that Wiggins had shut him out, and had refused to allow him to enter again. If this were so, and if Dudleigh had submitted to such exclusion, then all was indeed lost. But Edith would not yet believe it. She clung to hope, and since he had said "six or eight weeks," she thought that she might wait the extreme limit mentioned by him before yielding to despair.

Eight weeks passed.

On the day when those weeks had expired Edith found herself in a fever of suspense, devoured by the most intolerable impatience, with all her thoughts and feelings now centred upon Dudleigh, and her last hope fixed upon him only.

CHAPTER XXVII.

THE PROPOSAL.

EIGHT weeks passed.

Edith's impatience was uncontrollable. Thus far she had passed most of the time in her own room; but now the confinement was more than she could endure. She went out into the grounds, where she wandered day after day, watching and listening, restlessly and feverishly, for the approach of her friend. At length one day, as she was walking down the avenue, a well-known figure came up advancing toward her, at sight of which a thrill of joy passed through her. It was he. At last Little Dudleigh!

In her great joy she did not seek to conceal her feelings, or to maintain that reserve which thus far she had manifested in her interviews with him. All this was thrown aside. Here stood at last her one true friend, the one whose loss she had lamented, whose return she had looked for so eagerly; the one friend coming to her through the enemies who intervened. With a rapid step she advanced toward him. She held out her hands, and pressed his warmly. Her lips quivered, tears started to her eyes, but she did not speak.

"I am back again, Miss Dalton," said Little Dudleigh, joyously. "But how changed you are! You have suffered. I see it in your face. What is the matter? Has any thing new happened? Has that villain dared to offer insult? Ah, why was I not here before? But I could not come. I came as soon as I could."

Edith murmured a few words in reply, and then they walked together at a slow pace along the avenue. Edith did not care to go back to the Hall, where all was so gloomy, but preferred the fresh pure air, and the cheering face of nature.

As they walked on together Edith recounted the events of her life since she had last seen him. Now all her long pent-up feelings burst forth without restraint. At last she had some one to whom she could confide her sorrows, and she found it sweet to talk to one whom she knew to be so full of sympathy. To all this Dudleigh listened with the profoundest attention, and with visible agitation.

In all that she said and in all her manner Edith freely expressed the joy that she felt at once more meeting with a friend so tried, so true, so valued, in whom she could trust so implicitly, and from whom she could find sympathy. She had struggled so long in silence and in loneliness that Dudleigh's sympathy seemed doubly sweet.

When she ceased a long silence followed. Dudleigh's agitation still continued. Several times he looked at her wistfully, inquiringly, doubtfully, as if about to speak, and each time he hesitated. But at last, with a strong effort, he spoke.

"I must say it, Miss Dalton," said he. "I am compelled to. I came here this day —for the sole purpose of saying—something which—you—may be unwilling to hear. I have hesitated long, and staid away longer on this account, yet I must say it now. You are in a fearful position, Miss Dalton. You are in the power of an unprincipled and a desperate man. I feel for you most deeply. You are always in my thoughts. In order to assist you I have done all that I could. I do not wish to make any allusions to what I have done, but rather to what I have felt, and shall feel. You have become very dear to me. I know I am not worthy of you. You are above me. I am only a humble lieutenant; you are the lady of Dalton Hall; but I can not bear to—to go away and leave one whom I love in the power of a villain. Dare I offer you my protection? Will it be too much to ask you to be mine? I do not hope that you can look upon me just yet with any such feelings as love, but I see that you treat me as a friend, and you have honored me with your confidence. I have never said any thing about my love to you, but perhaps you have not been altogether without suspicion about it. Had I found Sir Lionel, or had I thought that he was at all accessible, I would never have made my humble confession until you were in a different position. I am ashamed to make it now, for though I know that you would not suspect me of any thing base, yet it looks as if I were taking advantage of your necessities. But I know that to a mind like yours such a suspicion would never come; and I am comforted by the thought that if you do listen to my request it will lead to your safety. I think, too, that if it were possible for you to consent, even if you felt no very tender sentiment toward me, you would have from me a devotion such as few others are capable of feeling. Under such circumstances you might not be altogether unhappy."

All this Dudleigh had spoken with feverish rapidity, and with every sign of the strongest agitation, occasionally stopping, and then resuming his remarks in a headlong way. But if he had felt agitation, Edith had felt at least quite as much. At the first mention of his proposal her head sank forward, and she looked fixedly upon the ground with downcast eyes, while her tears fell abundantly. She said nothing. Dudleigh in his frequent pauses seemed to expect that she would say something, but she did not.

Edith's feelings were of the most distressing kind. She had, of course, anticipated something like this, but had never yet been able to decide what she should do in the event of such a confession. She did not love him. Her feelings toward him were of a totally different kind. It seemed to her that such a feeling as love could never by any possibility be felt by her for him. And yet she had a very strong regard for him. His society was very pleasant to her. She would have done much and sacrificed much for his sake. But to be his wife, that was a thing which seemed odious.

Yet what could she do? Her position was intolerable and full of peril. If she were his wife, in one moment she would be safe, free, and under the protection of one who loved her with utter devotion. True, she had no such sentiment toward him as a wife should have for a husband, but he himself was aware of that, and in spite of that was willing, nay, eager, to take her. She was touched to the heart by his self-depreciation and profound respect.

Then, again, she thought, ought not he himself to be considered? Had he no claims? He had given himself up to her; he had done much for her. He had offered again and again to give up his life for her. Ought not such rare devotion to meet with some reward? And what reward could she ever give? There was only one which he wanted—herself. Could she refuse him that?

Dudleigh said not another word, and in that long and most embarrassing silence he looked away so as not to add to her confusion. Edith did not know what to do or say. Could she refuse him? Then how ungrateful she would be to her best friend! But if he should leave her? What then? A life of despair! The complete triumph of Wiggins. A living death.

Was it at all singular that she recoiled from such an alternative? She could not endure this captivity any longer. And was it, then, so dreadful to give herself to the man who adored her? No. If she did not love him, she at least had a strong friendship, and this in time might change to love.

She had a greater regard for him than for any other man. Distasteful? It was. Yes. But it was far better than this imprisonment. She must take him as her husband, or lose him forever. He could do no more for her unless she became his wife. He could only save her by marrying her.

She was touched by his present attitude. He was waiting so patiently, so humbly. She saw his deep agitation.

Suddenly, by a quick movement, she turned toward him and held out her hand. Dudleigh took it, and for a moment each gazed into the other's eyes, regardless of observation. Dudleigh's face was deathly pale, and his hand as cold as ice.

"Oh, my friend," said Edith, in a low, hesitating voice, "what can I say to you? I can not give you love. I have no such feeling, but I feel deep gratitude. I know your worth. You have done so much, and I wish I could feel different. If you take me as I am, I—I—I am—yours. But I am not worthy. No, I am not—not worthy of such devotion. You love me, but I do not love you. What can I do? Yet in spite of this, if you ask me, I am—yours."

Edith spoke with downcast eyes and deep embarrassment and frequent hesitation. Her last words died away almost into a whisper. But the agitation of Dudleigh was now even greater than her own. A change came over him that was terrible to witness. As he took her hand he trembled, almost convulsively, from head to foot. His face became ghastly white, he pressed his hand against his heart, his breathing was thick and oppressed, big drops of perspiration started forth upon his brow, and at last, to Edith's amazement, he burst into tears, and sobbed aloud. Then he dropped her hand, and turned away, murmuring some inarticulate words.

At this Edith's confusion passed away, and changed to wonder. What was the meaning of this? Tears and sobs—and from a man! But the thought at once occurred that this was his sensitiveness, and that it arose from her telling him so plainly that she did not love him. "I can not love him, and he knows it," she thought, "and it breaks his heart, poor fellow! How I wish I could console him!"

Suddenly Dudleigh dashed his hand across his eyes, and walked swiftly onward. Edith followed as fast as she could, keeping him in sight, but falling farther and farther behind. At length he turned and came back to meet her. His eyes were downcast, and there was misery unspeakable on his white face. As he came up to her he held out his hand, and looked at her with a strange, woful gaze.

Edith took the hand which he held out.

"Miss Dalton," said he, "you said you would be mine."

"THEN HE DROPPED HER HAND, AND TURNED AWAY."

Edith's lips moved, but no sound escaped them.

"All that you have said, Miss Dalton," he continued, "I feel most deeply, most keenly; but how else could it have been? Yet if you will indeed be mine, I will give you my love and gratitude. I will save you from—from danger; I will—will—bless you." He stopped, and looked at her with quivering lips, while an expression of agony came across his face.

But Edith's eyes were downcast now, and she did not see this new anguish of his; her own distress was too great.

Dudleigh dropped her hand again.

"Where shall it be?" said he, hurriedly and nervously. "It can not be in the Hall. Will you venture to pass the gates with me? —I will force my way through—or are you afraid?"

"I can not consent to bloodshed," said Edith.

"I thought of that," said Dudleigh, "and I have one more plan—if you will only consent. It is not much to you who have suffered so much. It will make your way to freedom easy. Can we not meet in the park somewhere—in some secluded place?"

"In the park?" repeated Edith, abstractedly.

"I can bring a clergyman inside," said Dudleigh, in a low voice.

Edith shuddered. The idea was not yet less repugnant than it had been. But she had consented, and here was this man—her only friend, her adorer—with all his love and devotion. If she did not love him, she must pity him. She had also given her word. As to the way in which this promise might be carried out, it was a matter of indifference. At any rate, she would escape from her hateful prison. And what mattered it how, or where, or when the ceremony might be performed?

"Oh, Miss Dalton," said Dudleigh, "forgive me! forgive me! I must go away in two days. Could you consent to let this be—to-morrow?"

Edith made no reply. She trembled. Her head sank down lower.

"There is one place," said Dudleigh, and then hesitated. Edith said nothing. There was anguish in her face and in her heart.

"The chapel—"

"The chapel," she repeated, dreamily. "It is hidden among the trees. Do you know it? It is away from all observation." Edith bowed her head. She knew it well. It was off the main avenue—not far away from the Hall.

"Can you get out of the house after dark?" said Dudleigh, in a feverish whisper. "It must be after dark, and we must be unobserved. For if Wiggins were to see us he would come as your guardian and take you back, and shut you up—perhaps for life."

This suggestion about Wiggins chimed in with Edith's own fears. It made her desperate. The marriage seemed less abhorrent; it was eclipsed by the horrors of imprisonment for life. Discovery now—after that last threat of his—would bring a closer restraint, stricter imprisonment, the loss of all hope.

"I can get out," she said, hurriedly.

"Where shall I find you?"

"There is a private door at the east end—"

"I know the door."

"I can get out through that. No one will think of my leaving the Hall after dark."

"I will meet you there."

Edith sighed heavily.

"To-morrow evening," said Dudleigh, "at ten o'clock. It will be dark then. Will you meet me?"

"I will," said Edith, calmly.

"I shall only hope, then," said he, "that no new restraint may be imposed upon you to prevent your coming. And now I will go—to meet you to-morrow."

He seized her hand in his icy grasp, wrung it convulsively, and bowing with his pallid face, walked quickly away.

There was a weight on Edith's heart; but in spite of this, Dudleigh's last look, his agitated manner, and his deep love filled her with pity, and made her anxious to carry out her act of self-sacrifice for so dear and so true a friend.

CHAPTER XXVIII.

A MARRIAGE IN THE DARK.

THE chapel referred to was a sombre edifice over the graves of the Daltons. Beneath it were the vaults where reposed the remains of Edith's ancestors. The chapel was used for the celebration of burial rites. It was in this place that the marriage was to take place. Edith, in her gloom, thought the place an appropriate one. Let the marriage be there, she thought—in that place where never any thing but burials has been known before. Could she have changed the one service into the other, she would have done so. And yet she would not go back, for it was the least of two evils. The other alterna-

"SHE SAW THROUGH THE GLOOM A FIGURE."

tive was captivity under the iron hand of Wiggins—Wiggins the adventurer, the forger, the betrayer of her father, whose power over herself was a perpetual insult to that father's memory—a thing intolerable, a thing of horror. Why should she not give herself to the man who loved her, even if her own love was wanting, when such an act would free her from so accursed a tyranny?

Agitated and excited, she lingered through the hours of the day after parting with Dudleigh. Night came, but brought no rest; and the following day dawned, and the irrevocable hour drew nigh. That day was one filled with strange fears, chief among which was the thought that Wiggins might discover all, or suspect it, and arrest her flight. But time passed, and evening came, and Wiggins had done nothing.

All was still. The house was always still, and surrounded her—a vast solitude. Mrs. Dunbar was in her own room: it was always her habit to retire early. Wiggins was far away, at the west end of the Hall. Hugo was in his remote quarters in the attic. The vigilance which her keepers maintained by day was relaxed at night, for they never suspected her of any design of leaving the house after dark. Her interview with Dudleigh must have been seen and reported, but no action that she was aware of had been taken. Perhaps Wiggins was waiting for him to make another call, when he would step forth and formally lock her up in her room.

And now, as Edith prepared to carry her plan into execution, there was nothing all around but the most profound stillness. Underneath the story on which her room was there extended a hall, at the east end of which there was a private stairway leading down to a small door which opened out into the park. Leaving her room noiselessly, she descended to the lower hall, traversed it, and descended the stairway to the door. It was secured by a bolt only. This she drew back as noiselessly as possible—not, however, without an unpleasantly loud grating sound. The door opened without much difficulty. She passed through it. She shut it after her. Then she turned to step down upon the grass. She saw through the gloom a figure. She recognized it. It was Dudleigh.

He held out his hand and took hers. As before, his hand was icy cold, and he trembled violently. But Edith also was trembling with excitement and agitation, and was therefore too much taken up with her own feelings to notice those of others. Dudleigh did not say a word, but started off at once, leading her by the hand.

Now that she had gone thus far, the act seemed too terrible to be endured, and she would have given any thing to go back. There came over her a frightful feeling of apprehension—a deep, dark horror, unutterable, intolerable. But it was now too late—she had to go on. And on she went, clinging to Dudleigh, who himself showed an agitation equal to hers. Thus they walked on in silence. Each might have heard the strong throbbing of the other's heart, had not the excitement of each been so overwhelming. In this way they went on, trembling, horror-stricken, till at length they reached the chapel.

It was a dark and sombre edifice, in the Egyptian style, now darker and more sombre in the gloom of evening and the shadows of surrounding trees. The door was open. As they entered, two figures advanced from the shadows of the trees. One of these wore a white surplice; the other was undistinguishable in the gloom, save that his stature was that of a tall, large man.

"The clergyman and the—witness," said Dudleigh, in a tremulous whisper.

As these two entered, one of them closed the door. The dull creaking of the hinges grated harshly on Edith's ears, and struck fresh horror to her heart. She faltered and trembled. She sank back.

"Oh, I can not, I can not!" she moaned.

"Courage, dear one; it will soon be over," whispered Dudleigh, in an agitated voice.

Edith made a violent effort to regain her composure. But she felt helpless. Her senses seemed leaving her; her heart throbbed still more painfully; her brain whirled. She clung to Dudleigh. But as she clung to him she felt that he trembled as violently as she herself did. This made her feel calmer. She pitied him. Poor fellow, she thought,

he sees my agitation. He thinks I hate him. He is broken-hearted. I must be calmer for his sake.

"Where are the lights?" asked the clergyman.

"Lights?" repeated Dudleigh.

"Yes."

"Well, it won't do to have lights," said he, in the same agitated voice. "I—I explained all that. The light will show through the window. We must go down into the vaults."

Outside, it was very obscure; inside, it was quite dark. Edith could see the outline of a large window and the white sheen of the clergyman's surplice; nothing more was visible.

The clergyman stood waiting. Dudleigh went to the witness and conversed with him in a low whisper.

"The witness," said Dudleigh, as he came back, "forgot to bring lights. I have none. Have you any?"

"Lights?—no," said the clergyman.

"What shall we do?"

"I don't know."

"We can't go down into the vaults."

"I should say," remarked the clergyman, "that since we have no lights, it is far better for us to remain where we are."

"But we may be overheard."

"I shall speak low."

"Isn't it a little too dark here?" asked Dudleigh, tremulously.

"It certainly is rather dark," said the clergyman, "but I suppose it can't be helped, and it need not make any difference. There is a witness who has seen the parties, and as you say secrecy is needed, why, this darkness may be all the more favorable. But it is no concern of mine. Only I should think it equally safe, and a great deal pleasanter, to have the ceremony here than down in the vaults."

All this had been spoken in a quick low tone, so as to guard against being overheard. During this scene Edith had stood trembling, half fainting, with a kind of blank despair in her soul, and scarcely any consciousness of what was going on.

The witness, who had entered last, moved slowly and carefully about, and walked up to where he could see the figure of Edith faintly defined against the white sheen of the clergyman's surplice. He stood at her right hand.

"Begin," said Dudleigh; and then he said, "Miss Dalton, where are you?"

She said nothing. She could not speak.

"Miss Dalton," said he again.

She tried to speak, but it ended in a moan.

Dudleigh seemed to distinguish her now, for he went toward her, and the next moment she felt the bridegroom at her side.

A shudder passed through Edith. She

could think of nothing but the horror of her situation. And yet she did not think of retreating. No. Her plighted word had been given, and the dark terror of Wiggins made it still more impossible. Yet so deep was her agitation that there was scarce any thought on her mind at all.

And now the clergyman began the marriage service. He could not use his book, of course, but he knew the service by heart, and went on fluently enough, omitting here and there an unimportant part, and speaking in a low voice, but very rapidly. Edith scarcely understood a word.

Then the clergyman said:

"Leon, wilt thou have this woman to thy wedded wife, to live together after God's ordinance in the holy estate of matrimony? Wilt thou love her, comfort her, honor, and keep her in sickness and in health; and forsaking all other, keep thee only unto her, so long as ye both shall live?"

The bridegroom answered, in a whisper, "I will."

"Edith, wilt thou have this man to thy wedded husband, to live together after God's ordinance in the holy estate of matrimony? Wilt thou obey him and serve him, love, honor, and keep him in sickness and in health; and forsaking all other, keep thee only unto him, so long as ye both shall live?"

Edith tried to say "I will," but only an unintelligible sound escaped her.

Then the clergyman went on, while the bridegroom repeated in a whisper these words:

"I, Leon, take thee, Edith, to my wedded wife, to have and to hold, from this day forward, for better for worse, for richer for poorer, in sickness and in health, to love and to cherish, till death us do part, according to God's holy ordinance; and thereto I plight thee my troth."

The clergyman then said the words for Edith, but she could not repeat the formula after him. Here and there she uttered a word or two in a disjointed way, but that was all.

Then Edith felt her hand taken and a ring put on her finger.

Then the clergyman said the next formula, which the bridegroom repeated after him in a whisper as before:

"With this ring I thee wed, with my body I thee worship, and with all my worldly goods I thee endow," etc., etc.

Then followed a prayer, after which the clergyman, joining their right hands together, said,

"Those whom God hath joined together, let no man put asunder."

Then followed the remainder of the service, and at its conclusion the clergyman solemnly wished them every happiness.

"I suppose I may go now," said he; and as there was no answer, he groped his way to the door, flung it open, and took his departure.

During all this service Edith had been in a condition verging upon half unconsciousness. The low murmur of voices, the hurried words of the clergyman, the whispers of the bridegroom, were all confused together in an unintelligible whole, and even her own answers had scarce made any impression upon her. Her head seemed to spin, her brain to whirl, and all her frame to sink away. At length the grating of the opening door, the clergyman's departing footsteps, and the slight increase of light roused her.

She was married!

Where was her husband?

This thought came to her with a new horror. Deep silence had followed the clergyman's departure. She in her weakness was not noticed. Dudleigh, the loving, the devoted, had no love or devotion for her now. Where was he? The silence was terrible.

But at last that silence was broken—fearfully.

"Come," said a voice which thrilled the inmost soul of Edith with horror unspeakable; "I'm tired of humbugging. I'm going home. Come along, Mrs. Dudleigh."

The horror that passed through Edith at the sound of this voice for a moment seemed to paralyze her. She turned to where the voice sounded. It was the man beside her who spoke—the bridegroom! He was not Dudleigh—not Little Dudleigh! He was tall and large. It was the witness. What frightful mockery was this? But the confusion of thought that arose was rudely interrupted. A strong hand was laid upon hers, and again that voice spoke:

"Come along, Mrs. Dudleigh!"

"What is—this?" gasped Edith.

"Why, you're married, that's all. You ought to know that by this time."

"Away!" cried Edith, with a sharp cry. "Who are you? Dudleigh! Dudleigh! where are you? Will you not help me?"

"That's not very likely," said the same voice, in a mocking tone. "His business is to help me."

"Oh, my God! what is the meaning of this?"

"Oh, it's simple enough. It means that you're my wife."

"Your wife! Oh, Dudleigh! oh, my friend! what does all this mean? Why do you not speak?"

But Dudleigh said nothing.

"I have no objections to explaining," said the voice. "You're actually married to me. My name is not Mowbray. It's Leon Dudleigh, the individual that you just plighted your troth to. My small friend here is not Leon Dudleigh, whatever other Dudleigh he may call himself. He is the witness."

"It's false!" cried Edith. "Lieutenant Dudleigh would never betray me."

"Well, at any rate," said Leon, "I happen to be the happy man who alone can claim you as his bride."

"Villain!" shrieked Edith, in utter horror. "Cursed villain! Let go my hand. This is all mockery. Your wife!—I would die first."

"Indeed you won't," said Leon—"not while you have me to love and to cherish you, in sickness and in health, till death us do part, and forsaking all others, keep only unto you, in the beautiful words of that interesting service."

"It's a lie! it's a lie!" cried Edith. "Oh, Lieutenant Dudleigh, I have trusted you implicitly, and I trust you yet. Come to me—save me!"

And in her anguish Edith sank down upon her knees, and held out her arms imploringly.

"Dudleigh!" she moaned. "Oh, my friend! Oh, only come—only save me from this villain, and I will love—I will love and bless you—I will be your menial—I will—"

"Pooh!" said Leon, "I'm the only Dudleigh about. If you knew half as much about my dear friend the lieutenant as I do, you would know what infernal nonsense you are talking;" and seizing her hand, he tried to raise her. "Come," said he, "up with you."

Edith tried to loosen her hand, whereupon Leon dashed it away.

"Who wants your hand?" he cried: "I'm your husband, not your lover."

"Lieutenant Dudleigh!" moaned Edith.

"Well, lieutenant," said Leon, "speak up. Come along. Tell her, if you like."

"Lieutenant Dudleigh, save me."

"Oh, great Heaven!" said a voice like that of the one whom Edith knew as Lieutenant Dudleigh—"oh, great Heaven! it's too much."

"Oh ho!" cried Leon: "so you're going to blubber too, are you? Mind, now, it's all right if you are only true."

"Oh, Leon, how you wring my heart!" cried the other, in a low, tremulous voice.

"Lieutenant Dudleigh!" cried Edith again. "Oh, my friend, answer me! Tell me that it is all a lie. Tell me—"

But Lieutenant Dudleigh flung himself on the stone pavement, and groaned and sobbed convulsively.

"Come," said Leon, stooping and lifting him up; "you understand all this. Don't you go on blubbering in this fashion. I don't mind her, and you mustn't. Come, you tell her, for she'll keep yelling after you all night till you do."

Lieutenant Dudleigh rose at this, and leaned heavily upon Leon's arm.

"You were not—married—to—to—me," said he at last.

"What! Then you too were false all along?" said Edith, in a voice that seemed to come from a broken heart.

The false friend made no reply.

"Well, Mrs. Dudleigh," said Leon, coolly, "for your information I will simply state that the—ahem—lieutenant here is my very particular friend—in fact, my most intimate and most valued friend—and in his tender affection for me he undertook this little affair at my instigation. It's all my act, all through, every bit of it, but the carrying out of the details was—ahem—his. The marriage, however, is perfectly valid. The banns were published all right. So you may feel quite at ease."

"Oh," cried Edith, "how basely, how terribly, I have been deceived! And it is all lies! It was all lies, lies, lies from the beginning!"

Suddenly a fierce thrill of indignation flashed through her. She started to her feet.

"It is all a lie from beginning to end!" she exclaimed, in a voice which was totally changed from that wail of despair which had been heard once before. It was a firm, proud, stern voice. She had fallen back upon her own lofty soul, and had sought refuge in that resolute nature of hers which had sustained her before this in other dire emergencies. "Yes," she said, sternly, "a lie; and this mock-marriage is a lie. Villains, stand off. I am going home."

"Not without me," said Leon, who for a moment stood silent, amazed at the change in Edith's voice and manner. "You must not leave your husband."

"You shall not come to Dalton Hall," said Edith.

"I shall not? Who can keep me out?"

"Wiggins," said Edith. "I will ask his protection against you."

"Wiggins!" sneered Leon. "Let him try it if he dares."

"Do not interfere with me," said Edith, "nor touch me."

"You shall not go without me."

"I shall go, and alone."

"You shall not."

Edith at once walked to the door. Just as she reached it Leon seized her arm. She struggled for a moment to get free, but in vain.

"I know," said she, bitterly, "what a coward you are. This is not the first time that you have laid hands on me. Let me go now, or you shall repent."

"Not the first time, and it won't be the last time!" cried Leon, with an oath.

"Let me go," cried Edith, in a fierce voice, "or I will stab you to the heart!"

As she said this she raised her right hand swiftly and menacingly, and by the dim light of the doorway Leon plainly saw a long keen dagger. In an instant he recoiled from the sight, and dropping her arm, he started back.

"Curse you!" he cried, in an excited voice; "who wants to touch you? It isn't you I've married, but the Hall!"

"Leon," cried Lieutenant Dudleigh, "I will allow no violence. If there is any more, I will betray you."

"You!" cried Leon, with a bitter sneer. "Pooh, you dare not."

"I dare."

"You will betray yourself, then."

"I don't care. After what I've suffered for you these two days past, and especially this night, I have but little care left about myself."

"But won't you get your reward, curse it all?"

"There can be no reward for me now, after this," said the other, in a mournful voice. "Is that the way you talk to me?" said Leon, in a tone of surprise.

"Miss Dalton has been wronged enough," said the other. "If you dare to annoy her further, or to harm a hair of her head, I solemnly declare that I will turn against you."

"You!" exclaimed Leon.

"Yes, I."

"Why, you're as bad as I am—in fact, worse."

"Well, at any rate, it shall go no further. That I am resolved on."

"Look out," cried Leon; "don't tempt me too far. I'll remember this, by Heaven! I'll not forget that you have threatened to betray me."

"I don't care. You are a coward, Leon, and you know it. You are afraid of that brave girl. Miss Dalton can take care of herself."

"Miss Dalton? Pooh!—Mrs. Dudleigh, you mean."

"Leon, you drive me to frenzy," cried Lieutenant Dudleigh, in a wild, impatient voice.

"And you—what are you?" cried Leon, morosely. "Are you not always tormenting me? Do you think that I'm going to stand you and your whims forever? Look out! This is more of a marriage than you think."

"Marriage!" cried the other, in a voice of scorn.

"Never mind. I'll go with my wife," said Leon.

Edith had waited a few moments as this altercation arose, half hoping that in the quarrel between these two something might escape them which could give her some ray of hope, but she heard nothing of that kind. Yet as she listened to the voices of the two, contrasting so strangely in their tones, and to their language, which was so very peculiar, a strange suspicion came to her mind. Then she hurried away back to the Hall.

"I'll go with my wife," said Leon.

"Coward and villain!" cried his compan-

ion, "Miss Dalton has a dagger. You're afraid of her. I'll go too, so that you may not annoy her."

Edith hurried away, and the others followed for a short distance, but she soon left them behind. She reached the little door at the east end. She passed through, and bolted it on the inner side. She hurried up to her rooms, and on reaching them fell fainting to the floor.

CHAPTER XXIX.

THE WIFE OF LEON DUDLEIGH.

SICKNESS and delirium came mercifully to Edith; for if health had continued, the sanity of the body would have been purchased at the expense of that of the mind. Mrs. Dunbar nursed her most tenderly and assiduously. A doctor attended her. For long weeks she lay in a brain-fever, between life and death. In the delirium that disturbed her brain, her mind wandered back to the happy days at Plympton Terrace. Once more she played about the beautiful shores of Derwentwater; once more she rambled with her school-mates under the lofty trees, or rode along through winding avenues. At times, however, her thoughts reverted to the later events of her life; and once or twice to that time of horror in the chapel.

The doctor came and went, and satisfied himself with seeing after the things that conduced to the recovery of his patient. He was from London, and had been sent for by Wiggins, who had no confidence in the local physicians. At length the disease was quelled, and after nearly two months Edith began to be conscious of her situation. She came back to sensibility with feelings of despair, and her deep agitation of soul retarded her recovery very greatly; for her thoughts were fierce and indignant, and she occupied herself, as soon as she could think, with incessant plans for escape. At last she resolved to tell the doctor all. One day when he came she began, but, unfortunately for her, before she had spoken a dozen words she became so excited that she almost fainted. Thereupon the doctor very properly forbade her talking about any of her affairs whatever until she was better. "Your friends," said he, "have cautioned me against this, and I have two things to regard—their wishes and your recovery." Once or twice after this Edith tried to speak about her situation, but the doctor promptly checked her. Soon after he ceased his visits.

In spite of all drawbacks, however, she gradually recovered, and at last became able to move about the room. She might even have gone out if she had wished, but she did not feel inclined.

THE LIVING LINK.

One day, while looking over some of her books which were lying on her table, she found a newspaper folded inside one of them. She took it and opened it carelessly, wondering what might be going on in that outside world of which she had known so little for so long a time. A mark along the margin attracted her attention. It was near the marriage notices. She looked there, and saw the following:

"On the 12th instant, at the Dalton family chapel, by the Rev. John Munn, of Dalton, Captain Leon Dudleigh, to Edith, only daughter of the late Frederick Dalton, Esquire, of Dalton Hall."

This paper was dated November 20, 1840. This was, as she knew, February 26, 1841.

The horror that passed through her at the sight of this was only inferior to that which she had felt on the eventful evening itself. Hitherto in all her gloom and grief she had regarded it as a mere mockery—a brutal kind of practical joke, devised out of pure malignity, and perhaps instigated or connived at by Wiggins. She had never cared to think much about it. But now, on being thus confronted with a formal notice in a public newspaper, the whole affair suddenly assumed a new character—a character which was at once terrible in itself, and menacing to her whole future. This formal notice seemed to her like the seal of the law on that most miserable affair; and she asked herself in dismay if such a ceremony could be held as binding.

She had thought much already over one thing which had been revealed on that eventful evening. The name Mowbray was an assumed one. The villain who had taken it now called himself Leon Dudleigh. Under that name he married her, and under that name his marriage was published. His friend and her betrayer—that most miserable scoundrel who had called himself Lieutenant Dudleigh—had gained her consent to this marriage for the express purpose of betraying her into the hands of her worst enemy. His name might or might not be Dudleigh, but she now saw that the true name of the other must be Dudleigh, and that Mowbray had been assumed for some purpose. But how he came by such a name she could not tell. She had no knowledge whatever of Sir Lionel; and whether Leon was any relation to him or not she was totally ignorant.

This gave a new and most painful turn to all her thoughts, and she began to feel anxious to know what had occurred since that evening. Accordingly, on Mrs. Dunbar's return to her room, she began to question her. Thus far she had said but little to this woman, whom for so long a time she had regarded with suspicion and aversion. Mrs. Dunbar's long and anxious care of her, her constant watchfulness, her eager inquiries after her health—all availed nothing, since all seemed to be nothing more than the selfish anxiety of a jailer about the health of a prisoner whose life it may be his interest to guard.

"Who sent this?" asked Edith, sternly, pointing to the paper.

Mrs. Dunbar hesitated, and after one hasty glance at Edith her eyes sought the floor.

"The captain," said she at length.

"The captain?—what captain?" asked Edith.

"Captain—Dudleigh," said Mrs. Dunbar, with the same hesitation.

Edith paused. This confirmed her suspicions as to his true name. "Where is he now?" she asked at length.

"I do not know," said Mrs. Dunbar, "where he is—just now."

"Has he ever been here?" asked Edith, after another pause.

"Ever been here?" repeated Mrs. Dunbar, looking again at Edith with something like surprise. "Why, he lives here—now. I thought you knew that."

"Lives here!" exclaimed Edith.

"Yes."

Edith was silent. This was very unpleasant intelligence. Evidently this Leon Dudleigh and Wiggins were partners in this horrible matter.

"How does he happen to live here?" she asked at length, anxious to discover, if possible, his purpose.

Mrs. Dunbar again hesitated. Edith had to repeat her question, and even then her answer was given with evident reluctance.

"He says that you—I mean that he—is your—that is, that he is—is master," said Mrs. Dunbar, in a hesitating and confused way.

"Master!" repeated Edith.

"He says that he is your—your—" Mrs. Dunbar hesitated and looked anxiously at Edith.

"Well, what does he say?" asked Edith, impatiently. "He says that he is my—what?"

"Your—your husband," said Mrs. Dunbar, with a great effort.

At this Edith stared at her for a moment, and then covered her face with her hands, while a shudder passed through her. This plain statement of the case from one of her jailers made her situation seem worse than ever.

"He came here," continued Mrs. Dunbar, in a low tone, "the day after your illness. He brought his horse and dog, and some things."

Edith looked up with a face of agony.

"He said," continued Mrs. Dunbar, "that you were—married—to—him; that you were now his—his wife, and that he intended to live at the Hall."

"Is that other one here too?" asked Edith, after a long silence.

"What other one?"

"The smaller villain—the one that used to call himself Lieutenant Dudleigh."

Mrs. Dunbar shook her head.

"Do you know the real name of that person?"

"No."

Edith now said nothing for a long time; and as she sat there, buried in her own miserable thoughts, Mrs. Dunbar looked at her with a face full of sad and earnest sympathy—a face which had a certain longing, wistful expression, as though she yearned over this stricken heart, and longed to offer some consolation. But Edith, even if she had been willing to receive any expressions of sympathy from one like Mrs. Dunbar, whom she regarded as a miserable tool of her oppressor, or a base ally, was too far down in the depths of her own profound affliction to be capable of consolation. Bad enough it was already, when she had to look back over so long a course of deceit and betrayal at the hands of one whom she had regarded as her best friend; but now to find that all this treachery had culminated in a horror like this, that she was claimed and proclaimed by an outrageous villain as his wife—this was beyond all endurance. The blackness of that perfidy, and the terror of her memories, which till now had wrung her heart, fled away, and gave place to the most passionate indignation.

And now, at the impulse of these more fervid feelings, her whole outraged nature underwent a change. Till now she had felt most strongly the emotions of grief and melancholy; now, however, these passed away, and were succeeded by an intensity of hate, a vehemence of wrath, and a hot glow of indignant passion that swept away all other feelings. All the pride of her haughty spirit was roused; her soul became instinct with a desperate resolve; and mingling with these feelings there was a scorn for her enemies as beings of a baser nature, and a stubborn determination to fight them all till the bitter end.

All this change was manifest in her look and tone as she again addressed Mrs. Dunbar.

"You have all mistaken me," said she, with bitter hostility; "you have imagined that you had to deal with some silly child. But this shall do none of you any good. You may kill me among you, but I am not afraid to die. Death itself will be welcome rather than submission to that foul miscreant, that vulgar coward, who takes advantage of a contemptible trick, and pretends that there was a marriage. I say this to you—that I defy him and all of you, and will defy you all—yes, to the bitter end; and you may go and tell this to your wretched confederates."

As Edith said this, Mrs. Dunbar looked at her; and if there could have appeared upon that face the signs of a wounded heart—a heart cut and stung to its inmost fibre—the face that confronted Edith showed all this at that moment.

"Confederates!" she repeated.

"Yes, you and Wiggins and this villain who, you say, is now living here."

"What, Leon?"

"Leon! Is that his name? Leon Dudleigh? Well, whatever name he chooses to bear, it is all the same; though it seems strange that he should adopt a stainless name like that of Dudleigh."

"Yes, that is his name," said Mrs. Dunbar, wearily.

"Till he assumes some other," said Edith. "But they are all assumed names," she continued, bitterly—"Mowbray and Dudleigh and Dunbar also, no doubt. Why you should call yourself Dunbar I can't imagine. You seem to me to be Mrs. Wiggins. Wiggins at least can not be an assumed name."

At these words, which were spoken on the spur f the moment, out of mere hostility toward Mrs. Dunbar, and the desire to wound her, the latter recoiled as though from some sudden blow, and looked at Edith with awful eyes.

"You are terrible," she said, in a low voice —"you are terrible. You can not imagine what horrors you give expression to."

To this Edith paid no attention. It sounded old. It was like what Wiggins had frequently said to her.

"I can not imagine," she continued, "any human being so utterly bad-hearted, so altogether vile and corrupt, as this man who now calls himself Leon Dudleigh. In pure fiendish malignity, and in all those qualities which are abhorrent and shameful, he surpasses even that arch-villain Wiggins himself."

"Stop, stop!" cried Mrs. Dunbar. "I can not bear this. You must not talk so. How do you know? You know nothing about Leon. Oh, how you wrong him! Leon has had bad associates, but he himself is not bad. After all, Leon has naturally a noble heart. He was a brave, high-minded boy. Oh, if you could but know what he once was. You wrong Leon. You wrong him most deeply. Oh, how deeply you wrong him!"

Mrs. Dunbar had said all this in a kind of feverish agitation, speaking quickly and vehemently. Never before had Edith seen any thing approaching to excitement in this strong-hearted, vigilant-eyed, self-contained woman, and the sight of such emotion amazed her. But for this woman and her feelings she cared nothing whatever; and so in the midst of her words she waved her hand and interrupted her.

"I'm tired," she said; "I can not stand any more excitement just now. I wish to be alone."

At this Mrs. Dunbar arose and walked wearily out of the room.

One thing at least Edith considered as

quite evident from Mrs. Dunbar's agitation and eager championship of "Leon," and that was that this Leon had all along been a confederate of Wiggins and this woman, and that the so-called "Lieutenant Dudleigh" had been one of the same band of conspirators. It seemed evident now to her that the whole plot had been contrived among them. Perhaps Wiggins was to get one half of the estate, and this Leon Dudleigh the other half.

Still she did not feel altogether sure, and in order to ascertain as near as possible the truth as to her present position and prospects, she determined to see Wiggins himself.

CHAPTER XXX.

JAILER AND CAPTIVE.

On the following day Edith felt stronger, and calling Mrs. Dunbar, she sent her to Wiggins with a request that the latter should meet her in the drawing-room. She then walked through the long hall on her way down stairs. Every thing looked as it did before her illness, except that one change had taken place which arrested her attention the moment she entered the drawing-room.

Over the chimney-piece a portrait had been hung—a portrait in a large gilt frame, which looked as though it had been painted but recently. It was a portrait of Leon Dudleigh. On catching sight of this she felt as if she had been rooted to the spot. She looked at it for a short time with compressed lips, frowning brow, and clinched hands, after which she walked away and flung herself into a chair.

Wiggins was evidently in no hurry, for it was more than half an hour before he made his appearance. Edith sat in her chair, waiting for his approach. The traces of her recent illness were very visible in the pallor of her face, and in her thin, transparent hands. Her large eyes seemed larger than ever, as they glowed luminously from their cavernous depths, with a darker hue around each, as is often seen in cases of sickness or debility, while upon her face there was an expression of profound sadness that seemed fixed and unalterable.

But in the tone with which she addressed Wiggins there was nothing like sadness. It was proud, cold, stern, and full of bitterest hostility.

"I have sent for you," she began, "because you, Wiggins, are concerned as much as I myself am in the issue of this business about which I am going to speak. I have suffered a very gross outrage, but I still have confidence both in a just Heaven and in the laws of the land. This ruffian, who now it seems calls himself Leon Dudleigh—your confederate—has, with your assistance, cheated

me into taking part in a ceremony which he calls a marriage. What you propose to gain for yourself by this I can not imagine; for it seems to me that it would have been rather for your advantage to remain the sole master of your ward than to help some one else to share your authority. But for your purposes I care nothing—the evil is done. Yet if this Leon Dudleigh or you think that I will sit tamely down under such an intolerable wrong, you are miserably mistaken. Sooner or later I shall be avenged. Sooner or later I shall gain my freedom, and then my turn shall come. I wish you to see that there is danger before you; and I wish you also to understand that it is for your interest to be my sole master, as you were before. I have sent for you, then, to ask you, Wiggins, to expel this man Leon Dudleigh from the house. Be my guardian again, and I will be your ward. More: I agree to remain here in a state of passive endurance for a reasonable time—one or two years, for instance; and I promise during that time to make no complaint. Do this—drive this man away—and you shall have no reason to regret it. On the other hand, remember there is an alternative. Villain though this man is, I may come to terms with him, and buy my liberty from him by giving him half of the estate, or even the whole of it. In that case it seems to me that you would lose every thing, for Leon Dudleigh is as great a villain as yourself."

As Edith spoke, Wiggins listened most attentively. He had seated himself not far from her, and after one look at her had fixed his eyes on the floor. He waited patiently until she had said all she wished to say. Edith herself had not hoped to gain much by this interview, but she hoped at least to be able to discover something concerning the nature of the partnership which she supposed to exist among her enemies, and something perhaps about their plans. The averted face of Wiggins seemed to her the attitude of conscious guilt; but she felt a little puzzled at signs of emotion which he exhibited, and which seemed hardly the result of conscious guilt. Once or twice a perceptible shudder passed through his frame; his bent head bowed lower; he covered his face with his hands; and at her last words there came from him a low moan that seemed to indicate suffering.

"It's his acting," she thought. "I wonder what his next pretense will be?"

Wiggins sat for some minutes without saying a word. When at length he raised his head he did not look at Edith, but fastened his eyes on vacancy, and went on to speak in a low voice.

"Your remarks," said he, "are all based on a misconception. This man is no confederate of mine. I have no confederate. I—I work out my purpose—by myself."

"I'm sure I wish that I could believe this," said Edith; "but unfortunately Mrs. Dunbar espouses his cause with so much warmth and enthusiasm that I am forced to conclude that this Leon Dudleigh must be a very highly valued or very valuable friend to both of you."

"In this case," said Wiggins, "Mrs. Dunbar and I have different feelings."

Instead of feeling gratified at this disclaimer of any connection with Leon Dudleigh, Edith felt dissatisfied, and somewhat disconcerted. It seemed to her that Wiggins was trying to baffle her and throw her off the right track. She had hoped that by speaking out frankly her whole mind she might induce him to come to some agreement with her; but by his answers she saw that he was not in the least degree affected by her warnings, or her threats, or her offers.

"This Leon Dudleigh," said she, "has all along acted sufficiently like a confederate of yours to make me think that he is one."

"How?"

"By coming into these grounds at all times; by having privileges equal in all respects to your own; by handing over those privileges to his spy and emissary—the one who took the name of Lieutenant Dudleigh. Surely all this is enough to make me think that he must be your confederate."

"You are altogether mistaken," said Wiggins, quietly.

"He told some idle story once," said Edith, anxious to draw more out of Wiggins than these short answers, "about some power which he had over you. He asserted that you were afraid of him. He said that you dared not keep him out of the park. He said that his power over you arose from his knowledge of certain past crimes of yours."

"When he said that," remarked Wiggins, "he said what was false."

"Why, then, did you allow him to come here?"

"I did so for reasons that I do not feel at liberty to explain—just now. I will only say that the reasons were altogether different from those which he stated."

Of this Edith did not believe a word; yet she felt completely baffled, and did not know what to say to this man, who thus met all her assertions with denials, and spoke in the calm, lofty tone of conscious truth. But this, she thought, was only his "acting."

"I only hope that this is so," said she; "but supposing that it is so, I should like very much to know what you feel disposed to do. The claim that this man asserts over me is utterly false. It is a mockery. If he is really not your confederate, you will see, I am sure, that it is not for your own interest to sustain him in his attempt to maintain his claim. I wish, therefore, to know exactly what it is that you feel willing to do."

"Your situation," said Wiggins, "is a

most unhappy one. I will do all that I can to prevent it from becoming more so. If this man annoys you, I will defend you against him, whatever it may cost."

This sounded well; yet still Edith was not satisfied. It seemed to her too much like an empty promise which he had no idea of fulfilling.

"How will you defend me?" she asked.

"This man lives here now. He asserts that he has the right to do so. He has published what he calls my marriage to him in the newspapers. He calls himself my husband. All this is a wrong and an insult to me. His presence here is a perpetual menace. When he is absent he leaves a reminder of himself," she continued, in a more bitter tone, glancing toward the portrait. "Now I wish to know what you will do. Will you prevent him from coming here? Will you send him away, either in your name or in mine? You are easily able to keep out my friends; will you keep out my enemies?"

"This man," said Wiggins, "shall soon give you no more trouble."

"Soon—what do you mean by soon?" asked Edith, impatiently.

"As soon as my plans will allow me to proceed to extremities with him."

"Your plans!" repeated Edith. "You are always bringing up your plans. Whatever is concerned, you plead your plans. They form a sufficient excuse for you to refuse the commonest justice. And yet what I ask is certainly for your own interests."

"If you knew me better," said Wiggins, "you would not appeal to my interests. I have not generally fashioned my life with regard to my own advantage. Some day you will see this. You, at least, should be the last one to complain of my plans, since they refer exclusively to the vindication of your injured father."

"So you have said before," said Edith, coldly. "Those plans must be very convenient, since you use them to excuse every possible act of yours."

"You will not have to wait long now," said Wiggins, in a weary voice, as though this interview was too much for his endurance—"not very long. I have heard to-day of something which is very favorable. Since the trial certain documents and other articles have been kept by the authorities, and an application has been made for these, with a view to the establishment of your father's innocence. I have recently heard that the application is about to be granted."

"You always answer my appeals for common justice," said Edith, with unchanged coldness, "by some reference to my father. It seems to me that if you had wished to vindicate his innocence, it would have been better to do so while he was alive. If you had done so, it might have been better for yourself in the end. But now these allu-

G

sions are idle and worse than useless. They have no effect on me whatever. I value them at what they are worth."

With these words Edith rose and left the room. She returned to her own apartments with a feeling of profound dejection and disappointment. Of Wiggins she could make nothing. He promised, but his promises were too vague to afford satisfaction.

Leon Dudleigh was away now, but would probably be back before long. As she had failed with Wiggins, only one thing remained, and that was to see Leon. She was resolved to meet him at once on his arrival, and fight out once for all that battle which was inevitable between herself and him.

CHAPTER XXXI.

THE IRREPRESSIBLE STRUGGLE.

ABOUT a month passed away, during which time Edith, in spite of her troubles, grew stronger every day. Youth and a good constitution were on her side, and enabled her to rally rapidly from the prostration to which she had been subjected.

At length one morning she learned that Leon had arrived at the Hall. This news gave her great satisfaction, for she had been waiting long, and felt anxious to see him face to face, to tell him her own mind, and gather from him, if possible, what his intentions were. An interview with him under such peculiar circumstances might have been painful had she been less courageous or less self-possessed; but to one with such lofty pride as hers, and filled as she was with such scorn of Leon, and convinced as she was that he was at heart an arrant coward, such an interview had nothing in it to deter her. Suspense was worse. She wished to meet that man.

She sent word to him that she wished to see him, after which she went down to the drawing-room and waited. Leon certainly showed no haste, for it was as much as an hour before he made his appearance. On entering he assumed that languid air which he had adopted on some of his former visits. He looked carelessly at her, and then threw himself into a chair.

"Really, Mrs. Dudleigh," said he, "this is an unexpected pleasure. 'Pon my life, I had no idea that you would volunteer to do me so much honor!"

"I am not Mrs. Dudleigh," said Edith, "as you very well know. I am Miss Dalton, and if you expect me to have any thing to say to you, you must call me by my proper name. You will suffer dearly enough yet for your crimes, and have no need to add to them."

"Now, my dear," said Leon, "that is kind and wife-like, and all that. It reminds me

of the way in which wives sometimes speak in the plays."

"Speak to me as Miss Dalton, or you shall not speak to me at all."

"It's quite evident," said Leon, with a sneer, "that you don't know into whose hands you've fallen."

"On the contrary," said Edith, contemptuously, "it has been my fortune, or my misfortune, to understand from the first both you and Wiggins."

Leon gave a light laugh.

"Your temper," said he, "has not improved much, at any rate. That's quite evident. You have always shown a very peculiar idea of the way in which a lady should speak to a gentleman."

"One would suppose by that," said Edith, "that you actually meant to hint that you considered yourself a gentleman."

"So I am," said Leon, haughtily.

"As you have no particular birth or family," said Edith, in her most insolent tone, "I suppose you must rest your claims to be a gentleman altogether on your good manners and high-toned character."

"Birth and family!" exclaimed Leon, excitedly—"what do you know about them? You don't know what you're talking about."

"I know nothing about you, certainly," said Edith. "I suppose you are some mere adventurer."

Leon looked at her for a moment with a glance of intense rage; and as she calmly returned his gaze, she noticed that peculiarity of his frowning brow—a red spot in the middle, with deep lines.

"You surely in your wildest dreams," said she, "never supposed that I took you for a gentleman."

"Let me tell you," cried Leon, stammering in his passion—"let me tell you that I associate with the proudest in the land."

"I know that," replied Edith, quietly. "Am I not here? But you are only tolerated."

"Miss Dalton," cried Leon, "you shall suffer for this."

"Thank you," said Edith: "for once in your life you have spoken to me without insulting me. You have called me by my right name. I could smile at your threat under any circumstances, but now I can forgive it."

"It seems to me," growled Leon, "that you are riding the high horse somewhat, and that this is a rather queer tone for you to assume toward me."

"I always assume a high tone toward low people."

"Low people! What do you mean?" cried Leon, his face purple with rage.

"I really don't know any name better than that for you and your friends."

"The name of Dudleigh," said Leon, "is one of the proudest in the land."

"Certainly it is—but how did you come by it?"

"What do you mean?" cried Leon, with an oath.

"Well, captain," said Edith, "or whatever else you call yourself, are you quite sure that you know yourself whether your name is Mowbray or Dudleigh? How am I to know any thing about a person who has so many aliases?"

At this Leon started from his seat with a menacing gesture.

"This seems like real excitement," said Edith, coolly. "You are usually so languid, you know. But how strange it is that you should become excited about such things as these—mere names, which you amuse yourself by adopting and changing from time to time."

"You don't appear to have found out who I am," said Leon. "You'll know soon enough, however, and so there's no need for me to take the trouble to tell you. Meanwhile some one appears to have stuffed you with some infernal lies about me."

"What I have heard about you may possibly have been of that character; for it certainly belonged to every thing I have ever heard from you."

"Do you dare to hint that I am a liar?"

"The hint was rather a strong one," said Edith, quietly.

"You shall suffer for this!"

"There will be suffering somewhere, beyond a doubt, before this is over."

"You don't know me yet, my lady," said Leon, fiercely.

"That's the second time you've taken the trouble to say that. Pray what possible difference can it make to me whether I do or not?"

"You'll see," muttered Leon, savagely. "What others have felt, you shall feel."

"You are really quite tragic," said Edith, who was deliberately bent on taunting him to the utmost, in the hope that in his anger she might make him disclose something that would be of use to her. "You are quite tragic. Have you ever been on the stage, pray? It looks a little like it."

"You shall suffer for all this!" growled Leon again.

"I have no doubt that you will do your best to make me suffer, under any circumstances," said Edith.

"Yes," said Leon, with a sneer, "I think I can flatter myself that I have already done something in that way. For instance, how do you like it, Mrs. Dudleigh, to see me as your husband? How do you like that, oh?"

"I imagine," said Edith, with unalterable placidity, "that you have as much right to the title of husband as you have to any one of your other pretended names, such as Mowbray or Dudleigh. As to what you

have done, that will be accounted for when the time comes."

"Oh yes—ha, ha—when the time comes. Well, if you can wait, I can."

Edith rose.

"Wiggins and you," said she, contemptuously, "have some sort of partnership or understanding just now, but you don't seem to agree very well together; you will have trouble before long. If I chose to rely upon that, I might feel quite secure; but fortunately there are other resources left me; and so I will recommend you to be a little more careful about your proceedings in this house, from which, I assure you, you will soon be ejected."

After saying this Edith was about to go, but Leon jumped up and put himself before her.

"Wait a minute, Mrs. Dudleigh," said he —"wait a minute, if you please. If you can only hold that devilish tongue of yours for one moment, so as to give me time to speak, I shall feel obliged—yes, infinitely obliged."

Edith waited in some curiosity, and Leon drew forth from his pocket a parcel of papers.

"Here," said he, flinging them on the table. "No nonsense now! sign these."

He spoke in a quick, sharp, peremptory tone, but Edith only smiled.

"And pray what are these?" she asked.

"Oh—some papers."

"Is it possible! Well, I can see that much for myself."

"Oh, well, if you're so infernally particular, they're papers of a—a business character—that require your signature."

"Do they, really! And who sent you to me with them? Was it Wiggins?"

"I brought them myself," said Leon, haughtily. "Wiggins has nothing to do with them."

"So you did. I saw you bring them into the room. But who sent you?"

"I tell you no one sent me. They are my own concern."

"And pray why should I take any interest in these more than in the papers of Wiggins, or the porter, or black Hugo?"

"I tell you," cried Leon, impatiently, "I'm your husband; and I am now the—the manager of this estate. These papers refer to estate business."

"I dare say they belong to your business, but of what concern is that to me? You do not appear to know that you are talking nonsense."

"Nonsense?"

"Certainly. I have no husband. I am Miss Dalton."

"You are not Miss Dalton. You are Mrs. Dudleigh."

Edith looked at him with a smile of scorn.

Leon fixed his gray eyes upon her with a fierce glance, and said, in vehement tones,

"SHE CONFRONTED HIM WITH A COLD, STONY GLARE."

"I swear by all that's holy that you are really my wife. The marriage was a valid one. No law can break it. The banns were published in the village church. All the villagers heard them. Wiggins kept himself shut up so that he knew nothing about it. The clergyman is the vicar of Dalton—the Rev. Mr. Munn. It has been published in the papers. In the eye of the law you are no longer Miss Dalton. You are Mrs. Leon Dudleigh. You are my wife!"

At these words, in spite of Edith's pride and courage, there came over her a dark fear that all this might indeed be as he said. The mention of the published banns disturbed her, and shook that proud and obstinate conviction which she had thus far entertained that the scene in the chapel was only a brutal practical joke. It might be far more. It might not be a mockery after all. It might be good in the eye of the law—that law whose injustice had been shown to her in the terrible experience of her father; and if this were so, what then?

A pang of anguish shot through her heart as this terrific thought occurred. But the pang passed away, and with it the terror passed also. Once more she called to her aid that stubborn Dalton fortitude and Dalton pride which had thus far so well sustained her.

"*Your* wife!" she exclaimed, with a loathing and a scorn in her face and in her voice that words could not express, at the sight of which even Leon, with all his insolence, was cowed—"*your* wife! Do you think you can affect me by lies like these?"

"Lies!" repeated Leon—"it's the truth. You are my wife, and you must sign these papers."

"I don't think so," said Edith, resuming her former coolness.

"Do you dare to refuse me this?"

"I don't see any daring about it. Of course I refuse."

"Sign them!" roared Leon, with an oath.

Edith smiled lightly and turned away.

Leon rushed toward her with a menacing gesture. But Edith was aware of this. In an instant she turned, snatched a dagger from her breast which had been concealed there, and confronted him with a cold, stony glare. "I well know," said she, "what an utter coward you are. While I have this you will not dare to touch me. It is better for you, on the whole, just now, that you are a coward, for this dagger—which, by-the-way, I always carry—is poisoned. It is an old family affair—and that shows you one of the advantages of having a family—and so deadly is the poison that a scratch would kill you. Yes, there is some advantage in being a coward, for if you dared to touch me I should strike you with this as I would strike a mad dog!"

Leon stood before her, a coward, as she knew and as she said, not daring to come within reach of her terrible weapon, which she upheld with a deadly purpose plainly visible in her eye. Yet it seemed as though, with his great muscular power, he might easily have grasped that slender arm and wrenched the dagger away. But this was a thing which he did not dare to attempt; the risk was too great. He might have received a scratch in the struggle with that young girl who confronted him so steadily, and who, with all her fragile beauty, was so calm, so proud, and so resolute.

Edith waited for a few moments, and then walked quietly away, trusting implicitly to Leon's cowardice, and without another word, or even another look, she left the room and returned to her own apartments.

CHAPTER XXXII.
A FIGHT IN THE ENEMY'S CAMP.

It will have been seen already that Leon had taken up his abode at Dalton Hall immediately after that marriage ceremony as the husband of Edith. Her illness had hitherto prevented him from having any understanding with her, and his own affairs called him away before her recovery. With Wiggins he remained on the same footing as before; nor did he find himself able to alter that footing in the slightest degree. Whatever Wiggins may have thought or felt on the subject of the marriage, he revealed it to no one; and Leon found himself compelled to wait for Edith's recovery before he could accomplish any thing definite with regard to his own position. On his return to Dalton Hall he learned that she was convalescent, and he was much surprised at her immediate request for an interview.

With the result of that interview he had but little reason to be satisfied. He felt disappointed, enraged, and humiliated. Edith had been perfectly free from all fear of him. The young girl had shown herself a virago. His insults she had returned with mocking sarcasms, his threats she had treat-

ed with utter contempt, and finally she had proved him to his own face to be a coward. Over the recollection of that scene he could only gnash his teeth in fruitless rage. The more he thought of that interview, the more bitter grew his mortification; and at length he resolved to force matters to a climax at once by coming to a distinct and final understanding with Wiggins himself.

Leon had enjoyed the freedom of the house long enough to know where Wiggins's room was, and into that room he intruded himself abruptly on the following day. It was in this room that Wiggins spent the greater part of his time, carrying on a vigorous though not very extensive correspondence, and moving the wires of those plans at which he had hinted to Edith. He was here now, and as Leon entered he looked up with a silent stare.

"I'll not stand this any longer," burst forth Leon, abruptly and vehemently. "I'm in terrible difficulties. I've been waiting long enough. You must side with me actively, for your assistance is absolutely necessary to bring that mad girl to terms. I'm married to her. She's my wife. I must have control of this place at once; and I'll tolerate no further opposition from her, or humbug from you. I've come now to tell you this finally and peremptorily."

"She is not your wife," said Wiggins, coldly.

"She is."

"It was a trick. The ceremony was a miserable sham."

"It was no sham. It was done legally, and can not be undone."

"Legally! Pooh! The whole thing was a farce. It's no marriage. Legally! Why, what has that miserable affair to do with the law?"

"What has it to do? It has every thing to do. The whole thing was done in a perfectly legal manner. The banns were regularly published by the vicar of Dalton in Dalton Church, and in that chapel Edith Dalton was regularly and legally married to Leon Dudleigh by the Rev. Mr. Munn. What more is wanting to make it legal? Go and ask Mr. Munn himself."

"The banns!" exclaimed Wiggins.

"Yes, the banns," said Leon. "You never heard of that, perhaps. If you doubt me, go and ask Munn."

"It was not you that she married!" cried Wiggins, after a pause, in which he seemed struck rather painfully by Leon's last information. "It was not you—it was that other one. He called himself Dudleigh—a miserable assumed name!"

"You know nothing about it," said Leon, "whether it was assumed or not. And as to the marriage, it was to me. I held her hand; I put the ring on her finger; she married me, and no other. But I'm not going to talk about that. I've simply come here to insist on your active help. I won't stand any more of this humbug. I've already told you that I know you."

Wiggins remained silent for some time.

"So you did," said he at last, in a low voice; "but what of that?"

"Why, only this: you had to let me do what I chose. And I intend to keep a good hold of you yet, my fine fellow."

Wiggins placed both his elbows on the table in front of him, and looked fixedly at Leon for some time.

"You did say once," said he, slowly, "that you knew me, and the possibility that it might be true induced me to tolerate you here for some time. I trusted to Miss Dalton's innate good sense to save her from any danger from one like you; but it appears that I was mistaken. At the present moment, however, I may as well inform you that you have not the slightest idea who I am, and more than this, that I have not the slightest objection to tell you."

"Pooh!" said Leon, with ill-disguised uneasiness, "it's all very well for you to take that tone, but it won't do with me. I know who you are."

"Who am I?"

"Oh, I know."

"Who? who? Say it! If you did know, you would not imagine that you had any power over me. Your power is a dream, and your knowledge of me is a sham. Who am I?"

"Why," said Leon, with still greater uneasiness and uncertainty in his face and voice, "you are not John Wiggins."

"Who do you think I am?" asked Wiggins.

"Who? who? Why, you came from Australia."

"Well, what of that?"

"Well, you are some convict who got acquainted with Dalton out there, and have come back here to try to get control of these estates."

"But how could I do that? If this were so, do you suppose that Wiggins of Liverpool would allow it?"

"Oh, he has a share in the business. He goes halves with you, perhaps."

"If he wanted any share at all in such a transaction, he might have all, and therefore he would be a fool to take half. Your theory, I infer, is somewhat lame. And what of Mrs. Dunbar? Is she an Australian convict too?"

"Mrs. Dunbar?—who is she? What! that crazy housekeeper? She looks as though she may have just been released from some lunatic asylum."

Wiggins made no immediate reply, and sat for a few moments in thought. Then he looked at Leon and said:

"Well, you have got hold of part of the

truth—just enough to mislead you. It is true that I have been in Australia, though why you should suppose that I was a convict I do not know. More: I went out there on account of Dalton, and for no other reason. While there I saw much of him, and gained his whole confidence. He told me his whole story unreservedly. He believed me to be his friend. He confided everything to me. You must have heard of his trial, and his strange persistence in refusing to say who the guilty party was."

"Oh yes," said Leon, with a laugh. "A good idea that, when the guilty party was himself."

"It was not himself," said Wiggins, "and before long the world shall know who it was, for that is the one business of my life since my return, to which I have sacrificed all other concerns. In my attention to this I have even neglected Miss Dalton."

"She does not appear to think that you have neglected her," said Leon, with a sneer.

To this Wiggins paid no attention.

"Dalton," said he, "told me all before he died. He thought of his daughter, and though he had suffered himself, yet he thought on his death-bed that it would be a sin to leave to her such a legacy of shame. It was this that broke his obstinate silence, and made him tell his secret to me. And here, Leon Dudleigh, is a thing in which you are concerned."

"I!" exclaimed Leon, in astonishment, not unmingled with alarm.

"I will tell you presently. I will simply remark now that I am following out his wishes, and am working for Miss Dalton, as he himself would have worked, to redeem her name."

"The name is hers no longer," said Leon. "She seems to give you a precious hard time of it too, I should say, and does not altogether appreciate your self-denying and wonderfully disinterested efforts."

"I have not treated her with sufficient consideration," said Wiggins. "I misunderstood her character. I began altogether wrong. I see now that I ought to have given her more of my confidence, or, better yet, that I ought not to have brought her here till the work was done. Well," he added, with a sigh, "my chief consolation is that it will be all right in the end."

"This is all rubbish," said Leon. "You are not what you pretend to be. You are not her guardian. You are an interloper and a swindler. You shall remain here no longer. I am her husband, and I order you off the premises at once."

"You are not her husband, and I am her guardian," said Wiggins, calmly. "I was appointed by her father on his death-bed."

"I don't believe it. Besides, your name is not Wiggins at all."

"How do you know? You know nothing."

"DOTARD! DO YOU TALK OF VENGEANCE?"

"I know Wiggins."

"Wiggins of Liverpool, perhaps, but there are more Wigginses in the world than that."

"A court of law will show that—"

"You will not go to a court of law. That is my task. And mark me," continued Wiggins, with thrilling emphasis, "when a court of law takes up the subject of the Dalton estates or the Dalton name, then it will be the turn for you and yours to tremble."

"Tremble!" exclaimed Leon, scornfully.

"Yes," repeated Wiggins. "Your father—"

"Pooh!" said Leon.

"When Dalton died," continued Wiggins, "he left his papers. Among them was a letter of which he himself told me. If he had produced that letter on his trial, he would have escaped, and the guilty man would have been punished. The letter was written by the real forger. It inclosed the forged check to Dalton, asking him to draw the money and pay certain pressing debts. The writer of that letter was your own father—Lionel Dudleigh!"

"It's a lie!" cried Leon, starting up, with terrible excitement in his face—an excitement, too, which was mingled with unspeakable dread.

"It's true," said Wiggins, calmly, "and the letter can be proved."

"It can not."

"It can, and by the best of testimony."

"I don't believe it."

"Perhaps not; but there is something more. With the murder trial you are no doubt familiar. In fact, I take it for granted that you are familiar with Dalton's case in all its bearings," added Wiggins, in a tone of deep meaning. "In that murder trial, then, you are aware that a Maltese cross was found on the scene of murder, and created much excitement. You know what part it had in the trial. I now inform you that I have proof which can show beyond a doubt that this Maltese cross was the property of your father—Lionel Dudleigh."

"It's a lie—an infernal lie!" said Leon, in a hoarse voice. His excitement had now become terrible.

"It's true—all true," continued Wiggins. "It can all be proved by a witness that can not be impeached. Yes, Leon Dudleigh, you yourself would be forced to accept the testimony of that witness."

"What witness?" said Leon, in a voice that was scarcely audible from conflicting emotions.

Wiggins looked at him earnestly, and then said, in a low, deep, solemn voice,

"Leon Dudleigh, that witness is your mother!"

The other started as though he had been shot.

"My mother!" he almost screamed—"my mother! why, she—she is dead—dead long ago."

"When did you find that out?" said Wiggins.

"She's dead! she's dead!" repeated Leon, as though by assertion he could make it true.

"She is not dead," said Wiggins, in an awful voice, "though all these years she has lived a living death. She is not dead. She is alive, and she now stands ready, when the hour comes, though with an agonized heart, to give that testimony which, years ago, she dared not and could not give. She has allowed the innocent to suffer, and the guilty to go free, but now she will do so no longer. The work upon which I have been engaged is almost complete. The preparations are made, and this very day I am going to Liverpool to perform the last acts that are necessary toward vindicating the memory of Dalton, establishing his innocence, and punishing the guilty. As for you, you can do nothing here, and I have resolved to punish you for what you have done. I shall show you no mercy. If you want to save yourself, leave the country, for otherwise I swear you will never be safe from my vengeance."

"Vengeance!" said Leon, in low, menacing tones. "Dotard! do you talk of vengeance? You do not understand the meaning of that word. Wait till you see what I can do."

And with these words he left the room.

That evening Wiggins left for Liverpool.

CHAPTER XXXIII.

THE HUSBAND'S LAST APPEAL.

EARLY on the following day Edith received a request from Leon for another interview. This request was acceptable in every way, for the last interview had been no more satisfactory to her than to him, and she could not help hoping that something more definite might result from a new one. She therefore went down, and found him already in the room.

On this occasion Leon showed nothing of that languor which he had previously affected. He appeared, on the contrary, uneasy, nervous, and impatient. So abstracted was he by his own thoughts that he did not notice her entrance. She sat down and waited for a little while, after which she said, quietly,

"Did you wish to see me, Captain—a—Dudleigh?"

Leon started, then frowned; then, after a little silence, he began abruptly:

"You may deny it as much as you choose, but it's no use. You are actually married to me. You are really and truly my wife, both in the eyes of man and in the eyes of the law. From that marriage nothing can ever deliver her but a divorce."

"You are mistaken," said Edith, quietly. "Even if that miserable performance should turn out to be a marriage—which is absurd

—still there is one other thing that can free me."

"Ah!—and what may that be?"

"Death!" said Edith, solemnly.

Leon turned pale. "Is that a threat?" he asked at length, in a trembling voice. "Whose death do you mean?"

Edith made no reply.

"Yes," said Leon, after a pause, going on with his former train of thought, "at any rate you are my wife, and you can not help it. You may deny it as much as you please, but that will not avail. In spite of this, however, I do not molest you, although I might so easily do it. I never trouble you with my presence. I am very forbearing. Few would do as I do. Yet I have rights, and some of them, at least, I am determined to assert. Now, on the whole, it is well for you—and you ought to see it—that you have one here who occupies the peculiar position toward you which I do. If it were not for me you would be altogether in the power of Wiggins. He is your guardian or your jailer, whichever you choose to call him. He could shut you up in the vaults of Dalton Hall if he chose—and he probably will do that very thing before long—for who is there to prevent him? I am the only one who can stand between you and him. I am your only hope. You do not know who and what this man is. You think you know him, but you don't. You think of him as a villain and a tyrant. Let me tell you that in your bitterest hate of that man you have never begun to conceive the fraction of his villainy. Let me tell you that he is one who passes your comprehension. Let me tell you that, however much you may hate me, if I were to tell you what Wiggins is, the feelings that you have toward me would be almost affection, compared to those which you would have toward him."

Leon paused. He had spoken most earnestly and vehemently; but upon Edith these words produced no effect. She believed that this was a last effort to work upon her feelings by exciting her fears of Wiggins. She did not believe him capable of speaking the truth to her, and thus his words produced no result.

"If you had not been married to me when you were," continued Leon, "I solemnly assure you that by this time you would have been where hope could never reach you."

"Well, really," said Edith, "Captain—a—Dudleigh, all this is excessively childish. By such an absurd preamble as this you, of course, must mean something. All this, however, can have no possible effect on me, for the simple reason that I consider it spoken for effect. I hope, therefore, that you will be kind enough to come at once to business, and say precisely what it is that you want of me."

"It is no absurd preamble," said Leon,

gloomily. "It is not nonsense, as I could soon show you. There is no human being who has done so much wrong to you and yours as this Wiggins, yet you quietly allow him to be your guardian."

"I?" said Edith. "I allow him? Let me be free, and then you will see how long I allow him."

"But I mean here—in Dalton Hall."

"I do not allow him any thing. I am simply a prisoner. He is my jailer, and keeps me here."

"You need not be so."

"Pray how can I escape?"

"By siding with me."

"With you?" asked Edith—"and what then?"

"Well, if you side with me I will drive him out."

"You seem incapable of understanding," said Edith, "that of the two, you yourself, both by nature and by position, are by far the more abhorrent to me. Side with you! And is this the proposal you have to make?"

"I tell you that you are in no danger from me, and that you are from him."

"Really, as far as danger is concerned, my prospects with Wiggins are far preferable to my prospects with you."

"But you don't know him. He has done terrible things—deeds of horror."

"And you—what have you done? But perhaps I have mistaken you. When you ask me to side with you, you may perhaps mean that I shall be at liberty, and that when you expel Wiggins you will allow me to go also."

At this Leon looked down in evident embarrassment.

"Well—not—yet," he said, slowly. "In time, of course; but it can not all be done just at once, you know."

"What can not be done at once?"

"Your—your freedom."

"Why not?"

"Well, there are—a—certain difficulties in the way."

"Then what can I gain by siding with you? Why should I cast off Wiggins, and take a new jailer who has done to me a wrong far more foul and far more intolerable than any that Wiggins ever attempted?"

"But you mistake me. I intend to let you go free, of course—that is, in time."

"In time!"

"Yes; every thing can not be done in a moment."

"This is mere childishness. You are trifling. I am astonished that you should speak in this way, after what you know of me."

"But I tell you I will set you free—only I can not do that until I get what I want."

"And what is it that you want?"

"Why, what I married you for."

"What is that?"

"Money," said Leon, abruptly.

"Money?" repeated Edith, in surprise.

"Yes, money," said Leon, harshly.

"You must really apply to Wiggins, then," said she, carelessly.

"No; you yourself are the only one to whom I must apply."

"To me? I have no money whatever. It is of no use for me to inform you that Wiggins is all-powerful here. I thought by your professed knowledge of his wonderful secrets that you had some great power over him, and could get from him whatever you want."

"Never mind what you thought," growled Leon. "I come to you, and you only, and I ask you for money."

"How can I give it?"

"By signing your name to a paper, a simple paper, which I can use. Your signature is necessary to effect what I wish."

"My signature? Ah! And what possible inducement can you offer me for my signature?"

"Why, what you most desire."

"What? My freedom?"

"Yes."

"Very well. Will you drive me to the village at once?"

Leon hesitated.

"Well, not just at once, you know. You must remain here a short time, and go through certain formalities and routine work, and attest certain things before a lawyer."

Edith smiled.

"What a simpleton you must still think me! How easy you must think it is to impose upon me! Perhaps you think me so credulous, or so much in the habit of confiding in you, that no such thing as doubt ever enters my mind."

Leon glared angrily at her.

"I tell you I must have it," he cried, in excited tones. "I must have it—by fair means or foul."

"But of the two ways I presume you have a preference for the latter," said Edith.

"I tell you I must and will have it," reiterated Leon.

"I don't see how you can get my signature very well—unless you forge it; but then I suppose that will not stand in your way."

"Now by all that is most holy," cried Leon, vehemently, "you make me hate you even worse than I hate Wiggins."

"Really, these feelings of yours are a subject in which I do not take the smallest interest."

"I tell you," cried Leon, struggling to repress his rage, "if you sign this paper you shall be free."

"Let me be free first, and then I will think about it."

"If you get free you'll refuse to sign," said Leon.

"But if I were to sign first I should never be free."

"You shall be free. I promise you on the honor of a gentleman," cried Leon, earnestly.

"I'm afraid," said Edith, in a tone of quiet contempt, "that the security is of too little value."

Leon looked at her with fury in his eyes.

"You are driving me to the most desperate measures," he cried.

"It seems to me that your measures have all along been as desperate as they well can be."

"I swear by all that's holy," thundered Leon, "that I'll tame you yet. I'll bring you into subjection."

"Ah! then in that case," said Edith, "my comfort will be that the subjection can not last long."

"Will it not?" asked Leon.

"No, it will not, as you very well know," said Edith, in cold, measured tones, looking steadfastly at him with what seemed like a certain solemn warning. She rose as she said this, still looking at Leon, while he also rose in a state of vehement excitement.

"What do you mean?" he cried. "You look as blood-thirsty as an assassin."

"I may yet become one," said Edith, gloomily, "if this lasts much longer. You have eyes, but you will not see. You treat me like some silly, timid child, while I have all the time the spirit of a man. This can only end in one way. Some one must die!"

Leon looked at her in astonishment. Her voice and her look showed that she was in earnest, but the fragile beauty of her slender form seemed to belie the dark meaning of her words.

"I came with a fair offer," said he, in a voice hoarse with passion.

"You!" said Edith, in cold scorn; "you with a fair offer! Fairness and honor and justice and truth, and all such things, are altogether unknown to such as you."

At this Leon frowned that peculiar frown of his, and gnawed his mustache in his rage.

"I have spared you thus far," said he—"I have spared you; but now, by Heaven, you shall feel what it is to have a master!"

"You!" she cried—"you spared me! If I have escaped any injury from you, it has been through my own courage and the cowardice of your own heart. You my master! You will learn a terrible lesson before you become that!"

"I have spared you," cried Leon, now beside himself with rage—"I have spared you, but I will spare you no longer. After this you shall know that what I have thus far done is as nothing to that which is yet before you."

"What you have done!" said Edith, fixing her great wrathful eyes more sternly upon Leon, with a look of deadly menace, and with burning intensity of gaze, and speaking in a low tone that was tremulous with repressed indignation—"what you have done! Let me tell you, Captain Dudleigh, your heart's blood could never atone for the wrongs you have done me! Beware, Sir, how you drive me to desperation. You little know what I have in my mind to do. You have made me too familiar with the thought of death!"

At these words Leon stared at her in silence. He seemed at last to understand the full possibility of Edith's nature, and to comprehend that this one whom he threatened was capable, in her despair, of making all his threats recoil on his own head. He said nothing, and in a few moments afterward she left the room.

As she went out of the door she encountered Hugo. He started as she came noiselessly upon him. He had evidently been listening to all that had been said. At this specimen of the way in which she was watched, though it really showed her no more than what she had all along known, there arose in Edith's mind a fresh sense of helplessness and of peril.

EDITH SET TO WORK.

CHAPTER XXXIV.

THE FUGITIVE AND THE PURSUER.

On returning to her own room from that interview with Leon, Edith sat for a long time involved in thought. It was evident to her now that her situation was one full of frightful peril. The departure of Wiggins, of which she was aware, seemed to afford additional danger. Between him and Leon there had been what seemed to her at least the affectation of dislike or disagreement, but now that he was gone there remained no one who would even pretend to interpose between herself and her enemy.

THE LIVING LINK.

Even if Mrs. Dunbar had been capable of assisting her against Leon, Edith knew that no reliance could be placed upon her, for she had openly manifested a strong regard for him.

This departure of Wiggins, which thus seemed to make her present position more perilous, seemed also to Edith to afford her a better opportunity than any she had known since her arrival of putting into execution her long-meditated project of flight. True, there was still the same difficulty which had been suggested once before—the want of money—but Edith was now indifferent to this. The one thing necessary was to escape from her new perils. If she could but get out of the Dalton grounds, she hoped to find some lawyer who might take up her cause, and allow her enough to supply her modest wants until that cause should be decided. But liberty was the one thought that eclipsed all others in her estimation; and if she could but once effect her escape from this horrible place, it seemed to her that all other things would be easy.

The present appeared to be beyond all others the fitting time, for Wiggins was away, and it seemed to her that in his absence the watch over her would probably be relaxed. Her long illness would of itself have thrown them to some extent off their guard, and render her purpose unsuspected. By this time it would doubtless be forgotten that she had once left the Hall by night, and it was not likely that any precaution would be taken against a second flight on the part of one so weak as she was supposed to be. A few days before she had made a stealthy visit to that door, and had found, to her great relief, that no additional fastenings had been put there. Her illness had evidently rendered any such precaution unnecessary for the time; and since her recovery Wiggins had no doubt been too much occupied with other things to think of this.

Now was the time, then, for flight. The danger was greater than ever before, and the opportunity for escape better. Leon was master in the house. The other inmates were simply his creatures. Leon Dudleigh, as he called himself, claimed to be her husband. He asserted that claim insolently and vehemently. She had defied him, but how long would she be able to maintain that defiant attitude? How long could her frail strength sustain her in a life of incessant warfare like this, even if her spirit should continue to be as indomitable as ever? The scene of this day, and her last parting with him, made the danger seem so imminent that it nerved her resolution, and made her determine at all hazards to attempt her escape that night.

But how should she escape?

Not for the first time did this question occur. For a long time she had been brooding over it, and as she had thought it over she had devised a plan which seemed to hold out to her some prospect of success.

In the first place, it was evident that she would have to climb over the wall. To obtain any key by which she could open the gates was impossible. She could find none that were at all likely to do so; besides, she was afraid that even if she had a key, the attempt to unlock the gates might expose her to detection and arrest by the watchful porter. The wall, therefore, was her only hope.

Now that wall could not be climbed by her unassisted strength, but she knew that if she had any sort of a ladder it might easily be done. The question that arose, then, was how to procure this ladder. A wooden one could not be of any service, for she could not carry it so far, and she saw plainly that her attempt must be made by means of some sort of a rope-ladder.

Having reached this conclusion, she began a diligent search among all the articles at her disposal, and finally concluded that the bed-cord would be exactly what she needed. In addition to this, however, something more was required—something of the nature of a grapple or hook to secure her rope-ladder to the top of the wall. This required a further search, but in this also she was successful. An iron rod on the curtain pole along which the curtains ran appeared to her to be well suited to her needs. It was about six feet long and a quarter of an inch thick. The rod rested loosely on the pole, and Edith was able to remove it without difficulty.

All these preliminaries had been arranged or decided upon before this evening, and Edith had now only to take possession of the rod and the rope, and adapt them to her wants. For this purpose she waited till dark, and then began her work.

It was moonlight, and she was able to work without lighting a lamp, thus securing additional secrecy. This moonlight was both an advantage and a disadvantage, and she did not know whether to be glad or sorry about it. It certainly facilitated her escape by showing the way, but then, on the other hand, it rendered discovery easier.

Edith set to work, and, first of all, she removed the bed-cord. It was as strong as was desirable, and far longer than was necessary. She doubled part of this, and tied knots at intervals of about a foot, and in this simple way formed what was a very good step-ladder about three yards long, which was sufficient for her purpose. Then she removed the iron curtain rod, and bent this in such a way that it formed a hook or grapple strong enough for her wants. She thus had a rope-ladder, with a grappling-iron attached, of rude construction, it is true, yet perfectly well suited to the task

before her, and so light as to be quite port-
able.

These preparations did not take up much
time. After taking what she wanted of the
bed-cord, there was enough left to replace in
the bedstead so as to hold up the bed. She
did not know what might happen, and wished to preserve appearances in the event of
Mrs. Dunbar's entrance, or in case of her
being compelled to postpone her project.
From the same motive she also replaced the
curtain so as to look as it did before, securing it in its place by means of pins.

At length all these preparations were
completed, and it only remained for Edith
to wait for the proper time to start.

The hours passed on.

Midnight came, but even at that hour
Edith thought that it was too early. Leon
probably kept late hours, and might be
wandering about. She determined to wait
longer.

The moon was still shining. There were
only a few scattered clouds in that clear
sky.

Could she find her way to the wall? She
felt confident of that. She intended to go
down the avenue, keeping close to the trees,
so as to fly to their shelter in case of pursuit.
When she reached the neighborhood of the
porter's lodge, she would go through the
trees to the wall, trusting to fortune to find
her way for that short distance.

Such were the hopes and plans, made long
before, which now occupied her thoughts as
she waited.

At last two o'clock came. It seemed now
that it would be unwise to wait any longer,
since the time that was left between this
and daylight was barely sufficient to allow
for contingencies. Without any further delay, therefore, she prepared to depart.

It was with a painful feeling of suspense
and agitation that she set forth upon this
attempt at flight, which she knew must be
a final one. Over her left arm she threw
the rope-ladder, while in her left hand she
held that ancestral dagger which had already done her such good service in her
dealings with Leon. Her right hand was
thus free to grope in the dark for her way,
to open bolts, or to seize the dagger from
her other hand whenever the need for it
might arise. For this last dread necessity
she had thoroughly prepared herself. By
the desperation of her position, and by the
dark menaces of Leon, she had been nerved
to a courage beyond even that elevated
standard which her high spirit ordinarily
reached, and she had resolved that if any
one interposed between herself and that
liberty for which she longed, to use that
dagger, and to strike without scruple.

On leaving her room she stood for a moment in the outer hall and listened. All
was still. She glided noiselessly along, and

reached the stairway. Once more she stood
and listened before descending. There was
silence yet. She now descended the stairs
as noiselessly as before, and reached the
lower hall, where she walked quickly toward the east end, and came to the narrow
stairway that led down to the door. Here
once more she paused. A fearful thought
came to her as she looked down. What if
some one should be waiting there in the
dark! What if Leon should be there! In
spite of herself a shudder passed through
her at that thought.

Suddenly, as she stood there, she heard a
sound—a sound which roused her once more
to action, and inspired new fears. It was
the sound of a footfall—far away, indeed, inside the house, but still a footfall—a heavy
tread, as of some one in pursuit, and its sound
was loud and menacing to her excited senses.
There was only one to whom she could at-
tribute it—Leon!

He had heard her, then!

She was pursued!

Like lightning this thought came to her,
and brought terror with it. She could delay no longer. Down the narrow stairway
she hurried through the darkness, and reached the door. In her panic she forgot her
usual caution. With a jerk she drew the
bolt back, and a harsh grating sound arose.
She flung open the door, which also creaked
on its unused hinges. Then leaping out,
she hastily banged the door after her, and
ran straight on.

In front of Dalton Hall there was a wide
lawn and a pond. Beyond this arose the
trees of the park. Toward the shelter of
these shadowy trees Edith hurried, with
the dread sense in her soul that she was being pursued by a remorseless enemy. This
thought lent additional speed to her footsteps as she flew over the intervening space.
The moon was shining brightly, and she
knew that she could easily be seen by any
watcher; but she sought only the more to
reach the trees, and thus escape observation. The time seemed long indeed to her
in those moments of dread suspense; but
the space was at last traversed, the trees
were reached, and plunging into the midst
of them, she ran along, occasionally stum-
bling, until at length, partly from exhaustion and partly from a desire to see where
her enemy might be, so as to elude him better, she stopped.

Her course had been a circuitous one, but
she had kept along the edge of the wood, so
that now, as she stopped, she found herself
under the shadow of the trees, and immediately opposite the portico of Dalton Hall,
between which and herself lay the pond.
Here she stood, and looked over the intervening space.

As she looked, she at first saw no appearance of any human being, and she began to

think that her fears all along had been unfounded; but in a little while, as her eyes wandered over the front of the Hall, she saw something which at once renewed all her excitement, and showed her that her fears were true.

Upon the portico stood a figure, the general outlines of which were now visible to her as she looked carefully, and seemed to be the figure of Leon. She could recognize the gray dress which he usually wore, and also understood why she had not noticed him before, for the color of his clothes had made him but faintly visible against the gray stone mass of the background. He was now standing there with his face turned in her direction.

"He has heard me," she thought. "He has seen me. Instead of chasing me at once, he has stopped to listen, so as to judge of my course. He knows that I am here now in this spot, and is still listening to find out if I go any further."

In a few moments her attention was attracted by a dark object lying on the portico near Leon.

It was the dog!

She knew it well. Her heart sank within her.

"He is going to track me with the dog!" she thought.

What could she do?

Nothing. Flight was now worse than useless. All seemed lost, and there was nothing now left to her in that moment of despair but the resolve to resist to the end.

After a short time, which to Edith seemed prolonged to a terrible degree, the figure came down the steps, followed by the dog.

Edith watched.

He walked on; he rounded the end of the pond; he came nearer!

She could now recognize his face as the moon shone down.

It was Leon. There was no longer the slightest doubt of that. He was coming toward her, and the huge dog followed.

Edith involuntarily shrank back among the trees, and grasping her dagger with desperate resolve, awaited the approach of her enemy.

CHAPTER XXXV.

THE EMPTY ROOMS.

ON the following morning Mrs. Dunbar waited a long time for Edith's appearance. But she did not make her appearance, and the time passed, until it at length grew so late that she determined to see what was the matter. Full of fear lest some new illness had been the result of the new excitement to which she had been subjected, Mrs. Dunbar passed cautiously through Edith's sitting-room, and knocked at her bedroom door.

There was no answer.

She knocked again and again, and still receiving no answer, she opened the door and looked in.

To her amazement the room was empty. What was more surprising was the fact that the bed did not appear to have been slept in. There was no disorder visible in the room. Every thing was in its usual place, but Edith was not there, and in that one glance which Mrs. Dunbar gave she took in the whole truth.

Edith had fled!

She knew also that she must have fled during the night; that the event against which such precautions had been taken had occurred at last, and that she was responsible. Over that sorrowful anxious face there came now a deeper sorrow and a graver anxiety at that discovery, and sitting down upon a chair, she tried to conjecture Edith's possible course, and wondered how she could get over the wall and out of the grounds.

At length she left this room, and going down stairs, called Hugo.

"Hugo," said she, "has the captain come down?"

"I habn't seen him, ma'am," said Hugo, respectfully.

"He always rises early," said Mrs. Dunbar. "I wonder what's the matter. He certainly must be up."

Turning away, she ascended the stairs, and went to the room which was occupied by Leon. The door was open. She entered. The room looked as though it had just been left by its occupant. The bed bore signs of having been occupied. The valise was lying there open. Upon the toilet-table was a pocket-book, and hanging from the screw of the looking-glass was his watch. His riding whip and gloves and top-boots were lying in different places.

As Mrs. Dunbar saw all this, she concluded at first that he had gone out for a walk, and would soon be back; but the lateness of the hour made that idea seem absurd, and showed her that there must be some other cause. The flight of Edith thereupon occurred to her, and was very naturally associated in her mind with the departure of Leon. Had he been watching? Had he detected her flight, and gone in pursuit? It seemed so. If so, he was doubtless yet in pursuit of the fugitive, who must have fled fast and far to delay him so long.

Then another thought came—the idea of violence. Perhaps he had caught the fugitive, and in his rage and vindictive fury had harmed her. That he was fierce enough for any atrocity she well knew; and the thought that he had killed her, and had fled, came swift as lightning to her mind.

The idea was terrible. She could not endure it. She left the room and hurried down stairs again.

"Hugo," said she, "go down and ask the porter if he has seen the captain or Miss Dalton."

"Miss Dalton!" exclaimed Hugo.

"Yes; she's gone."

"Gone!" repeated Hugo, in amazement.

He said no more, but hurried down to the gates, while Mrs. Dunbar, who felt restless and ill at ease, walked up the stairs, and feeling fatigued, stopped on the landing, and leaned against the window there, looking out upon the ground in the rear of the Hall.

Standing here, her eyes were attracted by a sight which made her start. It was the Newfoundland dog. He was standing at some distance from the house, looking straight ahead at vacancy, in a rigid attitude. The sight of this animal, who was always the inseparable companion of his master, standing there in so peculiar a fashion by himself, excited Mrs. Dunbar; and forgetful of her weariness, she descended the stairs again, and quitting the Hall, approached the spot where the dog was standing.

As she approached, the dog looked at her and wagged his tail. She called him. He went on wagging his tail, but did not move from the spot. She went up to him and stroked him, and looked all around, hoping to see some signs of his master. She looked in the direction in which the dog had been staring when she first noticed him. The stables seemed to be the place. Toward these she walked, and tried to induce the dog to follow, but he would not. She then walked over to the stables, and looked through them, without seeing any trace of the object of her search. Upon this she returned to the house.

On coming back she found Hugo. He had been to the gates, he said; but the porter had seen nothing whatever either of the captain or Miss Dalton.

This intelligence deepened the anxious expression on Mrs. Dunbar's face.

"His dog is here," said she, in a tremulous voice.

"His dog!" said Hugo. "Oh yes; he's ben out dar all de mornin'. Dunno what de matta wid dat ar animal at all. Stands dar like a gravy statoo."

For the rest of that day Mrs. Dunbar was restless and distressed. She wandered aimlessly about the house. She sent Hugo off to scour the grounds to see if he could find any trace of either of the fugitives. Every moment she would look out from any window or door that happened to be nearest, to see if either of them was returning. But the day passed by, and Hugo came back from his long search, but of neither of the fugitives was a single trace found.

What affected Mrs. Dunbar as much as anything was the behavior of the dog. Through all that day he remained in the same place, sometimes standing, sometimes lying down,

but never going away more than a few feet. That the dog had some meaning in this singular behavior, and that this meaning had reference to the flight of one or the other of the late inmates of the house, was very evident to her. No persuasion, or coaxing, or even threatening could draw the dog away; and even when Hugo fired a gun off close to his head, he quivered in every nerve, but only moved back a foot or two. Food and drink were brought to him, of which he partook with a most eager appetite, but no temptation could draw him any distance from his post.

That night was a sleepless one for Mrs. Dunbar; and it was with a feeling of great relief that she heard the noise of a carriage early on the following day, and knew that Wiggins had returned.

She hurried down at once, and met him in the great hall. In a few words she told him all.

For such intelligence as this Wiggins was evidently unprepared. He staggered back and leaned against the wall, staring at Mrs. Dunbar with a terrible look.

"What! Gone!" he said, slowly. "Edith!"

"Yes; and Leon."

"Edith gone!" gasped Wiggins once more. "Did you hear nothing in the village?"

"I drove through without stopping. Did you send to the village?"

"I did not think that they could have got out of the grounds."

"They! There's no trouble about Leon!"

"I'm afraid—for him," said Mrs. Dunbar, in a faint voice.

"For him!" exclaimed Wiggins. "What can happen to him? For her, you mean."

"They must have gone off together."

"Together! Do you think Edith would go with him? No; she has fled in her madness and ignorance, turning her back on happiness and love, and he has pursued her. O Heavens!" he continued, with a groan, "to think that it should end in this! And cursed be that scoundrel—"

"Stop!" cried Mrs. Dunbar. "He is not a scoundrel. He would not harm her. You don't know Leon. He has not left the place; his dog is here."

"His dog!"

Mrs. Dunbar explained.

Upon this Wiggins went through the hall to the rear, and there, in the same place as where Mrs. Dunbar last saw him, was the dog. He was lying down now. He wagged his tail in friendly recognition as they came up. Wiggins patted him and stroked him and tried to coax him away. The result was precisely the same as it had been before. The dog received all advances in the most friendly manner possible. He wagged his tail, rolled over on his back, licked their hands, sat up on his hind-quarters, and did every thing which dogs usually do when petted or played with, but nothing would induce him to leave the place. He did not appear to be in any trouble. He seemed simply to have made up his mind to stay there, and this resolution he maintained most obstinately.

Wiggins could make nothing of it; but the sight of the dog renewed the terrors of Mrs. Dunbar.

"I'm afraid," said she—"I'm afraid that something's happened to Leon."

"To Leon!" exclaimed Wiggins, impatiently; "what could happen to him? I told him to quit this place, and he has probably concluded to do so."

"But what do you think of his flight at the same time with Edith?"

"I don't know what to think of it. I only know this, that if he has harmed one hair of her head, I—I'll—kill him! My own injuries I will forgive, but wrongs done to her I will avenge!"

At this Mrs. Dunbar shrank away, and looked at Wiggins in fear.

"But it may be all the other way," said she, in a tremulous voice. "Edith was terrible in her fury. She was no timid, faltering girl; she was resolute and vindictive. If he has followed her, or laid hands on her, she may have—" She hesitated.

"May have what?" asked Wiggins.

"She may have done him some harm."

"She may have done him some harm!" repeated Wiggins, with a sneer. "What! and when he had his big dog to protect him? Pooh!"

And with a scornful laugh he turned away. Mrs. Dunbar followed him.

"She was so terrible in her despair," said she, as she followed him; "she looked like a fury—beautiful, yet implacable."

"Silence!" cried Wiggins. "Stop all that nonsense, or you'll drive me mad. Are you crazy? When I am almost broken-hearted in my anxiety about her, what do you mean by turning against that wronged and injured girl, who I now see has been driven to despair by my own cursed mistakes, and pretending that she is the aggressor, and your scoundrel Leon the victim?"

In the midst of this Wiggins was interrupted by the approach of Hugo.

"A gen'l'man, Sah, wants to see you, Sah," said he.

"A gentleman," repeated Wiggins. "Who is he? How did he come here?"

"Dunno, Sah, nuffin 'bout dat, Sah."

"It's about Edith!" exclaimed Wiggins; and he hurried into the house.

CHAPTER XXXVI.

THE VICAR OF DALTON.

WIGGINS entered the drawing-room, and found his visitor there. He was a slight man, with light hair, watery gray eyes, and

very mild demeanor. The timidity of the man seemed very marked; there was an apologetic air about him; and his very footfall as he advanced to greet Wiggins seemed to deprecate some anticipated rough treatment. He spoke a few words, and at Wiggins's request to be seated he sat down, while his agitation increased; and he had that hesitating, half-abstracted manner which marks the man who is on the point of giving unpleasant information, about the effect of which he is doubtful.

Wiggins, on his part, did not seem to notice this. He sat down, and looked with earnest inquiry at his visitor. He seemed to know what was the object of this visit, and yet to dread to ask it.

The visitor had given his name as the Rev. Mr. Munn, and Wiggins recognized that name as belonging to the parish vicar. That name excited strange emotions within him, for it was the same name that had appeared in the papers in connection with Edith's marriage.

"Well?" said Wiggins at last, in some impatience.

Mr. Munn cleared his throat.

"I have come here," he began, "to tell you very distressing news."

Wiggins was silent.

"I refer to—a—a—Mrs. Dudleigh," said Mr. Munn.

"Well?" said Wiggins, in a scarcely audible voice.

"She is at the village inn."

"At the village inn!" repeated Wiggins, in evident agitation, drawing a long breath.

"She is alive, then?" he added, eagerly.

"Oh yes," said Mr. Munn; "she came there early yesterday morning." And then he went on to tell his story, the substance of which was as follows:

On the previous morning about dawn the people at the Dalton Inn were aroused by a hurried knock. On going to the door they found Mrs. Dudleigh. The moment that the door was opened she sprang in and fell exhausted to the floor. So great was her weakness that she could not rise again, and had to be carried up to one of the bedrooms. She was so faint that she could scarcely speak; and in a feeble voice she implored them to put her to bed, as it was a long time since she had had any rest, and was almost dead with fatigue.

Her condition was most pitiable. Her clothes were all torn to shreds, and covered with mud and dust; her hands were torn and bleeding; her shoes had been worn into rags; and she looked as though she had been wandering for hours through woods and swamps, and over rocks and sand. To all their inquiries she answered nothing, but only implored them to put her to bed and let her rest; above all, she prayed most piteously that they would tell no one that she was there. This they promised to do; and, indeed, it would have been difficult for them to have informed about her, since none at the inn had ever seen her before, or had the remotest idea who she could be.

Full of pity and sympathy, they put her to bed, and the landlady watched over her most assiduously. All the morning she slept profoundly; but at about noon she waked with a scream, like one who has been roused from some fearful dream.

After that she grew steadily worse. Fever set in, and became more and more violent every moment. In their anxiety to do what she had requested, and keep her secret, they did not send immediately for a doctor. But her condition soon became such that further delay was out of the question, so they sent for the village physician.

When he arrived she was much worse. She was in a high fever, and already delirious. He pronounced her situation to be dangerous in the extreme, urged upon them the greatest care, and advised them to lose no time in letting her friends know about her condition. Here was a dilemma for these worthy people. They did not know who her friends were, and therefore could not send for them, while it became impossible to keep her presence at the inn a secret. Not knowing what else to do, they concluded to send for the vicar.

When Mr. Munn came he found them in great distress. He soon learned the facts of the case, and at once decided that it should be made known to Captain Dudleigh or to Wiggins. For though he did not know Edith's face, still, from the disconnected words that had dropped from her during her delirium, reported to him by the inn people, he thought it probable that she was the very lady whom he had married under such mysterious circumstances. So he soothed the fears of the landlady as well as he could, and then left. It was late at night when he went from the inn, and he had waited till the morning before going to Dalton Hall. He had some difficulty in getting in at the gate, but when the porter learned the object of his visit he at once opened to him. From the porter he learned of the disappearance of Captain Dudleigh also. Nothing was then left but to see Wiggins. Accordingly he had come to the Hall at once, so as to tell his message with the shortest possible delay.

To this recital Wiggins listened with gravity. He made no gesture, and he spoke no word, but sat with folded arms, looking upon the floor. When Mr. Munn had ended, he, after a long silence, turned toward him and said, in a severe tone,

"Well, Sir, now I hope you see something of the evil of that course which you chose to pursue."

"Evil? course?" stammered Mr. Munn. "I don't understand you."

"Oh, I think you understand me," said Wiggins, gloomily. "Has not your conscience already suggested to you the probable cause of this strange course of her whom you call Mrs. Dudleigh?"

"My conscience!" gasped Mr. Munn; "what has my conscience to do with it?"

"How long is it since that wretched mockery at which you officiated?" asked Wiggins, sternly.

"I really—I think—a few months only."

"A few months," repeated Wiggins. "Well, it has come to this. That is the immediate cause of her flight, and of her present suffering."

"I—I—married them," stammered Mr. Munn; "but what of that? Is her unhappiness my fault? How can I help it? Am I responsible for the future condition of those couples whom I marry? Surely this is a strange thing to say."

"You well know," said Wiggins, "what sort of a marriage this was. It was no common one. It was done in secret. Why did you steal into these grounds like a thief, and do this infamous thing?"

"Why—why," faltered the unhappy vicar, growing more terrified and conscience-stricken every minute—"Captain Dudleigh asked me. I can not refuse to marry people."

"No, Sir, you can not when they come to you fairly; you can not, I well know, when the conditions of the law are satisfied. But was that so here? Did you not steal into these grounds? Did you not come by night, in secret, conscious that you were doing wrong, and did you not have to steal out in the same way? And your only excuse is that Captain Dudleigh asked you!"

"He—he—showed very strong reasons why I should do so," said Mr. Munn, who by this time was fearfully agitated—"very strong reasons, I do assure you, Sir, and all my humanity was—a—aroused."

"Your humanity!" sneered Wiggins. "Where was your humanity for her?"

"For her!" exclaimed the vicar. "Why, she wanted it. She loved him."

"Loved him! Pooh! She hated him worse than the devil."

"Then what did she marry him for?" cried Mr. Munn, at his wits' end.

"Never mind," said Wiggins; "you went out of your way to do a deed the consequences of which can not yet be seen. I can understand, Sir, how Captain Dudleigh could have planned this thing; but how you, a calm, quiet clergyman, in the full possession of your faculties, could have ever been led to take part in it, is more than I can comprehend. I, Sir, was her guardian, appointed as such by her father, my own intimate friend. Captain Dudleigh was a villain. He sought out this thoughtless child merely for her money. It was not her that he wanted, but her estate. I could easily have saved her from this danger. He had no chance with me. But you come forward—you, Sir—suddenly, without cause, without a word of warning—you sneak here in the dark, you entice her to that lonely place, and there you bind her body and soul to a scoundrel. Now, Sir, what have you got to say for yourself?"

Mr. Munn's teeth chattered, and his hands clutched one another convulsively. "Captain Dudleigh told me that she was under restraint here by—by you—and that she loved him, and that her only refuge was to be married to him. I'm sure I didn't mean to do any harm."

"Rubbish!" said Wiggins, contemptuously. "The law gives a guardian a certain right to parental restraint for the good of the ward. The slight restraint to which she was subjected was accompanied by the deepest love of those who cared for her here. I had hoped, Sir, that you might have something different to tell me. I did not know that you had actually acted so madly. I thought the story which I heard of that marriage was incredible, and I have always spoken of it as a mockery. But from what I now gather from you, it seems to have been a bona fide marriage, true and valid."

"I—I'm afraid it—it was," said Mr. Munn.

Wiggins gave something that was almost like a groan.

"Fiends," he cried, passionately, rising from his chair—"fiends from the bottomless pit could not have more foully and fatally deceived that poor, thoughtless, trustful child. But all their trickery and treachery could never have succeeded had they not found a paltry tool in a senseless creature like you—you, Sir—who could stand there and go mumbling your marriage service, and never see the infernal jugglery that was going on under your very eyes. Yes, you, Sir, who now come to wring and break my heart by the awful tidings that you now tell me. Away! Begone! I have already borne more than my share of anguish; but this, if it goes on, will kill me or drive me mad!"

He turned away, with his head bent, with an unsteady step, and walked toward the window, where he stood leaning against it heavily, and staring out at vacancy.

As for Mr. Munn, he gave one glance of horror at Wiggins, and then, with a swift, frightened step, he hurried from the Hall.

CHAPTER XXXVII.

THE HOUSE OF REFUGE.

THE illness of Edith was of no light or common kind. Her old glow of health had not yet returned. The state of affairs at

Dalton Hall had retarded any thing like a complete recovery, and when she started off on her desperate flight, she was unfit for such a venture. Through that terrible night she had undergone what might have laid low a strong man, and the strength which had barely carried her to the door of the inn had there left her utterly; and so fierce was the attack that was now made upon her by this new illness that recovery seemed scarce possible.

The doctor was as non-committal as doctors usually are in a really dangerous case. It was evident, however, from the first, that her situation awakened in his mind the very deepest anxiety. He urged the landlady to keep the house in the quietest possible condition, and to see that she was never left without attendants. This the landlady promised to do, and was unremitting in her attentions.

But all the care of the attendants seemed useless. Deeper and deeper Edith descended into the abyss of suffering. Day succeeded to day, and found her worse. Fortunately she was not conscious of what she had to endure; but in that unconsciousness her mind wandered in delirium, and all the sorrows of the past were lived over again.

They knew not, those good kind souls who waited and watched at her bedside, what it was that thus rose before her, and distressed her in the visions of her distempered brain, but they could see that these were the result of deep grief and long sorrow, and therefore they pitied her more than ever. As her mind thus wandered, she talked incessantly, often in broken words, but often also in long connected sentences, and all these were intermingled with moans and sighs.

"This is heart-rending," said the doctor once. "It is her mind, poor lady, that has brought on this illness. In this case medicine is of no use. You can do more than I can. You must watch over her, and keep her as quiet as she can be kept."

All of which the landlady promised more fervently than ever, and kept her promise too.

But in spite of all this care, the fever and the delirium grew worse. The events of her Dalton life rose before her to the exclusion of all other memories, and filled all her thoughts. In her fancies she again lived that life of mingled anxiety and fear, and chafed and raged and trembled by turns at the restraint which she felt around her. Then she tried to escape, but escape was impossible. Then she seemed to speak with some one who promised deliverance. Eagerly and earnestly she implored this one to assist her, and mentioned plans of escape.

Most of all, however, her thoughts turned to that scene in the Dalton vaults. The dead seemed all around. Amidst the darkness she saw the ghosts of her ancestors. They

H

114 THE LIVING LINK.

frowned menacingly upon her, as on one who was bringing dishonor upon a noble name. They pointed at her scornfully with their wan fingers. Deep moans showed the horror of her soul, but amidst these moans she protested that she was innocent. Then her flight from the Hall came up before her. She seemed to be wandering through woods and thickets and swamps, over rocks and fallen trees. "Shall I never get out?" she murmured. "Shall I never get to the wall? I shall perish in this forest. I am sinking in this mire." Then she saw some enemy. "It is he!" she murmured, in low thrilling tones. "He is coming! I will never go back—no, never! I will die first! I have my dagger—I will kill him! He shall never take me there —never, never, never! I will kill him—I will kill him!"

After which came a low groan, followed by a long silence.

So she went on in her agony, but her delirious words carried no connected meaning to her attendants. They could only look at one another inquiringly, and shake their heads. "She has been unhappy in her married life, poor dear," said the landlady once, with a sigh; and this seemed to be the general impression, and the only one which they gathered from her words.

Thus a fortnight passed away.

At length the lowest stage of the disease was reached. It was the turning-point, and beyond that lay either death or recovery. All night long the landlady watched beside the bed of the poor sufferer, who now lay in a deep sleep, scarce breathing, while the doctor, who came in at midnight, remained till morning.

Morning came at length, and Edith awaked. The delirium had passed. She looked around inquiringly, but could recall nothing.

"Auntie dear," she said, feebly, "where are you?"

"There isn't no auntie, dear," said the landlady, gently. "You are at Dalton Inn. But don't speak, dearie—you are too weak."

"Dalton Inn," repeated Edith, in a faint voice. She looked puzzled, for she was as yet too confused to remember. Gradually, however, memory awaked, and though the recollection of her illness was a blank, yet the awful life that she had lived, and her flight from that life, with all its accompaniments, came gradually back.

She looked at the landlady with a face of agony.

"Promise," said she, faintly.

"Promise what, dearie?"

"Promise—that—you will not—send me away."

"Lord love you! send you away? Not me."

"Promise," said Edith, in feverish impa-

tience, "that you will not let them take me —till I want to go."

"Never; no one shall touch a hair of your head, dearie—till you wish it."

The tone of the landlady gave Edith even more confidence than her words. "God bless you!" she sighed, and turned her head away.

A week passed, and Edith continued to get better every day. Although her remembrances were bitter and her thoughts most distressing, yet there was something in her present situation which was, on the whole, conducive to health. For the first time in many months she felt herself free from that irksome and galling control which had been so maddening to her proud nature. Her life in Dalton Hall had been one long struggle, in which her spirit had chafed incessantly at the barriers around it, and had well-nigh worn itself out in maintaining its unconquerable attitude. Now all this was over. She trusted this honest and tenderhearted landlady. It was the first frank and open face which she had seen since she left school. She knew that here at last she would have rest, at least until her recovery. What she might do then was another question, but the answer to this she chose to put off.

But all this time, while Edith had been lying prostrate and senseless at the inn, a great and mighty excitement had arisen and spread throughout the country, and all men were discussing one common subject—the mysterious disappearance of Captain Dudleigh.

He had become well known in the village, where he had resided for some time. His rank, his reputed wealth, and his personal appearance had all made him a man of mark. His marriage with Miss Dalton, who was known to be his cousin, had been publicly announced, and had excited very general surprise, chiefly because it was not known that Miss Dalton had returned. The gentry had not called on the bride, however, partly on account of the cloud that hung over the Dalton name, but more especially on account of the air of mystery that hung about the marriage, and the impression that was prevalent that calls were not expected.

The marriage had been largely commented upon, but had been generally approved. It had taken place within the family, and the stain on the Dalton name could thus be obliterated by merging it with that of Dudleigh. It seemed, therefore, wise and appropriate and politic, and the reserve of the married couple was generally considered as a mark of delicacy, good taste, and graceful respect for public opinion.

Captain Dudleigh had at first been associated with a friend and relative of his, Lieutenant Dudleigh, who had made himself quite popular in the outside world.

Neither of them, however, had gone into society. It was understood that Lieutenant Dudleigh had come simply for the purpose of being the captain's groomsman, and when, after the marriage, he disappeared, nothing more was thought about him.

Occupying as he did this place in the attention of the county people, Captain Dudleigh's disappearance created an excitement which can easily be imagined. Who first started the report could not be found out, but no sooner had it been started than it spread like wild-fire.

Moreover, in spite of the landlady's care, they had heard of Edith's flight and illness, and naturally associated these two startling facts together. The Dalton name was already covered with deep disgrace, and that another tragedy should take place in connection with it was felt to be very natural. Week after week passed on, and still there were no tidings of the missing man. With the lapse of each week the excitement only increased. Throughout the whole county this was the common topic of conversation. It was matter for far more than the ordinary nine days' wonder, for about this there was the fascination and the horror of an impenetrable mystery.

For it was universally felt that in some way or other this mystery was connected with Edith, and that its solution lay with her. It was universally known that she had fled from Dalton Hall in a most suspicious and unaccountable manner, and that Captain Dudleigh had disappeared on that very night. It was natural, therefore, that every body should think of her as being, to some extent at least, aware of the fate of Dudleigh, and that she alone could account for it.

And so the excitement grew stronger and stronger every day. Gradually the whole public came to know something about the circumstances of the ill-fated marriage. There seemed to be some power at work which sent forth fresh intelligence at various intervals to excite the public mind. It was not Wiggins, for he kept himself in strict seclusion; and people who went to stare at the gates of Dalton Park found nothing for their pains. It could not have been the vicar, for his terror had reduced him to a state of simple imbecility. There was some other cause, and that cause seemed always at work.

From this mysterious cause, then, the public gained a version of the story of that marriage, which was circulated every where. Miss Dalton, it was said, had fallen in love with Captain Dudleigh, but her guardian, Wiggins, had resisted her inclinations. She determined to get married in spite of him, and Captain Dudleigh had a clergyman brought into the park, who performed the ceremony secretly. After the marriage, however, it was said, Captain Dudleigh treated his wife badly, and clamored for money to pay his debts. His wife suspected that he had married her for this sole purpose. They quarreled incessantly. Her health broke down through grief and disappointment, and she was ill for a long time. After her recovery they had several stormy interviews, in which she had threatened his life. It was said that she always carried a dagger, with which she had sworn to kill him. She had told him to his face that she would have "his heart's blood."

Such was the story that circulated far and wide among all classes. None had seen Edith personally except the doctor and those at the inn; and the general impression about her was that she was a fierce, bold, impetuous woman, with iron resolution and masculine temper. So, on the whole, public opinion ran high against her, and profound sympathy was felt for the injured husband.

All this was not confined to the county. The metropolitan papers had mentioned it and discussed it, and the "Continued Disappearance of Captain Dudleigh" was for a long time the standing heading of many paragraphs.

But during all this time Edith remained at the inn in complete seclusion, recovering slowly but surely. In that seclusion she was utterly ignorant of the excitement which she had caused, and, indeed, was not aware that she was talked of at all. The papers were all kindly kept out of her sight, and as she had never been accustomed to read them, she never thought of asking for them. But the public feeling had at last reached that point at which it demanded, with resistless voice, an inquiry after the missing man.

CHAPTER XXXVIII.
THE OLD WELL.

PUBLIC feeling had grown so strong that it could no longer be disregarded, and the authorities had to take up the case. It was enforced upon their attention in many ways. The whole county urged it upon them, and journals of note in different parts of the kingdom denounced their lethargy. Under these circumstances they were compelled to take some action.

Wiggins had foreseen this, and to guard against this necessity he had himself done all in his power to search after the missing man. He had put the case in the hands of detectives, who had carried on an investigation in all quarters, and in every possible way; but to no purpose, and with no result. When at length the authorities came, he informed them of his search and its failure, but assured them that he still believed that Captain Dudleigh was alive. His theory was that, being heavily in debt, he had taken this mode of eluding his creditors, and after causing it to be believed that he was dead, he had quietly disappeared, and was now enjoying himself somewhere on the Continent. No one else, however, shared this opinion, and those who came to the search had no doubt that the missing man had been murdered. So they instituted a regular search over the whole estate. They began with the Hall, and went through every part of it. Then they turned their attention to the grounds. These were extensive, and it seemed probable that somewhere among the groves or swamps the remains might be found. They searched the chapel and the vaults. They dragged the pond in front of the house. In all this Wiggins lent his active assistance toward furthering the ends of justice, but at the same time retained the firmest conviction that it was a trick of Dudleigh's, and that he was now in foreign parts.

At length some of those who had been going the rounds of the wall returned to the house, carrying something, the sight of which produced a profound excitement. It was the hook and rope by which Edith had sought to escape. They found it hanging upon the wall, and every one recognized at a glance the intention of this rope-ladder. But the thing that produced the strongest excitement was something else. They had found it lying among the grass at the foot of the ladder, having evidently been dropped by some fugitive as an impediment, or thrown away as useless. It was a dagger, which, from being so long exposed to the weather, was covered with rust, but was still sharp and deadly.

This dagger seemed at once to confirm the general impression. It showed that one of the fugitives of that night—the one who had escaped—had been armed with a deadly weapon. Every one knew who the one was who had escaped. Every one had already suspected her. Her wild flight, her terrible agitation, her long illness—all had been known. What else could cause such a state of things but the dread remembrance of some dark crime? And now this dagger lay before them, the silent proof of the guilt of her who had left it there.

Upon Wiggins the effect was crushing. His tongue was paralyzed. He kept aloof after that, with despair on his face, and surveyed the proceedings at a distance. Not so Mrs. Dunbar. All this time she had been feverish and agitated, sometimes following the officers, at other times retiring. Upon her the sight of that dagger acted like something that confirmed the worst of her fears, and she burst forth into wild wails and lamentations. She then urged the officers to renewed search, and finally told them all about her own discovery of the empty rooms on that eventful morning, and the singular behavior of the dog.

The mention of this created new excitement, and they at once asked where the dog now was. Mrs. Dunbar did not know. The dog had disappeared most mysteriously, and they had seen nothing of him for a long time. They then asked to be taken to the place where the dog had stationed himself. Mrs. Dunbar, still wild with excitement, led the way there. Arriving at the spot, they examined it narrowly, but found nothing. It was grass, which had not been touched for years. No body lay buried beneath that old turf, as was plainly evident. They then went to the out-houses, toward which Mrs. Dunbar told them the dog had kept his face turned for some time when she had first seen him; but here they found nothing whatever.

It was now late, and they began to think of retiring, when suddenly one of the party, who had been walking in the rear of the stables, gave a call which drew them all in that direction. Upon reaching him they found him standing at the edge of a pit, which looked like an old well. Over this there was still the frame of what had been the well-house, and the well itself was very deep. Kneeling, they all peered into the black depths beneath them, but discovered nothing. One of them dropped a stone, and the sound far below showed that the bottom lay at least sixty or eighty feet from the surface.

"How long since this well has been used?" asked the sheriff.

"Many years," said Mrs. Dunbar.

"Did you examine it?"

"We never thought of doing so."

"Well, we may as well try it. Can we have a rope?"

"Certainly," said Mrs. Dunbar, who at once went to the house, and soon returned with Hugo, who carried a long stout rope.

Now it remained to explore the well, and to do this it would be necessary for some one to descend. But no difficulty was found in this. By this time all had been stimulated to the highest degree by the excitement of the search, and there was something in the look of the well which made it seem like the very place for the hurried disposal of a body. Here, then, they were all convinced, if any where, they would be sure to come upon that which they sought. Accordingly several volunteered to go down; but the sheriff chose from among them the one who seemed fittest for that purpose, and to the others was allotted the task of lowering him. Some further time was taken up in making the necessary preparations for this; but at length these were all completed, and the man who was to go down, after binding one end of the rope about his chest and giving the other end to his companions, prepared to descend.

The well was not very wide, and was lined around its sides with rough stones. In the interstices between these he inserted his feet and hands, and thus he let himself down, descending gradually.

The others knelt around the mouth of the well, holding the rope, and letting it pass through their hands as their companion descended, peering silently into the dark with eager eyes, and listening breathlessly to the dull sounds made by the man below as he descended further and further.

At last all was still. From below there came no sound. He had reached the bottom. More anxiously than ever they tried to pierce through the gloom, but that gloom was impenetrable. Their companion delayed long. They began to feel uneasy.

At length they heard sounds, and knew that he was ascending. With what intelligence? What had he found in that awful abyss? This was the question which was suggested to every heart, but a question which no one could answer. They lent their assistance, and pulled at the rope to help their companion. Nearer and nearer he came, and still nearer, until at last he was within reach. A few moments more and he emerged from the mouth of the well, and falling forward, he lay for a moment motionless.

They all rushed to his assistance, but he shook them off and rose to his feet.

"Did you find any thing?"

"Yes," said the man, in a hollow voice.

"What?" cried all, in breathless suspense.

"You shall see. Bring lights here, somebody. It's getting too dark for this business."

Hugo was at once dispatched to the Hall by Mrs. Dunbar for lights. There was by this time every necessity for them. Much time had been taken up with their preparations, and the shadows of evening had already gathered about them. While Hugo was gone they all questioned their companion, but he refused to say any thing.

"Don't ask me," he replied. "Wait and see for yourselves."

At this answer there was but one conviction in the minds of all, which was that the object of their search had been found. But there was now no further delay. Hugo soon returned with a lantern, and the man prepared to descend once more. The lantern he hung about his neck, and taking another piece of rope with him, the end of which was left with those above, he again went down. This time he was gone longer than before. Those above peering through the gloom could see a faint light far below, and the shadowy outline of their companion. At length he began to ascend, and in due time reached the top.

"There," said he; "you may pull on that line. I have fastened it so that it 'll hold."

Saying this, he flung himself exhausted on the grass, and unslung the lantern and unbound the rope.

The others pulled. There was a heavy weight at the end of the rope. They could all conjecture well what that dead-weight might be. But the fierce curiosity that now animated them stimulated them to put forth all their strength in a series of vigorous pulls. Nearer and nearer came that weight to the top. At last it hung just beneath them. Half a dozen hands were stretched out, and in an instant it was jerked out and lay upon the grass.

The sheriff seized the lantern and held it up. The scene was one of horror. All around was the gloom of night, the shadowy outline of trees and of the out-houses. A flickering light revealed a group of men surrounding some object on the grass, upon which they gazed in silent awe.

It was a shapeless, sodden mass, but the human outline was preserved, and the clothes were there, recognizable. It was a grisly, a hideous sight, and it held them all spellbound.

But suddenly the silence was broken. A wild shriek burst forth from Mrs. Dunbar, who the next instant fell forward upon the hideous object. Hugo seized her and raised her up. She was senseless.

"What is this?" cried the stern voice of Wiggins, who at that moment had come to the place.

"Mrs. Dunbar has fainted," said the sheriff; and then he pointed silently to the Thing that lay in the midst of the circle of spectators.

Wiggins looked at it, and seemed turned to stone. Then a shudder passed through him. Then he turned away.

As he walked he staggered like one who has received some terrible blow, and staggering on in this way, he passed out of sight into the gloom. After this Mrs. Dunbar was carried into the house by Hugo.

There was silence for a long time.

"The head is gone!" said the sheriff at length, in a low voice.

"Yes," said another; "it's been long in the water."

"Water couldn't do it," said the sheriff; "it was gone before it went into the water."

"What was that for?"

"To prevent identification," said the sheriff, in a significant tone.

The remains were in due time conveyed to an appropriate place, together with the rope and the dagger. On the following day a search was made for the missing head. The well was pumped dry, a task in which there was little difficulty, as there was little more than two feet of water in it, but nothing of the kind was found. Then they dragged the pond, but without result. The search was also continued elsewhere, but it was equally unsuccessful.

It was then concluded that the murderer had removed the head of his victim to prevent identification, and had buried it somewhere, but that the traces of burial had been obliterated by the lapse of time. The only wonder was that the clothes should have been allowed to remain by one who had been so much on his guard as to decapitate his victim.

CHAPTER XXXIX.

THE CORONER'S INQUEST.

THE remains were deposited in a proper place, and a coroner's inquest was held at once, at which the usual examination of witnesses was conducted.

Wiggins was examined first. He showed great constraint. He had not much to say, however, about the disappearance of Captain Dudleigh, for he had been absent at that time, and he could only state what took place after his return. But in the course of these inquiries much was extorted from him relative to Edith's position at Dalton Hall, her marriage, and the terms on which she had been living with her husband. His answers were given with extreme hesitation and marked reluctance, and it was only by the utmost persistence that they were wrung from him.

The porter was examined, and in the course of the inquiry that scene at the gates when Edith tried to escape was revealed.

Hugo was examined. It was found out that he had overheard the conversation between Edith and Captain Dudleigh at their last interview. Hugo's answers were given with as much reluctance as those of Wiggins, but he was not able to evade the questions, and all that he knew was drawn from him. But Hugo's remembrance of words was not very accurate, and he could not give any detailed report of the conversation which he had overheard. Several things, however, had been impressed upon his memory. One was the occasion when Edith drew a dagger upon Captain Dudleigh, and left the room with it in her hand; another was when, in her last interview with him, she menaced his life, and threatened to have his "*heart's blood.*" So it was that Hugo had understood Edith's words.

Mrs. Dunbar was examined, and gave her testimony with less hesitation. She was deathly pale, and weak and miserable. She spoke with difficulty, but was eager to bear witness to the noble character of Captain Dudleigh. She certainly showed nothing like hate toward Edith, but at the same time showed no hesitation to tell all about her. She told about Captain Dudleigh's first visits, and about the visits of his friend, who had assumed his name, or had the same name.

She told how Edith had been warned, and how she scorned the warning. From her was elicited the story of Edith's return after her marriage, her illness, recovery, and desperate moods, in which she seemed transformed, as Mrs. Dunbar expressed it, to a "fury." The account of her discovery of the flight of Edith and the captain was given with much emotion, but with simple truth.

Mr. Munn was also examined about the marriage. He had not yet recovered from the agitation into which he had been thrown during his interview with Wiggins, but seemed in a state of chronic fright.

After these witnesses one other yet remained. It was one whose connection with these events was the closest of all—one upon whom that jury already looked as guilty of a terrible crime—as the one who had inflicted with her own hand that death whose cause they were investigating.

There was no doubt now in any mind. The remains had been identified by all the witnesses. The head had been removed, and had not been found, but the clothes were known to all. By these they judged the remains to be the body of Captain Dudleigh. Wiggins alone hesitated—but it was only hesitation; it was not denial.

When Edith was summoned before the coroner's jury, it was the very first intelligence that she had received of an event in which she was so deeply concerned. The landlady had heard all about the search and its results; but true to her determination to spare Edith all trouble, she had not allowed any news of these proceedings to be communicated to her. When the official appeared with his abrupt summons to attend, the shock was terrible, but there was nothing left except submission. A few brief answers to her hurried and agitated questions put her in possession of the chief facts of the case. On her way to the place she said not a word. The landlady went with her to take care of her, but Edith did not take any notice of her.

As she entered the room where the examination was going on, the scene that presented itself was one which might well have appalled a stouter heart than that of Edith, and which, coming as it did after the shock of this sudden surprise, and in the train of all that she had already suffered, gave to her a sharp pang of intolerable anguish, and filled her soul with horror unspeakable.

The rope-ladder lay there with its hook, with which she had effected her escape, and beside these was the dagger which more than once she had interposed between herself and her fierce aggressor; but it was not these that she saw; something else was there which fixed and enchained her gaze, which held her with a terrible fascination.

"WITH A LOUD CRY, SHE HALF TURNED."

A sheet was thrown over it, but the outlines of that which lay beneath indicated a human form, and the information which Edith had already received made her well aware whose that form was supposed to be. But she said nothing; she stood rigid, horror-stricken, overwhelmed, and looked at it with staring eyes and white lips.

The coroner made some remarks, consisting of the usual formulas, something like an apology for the examination, a hint that it might possibly affect herself, and a warning that she should be very careful not to say any thing that might inculpate herself.

To all this Edith paid no attention. She did not appear to have heard it. She stood, as the coroner spoke, in the same attitude as before, with her eyes set in the same rigid stare. As the coroner ceased, he stepped forward and drew away the sheet.

There it lay at last—unveiled, revealed to her eyes—the abhorrent Thing, whose faint outline had chilled her very soul, its aspect hideous, frightful, unendurable! As the sheet fell away, and all was revealed before her, she could restrain herself no longer; the strain was too great; with a loud cry, she half turned and tried to run. The next instant the landlady caught her as she was falling senseless to the floor.

The examination of Mrs. Dudleigh was postponed. On the whole, however, it was afterward considered unnecessary. Enough had been gathered from the other witnesses to enable the jury to come to a conclusion. It was felt, also, that Mrs. Dudleigh ought to have a chance; though they believed her guilty, they felt sorry for her, and did not wish her to criminate herself by any rash words. The result was that they brought in a verdict of murder against Mrs. Leon Dudleigh.

CHAPTER XL.
A STRANGE CONFESSION.

THE news of Edith's arrest spread like wild-fire, and the event became soon the subject of universal conversation. Rumors of all sorts arose, as is natural under such circumstances, most of which were adverse to the accused. People remembered against the daughter the crimes of the father. It was *bad blood*, they said, which she had inherited; it was an evil race to which she belonged, and the murderous tendency was hereditary.

The examination at the inquest had made known the general facts of her story, out of which public gossip constructed another story to suit itself. Mrs. Dudleigh had been found troublesome and dangerous all along, so much so that it became necessary to keep her within the grounds. When Captain Dudleigh was paying attentions to her, she treated him with perfect brutality. On one occasion she struck him with her whip, and tried to run away. Captain Dudleigh had sent his friend, or relative, Lieutenant Dudleigh, to bring about a reconciliation. This was so well managed that the two resumed their former relations, and she even consented to make a runaway match with him. This, however, was not out of love so much as to spite her guardian.

After this marriage she took a violent dislike to her husband, and pretended to be ill, or perhaps suffered real illness, the natural result of her fierce, unbridled temper. Her husband found it impossible to live with her. The few interviews which they had were very stormy. Over and over again she threatened his life. At length she beguiled him into the park on some unknown pretext, and there, with that dagger which she had so often flourished in his face, she shed that very "*heart's blood*" which she had threatened to take. The murder was evidently a preconcerted act. She must have done it deliberately, for she had prepared the means of secret escape. She deliberately tried to conceal her act, and after removing his head, and burying it, she had thrown the body into the old well. But "*murder will out,*" etc., etc.; and with this and other similar maxims Edith's condemnation was settled by the public mind.

Thus Edith was in prison, held there under a terrible charge, for which there was proof that was appalling in its character. The body found and identified seemed to plead against her; circumstances inculpated her; motives were assigned to her sufficiently strong to cause the act; her own words and acts all tended to confirm her guilt.

After all, however, this last blow was not so crushing a one as some others which she had received in the course of her life. The most terrible moment perhaps had been that one when she was taken and confronted with the horrible remains. After that shock had subsided she rallied somewhat; and when her arrest took place she was not unprepared.

If the shock of the arrest had thus been less severe than might be supposed, so also was she less affected by her imprisonment

than another person would have been in such a situation. The reason of this is evident. She had endured so much that this seemed an inferior affliction. The anguish which she had known could not be increased by this. At Dalton Hall she had become habituated to imprisonment, and of a far more galling kind to her than this. She had been in the power of a tyrant, at his mercy, and shut out from all means of communicating with the world at large. Her soul had perpetually fretted and chafed against the barriers by which she was confined, and the struggle within herself was incessant. Afterward there had been the worse infliction of that mock marriage, and the unspeakable dread of a new tyrant who called himself her husband. No prison could equal the horrors which she had known at Dalton Hall. Here in the jail her situation was at least known. From Wiggins she was saved; from her false husband rescued forever. She was now not in the power of a private tyrant, exercising his usurped authority over her from his own desire, and with his will as his only law; but she was in the hands of the nation, and under the power of the national law. So, after all, she knew less grief in that prison cell than in the more luxurious abode of Dalton Hall, less sorrow, less despair. Her mood was a calm and almost apathetic one, for the great griefs which she had already endured had made her almost indifferent to any thing that life might yet have to offer.

Two days after her arrest word was brought to Edith that a lady wished to see her. Full of wonder who it could be, and in doubt whether it could be Miss Plympton, or only Mrs. Dunbar, Edith eagerly directed that the visitor should be admitted.

Thereupon a lady dressed in black entered the chamber. A heavy black veil was over her face, which she raised as she entered, and stood before Edith with downcast eyes. There was something in that face which seemed strangely familiar to Edith, and yet she found herself quite unable to think who the lady could be. She thought over all the faces that she had known in her school days. She thought over the faces at Dalton Hall. Suddenly, as the lady raised her eyes, there was an additional revelation in them which at once told Edith all. She started back in amazement.

"Lieutenant Dudleigh!" she cried.

The lady bowed her head, and said, in a low voice,

"Fortescue is my real name."

A suspicion of this sort had once flashed across Edith's mind. It was during the altercation at the Dalton chapel. Still, as this suspicion was thus confirmed, her surprise was extreme, and she said not a word, but looked steadily at her. And in the midst of other thoughts and feelings she could not

"BUT EVEN NOW I WOULD BE WILLING TO DIE FOR HIM."

help seeing that great changes had come over Miss Fortescue, as she called herself, in addition to those which were consequent upon her resumption of feminine attire. She was pale and thin, and looked ten years older than she used to look. Evidently she had undergone great suffering. There were marks of deep grief on her face. Much Edith marveled to see that one who had acted so basely was capable of suffering such grief. She could not help being reminded of that expression which she had seen on this same face when they were arranging that false marriage; but now that deep remorse which then had appeared seemed stamped permanently there, together with a profound dejection that was like despair. All this was not without its effect on Edith. It disarmed her natural indignation, and even excited pity.

"Miss Dalton," said the visitor, in a voice that was quite different from the one which she remembered—a voice that was evidently her natural one, while that other must have been assumed—"Miss Dalton, I have come to try to do something, if possible, toward making amends for—for a frightful injury. I know well that amends can never be made; but at least I can do a little. Will you listen to me for a few moments, not with regard to me, but solely for your own sake?"

Edith said nothing, but bowed her head slightly. She did not yet know how far this betrayer might be sincere, and wished to hear and judge for herself.

"Will you let me, first of all, make a confession to you of my great sin?" she continued, slowly and painfully. "You will understand better your own present situation. I assure you it will be a help to you toward freeing yourself. I don't ask you to believe —I only ask you to listen."

Edith again bowed.

"I will tell you all, then. I was an actress in London; my name was Fortescue. I was a celebrity at Covent Garden. It was there that I first met Captain Dudleigh. I need say no more about him than this: I loved him passionately, with a frenzy and a devotion that you can not understand, and my fate is this—that I love him yet. I know that he is a coward and a villain and a traitor, but even now I would be willing to die for him."

The voice was different—how different!— and the tone and manner still more so. The careless "Little Dudleigh" had changed into a being of passion and ardor and fire. Edith tried to preserve an incredulous state of mind, but in vain. She could not help feeling that there was no acting here. This at least was real. This devoted love could not be feigned.

"He swore he loved me," continued Miss Fortescue. "He asked me to be his wife. We were married."

"Married!" cried Edith, in a tone of profoundest agitation.

"Yes," said Miss Fortescue, solemnly, "we were married. But listen. I believed that the marriage was real. He told some story about his friends being unwilling—about his father, who, he said, would disown him if he found it out. He urged a private marriage, without any public announcement. He knew a young clergyman, he said, who would do him that favor. For my part I had not the slightest objection. I loved him too well to care about a formal wedding. So wo were married in his rooms, with a friend of his for witness.

"He set up a modest little house, where we lived for about a year. At first my life was one of perfect happiness, but gradually I saw a change coming over him. He was terribly in debt, and was afraid of utter ruin. From hints that dropped from him, I began to suspect that he meditated some sort of treachery toward me. Then, for the first time, I was alarmed at the privacy of our marriage. Still, I was afraid to say any thing to him, for fear that it might hasten any treachery toward me which he might meditate. I loved him as dearly as ever, but I found out that he was base and unprincipled, and felt that he was capable of any thing. I had to content myself with watching him, and at the same time tried to be as cheerful as possible.

"At length he heard about you, and came to Dalton. His father sent him, he said. I followed him here. At first he was angry, but I persuaded him to take me as an assistant. He did not want to be known at the Hall, for he wished to see first what could be done with Wiggins. He made me disguise myself as a man, and so I called myself Lieutenant Dudleigh. He went to Dalton Hall, and discovered that the porter was some old criminal who had done his crime on the Dudleigh estates—poaching, I think, or murder, or both. On seeing Wiggins, he was able to obtain some control over him—I don't know what. He never would tell me.

"By this time I found out what I had all along suspected—that he came here for your sake. He was terribly in debt. A dark abyss lay before him. He began to feel me to be an incumbrance. He began to wish that he was a free man, so that he might marry you. I saw all this with a grief that I can not tell.

"We made several calls on you. I went as his mother, Mrs. Mowbray."

"Mrs. Mowbray! You?" exclaimed Edith, in wonder.

"Did I act my part well?" said Miss Fortescue, mournfully. "It was an easy enough part. I believe I succeeded in making myself utterly detestable. Captain Dudleigh was bitterly vexed at my manner. He wanted me to gain your confidence. That, however, I could not yet bring myself to do. His own intercourse with you was even worse. Your attempt to escape was a terrible blow

to his hopes. Yet he dared not let you escape. That would have destroyed his plans utterly. You would have gone to your friends—to Miss Plympton—and you would have found out things about him which would have made his projects with reference to you out of the question."

"Miss Plympton!" cried Edith. "How could I have gone to her? She is away."

"That was one of my lies," said Miss Fortescue. "Unfortunately, she is really ill, but she is still in the country, at her school. I myself went there to tell her about you only two days ago, but found that she had been ill for some time, and could not see any one."

Edith sighed heavily. For an instant hope had come, and then it had died out.

"He made me go again to see you, but with what result you know. I was fairly driven away at last. This made him terribly enraged against you and against me, but I quieted him by reminding him that it was only his own fault. It brought about a change in his plans, however, and forced him to put me more prominently forward. Then it was that he devised that plan by which I was to go and win your confidence. I can not speak of it; you know it all. I wish merely to show you what the pressure was that he put on me.

"'Dear wife,' said he to me one day, in his most affectionate tone—'my own Lucy, you know all about my affairs, and you know that I am utterly ruined. If I can not do something to save myself, I see no other resource but to blow my brains out. I will do it, I swear I will, if I can not get out of these scrapes. My father will not help me. He has paid all my debts twice, and won't do it again. Now I have a proposal to make. It's my only hope. You can help me. If you love me, you will do so. Help me in this, and then you will bind your husband to you by a tie that will be stronger than life. If you will not do this simple thing, you will doom me to death, for I swear I will kill myself, or at least, if not that, I will leave you forever, and go to some place where I can escape my creditors.'

"This was the way that he forced his plan upon me. You know what it was. I was to see you, and do—what was done.

"'You are my wife,' said he, earnestly. 'I can not marry her—I don't want to—but I do want to get money. Let me have the control of the Dalton estates long enough to get out of my scrapes. You can't be jealous of her. She hates me. I hate her, and love you—yes, better than life. When she finds out that I am married to her she will hate me still more. The marriage is only a form, only a means of getting money, so that I may live with my own true wife, my darling Lucy, in peace, and free from this intolerable despair.'

THE LIVING LINK. 123

"By such assurances as these—by dwelling incessantly upon the fact that I was his wife, and that this proposed marriage to you was an empty form—upon your hate for him, and the certainty of your still greater hate, he gradually worked upon me. He appealed to my love for him, my pity for his situation, and to every feeling that could move me in his favor. Then it was that he told me frankly the name of the clergyman who had married us, and the witness. The clergyman's name was Porter, and the witness was a Captain Reeves. So, in spite of my abhorrence of the act, I was led at last, out of my very love to him, and regard for his future, to acquiesce in his plan. Above all, I was moved by one thing upon which he laid great stress.

"'It will really be for her benefit,' he would say. 'She will not be married at all. I shall take some of her money, certainly; but she is so enormously rich that she will never feel it; besides, if I didn't get it, Wiggins would. Better for her cousin to have it. It will be all in the family. Above all, this will be the means, and the only means, of freeing her from that imprisonment in which Wiggins keeps her. That is her chief desire. She will gain it. After I pay my debts I will explain all to her; and what is more, when I succeed to my own inheritance, as I must do in time, I shall pay her every penny.'

"By such plausible reasoning as this he drove away my last objection, and so, without any further hesitation, I went about that task.

"But oh, how hard it was! Over and over again I felt like giving up. But always he was ready to urge me on, until at last it was accomplished, and ended as you remember."

Miss Fortescue paused here, and made no reply. Edith said not a word. Why should she? What availed this woman's repentance now?

"I came here," continued Miss Fortescue at length, "first of all to explain this, but to tell you other things also. I must now tell you something which makes your position more painful than I thought it would be. I soon found out the full depth of Captain Dudleigh's villainy. While I thought that you only were deceived, I found that I was the one who was most deceived.

"After that marriage in the chapel we went back to Dalton, and there he abused me in the most frightful manner. He pretended to be enraged because I rebuked him in the chapel. His rage was only a pretense. Then it all came out. He told me plainly that my marriage with him was a mockery; that the man Porter who had married us was not a clergyman at all, but a creature of his whom he had bribed to officiate; and that Reeves was not a captain, and that his testimony in any case would be useless. All

this was crushing. It was something that was so entirely in accordance with my own fears that I had not a word to say. He railed at me like a madman, and informed me that he had only tolerated me here at Dalton so as to use me as his tool. And this was our last interview. He left me there, and I have never seen him since. He said he was your husband, and was going to live at Dalton. I could do nothing. I went, however, to the gates, got sight of Wiggins, and for your sake I told him all. I thought it was better for you to remain under the authority of Wiggins than to be in the power of such a villain as Captain Dudleigh. I told Wiggins also that I still had a hope that my marriage was valid. I went back at once to London, and tried to find out clergymen named Porter. I have seen several, and written to many others whose names I have seen on the church list, but none of them know any thing about such a marriage as mine. I began, therefore, to fear that he was right, and if so—I was not his wife."

Silence followed now for some time. Miss Fortescue was waiting to see the effect of her story, and Edith was meditating upon the facts with which this strange revelation dealt. Although she had been so great a sufferer, still she did not feel resentment now against this betrayer. For this one was no longer the miserable, perfidious go-between, but rather an injured wife led to do wrong by the pressure put upon her, and by her own love.

"Then that was not a mock marriage?" said she at last.

"By justice and right it was no marriage," said Miss Fortescue; "but how the law may regard it I do not know."

"Has Sir Lionel been heard of yet?" asked Edith, after another pause.

"Sir Lionel!" said Miss Fortescue, in surprise. "Oh, I had forgotten. Miss Dalton, that, I grieve to say, was all a fiction. He was never out of the country."

"Did you ever speak a word of truth to me?" asked Edith, indignantly.

Miss Fortescue was silent.

"At any rate, it is of no consequence now," said Edith. "Sir Lionel is nothing to me; for he must look with horror on one whom he believes to be the slayer of his son."

"Oh, Miss Dalton!" burst forth Miss Fortescue, "do not despair; he will be found yet."

"Found! He has been found. Did you not hear?"

"Oh, I don't mean that. I do not believe that it was him. I believe that he is alive. This is all a mistake. I will search for him. I do not believe that this is him. I believe he is alive. Oh, Miss Dalton, if I could only do this for you, I should be willing to die. But I will try; I know how to get on his track; I know where to go; I must hear of him, if he is alive. Try to have hope; do not despair."

Edith shook her head mournfully.

Miss Fortescue tried still further to lessen Edith's despair, and assured her that she had hopes herself of finding him before it was too late, but her words produced no effect.

"I do not ask you to forgive me," said Miss Fortescue; "that would be almost insolence; but I entreat you to believe that I will devote myself to you, and that you have one whose only purpose in life now is to save you from this fearful fate. Thus far you have known me only as a speaker of lies; but remember, I pray you, what my position was. I was playing a part—as Mrs. Mowbray—as Lieutenant Dudleigh—as Barber the lawyer—"

"Barber!" exclaimed Edith. "What! Barber too?"

"Yes," said Miss Fortescue, sadly; "all those parts were mine. It was easy to play them before one so honest and so unsuspecting; but oh, Miss Dalton, believe me, it is in playing a part only that I have deceived you. Now, when I no longer play a part, but come to you in my own person, I will be true. I will devote myself to the work of saving you from this terrible position in which I have done so much to place you."

Edith made no reply, and soon after Miss Fortescue departed, leaving her to her own reflections.

"HE SAW HER HEAD FALL."

CHAPTER XLI.

A REVELATION.

IF any thing could have added to the misery of Edith and her general despondency, it would have been the revelations of Miss Fortescue. It had certainly been bad enough to recall the treachery of a false friend; but the facts as just revealed went far beyond what she had imagined. They revealed such a long course of persistent deceit, and showed that she had been subject to such manifold, long-sustained, and comprehensive lying, that she began to lose faith in human nature. Whom now could she believe? Could she venture to put confidence in this confession of Miss Fortescue? Was that her real name, and was this her real story, or was it all some new piece of acting, contrived by this all-accomplished actor for the sake of dragging her down to deeper abysses of woe? She felt herself to be surrounded by remorseless enemies, all of whom were plotting against her, and in whose hearts there was no possibility of pity or remorse. Wiggins, the archenemy, was acting a part which was mysterious just now, but which nevertheless, she felt sure, was aimed at her very life. Mrs. Dunbar, she knew, was more open in the mani-

festation of her feelings, for she had taken up the cause of the murdered man with a warmth and vindictive zeal that showed Edith plainly what she might expect from her. Her only friend, Miss Plympton, was still lost to her; and her illness seemed probable, since, if it were not so, she would not keep aloof from her at such a moment as this. Hopeless as she had been of late, she now found that there were depths of despair below those in which she had thus far been —"in the lowest deep, a lower deep."

Such were her thoughts and feelings through the remainder of that day and through the following night. But little sleep came to her. The future stood before her without one ray of light to shine through its appalling gloom. On the next day her despair seemed even greater; her faculties seemed benumbed, and a dull apathy began to settle down over her soul.

From this state of mind she was roused by the opening of the door and the entrance of a visitor. Turning round, she saw Wiggins.

This was the first time that she had seen him since she left Dalton Hall, and in spite of that stolid and apathetic indifference which had come to her, she could not help being struck by the change which had come over him. His face seemed whiter, his hair grayer, his form more bent; his footsteps were feeble and uncertain; he leaned heavily upon his walking-stick; and in the glance that he turned toward her there was untold sympathy and compassion, together with a timid supplication that was unlike any thing which she had seen in him before. Edith neither said any thing nor did any thing. She looked at him with dull indifference. She did not move. The thought came to her that this was merely another move in that great game of treachery and fraud to which she had been a victim; that here was the archtraitor, the instigator of all the lesser movements, who was coming to her in order to carry out some necessary part.

Wiggins sat down wearily upon one of the rude chairs of the scantily furnished room, and after a brief silence, looking at her sadly, began.

"I know," said he, "how you misunderstand me, and how unwelcome I must be; but I had to come, so as to assure you that I hope to find this man who is missing. I— I hope to do so before the—the trial. I have been searching all along, but without success—thus far. I wish to assure you that I have found out a way by which you —will be saved. And if you believe me, I trust that you will—try—to—cherish more hope than you appear to be doing."

He paused.

Edith said nothing at all. She was silent partly out of apathy, and partly from a determination to give him no satisfaction, for she felt that any words of hers, no matter how simple, might be distorted and used against her.

Wiggins looked at her with imploring earnestness, and seemed to wait for her to say something. But finding her silent, he went on:

"Will you let me ask you one question? and forgive me for asking it; but it is of some importance to—to me—and to you. It is this: Did—did you see him at all—that night?"

"I have been warned," replied Edith, in a dull, cold tone, "to say nothing, and I intend to say nothing."

Wiggins sighed.

"To say nothing," said he, "is not always wise. I once knew a man who was charged with terrible crimes—crimes of which he was incapable. He was innocent, utterly. Not only innocent, indeed, but he had fallen under this suspicion, and had become the object of this charge, simply on account of his active efforts to save a guilty friend from ruin. His friend was the guilty one, and his friend was also his sister's husband; and this man had gone to try and save his friend, when he himself was arrested for that friend's crimes."

Wiggins did not look at Edith; his eyes were downcast. He spoke in a tone that seemed more like a soliloquy than any thing else. It was a tone, however, which, though low, was yet tremulous with ill-suppressed agitation.

"He was accused," continued Wiggins, "and if he had spoken and told what he knew, he might have saved his life. But if he had done this he would have had to become a witness, and stand up in court and say that which would ruin his friend. And so he could not speak. His lips were sealed. To speak would have been to inform against his friend. How could he do that? It was impossible. Yet some may think—you may think—that this man did wrong in allowing himself to be put in this false position. You may say that he had more than himself to consider—he had his family, his name, his —his wife, his child!

"Yes," resumed Wiggins, after a long pause, "this is all true, and he did consider them, all—all—all! He did not trifle with his family name and honor, but it was rather on account of the pride which he took in these that he kept his silence. He was conscious of his perfect innocence. He could not think it possible that such charges could be carried out against one like himself. He believed implicitly in the justice of the courts of his country. He thought that in a fair trial the innocent could not possibly be proclaimed guilty. More than all, he thought that his proud name, his stainless character, and even his wealth and position, would have shown the world that the charges were simply impossible. He thought that all men would have seen that for him to have done such things would involve insanity."

As Wiggins said this his voice grew more earnest and animated. He looked at Edith with his solemn eyes, and seemed as though he was pleading with her the cause of his friend—as though he was trying to show her how it had happened that the father had dishonored the name which the child must bear—as though he was justifying to the daughter, Edith Dalton, the acts of the father, Frederick Dalton.

"So he bore it all with perfect calmness," continued Wiggins, "and had no doubt that he would be acquitted, and thought that thus he would at least be able, without much suffering, to save his friend from ruin most terrific—from the condemnation of the courts and the fate of a felon."

Wiggins paused once more for some time. He was looking at Edith. He had expected some remark, but she had made none. In fact, she had regarded all this as a new trick of Wiggins—a transparent one too—the aim of which was to win her confidence by thus pretending to vindicate her father. He had already tried to work on her in that way, and had failed; and on this occasion he met with the same failure.

"There is no occasion for you to be silent, I think," said Wiggins, turning from the subject to the situation of Edith. "You have no friend at stake; you will endanger no one, and save yourself, by telling whether you are innocent or not."

These last words roused Edith. It was an allusion to her possible guilt. She determined to bring the interview to a close. She was tired of this man and his attempts to deceive her. It was painful to see through all this hypocrisy and perfidy at the very moment when they were being used against herself.

She looked at him with a stony gaze, and spoke in low, cold tones as she addressed him. "This is all useless. I am on my guard. Why you come here I do not know. Of course you wish to entrap me into saying something, so that you may use my words against me at the trial. You ask me if I saw this man on that night. You ask me if I am innocent. You well know that I am innocent. You, and you only, know who saw him last on that night; for as I believe in my own existence, so I believe, and affirm to your face, that this Leon Dudleigh was murdered by you, and you only!"

He looked at her fixedly as she said this, returning her stony gaze with a mournful look—a pitying look, full of infinite sadness and tenderness. He raised his hand deprecatingly, but said nothing until she had uttered those last words.

"Stop!" he said, in a low voice—"stay! I can not bear it."

He rose from his seat and came close to her. He leaned upon his stick heavily, and looked at her with eyes full of that same strange, inexplicable tenderness and compassion. Her eyes seemed fascinated by his, and in her mind there arose a strange bewilderment, an expectation of something she knew not what.

"Edith," said he, in a sweet and gentle voice, full of tender melancholy—"Edith, it would be sin in me to let you any longer heap up matter for future remorse; and even though I go against the bright hope of my life in saying this now, yet I must. Edith—"

He paused, looking at her, while she regarded him with awful eyes.

"Edith!" he said again—"my—my—child!"

There were tears in his eyes now, and there was on his face a look of unutterable love and unspeakable pity and forgiveness. He reached out his hand and placed it tenderly upon her head.

"Edith," he said again, "my child, you will never say these things again. I—I do not deserve them. I—am your—your father, Edith!"

At these words a convulsive shudder passed through Edith. He felt her frail form tremble, he saw her head fall, and heard a low sob that seemed torn from her.

She needed no more words than these. In an instant she saw it all; and though bewildered, she did not for a moment doubt his words. But her whole being was overwhelmed by a sudden and a sharp agony of remorse; for she had accustomed herself to

hate this man, and the irrepressible tokens of a father's love she had regarded as hypocrisy. She had never failed to heap upon that reverend head the deepest scorn, contumely, and insult. But a moment before she had hurled at him a terrible accusation. At him! At whom! At the man whose mournful destiny it had been all along to suffer for the sins of others; and she it was who had flung upon him an additional burden of grief.

But with all her remorse there were other feelings—a shrinking sense of terror, a recoil from this sudden discovery as from something abhorrent. This her father! That father's face and form had been stamped in her memory. For years, as she had lived in the hope of seeing him, she had quickened her love for him and fed her hopes from his portrait. But how different was this one! What a frightful change from the father that lived in her memory! The one was a young man in the flush and pride of life and strength—the other a woe-worn, grief-stricken sufferer, with reverend head, bowed form, and trembling limbs. Besides, she had long regarded him as dead; and to see this man was like looking on one who had risen from the dead.

In an instant, however, all was plain, and together with the discovery there came the pangs of remorse and terror and anguish. She could understand all. He, the escaped convict, had come to England, and was supposed to be dead. He had lived, under a false name, a life of constant and vigilant terror. He kept his secret from all the world. Oh, if he had only told her! Now the letter of Miss Plympton was all plain, and she wondered how she had been so blind.

"Oh!" she moaned, in a scarce audible voice, "why did you not tell me?"

"Oh, Edith darling! my child! my only love!" murmured Frederick Dalton, bending low over her, and infolding her trembling frame in his own trembling arms; "my sweet daughter, if you could only have known how I yearned over you! But I delayed to tell you. It was the one sweet hope of my life to redeem my name from its foul stain, and then declare myself. I wanted you to get your father back as he had left you, without this abhorrent crime laid to his charge. I did wrong not to trust you. It was a bitter, bitter error. But I had so set my heart on it. It was all for your sake, Edith—all, darling, for your sake!"

Edith could bear no more. Every one of these words was a fresh stab to her remorseful heart—every tone showed to her the depth of love that lay in that father's heart, and revealed to her the suffering that she must have caused. It was too much; and with a deep groan she sank away from his arms upon the floor. She clasped his knees

—she did not dare to look up. She wished only to be a suppliant. He himself had prophesied this. His terrible warnings sounded even now in her ears. She had only one thought—to humble herself in the dust before that injured father.

Dalton tried to raise her up.

"My darling!" he cried, "my child! you must not—you will break my heart!"

"Oh," moaned Edith, "if it is not already broken, how can you ever forgive me?—how can you call me your child?"

"My child! my child!" said Dalton. "It was for you that I lived. If it had not been for the thought of you, I should have died long since. It was for your sake that I came home. It is for you only that I live now. There is nothing for me to forgive. Look up at me. Let me see your darling face. Let me hear you say one word—only one word—the word that I have hungered and thirsted to hear. Call me father."

"Father! oh, father! dear father!" burst forth Edith, clinging to him with convulsive energy, and weeping bitterly.

"Oh, my darling!" said Dalton, "I was to blame. How could you have borne what I expected you to bear, when I would not give you my confidence? Do not let us speak of forgiveness. You loved your father all the time, and you thought that I was his enemy and yours."

Gradually Edith became calmer, and her calmness was increased by the discovery that her father was painfully weak and exhausted. He had been overwhelmed by the emotions which this interview had called forth. He now sat gazing at her with speechless love, holding her hands in his, but his breath came and went rapidly, and there was a feverish tremulousness in his voice and a flush on his pale cheeks which alarmed her. She tried to lessen his agitation by talking about her own prospects, but Dalton did not wish to.

"Not now, daughter," he said. "I will hear it all some other time. I am too weary. Let me only look at your dear face, and hear you call me by that sweet name, and feel my child's hands in mine. That will be bliss enough for this day. Another time we will speak about the—the situation that you are in."

As he was thus agitated, Edith was forced to refrain from asking him a thousand things which she was longing to know. She wished to learn how he had escaped, how he had made it to be believed that he was dead, and whether he was in any present danger. But all this she had to postpone. She had also to postpone her knowledge of that great secret—the secret that had baffled her, and which he had preserved inviolable through all these years. She now saw that her suspicions of the man "John Wiggins" must have been unfounded, and indeed the personality of "Wiggins" became a complete puzzle to her.

He bade her a tender adieu, promising to come early on the following day.

But on the following day there were no signs of him. Edith waited in terrible impatience, which finally deepened into alarm as his coming was still delayed. She had known so much of sorrow that she had learned to look for it, and began to expect some new calamity. Here, where she had found her father, where she had received his forgiveness for that which would never cease to cause remorse to herself, here, in this moment of respite from despair, she saw the black prospect of renewed misery. It was as though she had found him for a moment, only to lose him forever.

Toward evening a note was sent to her. She tore it open. It was from Mrs. Dunbar, and informed her that her father was quite ill, and was unable to visit her, but hoped that he might recover.

After that several days passed, and she heard nothing. At length another note came informing her that her father had been dangerously ill, but was now convalescent.

Other days passed, and Edith heard regularly. Her father was growing steadily better. On one of these notes he had written his name with a trembling hand.

And so amidst these fresh sorrows, and with her feelings ever alternating between hope and despair, Edith lingered on through the time that intervened until the day of the trial.

CHAPTER XLII.

THE TRIAL.

AT length the day for the trial arrived, and the place was crowded. At the appearance of Edith there arose a murmur of universal sympathy and pity. All the impressions which had been formed of her were falsified. Some had expected to see a coarse masculine woman; others a crafty, sinister face; others an awkward, ill-bred rustic, neglected since her father's trial by designing guardians. Instead of this there appeared before them a slender, graceful, youthful form, with high refinement and perfect breeding in every outline and movement. The heavy masses of her dark hair were folded across her brow, and wreathed in voluminous folds behind. Her pallid face bore traces of many griefs through which she had passed, and her large spiritual eyes had a piteous look as they wandered for a moment over the crowd.

No one was prepared to see any thing like this, and all hearts were at once touched. It seemed preposterous to suppose that one like her could be otherwise than innocent.

The usual formulas took place, and the trial began. The witnesses were those who had already been examined. It was rumored that Sir Lionel Dudleigh was to be brought forward, and "Wiggins," and Mrs. Dunbar, but not till the following day.

At the end of that day the opinion of the public was strongly in favor of Edith; but still there was great uncertainty as to her guilt or innocence. It was generally believed that she had been subject to too much restraint, and in a foolish desire to escape had been induced to marry Dudleigh. But she had found him a worse master than the other, and had hated him from the first, so that they had many quarrels, in which she had freely threatened his life. Finally both had disappeared on the same night. He was dead; she survived.

The deceased could not have committed suicide, for the head was missing. Had it not been for that missing head, the theory of suicide would have been plausible.

The second day of the trial came. Edith had seen her father on the previous evening, and had learned something from him which had produced a beneficial effect, for there was less terror and dejection in her face. This was the first time that she had seen him since his illness.

There was one in the hall that day who looked at her with an earnest glance of scrutiny as he took his place among the witnesses.

It was Sir Lionel Dudleigh, who had come here to give what testimony he could about his son. His face was as serene as usual; there was no sadness upon it, such as might have been expected in the aspect of a father so terribly bereaved; but the broad content and placid bonhomie appeared to be invincible.

The proceedings of this day were begun by an announcement on the part of the counsel for the defense, which fell like a thunder-clap upon the court. Sir Lionel started, and all in the court involuntarily stretched forward their heads as though to see better the approach of the astonishing occurrence which had been announced.

The announcement was simply this, that any further proceedings were useless, since the missing man himself had been found, and was to be produced forthwith. There had been no murder, and the body that had been found must be that of some person unknown.

Shortly after a group entered the hall.

First came Frederick Dalton, known to the court as "John Wiggins." He still bore traces of his recent illness, and, indeed, was not fit to be out of his bed, but he had dragged himself here to be present at this momentous scene. He was terribly emaciated, and moved with difficulty, supported by Mrs. Dunbar, who herself showed marks of suffering and exhaustion almost equal to his.

But after these came another, upon whom all eyes were fastened, and even Edith's gaze was drawn away from her father, to whom she had longed to fly so as to sustain his dear form, and fixed upon this new-comer.

Dudleigh! The one whom she had known as Mowbray. Dudleigh!

Yes, there he stood.

Edith's eyes were fixed upon him in speechless amazement.

It was Dudleigh, and yet it seemed as though it could not be Dudleigh.

There was that form and there was that face which had haunted her for so long a time, and had been associated with so many dark and terrible memories—the form and the face which were so hateful, which never were absent from her thoughts, and intruded even upon her dreams.

Yet upon that face there was now something which was not repulsive even to her. It was a noble, spiritual face. Dudleigh's features were remarkable for their faultless outline and symmetry, and now the expression was in perfect keeping with the beauty of physical form, for the old hardness had departed, and the deep stamp of sensuality and selfishness was gone, and the sinister look which had once marred those features could be traced there no more.

It was thinner than the face which Edith remembered, and it seemed to her as if it had been worn down by some illness. If so, it must have been the same cause which had imparted to those features the refinement and high bearing which were now visible there. There was the same broad brow covered with its clustering locks, the same penetrating eyes, the same square, strong chin, the same firm, resolute mouth, but here it was as though a finer touch had added a subtle grace to all these; for about that month there lingered the traces of gentleness and kindliness, like the remnant of sweet smiles; the glance of the eye was warmer and more human; there was also an air of melancholy, and over all a grandeur of bearing which spoke of high breeding and conscious dignity.

This man, with his earnest and even melancholy face and lofty bearing, did not seem like one who could have plotted so treacherously against a helpless girl. His aspect filled Edith with something akin to awe, and produced a profound impression upon the spectators. They forgot the hatred which they had begun to feel against Dudleigh in the living presence of the object of their hate, and looked in silence first at Edith, then at the new-comer, wondering why it was that between such as these there could be any thing less than mutual affection. They thought they could understand now why she should choose him as a husband.

They could not understand how such a husband could become hateful.

In all the court but one object seemed to attract Dudleigh, and that was Edith. His eyes had wandered about at first, and finally had rested on her. With a glance of profoundest and most gentle sympathy he looked at her, conveying in that one look enough to disarm even her resentment. She understood that look, and felt it, and as she looked at him in return she was filled with wonder.

Could such things be? she thought. Was this the man who had caused her so much suffering, who had blasted and blighted the hopes of her life? or, rather, had the man who had so wronged her been transformed to this? Impossible! As well might a fiend become changed to an archangel. And yet here he was. Evidently this was Dudleigh. She looked at him in speechless bewilderment.

The proceedings of the court went on, and Dudleigh soon explained his disappearance. As he spoke his voice confirmed the fact that he was Dudleigh; but Edith listened to it with the same feelings which had been excited by his face. It was the same voice, yet not the same; it was the voice of Dudleigh, but the coldness and the mockery of its intonations were not there. Could he have been playing a devil's part all along, and was he now coming out in his true character, or was this a false part? No; whatever else was false, this was not—that expression of face, that glance of the eye, those intonations, could never be feigned. So Edith thought as she listened.

Dudleigh's explanation was a simple one. He had not been very happy at Dalton Hall, and had concluded to go away that night for a tour on the Continent. He had left so as to get the early morning train, and had traveled on without stopping until he reached Palermo, from which he had gone to different places in the interior of Sicily, which he mentioned. He had climbed over the gate, because he was in too much of a hurry to wake the porter. He had left his valise, as he intended to walk. He had, of course, left his dog at Dalton, because he couldn't take him to the Continent. He had forgotten his watch, for the reason that he had slept longer than he intended, and dressed and went off in a great hurry. The pocket-book which he left was of no importance—contained principally memoranda, of no use to any but himself. He had no idea there would have been such a row, or he would not have gone in such a hurry. He had heard of this for the first time in Sicily, and would have come at once, but, unfortunately, he had an attack of fever, and could not return before.

Nothing could have been more natural and frank than Dudleigh's statement. A few questions were asked, merely to satisfy public curiosity. Every one thought that a trip to Sicily was a natural enough thing for one who was on such bad terms with his wife, and the suddenness of his resolution to go there was sufficient to account for the disorder in which he had left his room.

But all this time there was one in that court who looked upon the new-comer with far different feelings than those which any other had.

This was Sir Lionel Dudleigh.

He had heard the remark of the counsel that Dudleigh had returned, and looked toward the door as he entered with a smile on his face. As he saw Dudleigh enter he started. Then his face turned ghastly white, and his jaw fell. He clutched the railing in front of him with both hands, and seemed fascinated by the sight.

Near him stood Mrs. Dunbar, and Dalton leaned on her. Both of these looked fixedly at Sir Lionel, and noticed his emotion.

At the sound of Dudleigh's voice Sir Lionel's emotion increased. He breathed heavily. His face turned purple. His knuckles turned white as he grasped the railing. Suddenly, in the midst of Dudleigh's remarks, he started to his feet, and seemed about to say something. Immediately in front of him were Dalton and Mrs. Dunbar. At that instant, as he rose, Mrs. Dunbar laid her hand on his arm.

He looked at her with astonishment. He had not seen her before. She fixed her solemn eyes on him—those eyes to which had come a gloom more profound, and a sadness deeper than before. But Sir Lionel stared at her without recognition, and impatiently tried to shake off her hand.

"Who are you?" he said, suddenly, in a trembling voice—for there was something in this woman's face that suggested startling thoughts.

Mrs. Dunbar drew nearer to him, and in a whisper that thrilled through every fibre of Sir Lionel's frame, hissed in his ear, "*I am your wife—and here is my brother Frederick!*"

Over Sir Lionel's face there came a flash of horror, sudden, sharp, and overwhelming. He staggered and shrank back.

"Claudine!" he murmured, in a stifled voice.

"Sit down," whispered Lady Dudleigh—now no longer Mrs. Dunbar—"sit down, or you shall have to change places with Frederick's daughter."

Sir Lionel swayed backward and forward, and appeared not to hear her. And now his eyes wandered to Dalton, who stood gazing solemnly at him, and then to Dudleigh, who was still speaking.

"Who is that?" he gasped.

"Your son!" said Lady Dudleigh.

At this instant Dudleigh finished. Sir Lionel gave a terrible groan, and flung up

I

"HE LOOKED AT HER WITH ASTONISHMENT."

his arms wildly. The next instant he fell heavily forward, and was caught in the arms of his wife. A crowd flew to his assistance, and he was carried out of court, followed by Lady Dudleigh.

There was a murmur of universal sympathy.

"Poor Sir Lionel! He has been heartbroken, and the joy of his son's safety is too much."

After this the proceedings soon came to an end.

Edith was free!

Dalton tried to get to her, but in his weakness sank upon a seat, and looked imploringly at his daughter. Seeing this, Dudleigh sprang to his assistance, and gave his arm. Leaning heavily upon this, Dalton walked toward Edith, who was already striving to reach him, and, with a low cry, caught her in his arms.

Sir Lionel had been taken to the inn, where Lady Dudleigh waited on him. After some time he recovered his senses, and began to rally rapidly. It had been feared that it was apoplexy, but, fortunately for the sufferer, it turned out to be nothing so serious as that. After this Lady Dudleigh was left alone with her husband.

Ten years of separation lay between these two—a separation undertaken from causes that still existed to alienate them beyond the hope of reconciliation. Yet there was much to be said; and Lady Dudleigh had before her a dark and solemn purpose.

On the next day Sir Lionel was able to drive out. Lady Dudleigh seemed to have constituted herself his guardian. Sir Lionel's face and expression had changed. The easy, careless bonhomie, the placid content, the serene joyousness, that had once characterized him, were gone. In the place of these there came an anxious, watchful, troubled look—the look of a mind ill at ease—the furtive glance, the clouded brow. It was as though in this meeting Lady Dudleigh had communicated to her husband a part of that expression which prevailed in her own face.

Sir Lionel seemed like a prisoner who is attended by an ever-vigilant guard—one who watches all his movements, and from whom he can not escape. As he rolled along in his carriage, the Black Care of the poet seemed seated beside him in the person of Lady Dudleigh.

While Sir Lionel thus recovered from the sudden shock which he had felt, there was another who had endured a longer and severer course of suffering, and who had rallied for a moment when his presence was required, but only to sink back into a relapse worse than the illness from which he had begun to recover. This was Frederick Dalton, who had crawled from his bed twice—once to his daughter's prison, and once to the scene of her trial. But the exertion was too much, and the agitation of feeling to which he had been subject had overwhelmed him. Leaning heavily on Dudleigh, and also on Edith, he was taken by these two to his carriage, and thence to the inn; but here he could walk no further. It was Dudleigh who had to carry him to his room and lay him on his bed—and Dudleigh, too, who would intrust to no other person the task of putting his prostrate form in that bed. Dudleigh's own father was lying in the same house, but at that moment, whatever were his motives, Dalton seemed to have stronger claims on his filial duty, and Edith had to wait till this unlooked-for nurse had tenderly placed her father in his bed.

The doctor, who had found Sir Lionel's case so trifling, shook his head seriously over Frederick Dalton. Dudleigh took up his station in that room, and cared for the patient like a son. The day passed, and the night, and the next morning, but Dalton grew no better. It was a strange stupor which affected him, not like paralysis, but arising rather from exhaustion, or some affection of the brain. The doctor called it congestion. He lay in a kind of doze, without sense and without suffering, swallowing any food or medicine that might be offered, but never noticing any thing, and never answering any questions. His eyes were closed at all times, and in that stupor he seemed to be in a state of living death.

Edith's grief was profound; but in the midst of it she could not help feeling wonder at the unexpected part which Dudleigh was performing. Who was he that he should take so large a part in the care of her father? Yet so it was; and Dudleigh seemed to think of nothing and see nothing but that old man's wasted and prostrate form.

For the present, at least, departure from the inn was of course out of the question. Edith's position was a very distressing one. Every feeling of her heart impelled her to be present at her father's bedside, but Dudleigh was present at that same bedside; and how could she associate herself with him even there? At first she would enter the room, and sit quietly by her father's bedside, and on such occasions Dudleigh would respectfully withdraw; but this was unpleasant, and she hardly knew what to do.

Two or three days thus passed, and on the third Dudleigh requested an interview, to ask her, as he said, something about "Mr. Wiggins"—for this was the name by which Mr. Dalton still was called. This request Edith could not refuse.

Dudleigh entered with an air of profound respect.

"Miss Dalton," said he, laying emphasis on that name, "nothing would induce me to intrude upon you but my anxiety about your father. Deep as your affection for him may be, it can hardly be greater than mine. I would gladly lay down my life for him. At the same time, I understand your feelings, and this is what I wish to speak about. I would give up my place at his bedside altogether if you wished it, and you should not be troubled by my presence; but I see that you are not strong enough to be sole nurse, or to undertake the work that would be required of you, and that your own affection for him would impose upon you. You yourself are not strong, and you must take care of yourself for his sake. I will not, therefore, give up to you all the care of your father, but I will absent myself during the afternoon, and you will then have exclusive care of him."

Edith bowed without a word, and Dudleigh withdrew.

This arrangement was kept up, and Edith scarcely saw Dudleigh at all. She knew, however, that his care for her father was incessant and uninterrupted. Every thing that could possibly be needed was supplied; every luxury or delicacy that could be thought of was obtained; and not only were London physicians constantly coming up, but from the notes which lay around, she judged that Dudleigh kept up a constant correspondence with them about this case.

CHAPTER XLIII.

SIR LIONEL AND HIS "KEEPER."

SIR LIONEL, who had come to this place with the face that indicated a mind at peace, thus found himself suddenly confronted by a grim phantom, the aspect of which struck terror to his heart. That phantom was drawn up from a past which he usually did not care to remember. Now, however, he could not forget it. There was one by his side to remind him of it always—one who had become his guard, his jailer—in fact, his keeper—a word which signifies better than any other the attitude which was assumed by Lady Dudleigh. For the feeling which Sir Lionel had toward her was precisely like that which the lunatic has toward his keeper, the feeling that this one is watching night and day, and never relaxes the terrible stare of those vigilant eyes. There are those who on being thus watched would grow mad; and Sir Lionel had this in addition to his other terrors—this climax of them all, that upon him there was always the maddening glare of his "keeper's" eyes. Terrible eyes were they to him, most terrible—eyes which he dared not encounter. They were the eyes of his wife—a woman most injured; and her gaze reminded him always of a past full of horror. That gaze he could not encounter. He knew without looking at it what it meant. He felt it on him. There were times when it made his flesh crawl, nor could he venture to face it.

A few days of this reduced him to a state of abject misery. He began to fear that he was really growing mad. In that case he would be a fit subject for a "keeper." He longed with unutterable longing to throw off this terrible restraint; but he could not and dared not. That woman, that "keeper," wielded over him a power which he knew and felt, and dared not defy. It was the power that arises from the knowledge of secrets of life and death, and her knowledge placed his life in her hands.

This woman was inflexible and inexorable. She had suffered so much that she had no pity for his present sufferings. These seemed trivial to her. She showed a grand, strong, self-sufficient nature, which made her his superior, and put her above the reach of any influences that he might bring. He could remember the time when she was a fair and gentle young girl, with her will all subject to his; then a loving bride with no thought apart from him; but now years of suffering and self-discipline had transformed her to this, and she came back to him an inexorable Fate, an avenging Nemesis.

Yet Sir Lionel did not give up all hope. He could not drive her away. He could not fly away from her, for her watch was too vigilant; but he hoped for some chance of secret flight in which, if he once escaped, he might find his way to the Continent. With something of that cunning which characterizes the insane, and which, perhaps, is born of the presence of a "keeper," Sir Lionel watched his opportunity, and one day nearly succeeded in effecting his desire.

That day Lady Dudleigh was in her brother's room. Sir Lionel had waited for this, and had made his preparations. When she had been gone for a few minutes, he stole softly out of his room, passed stealthily down the back stairs of the inn, and going out of the back-door, reached the rear of the house. Here there was a yard, and a gate that led out to a road at the end of the house. A carriage had been waiting here for about an hour. Sir Lionel hurried across the yard, passed through the gate, and looked for the carriage.

He took one glance, and then a deep oath escaped him.

In the carriage was Lady Dudleigh.

How she could have detected his flight he could not imagine, nor did he now care. She had detected it, and had followed at once to circumvent him. She must have gone down the front stairs, out of the front-door, and reached the carriage before him. And there she was! Those hateful eyes were fixed on him—he felt the horrid stare—he cowered beneath it. He walked toward her.

"I thought I would go out too," said she.

Sir Lionel said not a word. He felt too much ashamed to turn back now, and was too politic to allow her to see any open signs that he was in full flight; so he quietly got into the carriage, and took his seat by her side.

Whipping up the horses, he drove them at a headlong rate of speed out through the streets into the country. His whole soul was full of mad fury. Rage and disappointment together excited his brain to madness; and the fierce rush of the impetuous steeds was in accordance with the excitement of his mind. At length the horses themselves grew fatigued, and slackened their pace. Sir Lionel still tried to urge them forward, but in vain, and at last he flung down the whip with a curse.

"I'll not stand this any longer!" he cried, vehemently, addressing his "keeper," but not looking at her.

"What?" said she.

"This style of being dogged and tracked and watched."

"You allude to me, I suppose," said Lady Dudleigh. "At any rate, you must allow that it is better to be tracked, as you call it, by me, than by the officers of the law."

"I don't care," growled Sir Lionel, gathering courage. "I'll not stand this style of thing any longer. I'll not let them have it all their own way."

"I don't see what you can do," said Lady Dudleigh, quietly.

"Do!" cried Sir Lionel, in a still more violent tone—"do! I'll tell you what I'll do. I'll fight it out."

"Fight!"

"Yes," cried Sir Lionel, with an oath. "Every one of you—every one. Every one without a single exception. Oh, you needn't think that I'm afraid. I've thought it all over. You're all under my power. Yes—ha, ha, ha! that's it. I've said it, and I say what I mean. You thought that I was under your power. Your power! Ha, ha, ha! That's good. Why, you're all under mine—every one of you."

Sir Lionel spoke wildly and vehemently, in that tone of feverish excitement which marks a madman. It may have been the influence of his "keeper," or it may have been the dawnings of actual insanity.

As for Lady Dudleigh, she did not lose one particle of her cold-bloodedness. She simply said, in the same tone,

"How?"

"How? Ha, ha! Do you think I'm going to tell you? That's my secret. But stop. Yes; I don't care. I'd just as soon tell as not. You can't escape, not one of you, unless you all fly at once to the Continent, or to America, or, better yet, back to Botany Bay. There you'll be safe. Fly! fly! fly! or else," he suddenly added, in a gloomy tone, "you'll all die on the gallows! every one of you, on the gallows! Ha, ha, ha! swinging on the gallows! the beautiful gallows!"

Lady Dudleigh disregarded the wildness of his tone, or perhaps she chose to take advantage of it, thinking that in his excitement he might disclose his thoughts the more unguardedly.

"You can do nothing," she said.

"Can't I, though?" retorted Sir Lionel. "You wait. First, there's Dalton."

"What can you do with him?"

"Arrest him," said Sir Lionel. "What is he? An outlaw! An escaped convict! He lives under an assumed name. He must go back to Botany Bay—that is, if he isn't hanged. And then there's that pale-faced devil of a daughter with her terrible eyes." He paused.

"What can you do to her?"

"Her! Arrest her too," cried Sir Lionel. "She murdered my boy—my son—my Leon. She must be hanged. You shall not save her by this trick. No! she must be hanged, like her cursed father."

A shudder passed through Lady Dudleigh. Sir Lionel did not notice it. He was too much taken up with his own vengeful thoughts.

"Yes," said he, "and there's that scoundrel Reginald."

"Reginald!" cried Lady Dudleigh, in a stern voice. "Why do you mention him?"

"Oh, he's one of the same gang," cried Sir Lionel. "He's playing their game. He is siding against his father, as he always did, and with his brother's murderers. He shall not escape. I will avenge Leon's death on all of you; and as for him, he shall suffer!"

It was with a strong effort that Lady Dudleigh restrained herself. But she succeeded in doing so, and said, simply, as before,

"How?"

"Arrest him!" cried Sir Lionel. "Arrest him too. He is guilty of perjury; and if he doesn't hang for it, he'll go back again to Botany Bay with that scoundrel with whom he sides against me—his own father—and against his brother."

"Are there any more?" asked Lady Dudleigh, as Sir Lionel ended.

"More! Yes," he said.

"Who?"

"You!" shouted Sir Lionel, with a voice of indescribable hate and ferocity. He turned as he spoke, and stared at her. His wild eyes, however, met the calm, cold, steady glance of those of his "keeper," and they fell before it. He seized the whip and began to lash the horses, crying as he did so, "You! yes, you! you! most of all!"

"What can you do to me?" asked Lady Dudleigh.

"You? Arrest you."

"What have I done?"

"You? You have done every thing. You have aided and abetted the escape of an outlaw. You have assisted him in his nefarious occupation of Dalton Hall. You have aided and abetted him in the imprisonment of Dalton's brat. You have aided and abetted him in the murder of my boy Leon. You have—"

"Stop!" cried Lady Dudleigh, in a stern, commanding voice. "You have been a villain always, but you have never been so outspoken. Who are you? Do you know what happened ten years ago?"

"What?" asked Sir Lionel. "Do you mean Dalton's forgery, and his assassination of that—that banker fellow?"

Lady Dudleigh smiled grimly.

"I am glad that you said that," said she. "You remove my last scruple. My brother's wrongs have well-nigh maddened me; but I have hesitated to bear witness against my husband, and the father of my children. I shall remember this, and it will sustain me when I bear my witness against you in a court of law."

"Me?" said Sir Lionel. "Me? Witness against me? You can not. No one will believe you."

"It will not be only your wife," said she, "though that will be something, but your own self, with your own hand."

"What do you mean?"

"I mean what you know very well—your letter which you wrote to Frederick, inclosing your forged check."

"I never forged a check, and I never wrote a letter inclosing one!" cried Sir Lionel. "Dalton forged that letter himself, if there is such a letter. He was an accomplished forger, and has suffered for it."

"The letter is your own," said Lady Dudleigh, "and I can swear to it."

"No one will believe you," cried Sir Lionel. "You shall be arrested for perjury."

Lady Dudleigh gave another grim smile, and then she added, "There is that Maltese cross. You forget that."

"What Maltese cross?" said Sir Lionel. "I never had one. That wasn't mine; it was Dalton's."

"But I can swear in a court of law," said Lady Dudleigh, "that this Maltese cross was yours, and that it was given to you by me as a birthday gift."

"No one will believe you!" cried Sir Lionel; "no one will believe you!"

"Why not? Will they refuse the oath of Lady Dudleigh?"

"I can show them that you are insane," said Sir Lionel, with a chuckle at the idea, which seemed to him like a sudden inspiration.

"You will not be able to show that Reginald is insane," said she.

"Reginald?"

"Yes, Reginald," repeated Lady Dudleigh. "Reginald knows that Maltese cross, and knows when I gave it to you. He too will be ready to swear to that in a court of law whenever I tell him that he may do so."

"Reginald?" said Sir Lionel, in a gloomy voice. "Why, he was—a child then."

"He was sixteen years old," said Lady Dudleigh.

This mention of Reginald seemed to crush Sir Lionel. He was silent for a long time. Evidently he had not been prepared for this in his plans for what he called a "fight." He sat in moody silence therefore. Once or twice he stole a furtive glance at her, and threw upon her a look which she did not see. It was a look full of hate and malignancy, while at the same time there was an expression of satisfaction in his face, as though he had conceived some new plan, which he intended to keep a secret all to himself.

CHAPTER XLIV.

LADY DUDLEIGH'S DECISION.

DURING the remainder of that drive nothing was said by either. Sir Lionel had his own thoughts, which, whatever they were, appeared to give him a certain satisfaction, and his brow was more unclouded when they reached the inn than it had been ever since the day of the trial. Evidently the new design which he had conceived, and which remained unuttered in his mind, was very satisfactory to him.

That evening he himself began the conversation with Lady Dudleigh, a thing which he had not before done.

"It's all very well," said he, "for you to carry on your own plans. You may carry them on and welcome. I won't prevent you; in fact, I can't. It's no use to deny it; I'm in your power. You're determined to crush me, and I must be crushed, I suppose. You are going to show to the world the strange spectacle of a wife and a son rising up against a husband and father, and swearing his life away. You will lead on, and Reginald will follow. This is the education that you have given him—it is to end in parricide. Very well; I must submit. Wife, slay your husband! mother, lead your son to parricide! Of course you comfort

your conscience with the plea that you are doing justice. In the French Revolution there were wives who denounced their husbands, and sons who denounced their fathers, in the name of 'humanity,' and for the good of the republic. So go on. See that justice be done. Come on yourself to assassinate your husband, and bring on your parricide! Take sides with those who have murdered your son—the son whom you bore to me, and once loved! Unsex yourself, and become a Fury! It is useless for me to make resistance, I suppose; and yet, woman! wife! mother! let me tell you that on the day when you attempt to do these things, and when your son stands by your side to help you, there will go up a cry of horror against you from outraged humanity!"

At this Lady Dudleigh looked at him, who, as usual, averted his eyes; but she made no reply.

"Bring him on!" said Sir Lionel—"your son—my son—the parricide! Do your worst. But at the same time allow me to inform you, in the mildest manner in the world, that if I am doomed, there is no reason why I should go mad in this infernal hole. What is more, I do not intend to stay here one single day longer. I'm not going to run away. That is impossible; you keep too sharp a look-out altogether. I'm simply going away from this place of horrors, and I rather think I'll go home. I'll go home—yes, home. Home is the place for me—Dudleigh Manor, where I first took you, my true wife—that is the place for me to be in when you come to me, you and your son, to hand me over, Judas-like, to death. Yes, I'm going home, and if you choose to accompany me, why, all that I can say is, I'll have to bear it."

"I'll go," said Lady Dudleigh, laconically.

"Oh, of course," said Sir Lionel, "quite a true wife; like Ruth and Naomi. Whither thou goest, I will go. You see, I'm up in my Bible. Well, as I said, I can not prevent you, and I suppose there is no need for me to tell you to get ready."

Whether under these bitter taunts Lady Dudleigh writhed or not did not at all appear. She seemed as cool and calm as ever. Perhaps she had so schooled her nature that she was able to repress all outward signs of emotion, or perhaps she had undergone so much that a taunt could have no sting for her, or perhaps she had already contemplated and familiarized herself with all these possible views of her conduct to such an extent that the mention of them created no emotion. At any rate, whatever she felt, Sir Lionel saw nothing.

Having discharged this shot, Sir Lionel went to his desk, and taking out writing materials, began to write a letter. He wrote rapidly, and once or twice glanced furtively at Lady Dudleigh, as though he was fearful that she might overlook his writing. But there was no danger of that. Lady Dudleigh did not move from her place. She did not seem to be aware that he was writing at all.

At length Sir Lionel finished, and then he folded, sealed, and addressed the letter. He finished this task with a face of supreme satisfaction, and stole a look toward Lady Dudleigh, in which there was a certain cunning triumph very visible, though it was not seen by the one at whom it was directed.

"And now," said he, waving the letter somewhat ostentatiously, and speaking in a formal tone, in which there was an evident sneer—"and now, Lady Dudleigh, I have the honor to inform you that I intend to go out and post this letter. May I have the honor of your company as far as the post-office, and back?"

Lady Dudleigh rose in silence, and hastily throwing on her things, prepared to follow him. Sir Lionel waited with mocking politeness, opened the door for her to pass out first, and then in company with her went to the post-office, where he mailed the letter, and returned with the smile of satisfaction still upon his face.

Early on the next morning Lady Dudleigh saw her son. He had watched all that night by Dalton's bedside, and seemed pale and exhausted.

"Reginald," said Lady Dudleigh, "Sir Lionel is going away."

"Going away?" repeated Reginald, absently.

"Yes; back to Dudleigh Manor."

Reginald looked inquiringly at his mother, but said nothing.

"I intend," said Lady Dudleigh, "to go with him."

"You?"

"Yes."

Reginald looked at her mournfully.

"Have you done any thing with him yet?" he asked.

Lady Dudleigh shook her head.

"Do you expect to do any thing?"

"I do."

"I'm afraid you will be disappointed."

"I hope not. I have at least gained a hold upon him, and I have certainly worked upon his fears. If I remain with him now I hope in time to extort from him that confession which will save us all from an additional sorrow; one perhaps as terrible as any we have ever known, if not even more so."

"Confession?" repeated Reginald. "How is that possible? He will never confess—never. If he has remained silent so long, and has not been moved by the thought of all that he has done, what possible thing can move him? Nothing but the actual presence of the law. Nothing but force."

"Well," said Lady Dudleigh, "it is worth trying—the other alternative is too terrible just yet. I hope to work upon his fears. I hope to persuade him to confess, and fly from the country to some place of safety. Frederick must be righted at all hazards, and I hope to show this so plainly to Sir Lionel that he will acquiesce in my proposal, confess all, save Frederick, and then fly to some place where he may be safe. If not, why, then we can try the last resort. But oh, Reginald, do you not see how terrible that last resort is?—I against my husband, you against your father—both of us bringing him to the gallows! It is only the intolerable sense of Frederick's long-sufferings that can make me think of doing so terrible a thing. But Frederick is even now in danger. He must be saved; and the question is between the innocent and the guilty. I am strong enough to decide differently from what I did ten years ago."

"Oh, I know—I feel it all, mother dear," said Reginald; "but at the same time I don't like the idea of your going away with him—alone."

"Why not?"

"I don't like the idea of your putting yourself in his power."

"His power?"

"Yes, in Dudleigh Manor, or any other place. He is desperate. He will not shrink from any thing that he thinks may save him from this danger. You will be his chief danger: he may think of getting rid of it. He is unscrupulous, and would stop at nothing."

"Oh, as for that, he may be desperate, but what can he possibly do? Dudleigh Manor is in the world. It is not in some remote place where the master is superior to law. He can do no more harm there than he can here."

"The man," said Reginald, "who for all these years has outraged honor and justice and truth, and has stifled his own conscience for the sake of his comfort, must by this time be familiar with desperate deeds, and be capable of any crime. I am afraid, mother dear, for you to trust yourself with him."

"Reginald," said Lady Dudleigh, "you speak as though I were a child or a schoolgirl. Does he seem now as though he could harm me, or do I seem to be one who can easily be put down? Would you be afraid to go with him?"

"I—afraid? That is the very thing that I wish to propose."

"But you could not possibly have that influence over him which I have. You might threaten, easily enough, and come to an open rupture, but that is what I wish to avoid. I wish to bring him to a confession, not so much by direct threats as by various constraining moral influences."

"Oh, as to that," said Reginald, "I have no doubt that you will do far better than I can; but at the same time I can not get rid of a fear about your safety."

"And do you really think, Reginald, that I would be less safe than you? or, from what you know of me, should you suppose that I have much of that woman's weakness about me which might make me an easy prey to one who wished to do me harm?"

"I know well what you are, mother dear," said Reginald, taking her hand tenderly in both of his. "You have the tenderness of a woman and the courage of a man; but still I feel uneasy. At any rate, promise me one thing. You will let me know what you are doing."

"I do not promise to write regularly," said Lady Dudleigh, "but I do promise to write the moment that any thing happens worth writing about."

"And if you are ill, or in danger?" said Reginald, anxiously.

"Oh, then, of course I shall write at once. But now I must go. I shall not see you again for some time. Good-by."

Lady Dudleigh kissed her son tenderly as she said this, and left him, and Reginald returned to his place by Frederick Dalton's bedside.

That same day, shortly after this interview, Sir Lionel and Lady Dudleigh drove away from the inn, en route for Dudleigh Manor.

CHAPTER XLV.

LADY DUDLEIGH IS SHOWN TO HER ROOM.

AFTER driving for about a mile Sir Lionel and Lady Dudleigh took the train, securing a compartment to themselves.

During this part of the journey Sir Lionel's face lost much of that gloom which of late had pervaded it, and assumed an expression which was less dismal, though not quite like the old one. The old look was one of serene and placid content, an air of animal comfort, and of easy-going self-indulgence; but now the expression was more restless and excited. There was a certain knowing look—a leer of triumphant cunning—combined with a tendency to chuckle over some secret purpose which no one else knew. Together with this there was incessant restlessness; he appeared perpetually on the look-out, as though dreading discovery; and he alternated between exultant nods of his head, with knowing winks at vacancy, and sudden sharp furtive glances at his companion. Changed as Sir Lionel's mood was, it can hardly be said that the change was for the better. It would have been obvious even to a more superficial observer than that vigilant "keeper" who accompanied him that Sir Lionel had lost his self-poise, and was in rather a dangerous way. Lady Dudleigh must have noticed this; but it made no difference in her, save that there was perhaps a stonier lustre in

her eyes as she turned them upon him, and a sharper vigilance in her attitude.

In this way they rode on for several hours; and whatever Sir Lionel's plans might have been, they certainly did not involve any action during the journey. Had he been sufficiently violent he might have made an assault upon his companion in the seclusion of that compartment, and effectually prevented any trouble ever arising to him from her. He might have done this, and made good his escape in the confusion of some station. But no such attempt was made; and so in due time they reached the place where they were to get out.

"This is the nearest station to Dudleigh Manor," said Sir Lionel, gayly. "This road has been made since your time."

Lady Dudleigh said nothing, but looked around. She saw nothing that was familiar. A neat wayside station, with the usual platform, was nearest; and beyond this arose trees which concealed the view on one side, while on the other there were fields and hedges, and one or two houses in the distance. It was a commonplace scene, in a level sort of country, and Lady Dudleigh, after one short survey, thought no more about it. It was just like any other wayside station.

A common-looking hack, with a rather ill-dressed driver, was waiting, and toward this Sir Lionel walked.

"This," said he, "is the Dudleigh coach. It isn't so grand an affair as it used to be; but my means have dwindled a good deal since your day, you know, and I have to economize—yes—ha, ha, ha!—economize—queer thing too, isn't it? Economizing—ha, ha, ha!"

Sir Lionel's somewhat flighty manner was not at all congenial to Lady Dudleigh, and she treated him as the vigilant "keeper" always treats his flighty prisoner—that is, with silent patience and persistent watchfulness.

In a few minutes they were both seated inside the coach, and were driving away. The coach was a gloomy one, with windows only in the doors. The rest was solid woodwork. These windows in the doors were small, and when let down were scarcely large enough for one to put his head through. When sitting down it was impossible for Lady Dudleigh to see the road. She could see nothing but the tops of the trees, between which the sky appeared occasionally. She saw that she was driving along a road which was shaded with trees on both sides; but more than this she could not see.

They drove for about an hour at a moderate pace, and during this time Sir Lionel preserved that same peculiar demeanor which has already been described, while Lady Dudleigh maintained her usual silent watchfulness.

At length they stopped for a moment. Voices sounded outside, and then Lady Dudleigh saw that she was passing through a gateway. Thinking that this was Dudleigh Manor, she made no remark, but calmly awaited the time when she should reach the house. She did not have to wait long. Sooner than she expected the coach stopped. The driver got down and opened the door. Sir Lionel sprang out with surprising agility, and held out his hand politely to assist his companion. She did not accept his offer, but stepped out without assistance, and looked around.

To her surprise, the place was not Dudleigh Manor at all, but one which was entirely different, and quite unfamiliar. It was a brick house of no very great size, though larger than most private houses, of plain exterior, and with the air of a public building of some sort. The grounds about were stiff and formal and forbidding. The door was open, and one or two men were standing there. It did not look like an inn, and yet it certainly was not a private residence.

"I have to stop here for a little while," said Sir Lionel, "to see a friend on business. We are not half-way to Dudleigh Manor yet; it's further than you think."

He turned and went up the steps. Lady Dudleigh looked around once more, and then followed him. The men at the head of the steps looked at her curiously as she went in. She took no notice of them, however, but walked past them, looking calmly beyond them.

On entering the house she saw a bare hall covered with slate-colored oil-cloth, and with a table against the wall. A gray-headed man came out of one of the rooms, and advanced to meet Sir Lionel, who shook hands with him very cordially, and whispered to him a few words. The gray-headed man wore spectacles, was clean shaven, with a double chin, and a somewhat sleek and oily exterior.

"Lady Dudleigh," said Sir Lionel, leading the gray-headed man forward by the arm, "allow me to make you acquainted with my particular friend, Dr. Leonard Morton."

Lady Dudleigh bowed slightly, and Dr. Morton made a profound obeisance that seemed like a caricature of politeness.

"Will you have the kindness to walk up stairs?" said he, and led the way, while the others followed him. Ascending the stairs, they reached a large room at the back of the house, which was furnished in the same stiff and formal way as the hall below. Over the mantel-piece hung an engraving, somewhat faded out, and on the table were a Bible and a pitcher of water.

The doctor politely handed Lady Dudleigh a chair, and made one or two remarks about the weather.

"Sir Lionel," said he, "if Lady Dudleigh will excuse us for a few moments, I should like to speak with you in private."

"Will you have the kindness, Lady Dudleigh," asked Sir Lionel, "to excuse us for a few moments? We shall not leave you long alone. And here is a book—an invaluable book—with which you may occupy your time."

He said this with such exaggerated politeness, and with such a cunning leer in his eyes, that his tone and manner were most grotesque; and as he concluded he took up the large Bible with ridiculous solemnity.

Lady Dudleigh merely bowed in silence.

"A thousand thanks," said Sir Lionel, turning away; and thereupon he left the room, followed by the doctor. Lady Dudleigh heard their footsteps descending the stairs, and then they seemed to go into some room.

For some time she forgot all about him. The place had at first surprised her, but she gave it little thought. She had too much to think of. She had before her a task which seemed almost impossible; and if she failed in this, there was before her that dread alternative which Sir Lionel had presented to her so plainly. Other things too there were besides her husband—connected with all who were dearest to her—her brother, perhaps, dying before he had accomplished his work; her son so mysteriously murdered; her other son awaiting her command to assist in bringing his father to death. Besides, there was the danger that even now might be impending over these—the danger of discovery. Sir Lionel's desperate threats might have some meaning, and who could tell how it might result if he sought to carry out those threats?

Brooding over such thoughts as these, she forgot about the lapse of time, and at last was roused to herself by the entrance of a woman. She was large and coarse and fat. At the door stood another woman.

"Your room's ready, missus," said the woman, bluntly.

Lady Dudleigh rose.

"I don't want a room," said she. "I intend to go in a few minutes."

"Anyway, ye'd better come to your room now, and not keep us waitin'," said the woman.

"You needn't wait," said Lady Dudleigh.

"Come along," said the woman, impatiently. "It's no use stayin' here all day."

Lady Dudleigh felt annoyed at this insolence, and began to think that Sir Lionel had run away while she had forgotten about him. She said nothing to the women, but walked toward the door. The two stood there in the way.

"I will go down," said she, haughtily, "and wait below. Go and tell Sir Lionel."

The women stared at one another.

"SHE WAS DRAGGED ALONG HELPLESSLY."

"Sir Lionel Dudleigh," said Lady Dudleigh, "is with Dr. Morton on business. Tell him that I am tired of waiting, or take me to the room where he is."

"Oh yes, 'm," said one of the women; and saying this, she went down stairs.

In a few moments Dr. Morton came up, followed by the women. The two men who had been standing at the door came into the hall, and stood there at the foot of the stairs.

"Where is Sir Lionel?" was Lady Dudleigh's first words.

The doctor smiled blandly.

"Well, he has just gone, you know; but he'll soon be back—oh yes, quite soon. You wait here, and you may go to your room." He spoke in an odd, coaxing tone, as though he were addressing some fretful child whom it was desirable to humor.

"Gone!" exclaimed Lady Dudleigh.

"Yes, but he'll soon be back. You needn't wait long. And these women will take you to your own room. You'll find it very pleasant."

"I have no room here," said Lady Dudleigh, haughtily. "If Sir Lionel has gone, I shall go too;" and with these words she tried to move past the woman who was in front of her. But the woman would not move, and the other woman and the doctor stood there looking at her. All at once the truth dawned upon her, or a part of the truth. She had been brought here, and they would keep her here. Who they were she could

not imagine, but their faces were not at all prepossessing.

"Oh, it's all right," said the doctor, in a smooth voice. "You shall go to-morrow. We'll send for Sir Lionel."

"Dr. Morton," said Lady Dudleigh, solemnly, "beware how you detain me. Let me go, or you shall repent it. I don't know what your motive is, but it will be a dangerous thing for you. I am Lady Dudleigh, and if you dare to interfere with my movements you shall suffer."

"Oh yes, oh yes," said the doctor. "You are Lady Dudleigh. Oh, of course. And now come, Lady Dudleigh; you shall be treated just like a lady, and have a nice room, and—"

"What do you mean?" cried Lady Dudleigh, indignantly. "This insolence is insufferable."

"Oh yes," said the doctor; "it'll be all right, you know. Come, now; go like a good lady to your room."

"Are you mad?" exclaimed Lady Dudleigh, in amazement.

The doctor smiled and nodded.

"What do you intend to do?" asked Lady Dudleigh, restraining herself with a strong effort.

"Oh, nothing; we shall put you in a nice room, you know—all so pleasant—for you are not very well; and so, Susan, you just take the lady's hand, and, Martha, you take the other, and we'll show her the way to her room."

At this each of the women seized one of Lady Dudleigh's hands quickly and dextrously, the result of long practice, and then they drew her out of the room. Lady Dudleigh resisted, but her strength was useless. She was dragged along helplessly, while all the time the doctor walked after her, prattling in his usual way about "the nice room," and how "comfortable" she would find it. At length they reached a room, and she was taken in. One of the women entered with her. Lady Dudleigh looked around, and saw that the walls were bare and whitewashed; the floor was uncarpeted; an iron bedstead and some simple furniture were around her, and a small grated window gave light.

It looked dreary enough, and sufficiently prison-like to appall any one who might be thus suddenly thrust in there. Lady Dudleigh sank into a chair exhausted, and the woman began to make her bed.

"My good woman," said Lady Dudleigh, anxious to get some clew to her position, "can you tell me what all this means?"

"Sure it's all for the good of your health," said the woman.

"But I'm not ill."

"No, not to say ill; but the body's often all right when the mind's all wrong."

"The mind? There's nothing the matter with my mind. Dr. Morton has been deceived. He would not dare to do this if he knew it."

"Sure, now, it's nothing at all, and ye'll be well soon."

At these simple words of the woman Lady Dudleigh began to understand the situation. This must be a lunatic asylum, a private one. Sir Lionel had brought her here, and told the doctor that she was insane. The doctor had accepted his statement, and had received her as such. This at once accounted for his peculiar mode of addressing her.

"There's a mistake," said Lady Dudleigh, quietly. "Dr. Morton has been deceived. Let me see him at once, please, and I will explain. He does not know what a wrong he is doing. My good woman, I am no more mad than you are."

"Dear, dear!" said the woman, going on placidly with her work; "that's the way they all talk. There's not one of them that believes they're mad."

"But I'm not mad at all," said Lady Dudleigh, indignant at the woman's obtuseness.

"There, there; don't you go for to excite yourself," said the woman, soothingly. "But I s'pose you can't help it."

"So this is a mad-house, is it?" said Lady Dudleigh, gloomily, after a pause.

"Well, 'm, we don't call it that; we call it a 'sylum. It's Dr. Morton's 'sylum."

"Now see here," said Lady Dudleigh, making a fresh effort, and trying to be as cool as possible, "I am Lady Dudleigh. I have been brought here by a trick. Dr. Morton is deceived. He is committing a crime in detaining me. I am not mad. Look at me. Judge for yourself. Look at me, and say, do I look like a madwoman?"

The woman, thus appealed to, good-naturedly acquiesced, and looked at Lady Dudleigh.

"'Deed," she remarked, "ye look as though ye've had a deal of sufferin' afore ye came here, an' I don't wonder yer mind give way."

"Do I look like a madwoman?" repeated Lady Dudleigh, with a sense of intolerable irritation at this woman's stupidity.

"'Deed, then, an' I'm no judge. It's the doctor that decides."

"But what do you say? Come, now."

"Well, then, ye don't look very bad, exceptin' the glare an' glitter of the eyes of ye, an' yer fancies."

"Fancies? What fancies?"

"Why, yer fancies that ye're Lady Dudleigh, an' all that about Sir Lionel."

Lady Dudleigh started to her feet.

"What!" she exclaimed. "Why, I am Lady Dudleigh."

"There, there!" said the woman, soothingly; "sure I forgot myself. Sure ye are Lady Dudleigh, or any body else ye like. It's a dreadful inveiglin' way ye have to trap a body the way ye do."

At this Lady Dudleigh was in despair. No further words were of any avail. The woman was determined to humor her, and assented to every thing she said. This treatment was so intolerable that Lady Dudleigh was afraid to say any thing for fear that she would show the excitement of her feelings, and such an exhibition would of course have been considered as a fresh proof of her madness.

The woman at length completed her task, and retired.

Lady Dudleigh was left alone. She knew it all now. She remembered the letter which Sir Lionel had written. In that he had no doubt arranged this plan with Dr. Morton, and the coach had been ready at the station. But in what part of the country this place was she had no idea, nor could she know whether Dr. Morton was deceived by Sir Lionel, or was his paid employé in this work of villainy. His face did not give her any encouragement to hope for either honesty or mercy from him.

It was an appalling situation, and she knew it. All the horrors that she had ever heard of in connection with private asylums occurred to her mind, and deepened the terror that surrounded her. All the other cares of her life—the sorrow of bereavement, the anxiety for the sick, the plans for Frederick Dalton—all these and many others now oppressed her till her brain sank under the

crushing weight. A groan of anguish burst
from her.

"Sir Lionel's mockery will become a reality," she thought. "I shall go mad!"

Meanwhile Sir Lionel had gone away.
Leaving Lady Dudleigh in the room, he had
gone down stairs, and after a few hurried
words with the doctor, he left the house and
entered the coach, which drove back to the
station.

All the way he was in the utmost glee, rub-
bing his hands, slapping his thighs, chuck-
ling to himself, laughing and cheering.

"Ha, ha, ha! ha, ha, ha!" he laughed.
"Outwitted! The keeper — the keeper
caught! Ha, ha, ha! Why, she'll never
get out—never! In for life, Lionel, my
boy! Mad? Why, by this time she's a raving maniac! Ha, ha, ha! She swear against
me! Who'd believe a madwoman, an idiot,
a lunatic, a bedlamite, a maniac—a howling,
frenzied, gibbering, ranting, raving, driveling, maundering, mooning maniac? And
now for the boy next—the parricide! Ha,
ha, ha! Arrest him? No. Shut him up
here—both—with my friend Morton—both
of them, mother and son, the two—ha, ha,
ha!—witnesses! One maniac! two maniacs!
and then I shall go mad with joy, and come
here to live, and there shall be *three maniacs!*
Ha, ha, ha! ha, ha, ha-a-a-a-a-a-a!"

Sir Lionel himself seemed mad now.

On leaving the coach, however, he became
calmer, and taking the first train that came
up, resumed his journey.

CHAPTER XLVI.

THE BEDSIDE OF DALTON.

FREDERICK DALTON remained in his prostrate condition, with no apparent change
either for the better or for the worse, and
thus a month passed.

One morning Dudleigh requested an interview with Edith.

On entering the room he greeted her with
his usual deep respect.

"I hope you will excuse me for troubling
you, Miss Dalton," he said, "but I wish very
much to ask your opinion about your father.
He remains, as you know, unchanged, and
this inn is not the place for him. The air
is close, the place is noisy, and it is impossible for him to have that perfect quiet which
he so greatly needs. Dudleigh Manor is too
far away, but there is another place close
by. I am aware, Miss Dalton, that Dalton
Hall must be odious to you, and therefore I
hesitate to ask you to take your father to
that place. Yet he ought to go there, and
at once. As for yourself, I hope that the
new circumstances under which you will live
there will make it less unpleasant; and, let
me add, for my own part, it shall be my

"THEIR HANDS TOUCHED."

effort to see that you, who have been so
deeply wronged, shall be righted—with all
and before all. As to myself," he continued,
"I would retire, and relieve you of my presence, which can not be otherwise than painful, but there are two reasons why I ought to
remain. The first is your father. You yourself are not able to take all the care of him,
and there is no other who can share it except myself. Next to yourself, no one can be
to him what I am, nor is there any one with
whom I would be willing to leave him. He
must not be left to a servant. He must be
nursed by those who love him. And so I
must stay with him wherever he is. In addition to this, however, my presence at Dalton Hall will effectually quell the vulgar
clamor, and all the rumors that have been
prevailing for the last few months will be
silenced."

Dudleigh spoke all this calmly and seriously, but beneath his words there was something in his tone which conveyed a deeper
meaning. That tone was more than respectful—it was almost reverential—as though
the one to whom he spoke required from
him more than mere courtesy. In spite of
his outward calm, there was also an emotion
in his voice which showed that the calm
was assumed, and that beneath it lay something which could not be all concealed.
In his eyes, as he fixed them on Edith, there
was that same reverential regard, which
seemed to speak of devotion and loyalty;
something stronger than admiration, something deeper than sympathy, was expressed
from them. And yet it was this that he
himself tried to conceal. It was as though
this feeling of his burst forth irrepressibly
through all concealment, as though the in-

tensity of this feeling made even his calmest words and commonest formulas full of a new and deeper meaning.

In that reverence and profound devotion thus manifest there was nothing which could be otherwise than grateful to Edith. Certainly she could not take offense, for his words and his looks afforded nothing which could by any possibility give rise to that.

For a whole month this man had been before her, a constant attendant on her father, sleeping his few hours in an adjoining chamber, with scarce a thought beyond that prostrate friend. All the country had been searched for the best advice or the best remedies, and nothing had been omitted which untiring affection could suggest. During all this time she had scarce seen him. In the delicacy of his regard for her he had studiously kept out of her way, as though unwilling to allow his presence to give her pain. A moment might occasionally be taken up with a few necessary arrangements as she would enter, but that was all. He patiently waited till she retired before he ventured to come in himself.

No; in that noble face, pale from illness or from sadness, with the traces of sorrow upon it, and the marks of long vigils by the bedside of her father—in that refined face, whose expression spoke only of elevation of soul, and exhibited the perfect type of manly beauty, there was certainly nothing that could excite repugnance, but every thing that might inspire confidence.

Edith saw all this, and remarked it while listening to him; and she thought she had never seen any thing so pure in its loyalty, so profound in its sympathy, and so sweet in its sad grace as that face which was now turned toward her with its eloquent eyes. She did not say much. A few words signified her assent to the proposal. Dudleigh said that he would make all the necessary arrangements, and that she should have no trouble whatever. With this he took his departure.

That same evening another visitor came. It was a pale, slender girl, who gave her name as Lucy Ford. She said that she had been sent by Captain Dudleigh. She heard that Edith had no maid, and wished to get that situation. Edith hesitated for a moment. Could she accept so direct a favor from Dudleigh, or give him that mark of confidence? Her hesitation was over at once. She could give him that, and she accepted the maid. The next day came a housekeeper and two or three others, all sent by Dudleigh, all of whom were accepted by her. For Dudleigh had found out somehow the need of servants at Dalton Hall, and had taken this way of supplying that prime requisite.

It then remained to move Dalton. He still continued in the same condition, not much changed physically, but in a state of mental torpor, the duration of which no one was able to foretell. Two short stages were required to take him to Dalton Hall. For this a litter was procured, and he was carried all the way. · Edith went, with her maid and housekeeper, in a carriage, Dudleigh on horseback, and the other servants, with the luggage, in various conveyances.

Dalton received no benefit from his journey, but his friends were happy enough that he had received no injury. The medical attendance at Dalton Hall was, as before, the best that could be obtained, and all the care that affection could suggest was lavished upon him.

From what has already been said, it will be seen that in making this migration to Dalton Hall, Dudleigh was regardful of many things besides the patient. He had made every arrangement for the comfort of the occupants. He had sought out all the domestics that were necessary to diffuse an air of home over such a large establishment, and had been careful to submit them to Edith for her approval. He had also procured horses and grooms and carriages, and every thing that might conduce to the comfort of life. The old solitude and loneliness were thus terminated. The new housekeeper prevented Edith from feeling any anxiety about domestic concerns, and the servants all showed themselves well trained and perfectly subordinate.

Dalton's room was at the west end of the building. Edith occupied her old apartments. Dudleigh took that which had belonged to his "double." The housekeeper took the room that had been occupied by Lady Dudleigh.

Dudleigh was as devoted as ever to the sick man. He remained at his bedside through the greater part of the nights and through the mornings. In the afternoons he retired as before, and gave place to Edith. When he was there he sometimes had a servant upon whom he could rely, and then, if he felt unusual fatigue, and circumstances were favorable, he was able to snatch a little sleep. He usually went to bed at two in the afternoon, rose at seven, and in that brief sleep, with occasional naps during the morning, obtained enough to last him for the day. With this rest he was satisfied, and needed, or at least sought for, no recreation. During the hours of the morning he was able to attend to those outside duties that required overseeing or direction.

But while he watched in this way over the invalid, he was not a mere watcher. That invalid required, after all, but little at the hands of his nurses, and Dudleigh had much to do.

On his arrival at Dalton Hall he had possessed himself of all the papers that his "double" had left behind him, and these he diligently studied, so as to be able to carry out with the utmost efficiency the purpose that he had in his mind. It was during the long watches of the night that he studied these papers, trying to make out from them the manner of life and the associates of the one who had left them, trying also to arrive at some clew to his mysterious disappearance. This study he could keep up without detriment to his office of attendant, and while watching over the invalid he could carry out his investigations. Sometimes, in the afternoons, after indulging in more frequent naps than usual during the mornings, he was able to go out for a ride about the grounds. He was a first-rate horseman, and Edith noticed his admirable seat as she looked from the windows of her father's room.

Thus time went on.

Gradually Dudleigh and Edith began to occupy a different position toward one another. At the inn their relations were as has been shown. But after their arrival at Dalton Hall there occurred a gradual change. As Edith came to the room on the first day, Dudleigh waited. On entering she saw his eyes fixed on her with an expression of painful suspense, of earnest, eager inquiry. In that eloquent appealing glance all his soul seemed to beam from his eyes. It was reverent, it was almost humble, yet it looked for some small concession. May I hope? it said. Will you give a thought to me? See, I stand here, and I hang upon your look. Will you turn away from me?

Edith did not repel that mute appeal. There was that in her face which broke down Dudleigh's reserve. He advanced toward her and held out his hand. She did not reject it.

It was but a commonplace thing to do—it was what might have been done before—yet between these two it was far from commonplace. Their hands touched, their eyes met, but neither spoke a word. It was but a light grasp that Dudleigh gave. Reverentially, yet tenderly, he took that hand, not venturing to go beyond what might be accorded to the merest stranger, but contenting himself with that one concession. With that he retired, carrying with him the remembrance of that nearer approach, and the hope of what yet might be.

After that the extreme reserve was broken down. Each day, on meeting, a shake of the hands was accompanied by something more. Between any others these greetings would have been the most natural thing in the world; but here it was different. There was one subject in which each took the deepest interest, and about which each had something to say. Frederick Dalton's health was precious to each, and each felt anxiety about his condition. This formed a theme about which they might speak.

As Dudleigh waited for Edith, so Edith waited for Dudleigh; and still there were the same questions to be asked and answered. Standing thus together in that sick-room, with one life forming a common bond between them, conversing in low whispers upon one so dear to both, it would have been strange indeed if any thing like want of confidence had remained on either side.

CHAPTER XLVII.
A BETTER UNDERSTANDING.

DUDLEIGH lived on as before, assiduous in his attendance, dividing his time chiefly between nursing and study of the papers already mentioned. He never went out of the grounds on those occasional rides, and if any one in the neighborhood noticed this, the recent sad events might have been considered an excuse. Thus these two were thrown upon one another exclusively. For each there was no other society. As for Edith, Dudleigh had done so much that she felt a natural gratitude; and more than this, there was in her mind a sense of security and of dependence.

Meanwhile Dudleigh's pale face grew paler. His sleep had all along been utterly inadequate, and the incessant confinement had begun to show its effects. He had been accustomed to an open-air life and vigorous exercise. This quiet watching at the bedside of Dalton was more trying to his strength than severe labor could have been.

The change in him was not lost on Edith, and even if gratitude toward him had been wanting, common humanity would have impelled her to speak about it.

One day, as she came in, she was struck by his appearance. His face was ghastly white, and he had been sitting with his head in his hands as she softly entered. In an instant, as he heard her step, he started up, and advanced with a radiant smile, a smile caused by her approach.

"I'm afraid that you are overtasking yourself," said Edith, gently, after the usual greeting. "You are here too much. The confinement is too trying. You must take more rest and exercise."

Dudleigh's face was suffused with a sudden glow of delight.

"It is kind of you to notice it," said he, earnestly, "but I'm sure you are mistaken. I could do far more if necessary. This is my place, and this is my truest occupation."

"For that very reason," said Edith, in tones that showed more concern than she would have cared to acknowledge—"for that very reason you ought to preserve yourself—for his sake. You confine yourself here too much, and take too little rest. I see that you feel it already."

"I?" said Dudleigh, with a light laugh, whose musical cadence sounded very sweet to Edith, and revealed to her another side of his character very different from that sad and melancholy one which he had thus far shown—"I? Why, you have no idea of my capacity for this sort of thing. Excuse me, Miss Dalton, but it seems absurd to talk of my breaking down under such work as this."

Edith shook her head.

"You show traces of it," said she, in a gentle voice, looking away from him, "which common humanity would compel me to notice. You must not do all the work; I must have part of it."

"You?" exclaimed Dudleigh, with infinite tenderness in his tone. "Do you think that I would allow you to spend any more time here than you now do, or that I would spare myself at the expense of your health? Never! Aside from the fact that your father is so dear to me, there are considerations for you which would lead me to die at my post rather than allow you to have any more trouble."

There was a fervor in Dudleigh's tones which penetrated to Edith's heart. There was a deep glow in his eyes as he looked at her which Edith did not care to encounter.

"You are of far more importance to Sir Lionel than I am," said she, after a pause which began to be embarrassing. "But what will become of him if—if you are prostrated?"

"I shall not be prostrated," said Dudleigh.

"I think you will if this state of things continues."

"Oh, I don't think there is any prospect of my giving up just yet."

"No. I know your affection for him, and that it would keep you here until—until you could not stay any longer; and it is this which I wish to avoid."

"It is my duty," said Dudleigh. "He is one whom I revere more than any other man, and love as a father. Besides, there are other things that bind me to him—his immeasurable wrongs, his matchless patience—wrongs inflicted by one who is my father; and I, as the son, feel it a holy duty, the holiest of all duties, to stand by that bedside and devote myself to him. He is your father, Miss Dalton; you have never known him as I have known him—the soul of honor, the stainless gentleman, the ideal of chivalry and loyalty and truth. This he is, and for this he lies there, and my wretched father it is who has done this deed. But that father is a father only in name, and I have long ago transferred a son's love and a son's duty to that gentle and noble and injured friend."

This outburst of feeling came forth from Dudleigh's inmost heart, and was spoken with a passionate fervor which showed how deeply he felt what he said. Every word

thrilled through Edith. Bitter self-reproach at that moment came to her, as she thought of her own relations to her father. What Dudleigh's had been she did not know, but she saw that in him her father had found a son. And what had his daughter been to him? Of that she dared not think. Her heart was wrung with sharp anguish at the memories of the past, while at the same time she felt drawn more closely to Dudleigh, who had thus been to him all that she had failed to be. Had she spoken what she thought, she would have thanked and blessed him for those words. But she did not dare to trust herself to speak of that; rather she tried to restrain herself; and when she spoke, it was with a strong effort at this self-control.

"Well," she said, in a voice which was tremulous in spite of all her efforts, "this shows how dear you must be to him, since he has found such love in you, and so for his sake you must spare yourself. You must not stay here so constantly."

"Who is there to take my place?" asked Dudleigh, quietly.

"I," said Edith.

Dudleigh smiled.

"Do you think," said he, "that I would allow that? Even if I needed more rest, which I do not, do you think that I would take it at your expense—that I would go away, enjoy myself, and leave you to bear the fatigue? No, Miss Dalton; I am not quite so selfish as that."

"But you will let me stay here more than I do," said Edith, earnestly. "I may as well be here as in my own room. Will you not let me have half the care, and occasionally allow you to take rest?"

She spoke timidly and anxiously, as though she was asking some favor. And this was the feeling that she had, for it seemed to her that this man, who had been a son to her father, had more claims on his love, and a truer right here, than she, the unworthy daughter.

Dudleigh smiled upon her with infinite tenderness as he replied:

"Half the care! How could you endure it? You are too delicate for so much. You do too much already, and I am only anxious to relieve you of that. I was going to urge you to give up half of the afternoon, and take it myself."

"Give up half the afternoon!" cried Edith. "Why, I want to do more."

"But that is impossible. You are not strong enough," said Dudleigh. "I fear all the time that you are now overworking yourself. I would never forgive myself if you received any harm from this."

"Oh, I am very much stronger than you suppose. Besides, nursing is woman's work, and would fatigue me far less than you."

"I can not bear to have you fatigue yourself in any way. You must not—and I would do far more rather than allow you to have any trouble."

"But even if my health should suffer, it would not be of much consequence. So at least let me relieve you of something."

"Your health?" said Dudleigh, looking at her with an earnest glance; "your health! Why, that is every thing. Mine is nothing. Can you suggest such a thing to me as that I should allow any trouble to come to you? Besides, your delicate health already alarms me. You have not yet recovered from your illness. You are not capable of enduring fatigue, and I am always reproaching myself for allowing you to stay here as much as you do. The Dudleighs have done enough. They have brought the father to this;" and he pointed mournfully to the bed. "But," he added, in a tremulous voice, "the daughter should at least be saved, and to have harm come to her would be worse than death itself—to me."

Edith was silent for a few moments. Her heart was beating fast. When she spoke, it was with an effort, and in as calm a voice as possible.

"Oh," she said, "I am quite recovered. Indeed, I am as well as ever, and I wish to spend more time here. Will you not let me stay here longer?"

"How can I? The confinement would wear you out."

"It would not be more fatiguing than staying in my own room," persisted Edith.

"I'm afraid there would be very much difference," said Dudleigh. "In your own room you have no particular anxiety, but here you would have the incessant responsibility of a nurse. You would have to watch your father, and every movement would give you concern."

"And this harassing care is what I wish to save you from, and share with you," said Edith, earnestly. "Will you not consent to this?"

"To share it with you?" said Dudleigh, looking at her with unutterable tenderness. "To share it with you?" he repeated. "It would be only too much happiness for me to do so, but not if you are going to overwork yourself."

"But I will not," said Edith. "If I do, I can stop. I only ask to be allowed to come in during the morning, so as to relieve you of some of your work. You will consent, will you not?"

Edith asked him this as though Dudleigh had exclusive right here, and she had none. She could not help feeling as if this was so, and this feeling arose from those memories which she had of that terrible past, when she ignorantly hurled at that father's heart words that stung like the stings of scorpions. Never could she forgive herself for that, and for this she now humbled herself

in this way. Her tone was so pleading that Dudleigh could refuse no longer. With many deprecatory expressions, and many warnings and charges, he at last consented to let her divide the morning attendance with him. She was to come in at eleven o'clock.

This arrangement was at once acted upon. On the following day Edith came to her father's room at eleven. Dudleigh had much to ask her, and much to say to her, about her father's condition. He was afraid that she was not strong enough. He seemed to half repent his agreement. On the other hand, Edith assured him most earnestly that she was strong enough, that she would come here for the future regularly at eleven o'clock, and urged him to take care of his own health, and seek some recreation by riding about the grounds. This Dudleigh promised to do in the afternoon, but just then he seemed in no hurry to go. He lingered on. They talked in low whispers, with their heads close together. They had much to talk about; her health, his health, her father's condition—all these had to be discussed. Thus it was that the last vestiges of mutual reserve began to be broken down.

Day succeeded to day, and Edith always came to her father's room in the morning. At first she always urged Dudleigh to go off and take exercise, but at length she ceased to urge him. For two or three hours every day they saw much of one another, and thus associated under circumstances which enforced the closest intimacy and the strongest mutual sympathy.

CHAPTER XLVIII.

CAPTAIN CRUIKSHANK.

WHILE these things were going on, the world outside was not altogether indifferent to affairs in Dalton Hall. In the village and in the immediate neighborhood rumor had been busy, and at length the vague statements of the public voice began to take shape.

This is what rumor said: Dudleigh is an impostor!

An impostor, it said. For the true Dudleigh, it asserted, was still missing. This was not the real man. The remains found in the well had never been accounted for. Justice had foregone its claims too readily. The act remained, and the blood of the slain called aloud for vengeance.

How such a strange report was first started no one knew; but there it was, and the Dalton mystery remained as obscure as ever.

Various circumstances contributed to increase the public suspicion. All men saw that Dudleigh was different from this man, or else he had greatly changed. For the former was always outside, in the world, while this man remained secluded and shut up in the Hall. Why did he never show himself? Why did he surround himself with all this secrecy? This was the question.

The servants were eagerly questioned whenever any of them made their appearance in the village, but as they were all new in the place, their testimony was of little value. They could only say that he was devoted to the invalid, and that he called Miss Dalton by that name, and had called her by that name when he engaged them for her service.

Soon public opinion took two different forms, and two parties arose. One of these believed the present Dudleigh to be an impostor; the other, however, maintained that he was the real man, and that the change in his character was to be accounted for on the grounds of the terrible calamities that had resulted from his thoughtlessness, together with his own repentance for the suffering which he had inflicted.

Meanwhile the subject of all this excitement and gossip was living in his own seclusion, quite apart from the outside world. One change, however, had taken place in his life which required immediate action on his part.

A great number of letters had come for "Captain Dudleigh." The receipt of these gave him trouble. They were reminders of various pecuniary obligations which had been contracted some time previously. They were, in short—duns. He had been at Dalton Hall some six weeks before these interesting letters began to arrive. After that time they came in clusters, fast and frequent. The examination of these formed no small part of his occupation when he was alone. Some of these letters were jocular in their tone, reminding him of his chronic impecuniosity, and his well-known impracticability in every thing relating to money. These jocular letters, however, never failed to remind him that, as he had made a rich match, there was no reason why he should not pay his debts, especially as the writers were hard up, and had waited so long without troubling him. These jocular letters, in fact, informed him that if a settlement was not made at once, it would be very much the worse for Dudleigh.

Others were from old sporting companions, reminding him of bets which had not been paid, expressing astonishment which was child-like in its simplicity, and requesting an immediate settlement. These were generally short, curt, and altogether unpleasant. Others were business letters, containing the announcement of notes falling due. Others were from lawyers, stating the fact that certain specified claims had been put in their hands for collection, and requesting early attention.

All these seemed to come together. Misfortunes, says the proverb, never come singly, and duns may fairly be reckoned among misfortunes. These duns, however, troublesome though they were, were one by one got rid of by the simple and effectual process of payment; for Dudleigh considered it on the whole safer and better, under these peculiar circumstances, to pay the money which was demanded than to expose himself to arrest or lawsuits.

In connection with these affairs an event occurred which at the time caused uneasiness, and gave the prospect of future trouble. One day a gentleman called and sent up his card. It was Captain Cruikshank. The name Dudleigh recognized as one which had been appended to several dunning letters of the most importunate kind, and the individual himself was apparently some sporting friend.

On going down Dudleigh saw a portly, bald-headed man, with large whiskers, standing in front of one of the drawing-room windows, looking out. He seemed midway between a gentleman and a blackleg, neither altogether one nor the other. At the noise of Dudleigh's entrance he turned quickly around, and with a hearty, bluff manner walked up to him and held out his hand.

Dudleigh fixed his eyes steadily upon those of the other man, and bowed, without accepting the proffered hand, appearing not to see it. His whole mien was full of aristocratic reserve, and cold, repellent distance of manner, which checked the other in the midst of a full tide of voluble congratulations into which he had flung himself. Thus interrupted, he looked confused, stammered, and finally said,

"'Pon my honor, Dudleigh, you don't appear to be overcordial with an old friend, that's seen you through so many scrapes as I have."

"Circumstances," said Dudleigh, "of a very painful character have forced me to sever myself completely from all my former associates—all, without exception."

"Well, of course—as to that, it's all right, I dare say," remarked the other, from whom Dudleigh never removed his eyes; "but then, you know, it seems to me that some friends ought to be—a—retained, you know, and you and I, you know, were always of that sort that we were useful to one another."

This was thrown out as a very strong hint on the part of Captain Cruikshank, and he watched Dudleigh earnestly to see its effect.

"I make no exceptions whatever," said Dudleigh. "What has occurred to me is the same as death. I am dead virtually to the world in which I once lived. My former friends and acquaintances are the same as though I had never known them."

"Gad! something has come over you, that's a fact," said Captain Cruikshank. "You're

K

"WELL, REALLY—YES, THIS IS IT."

a changed man, whatever the reason is. Well, you have a right to choose for yourself, and I can't be offended. At the same time, if you ever want to join the old set again, let me know, and I promise you there'll be no difficulty."

Dudleigh bowed.

"But then I suppose you're settled down in such infernally comfortable quarters," continued the other, "that it's not likely you'll ever trouble us again. Married and done for—that's the word. Plenty of money, and nothing to do."

"If you have any thing particular to say," said Dudleigh, coldly, "I should like to hear it; if not, I must excuse myself, as I am particularly engaged."

"Oh, no offense, no offense; I merely came to offer an old friend's congratulations, you know, and— By-the-way," continued Cruikshank, lowering his voice, "there's that little I O U of yours. I thought perhaps you might find it convenient to settle, and if so, it would be a great favor to me."

"What is the amount?" asked Dudleigh, who remembered this particular debt per-

fectly well, since it had been the subject of more than one letter of a most unpleasant character.

"The amount?" said Cruikshank. "Well, really—let me see—I don't quite remember, but I'll find out in a moment."

With these words he drew forth his pocket-book and fumbled among the papers. At length he produced one, and tried hard to look as if he had not known all along perfectly well what that amount was.

"Well, really—yes, this is it," he remarked, as he looked at a piece of paper. "The amount, did you say? The amount is just two hundred pounds. It's not much for you, as you are now situated, I should suppose."

"Is that the note?" asked Dudleigh, who was anxious to get rid of this visitor, and suspected all along that he might have a deeper purpose than the mere collection of a debt.

"That is the note," said Cruikshank.

"I will pay it now," said Dudleigh.

He left the room for a short time, and during his absence Cruikshank amused himself with staring at the portrait of "Captain Dudleigh," which hung in a conspicuous position before his eyes. He was not kept long waiting, for Dudleigh soon returned, and handed him the money. Cruikshank took it with immense satisfaction, and handed the note over in return, which Dudleigh carefully transferred to his own pocket-book, where he kept many other such papers.

Cruikshank now bade him a very effusive adieu. Dudleigh stood at the window watching the retreating figure of his visitor.

"I wonder how long this sort of thing can go on?" he murmured. "I don't like this acting on the defensive. I'll have to make the attack myself soon."

CHAPTER XLIX.

EDITH'S NEW FRIEND.

EVERY day Edith and Dudleigh saw more and more of one another. Now that the crust of reserve was broken through, and something like intimacy had been reached, the sick man's apartment was the most natural place for each to seek. It came at last that the mornings and afternoons were no longer allotted to each exclusively, but while one watched, the other would often be present. In the evenings especially the two were together there.

The condition in which Dalton was demanded quiet, yet needed but little direct attention. It was only necessary that some one should be in the room with him. He lay, as has been said, in a state of stupor, and knew nothing of what was going on. It was only necessary for those who might be with him to give him, from time to time, the medicines that had been prescribed by the physicians, or the nourishment which nature demanded. Apart from this there was little now to be done.

While Edith and Dudleigh were thus together, they were naturally dependent exclusively upon one another. This association seemed not unpleasant to either of them; every day it gained a new charm; and at length both came to look forward to this as the chief pleasure of their lives. For Edith there was no other companion than Dudleigh in Dalton Hall with whom she could associate on equal terms; he had strong claims now on her confidence, and even on her gratitude; and while he was thus the only one to whom she could look for companionship, she also bore the same relation to him.

There was something in the look and in the manner of Dudleigh in these interviews which might have moved a colder nature than that of Edith. Whenever he entered and greeted her, his face was overspread by a radiant expression that spoke of joy and delight. Whenever they met, his face told all the feelings of his heart. Yet never in any way, either by word or act, did he ven-

ture upon any thing which might not have been witnessed by all the world. There was something touching in that deep joy of his which was inspired simply by her presence, and in the peace and calm that came over him while she was near. Elsewhere it was different with him. Whenever she had seen his face outside—and that had been often—for she had often seen him riding or walking in front of the windows—she had marked how care-worn and sad its expression was; she had marked a cloud of melancholy upon his brow, that bore witness to some settled grief unknown to her, and had read in all the lineaments of his features the record which some mysterious sorrow had traced there. Yet in her presence all this departed, and the eyes that looked on her grew bright with happiness, and the face that was turned toward her was overspread with joy. Could it be any other than herself who made this change?

There was something in the manner of this man toward her which was nothing less than adoration. The delicate grace of his address, the deep reverence of his look, the intonations of his voice, tremulous with an emotion that arose from the profoundest depths of his nature, all bore witness to this. For when he spoke to her, even about the most trifling things, there was that in his tone which showed that the subject upon which he was speaking was nothing, but the one to whom he was speaking was all in all. He stood before her like one with a fervid nature, intense in its passion, and profound in all its emotion, who under a calm exterior concealed a glow of feeling which burned in his heart like a consuming fire—a feeling that was kept under restraint by the force of will, but which, if freed from restraint but for one moment, would burst forth and bear down all before it.

Weeks passed away, but amidst all the intimacy of their association there never appeared the slightest attempt on his part to pass beyond the limits which he had set for himself. Another man under such circumstances might have ventured upon something like a greater familiarity, but with this man there was no such attempt. After all their interviews he still stood in spirit at a distance, with the same deep reverence in his look, and the same profound adoration in his manner, regarding her as one might regard a divinity. For Dudleigh stood afar off, yet like a worshiper—far off, as though he deemed that divinity of his inaccessible—yet none the less did his devotion make itself manifest. All this was not to be seen in his words, but rather in his manner, in the expression of his face, and in the attitude of his soul, as it became manifest to her whom he adored.

For she could not but see it; in matters of this sort woman's eyes are keen; but here any one might have perceived the deep devotion of Dudleigh. The servants saw it, and talked about it. What was plain to them could not but be visible to her. She saw it—she knew it—and what then? Certainly it was not displeasing. The homage thus paid was too delicate to give offense; it was of that kind which is most flattering to the heart, which never grows familiar, but is insinuated or suggested rather than expressed.

It was consoling to her lonely heart to see one like this, who, whenever she appeared, would pass from a state of sadness to one of happiness; to see his eloquent eyes fixed upon her with a devotion beyond words; to hear his voice, which, while it spoke the commonplaces of welcome, was yet in its tremulous tones expressive of a meaning very different from that which lay in the words. Naturally enough, she was touched by this silent reverence which she thus inspired; and as she had already found cause to trust him, so she soon came to trust him still more. She looked up to him as one with whom she might confer, not only with reference to her father, but also with regard to the conduct of the estate. Thus many varied subjects grew up for their consideration, and gradually the things about which they conversed grew more and more personal. Beginning with Mr. Dalton, they at last ended with themselves, and Dudleigh on many occasions found opportunity of advising Edith on matters where her own personal interest or welfare was concerned.

Thus their intimacy deepened constantly from the very necessities of their position.

Then there was the constant anxiety which each felt and expressed about the health of the other. Each had urged the other to give up the allotted portion of attendance. This had ended in both of them keeping up that attendance together for a great part of the time. Nevertheless, the subject of one another's health still remained. Dudleigh insisted that Edith had not yet recovered, that she was nothing better than a convalescent, and that she ought not to risk such close confinement. Edith, on the contrary, insisted that she was able to do far more, and that the confinement was injuring him far more than herself. On one occasion she asked him what he thought would become of her if he too became ill, and the care of the two should thus devolve upon her.

At this remark, which escaped Edith in the excitement of an argument about the interesting subject of one another's health, Dudleigh's face lighted up. He looked at her with an expression that spoke more than words could tell. Yet he said nothing. He said nothing in words, but his eyes spoke an intelligible language, and she could well understand what was thus expressed.

What was it that they said?

O loved! and O adored beyond weak words! O divinity of mine! they said. If death should be the end of this, then such death would be sweet, if I could but die in your presence! O loved and longed for! they said. Between us there is an impassable barrier. I stand without; I seek not to break through; but even at a distance I love, and I adore!

And that was what Edith understood. Her eyes sank before his gaze. They sat in silence for a long time, and neither of them ventured to break that silence by words.

At length Dudleigh proposed that they should both go out for a short time each day together. This he had hesitated to do on account of Mr. Dalton. Yet, after all, there was no necessity for them to be there always. Mr. Dalton, in his stupor, was unconscious of their presence, and their absence could therefore make no difference to him, either with regard to his feelings or the attention which he received. When Dudleigh made his proposal, he mentioned this also, and Edith saw at once its truth. She therefore consented quite readily, and with a gratification that she made no attempt to conceal.

Why should she not? She had known enough of sorrow. Dalton Hall had thus far been to her nothing else than a prison-house. Why should it not afford her some pleasure as an offset to former pain? Here was an opportunity of obtaining at last some compensation. She could go forth into the bright free open air under the protection of one whose loyalty and devotion had been sufficiently proved. Could she hope for any pleasanter companion?

Thus a new turn took place in the lives of these two. The mornings they passed in Mr. Dalton's room, and in the afternoons, except when there was unpleasant weather, they went out together. Sometimes they strolled through the grounds, down the lordly avenues, and over the soft sweet meadows; at other times they went on horseback. The grounds were extensive and beautiful, but confinement within the park inclosure was attended with unpleasant memories, and so, in the ordinary course of things, they naturally sought the wider, freer world outside.

The country around Dalton Hall was exceedingly beautiful, and rich in all those peculiar English charms whose quiet grace is so attractive to the refined taste. Edith had never enjoyed any opportunity of seeing all this, and now it opened before her like a new world. Formerly, during her long imprisonment, she had learned to think of that outside world as one which was full of every thing that was most delightful; there freedom dwelt; and that thought was enough to make it fair and sweet to her. So the prisoner always thinks of that which lies beyond his prison walls, and imagines that if he were once in that outer world he would be in the possession of perfect happiness.

Horseback riding has advantages which make it superior to every other kind of exercise. On foot one is limited and restrained, for progress is slow; and although one can go any where, yet the pedestrian who wishes for enjoyment must only stroll. Any thing else is too fatiguing. But a small space can be traversed, and that only with considerable fatigue. In a carriage there is ease and comfort; but the high-road forms the limit of one's survey; to that he must keep, and not venture out of the smooth beaten track. But on horseback all is different. There one has something of the comfort of the carriage and something of the freedom of the pedestrian. Added to this, there is an exhilaration in the motion itself which neither of the others presents. The most rapid pace can alternate with the slowest; the highway no longer forms bounds to the journey; distance is no obstacle where enjoyment is concerned; and few places are inaccessible which it is desirable to see. The generous animal which carries his rider is himself an additional element of pleasure; for he himself seems to sympathize with all his rider's feelings, and to such an extent that even the solitary horseman is not altogether alone.

This was the pleasure which Edith was now able to enjoy with Dudleigh as her companion, and the country was one which afforded the best opportunity for such exercise. Dudleigh was, as has been said, a first-rate horseman, and managed his steed like one who had been brought up from childhood to that accomplishment. Edith also had always been fond of riding; at school she had been distinguished above all the others for her skill and dash in this respect; and there were few places where, if Dudleigh led, she would not follow.

All the pleasure of this noble exercise was thus enjoyed by both of them to the fullest extent. There was an exhilaration in it which each felt equally. The excitement of the rapid gallop or the full run, the quiet sociability of the slow walk, the perfect freedom of movement in almost any direction, were all appreciated by one as much as by the other. Then, too, the country itself was of that character which was best adapted to give pleasure. There were broad public roads, hard, smooth, and shadowed by overarching trees—roads such as are the glory of England, and with which no other country has any that can compare. Then there were by-roads leading from one public road to another, as smooth and as shadowy as the others, but far more inviting, since they presented greater seclusion and scenes of more quiet picturesque beauty.

Here they encountered pleasant lanes leading through peaceful sequestered valleys, beside gently flowing streams and babbling brooks, where the trees overarched most grandly and the shade was most refreshing. Here they loved best to turn, and move slowly onward at a pace best suited to quiet observation and agreeable conversation.

Such a change from the confinement of Dalton Hall and Dalton Park was unspeakably delightful to Edith. She had no anxiety about leaving her father, nor had Dudleigh; for in his condition the quiet housekeeper could do all that he would require in their absence. To Edith this change was more delightful than to Dudleigh, since she had felt those horrors of imprisonment which he had not. These rides through the wide country, so free, so unrestrained, brought to her a delicious sense of liberty. For the first time in many weary months she felt that she was her own mistress. She was free, and she could enjoy with the most intense delight all the new pleasures of this free and unrestrained existence. So in these rides she was always joyous, always gay, and even enthusiastic. It was to her like the dawn of a new life, and into that life she threw herself with an abandonment of feeling that evinced itself in unrestrained enjoyment of every thing that presented itself to her view.

Dudleigh, however, was very different. In him there had always appeared a certain restraint. His manner toward Edith had that devotion and respect which have already been described; he was as profound and sincere in his homage and as tender in his loyalty as ever; but even now, under these far more favorable circumstances, he did not venture beyond the limits of courtesy—those limits which society has established and always recognizes. From the glance of his eyes, however, from the tone of his voice, and from his whole mien, there could be seen the deep fervor of his feelings toward Edith; but though the tones were often tremulous with deep feeling, the words that he spoke seldom expressed more than the formulas of politeness. His true meaning lay behind or beneath his words. His quiet manner was therefore not the sign of an unemotional nature, but rather of strong passion reined in and kept in check by a powerful will, the sign and token of a nature which had complete mastery over itself, so that never on any occasion could a lawless impulse burst forth.

These two were therefore not uncongenial. —the one with her enthusiasm, her perfect abandon of feeling, the other with his self-command, his profound devotion. Their tastes were alike. By a common impulse they sought the same woodland paths, or directed their course to the same picturesque scenes; they admired the same beauties, or turned away with equal indifference from the commonplace, the tame, or the prosaic. The books which they liked were generally the same. No wonder that the change was a pleasant one to Edith. These rides began to bring back to her the fresh feeling of her buoyant school-girl days, and restore to her that joyous spirit and that radiant fancy which had distinguished her at Plympton Terrace.

Riding about thus every where, these two became conspicuous. The public mind was more puzzled than ever. Those who maintained that Dudleigh was an impostor felt their confidence greatly shaken, and could only murmur something about its being done "for effect," and "to throw dust into the eyes of people;" while those who believed in him asserted their belief more strongly than ever, and declared that the unhappy differences which had existed between husband and wife had passed away, and terminated in a perfect reconciliation.

CHAPTER L.

A TERRIBLE ADVENTURE.

THUS Dudleigh and Edith found a new life opening before them; and though this life was felt by both to be a temporary one, which must soon come to an end, yet each seemed resolved upon enjoying it to the utmost while it lasted.

On one of these rides a remarkable event occurred.

It chanced that Edith's horse dropped a shoe, and they went slowly to the nearest village to have him reshod. They came to one before long, and riding slowly through it, they reached the farthest end of it, and here they found a smithy.

A small river ran at this end of the village across the road, and over this there was a narrow bridge. The smithy was built close beside the bridge on piles half over the edge of the stream. It faced the road, and, standing in the open doorway, one could see up the entire length of the village.

Here they dismounted, and found the farrier. Unfortunately the shoe had been lost, and the farrier had none, so that he had to make one for the occasion. This took up much time, and Edith and Dudleigh strolled up and down the village, stood on the bridge, and wandered about, frequently returning to the smithy to see how the work was progressing.

The last time they came they found that the smith was nearly through his work. They stood watching him as he was driving in one of the last nails, feeling a kind of indolent curiosity in the work, when suddenly there arose in the road behind them a frightful outburst of shrieks and cries. The smith dropped the horse's foot and the hammer,

and started up. Dudleigh and Edith also turned by a quick movement to see what it might be.

A terrible sight burst upon them.

As they looked up the village street, they saw coming straight toward them a huge dog, which was being pursued by a large crowd of men. The animal's head was bent low, his jaw dropped, and almost before they fairly understood the meaning of what they saw, he had come close enough for them to distinguish the foam that dropped from his jaws, and his wild, staring, blood-shot eyes. In that moment they understood it. In that animal, which thus rushed straight toward them, and was already so near, they saw one of the most terrible sights that can appear to the eye of man—a mad dog!

The smith gave a yell of horror, and sprang to a window that looked out of the rear of the smithy into the stream. Through this he flung himself, and disappeared.

On came the dog, his eyes glaring, his mouth foaming, distancing all his pursuers, none of whom were near enough to deal a blow. They did not seem particularly anxious to get nearer to him, to tell the truth, but contented themselves with hurling stones at him, and shrieking and yelling from a safe distance in his rear.

On came the dog. There was no time for escape. Quick as thought Dudleigh flung himself before Edith. There was no time to seize any weapon. He had to face the dog unarmed, in his own unassisted strength. As for Edith, she stood paralyzed with utter horror.

On came the mad dog, and with a horrible snapping howl, sprang straight at Dudleigh. But Dudleigh was prepared. As the dog sprang he hit straight out at him "from the shoulder," and dealt him a tremendous blow on the throat with his clinched fist. The blow hurled the animal over and over till he fell upon his back, and before he could regain his feet, Dudleigh sprang upon him and seized him by the throat.

He was a large and powerful animal. He struggled fiercely in the grasp of Dudleigh, and the struggle was a terrific one. The villagers, who had now come up, stood off, staring in unspeakable horror, not one of them daring to interfere.

But the terror which had at first frozen Edith into stone now gave way to another feeling, a terror quite as strong, but which, instead of congealing her into inaction, roused her to frenzied exertion. Dudleigh's life was at stake! Terror for herself was paralysis to her limbs; terror for him was the madness of desperate exertion and daring.

She sprang toward one of the by-standers, who had a knife in his hand. This knife she snatched from him, and rushed toward Dudleigh. The dog was still writhing in his furious struggles. Dudleigh was still holding him down, and clutching at his throat with death-like tenacity. For a moment she paused, and then flinging herself upon her knees at the dog's head, she plunged the knife with all her strength into the side of his neck.

It was a mortal wound!

With a last howl, the huge animal relaxed his efforts, and in a few moments lay dead in the road.

Dudleigh rose to his feet. There was in his face an expression of pain and apprehension. The villagers stood aloof, staring at him with awful eyes. No word of congratulation was spoken. The silence was ominous; it was terrible. Edith was struck most of all by the expression of Dudleigh's face, and read there what she dared not think of. For a moment the old horror which had first seized upon her came upon her once more, paralyzing her limbs. She looked at him with staring eyes as she knelt, and the bloody knife dropped from her nerveless hands. But the horror passed, and once more, as before, was succeeded by vehement action. She sprang to her feet, and caught at his coat as he walked away.

He turned, with downcast eyes.

"O my God!" she exclaimed, in anguish, "you are wounded—you are bitten—and by that—" She could not finish her sentence. Dudleigh gave her an awful look.

"You will die! you will die!" she almost screamed. "Oh, can not something be done? Let me look at your arm. Oh, let me examine it—let me see where it is! Show me—tell me what I can do."

Dudleigh had turned to enter the smithy as Edith had arrested him, and now, standing there in the doorway, he gently disengaged himself from her grasp. Then he took off his coat and rolled up his sleeve.

Edith had already noticed that his coat sleeve was torn, and now, as he took off his coat, she saw, with unutterable horror, his white shirt sleeves red with spots of blood. As he rolled up that sleeve she saw the marks of bruises on his arm; but it was on one place in particular that her eyes were fastened—a place where a red wound, freshly made, showed the source of the blood stains, and told at what a terrible price he had rescued her from the fierce beast. He had conquered, but not easily, for he had carried off this wound, and the wound was, as he knew, and as she knew, the bite of a mad dog!

Edith gave a low moan of anguish and despair. She took his arm in her hands. Dudleigh did not withdraw it. Even at that moment of horror it seemed sweet to him to see these signs of feeling on her part; and though he did not know what it was that she had in her mind, he waited, to feel for a moment longer the clasp of those hands.

Edith held his arm in her hands, and the terrible wound fascinated her eyes with horror. It seemed to her at that moment that this was the doom of Dudleigh, the stamp of his sure and certain death. It seemed to her that this mark was the announcement to her that henceforth Dudleigh was lost to her; that he must die—die by a death so horrible that its horrors surpassed language and even imagination, and that this unutterable doom had been drawn down upon him for her.

It had been terrible. Out of pleasant thoughts and genial conversation and gentle smiles and happy interchange of sentiment, out of the joy of a glad day, out of the delight of golden hours and sunlight and beauty and peace—to be plunged suddenly into a woe like this!

There came to her a wild and desperate thought. Only one idea was in her mind—to save Dudleigh, to snatch this dear friend from the death to which he had flung himself for her sake. Inspired by this sole idea, there had come a sudden thought. It was the thought of that royal wife's devotion who, when her young husband lay dying from the poisoned dagger of an assassin, drew the poison from the wound, and thus snatched him from the very grasp of death. This it was, then, that was in the mind of Edith, and it was in her agonized heart at that moment to save Dudleigh even as Eleanor had saved Edward.

She bent down her head, till her face was close to his arm.

Dudleigh looked on as in a dream. He did not know, he could not even conceive, what she had in her heart to do for his sake. It would have seemed incredible, had he not seen it; nor could he have imagined it, had he not been convinced.

The discovery flashed suddenly, vividly across his mind. He recognized in that one instant the love, the devotion, stronger than death, which was thus manifesting itself in that slight movement of that adored one by his side. It was a thought of sweetness unutterable, which amidst his agony sent a thrill of rapture through every nerve.

It was but for a moment.

He gently withdrew his arm. She looked at him reproachfully and imploringly. He turned away his face firmly.

"Will you leave me for a moment, Miss Dalton?" said he, in a choking voice.

He pointed to the doorway.

She did not appear to understand him. She stood, with her face white as ashes, and looked at him with the same expression.

"Leave me—oh, leave me," he said, "for one moment! It is not fit for you."

She did not move.

Dudleigh could wait no longer. His soul was roused up to a desperate purpose, but the execution of that purpose could not be

"THERE WAS THE HISS OF SOMETHING SCORCHING."

delayed. He sprang to the fire. One of the irons had been imbedded there in the glowing coals. He had seen this in his despair, and had started toward it, when Edith detained him. This iron he snatched out. It was at a white heat, dazzling in its glow.

In an instant he plunged this at the wound. A low cry like a muffled groan was wrung from the spectators, who watched the act with eyes of utter horror.

There was the hiss of something scorching; a sickening smoke arose and curled up about his head, and ascended to the roof. But in the midst of this Dudleigh stood as rigid as Mucius Scævola under another fiery trial, with the hand that held the glowing iron and the arm that felt the awful torment as steady as though he had been a statue fashioned in that attitude. Thus he finished his work.

It was all over in a few seconds. Then Dudleigh turned, with his face ghastly white, and big drops of perspiration, wrung out by that agony, standing over his brow. He flung down the iron.

At the same moment Edith, yielding altogether to the horror that had hitherto overwhelmed her, fell senseless to the floor.

By this time some among the crowd had regained the use of their faculties, and these advanced to offer their services. Dudleigh was able to direct them to take Edith to some shelter, and while they did so he followed. Edith after some time revived. A doctor was sent for, who examined Dudleigh's arm, and praised him for his prompt action, while wondering at his daring. He bound it up, and gave some general directions.

Meanwhile a messenger had been sent to Dalton Hall for the carriage. Edith, though she had revived, hardly felt strong enough for horseback, and Dudleigh's arm was sufficiently painful to make him prefer as great a degree of quiet as possible. When the carriage came, therefore, it was with feelings of great relief that they took their seats and prepared to go back. Nor was their journey any the less pleasant from the fact that they had to sit close together, side by side—a closer union than any they had thus far known. It was an eventful day: nor was its conclusion the least so. But little was said during the drive home. Each felt what had been done by the other. Edith remembered how Dudleigh had risked the most terrible, the most agonizing of deaths to save her. Dudleigh, on his part, remembered that movement of hers, by which she was about to take the poison from his wound unto herself. The appalling event which had occurred had broken down all reserve. All was known. Each knew that the other was dearer than all the world. Each knew that the other loved and was loved; but yet in the midst of this knowledge there was a feeling of utter helplessness arising from the unparalleled position of Edith. It was a peculiar and at the same time a perilous one.

In the eyes of the world these two were nothing less than man and wife. In the eyes of the law, as Edith feared, she was the wife of Leon Dudleigh.

Now this man was not Leon ·Dudleigh. He was an impostor. Edith did not even know that his name was Dudleigh at all. She had never asked him the secret of his life; he had never volunteered to tell it. She did not know what his name really was.

As an impostor, she knew that he was liable to discovery, arrest, and punishment at any time. She knew that the discovery of this man would endanger herself. His arrest would involve hers, and she would once more be tried for her life, as the murderer of the missing man, with the additional disadvantage of having already eluded justice by a trick. She was liable at any moment to this, for the missing man was still missing, and it would go doubly hard for her, since she had aided and abetted for so long a time the conspiracy of an impostor.

Yet this impostor was beyond all doubt a man of the loftiest character, most perfect breeding, and profoundest self-devotion. From the very first his face had revealed to her that he had entered upon this conspiracy for her sake. And since then, for her sake, what had he not done?

Thus, then, they were both in a position of peril. They loved one another passionately. But they could not possess one another. The world supposed them man and wife, but the law made her the wife of another, of whom it also charged her with being the murderer. Around these two there were clouds of darkness, deep and dense, and their future was utterly obscure.

These things were in the minds of both of them through that drive, and that evening as they walked about the grounds. For since their mutual love had all been revealed, Dudleigh had spoken in words what he had repressed so long, and Edith had confessed what had already been extorted from her. Yet this mutual confession of love, with all its attendant endearments, had not blinded them to the dangers of their position and the difficulties that lay in their way.

"I can not endure this state of things," said Dudleigh. "For your sake, as well as my own, Edith darling, it must be brought to an end. I have not been idle, but I have waited to hear from those who have put themselves on the track of the man from whom we have most to dread. One has tried to find some trace of Leon; the other is my mother. Now I have not heard from either of them, and I am beginning to feel not only impatient, but uneasy."

CHAPTER LI.

IMPORTANT NEWS.

THE position of Edith and Dudleigh was of such a character that further inaction was felt to be intolerable, and it was only the hope of hearing from those who were already engaged in the work that made him capable of delaying longer. But several events now occurred which put an end to the present state of things.

The first of these was a marked improvement in the condition of Mr. Dalton. A successful operation performed upon him had the result of restoring him to consciousness, and after this a general increase of strength took place. His intense joy at the sight of Edith, and the delight which he felt at her presence and the reception of her loving and tender care, all acted favorably upon him; and as the sorrow which he had experienced had been the chief cause of his prostration, so the happiness which he now felt became a powerful agent toward restoring him to strength.

The joy of Edith was so great that the terror and perplexity of her position ceased to alarm her. Her greatest grief seemed now removed, for she had feared that her father might die without ever knowing how deeply she repented for the past and how truly she loved him. Now, however, he would live to receive from her those tender cares which, while they could never in her mind atone for the wrongs that she had inflicted upon him, would yet be the means of giving some happiness to him who had suffered so much.

A few days after her father's restoration to consciousness Dudleigh received a letter of a most important character, and as soon as he was able to see Edith during the walks that they still took in the afternoon or evening, he informed her with unusual emotion of the fact.

"She writes," he concluded, "that she has got at last on the track of Leon."

"Who? Your mother?"

"No. I have not heard from my mother. I mean Miss Fortescue."

"Miss Fortescue?" repeated Edith, in some surprise.

"Yes," said Dudleigh. "I did not mention her before, because I did not know what you might think about it. But the fact is, I saw her after the trial was over. She had come to give important testimony. She came to see me, and told me all about it. The information was of the most extraordinary kind. It appears that in the course of her own inquiries she had heard some gossip about a long box which had been put off at Finsbury from the train. This was called for by a teamster, who was accompanied by a Newfoundland dog, who took the box, and drove away from Finsbury to Dalton. Now, as no such teamster, or box, or dog, had been seen in Dalton, she began to suspect that it had something to do with the remains found in the well, and that this whole matter was a malignant scheme of Leon's to involve you or your father, or both, in some calamity. At any rate, she herself went cautiously about, and tried to investigate for herself. She had all along felt convinced that Leon was alive, and she felt equally convinced that he was capable of any malignant act for the purpose of wreaking his vengeance on you or your father. He had been baffled here, and had sworn vengeance. That much your father told me before the trial.

"So Miss Fortescue searched very carefully, and at length made a very important discovery. A few miles this side of Finsbury there is a grove, through which the Dalton Park wall runs. Here she happened to see the trace of heavy wheels, and the hedge which adjoins the wall, and is rather thin there, seemed to have been broken through, so as to form an opening wide enough to admit a cart. Struck by this, she followed the marks of the wheels into the grove for some distance, until they stopped. Here, to her surprise, she saw close by the Dalton Park wall an oblong box, just like the one which had been described to her. It was empty, and had been left here.

"Now why had it been left here? Miss Fortescue felt certain that Leon had brought a dead body in that box, that he had taken it stealthily into the park, and thrown it down into the well, and then, not wishing to be seen with such a very conspicuous thing as this box, he had left it behind him. She also thought that he had managed in a secret way to start the rumors that had prevailed, and to drop some hints, either by anonymous letters to the sheriff or otherwise, which turned their attention to the well. She saw at once how important this testimony would be in your favor, and therefore saw the Finsbury people who had told her of the teamster, and with these she came to the trial. But when she came she heard that the missing man had returned—and saw me, you know."

At this extraordinary information Edith was silent for some time.

"I have often tried to account for it," said she, "but I could hardly bring myself to believe that this was his work. But now when I recall his last words to me, I can understand it, and I am forced to believe it."

"His last words to you?" said Dudleigh, in an inquiring tone.

"Yes," said Edith, with a sigh. "The remembrance of that night is so distressing that I have never felt able to speak of it. Even the thought of what I suffered then almost drives me wild; but now—and to you, Reginald—it is different, and I have strength to speak of it."

As she said this she looked at him tenderly, and Reginald folded her in his arms. She then began to give an account of that eventful night, of her long preparations, her suspense, her departure, until that moment when she saw that she was pursued. The remainder only need be given here.

She had been right in her conjectures. Leon had suspected, or at least had watched, and discovered all. The moonlight had revealed her plainly as she stole across the open area, and when she fled into the woods the rustling and crackling had betrayed the direction which she had taken. Thus it was that Leon had been able to pursue her, and his first sneering words as he came up to her made her acquainted with her awkwardness. The trees were not so close but that her figure could be seen; the moonlight streamed down, and disclosed her standing at bay, desperate, defiant, with her dagger uplifted, and her arm nerved to strike. This Leon saw, and being afraid to venture close to her, he held aloof, and tried to conceal his cowardice in taunts and sneers.

Edith said nothing for some time, but at last, seeing that Leon hesitated, she determined to continue her flight in spite of him, and informed him so.

Upon this he threatened to set the dog on her.

"He will tear you to pieces," cried Leon. "No one will suspect that I had any thing to do with it. Every body will believe that in trying to run away you were caught by the dog."

This threat, however, did not in the least alarm Edith. She was not afraid of the dog. She had already gained the animal's affections by various little acts of kindness. So now, in response to Leon's threats, she held out her hand toward the dog and called him. The dog wagged his tail and made a few steps forward. At this Leon grew infuriated, and tried to set him at Edith. But the dog would not obey. Leon then held him, pointing his head toward Edith, and doing all in his power to urge him on. The effort, however, was completely useless. Edith, seeing this, hurried away. Leon rushed after her, followed by the dog, and once more she stood at bay, while the same efforts were repeated to set the dog at her. This was done several times over. At last Leon gave the dog a terrible beating. Wild with indignant rage at his cowardice, brutality, and persistent pursuit, full also of pity for the poor animal who was suffering for love of her, Edith sprang forward at Leon as though she would stab him. Whether she would have done so or not, need not be said; at any rate her purpose was gained, for Leon, with a cry of fear, started back.

Then standing at a safe distance, he hurled at her the most terrible threats of veugeauce. Among all these she remembered well one expression, which he repeated over and over.

"You've threatened my life!" he cried. "My life shall lie at your door, if I have to kill myself."

This he said over and over. But Edith did not wait much longer. Once more she started off, and this time Leon did not follow her. That was the last she saw or heard of him. After this she wandered about through woods and swamps for a long time, and at length, about the dawn of day, when she had almost lost all hope, she came to the wall. This she clambered over by means of her rope and hook, and reached the Dalton Inn in the condition already described.

Afterward, when she heard that Leon was missing, and when she was confronted with the remains, the whole horror of her situation burst upon her mind. Her first thought was that he had in his desperate rage actually killed himself; but the absence of the head showed that this was impossible. There remained after this a deep mystery, the solution of which she could not discover, but in the midst of which she could not fail to see how terribly circumstances bore against her. She was afraid to say any thing. She knew that if she told all she would be believed but in part. If she confessed that she had seen him, and had quarreled with him on that night, then all men would conclude that she had also murdered him so as to escape. She saw also how hopeless it was to look for any testimony in her favor. Every thing was against her. Being in ignorance of her father and Lady Dudleigh, she had supposed that they would be most relentless of all in doing her to death; and the excitement of the latter over the loss of Leon was never suspected by her to be the frenzied grief of a mother's heart over a sudden and most agonizing bereavement.

But now all these things were plain. Another shared her secret—one, too, who would lay down his life for her—and the efforts of Miss Fortescue had resulted in suggesting to her mind a new solution of the mystery.

After the natural comments which were elicited by Edith's strange story, Reginald showed her the letter which he had received from Miss Fortescue. It was not very long, nor was it very definite. It merely informed him that she had reason to believe that she had at last got upon the track of Leon; and requested him to come to her at once, as there was danger of losing this opportunity if there was any delay. She appointed a place at which she would meet him three days from the date of the letter, where she would wait several days to allow for all delay in his reception of the letter. The place which she mentioned was known to Reginald as the nearest station on the railway to Dudleigh Manor.

"This must decide all," said Reginald. "They are playing a desperate game, and the part which must be done by my mother and myself is a terrible one. If we fail in this, we may have to fly at once. But if I can only see Leon once, so as to drag him before the world, and show that he is alive—if I can only save you, darling, from your terrible position, then I can bear other evils in patience for a time longer."

"You have heard nothing from your mother, then?" said Edith.

"No," said he, with a sigh. "And I feel anxious—terribly anxious. I was very unwilling for her to go, and warned her against it; but she was determined, and her reasons for doing so were unanswerable; still I feel terribly alarmed, for Sir Lionel is a man who would stop at nothing to get rid of one whom he thinks is the only witness against him."

"THEY WERE STARTLED BY THE APPROACH OF SEVERAL MEN."

CHAPTER LII.

THE STORY OF FREDERICK DALTON.

AFTER Dudleigh's departure Edith was left more exclusively with her father, and had the satisfaction of seeing that under her tender care he grew stronger and more happy every day. In the long confidences between these two, who had once been so separated, all was gradually explained, and Edith learned not only the whole truth about that calamity which had befallen him in early life, but also the reason of that once inexplicable policy which he had chosen with regard to herself.

Lionel Dudleigh and he had been friends from boyhood, though the weak and lavish character of the former had gradually put them upon divergent lines of life, which even Lionel's marriage with his sister, Claudine Dalton, could not bring together again. For Lionel had fallen into evil courses, and had taken to the common road of ruin—the turf; and though it had been hoped that his marriage would work a reformation, yet those hopes had all proved unfounded. Years passed. Two children were born to Lionel Dudleigh—Reginald and Leon; yet not even the considerations of their future welfare, which usually have weight with the most corrupt, were sufficiently powerful to draw back the transgressor from his bad career.

He became terribly involved in debt. Twice already his debts had been paid, but this third time his father would assist him no longer. His elder brother, then heir to the estate, was equally inexorable; and Frederick Dalton was the one who came forward to save his sister's husband and his old friend from destruction.

On this occasion, however, Lionel was not frank with Dalton. Perhaps he was afraid to tell him the whole amount of his debts, for fear that Dalton would refuse to do any thing. At any rate, whatever the cause was, after Dalton had, as he supposed, settled every thing, Lionel was pressed as hard as ever by a crowd of creditors, whom this partial settlement had only rendered the more ravenous.

Pressed hard by one of these, the wretched man had forged a check on the Liverpool banker, Mr. Henderson, and this check he had inclosed in a letter to Frederick Dalton, requesting him to get the money and pay one or two debts which he specified. This Dalton did at once, without hesitation or suspicion of any sort.

Then came the discovery, swift and sudden, that it was a forgery. But one feeling arose in Dalton's mind, and that was a desire to save Lionel. He hurried off at once to see him. The wretched man confessed all. Dalton at once went to Liverpool, where he saw Mr. Henderson, and tried to save his friend. He came away from that interview, however, only to make known to Lionel the banker's obstinacy and resolution to have vengeance.

Dalton's solicitor in Liverpool was Mr. John Wiggins. Lionel's presence in Liverpool was not known to any one but Dalton. He had seen Wiggins once, and persuaded Lionel to see him also, to which the latter consented only with extreme difficulty. The interview never took place, however, nor was Wiggins aware of Lionel's presence in Liverpool, or of his guilt. Then the murder took place, and the paper was found which criminated Dalton, who was at once arrested.

Dalton was thunder-struck, not so much at his own arrest as at the desperation of his friend and his utter baseness. He knew perfectly well who the murderer was. The Maltese cross which had been found was not necessary to show him this. No other man could have had any motive, and no other man could have thought of mentioning his name in connection with the terrible deed. It was thus that Dalton found himself betrayed in the foulest manner, through no other cause than his own generosity.

The horror of Mrs. Dudleigh on hearing of her brother's arrest was excessive. She went off at once to see him. Even to her Dalton said nothing about Lionel's guilt, for he wished to spare her the cruel blow which such intelligence would give.

The feeling that now animated Dalton can easily be explained. In the first place, knowing that he was innocent, he had not the faintest doubt that he would be acquitted. He believed that where there was no guilt, no such thing as guilt could be proved. He relied also on his well-known reputation.

Feeling thus confident of his own innocence, and certain of acquittal, he had only to ask himself what he ought to do with reference to Lionel. Strict justice demanded that he should tell all that he knew; but there were other considerations besides strict justice. There was the future of Lionel himself, whom he wished to spare in spite of his baseness. More than this, there was his sister and his sister's children. He could not bring himself to inform against the guilty husband and father, and thus crush their innocent heads under an overwhelming load of shame. He never imagined that he himself, and his innocent wife and his innocent child, would have to bear all that which he shrank from imposing upon the wife and children of Lionel.

The trial went on, and then came forth revelations which showed all to Mrs. Dudleigh. That Maltese cross was enough. It was the key to the whole truth. She saw her brother, and asked him. He was silent. Frantic with grief, she hurried back to her husband. To her fierce reproaches he answered not a word. She now proceeded to Liverpool. Her brother entreated her to be calm and silent. He assured her that there was no possible danger to himself, and implored her, for the sake of her children, to say nothing. She allowed herself to be convinced by him, and to yield to entreaties uttered by the very accused himself, and in the name of her children. She believed in his innocence, and could not help sharing his confidence in an acquittal.

That acquittal did come—by a narrow chance, yet it did come; but at once, to the consternation of both brother and sister, the new trial followed. Here Dalton tried to keep up his confidence as before. His counsel implored him to help them in making his defense by telling them what he knew, but Dalton remained fatally obstinate. Proudly confiding in his innocence, and trusting to his blameless life, he still hesitated to do what he considered an act of merciless cruelty to his sister, and he still persuaded her also to silence, and still prophesied his own acquittal, and the rescue of her husband and children from ruin. Part of his prophecy was fulfilled. The husband and children of the sister were indeed saved, but it was at the expense of the innocent and devoted brother.

The effect was terrible. Dalton heard of his wife's illness. He had written to her before, full of confidence, and trying to cheer her; but from the first Mrs. Dalton had looked for the worst; not that she supposed her husband could possibly be otherwise than innocent, but simply because she was timid and afraid of the law. She had good reason to fear. Word was brought to Dalton that she was dying, and then the news came that she was dead.

Meanwhile Mrs. Dudleigh, more frenzied than ever, flew to see her husband. She found that he had gone to the Continent. She pursued him, and reached him in Italy. Here she called upon him to confess his guilt, and save his innocent friend. He refused. He dared not. She threatened to denounce him. She fell at her feet and implored her mercy in the name of their children. He entreated her to wait, to try other means first, to get a new trial—any thing. Mrs. Dudleigh's threats to inform against him were easy to make, yet not so easy to carry out. Turning from her husband in horror, she returned to England with the fixed intention of telling every thing. His letter to Dalton could have been shown, and the Maltese cross could have proved who the murderer was. But Mrs. Dudleigh's courage faltered when she reached her home and saw her children. Already she had heard of Mrs. Dalton's death; already she knew well that Edith Dalton was doomed to inherit a name of shame, a legacy of dishonor, and that she alone could now avert this. But to avert this she must doom her own children. Had it been herself only and her guilty husband, it would have been easy to be just; but here were her children standing in the way and keeping her back.

Her struggles were agonizing. Time passed on; the delay was fatal. Time passed, and the distracted mother could not make up her mind to deal out ruin and shame to her children. Time passed, and Dalton was taken away to that far-distant country to which he had been sentenced—transported for life.

Other changes also took place. Lionel's father and elder brother both died within a short time of one another, leaving him heir to the estate and the baronetcy. He was now Sir Lionel Dudleigh, and she was Lady Dudleigh; and her brother—the pure in heart, the noble, the devoted—what and where was he?

The struggle was terrible, and she could not decide it. It seemed abhorrent for her to rise up and denounce her husband, even to save her brother. She could not do it, but she did what she could. She wrote her husband a letter, bidding him farewell, and imploring him to confess; took her son Reginald, the eldest, leaving behind the younger, Leon, and prepared to go to her brother, hoping that if she could not save him, she might at least alleviate his sorrows. She took with her Hugo, a faithful old servant of the Dalton family, and with him and Reginald went to Australia.

Meanwhile Dalton had been in the country for a year. Before leaving he had not been unmindful of others even in that dire extremity. He had only one thought, and that was his child. He had learned that Miss Plympton had taken her, and he wrote to her, urging her never to tell Edith her father's story, and never to let the world know that she was his daughter. He appointed Wiggins agent for his estates and guardian of Edith before he left; and having thus secured her interests for the present, he went to meet his fate.

In Sydney he was treated very differently from the common convicts. Criminals of all classes were sent out there, and to the better sort large privileges were allowed. Dalton was felt by all to be a man of the latter kind. His dignified bearing, his polish and refinement, together with the well-known fact that he had so resolutely maintained his innocence, all excited sympathy and respect.

When Lady Dudleigh arrived there with Hugo and her son, she soon found out this, and this fact enabled her to carry into execution a plan which she had cherished all along during the voyage. She obtained a sheep farm about a hundred miles away, applied to the authorities, and was able to hire Dalton as a servant. Taking him in this capacity, she went with him to the sheep farm, where Hugo and Reginald also accompanied them. One more was afterward added. This was the man "Wilkins," who had been sentenced to transportation for poaching, and had come out in the same ship with Dalton. Lady Dudleigh obtained this man also, under Dalton's advice, and he ultimately proved of great assistance to them.

Here in this place years passed away. Dalton's only thought was of his daughter. The short formal notes which were signed "John Wiggins," all came from him. He could not trust himself to do any more. The sweet childish letters which she wrote once or twice he kept next his heart, and cherished as more precious than any earthly possession, but dared not answer for fear lest he might break that profound secret which he wished to be maintained between her and himself—her, the pure young girl, himself, the dishonored outcast. So the years passed, and he watched her from afar in his thoughts, and every year he thought of her age, and tried to imagine what she looked like.

During these years there was rising among them another spirit—a character—whose force was destined to change the fortune of all.

This was Reginald.

From the first he had known the whole story—more than Leon had known. Leon had known his father's guilt and Dalton's innocence, but Reginald had been the confidant of his mother, the witness of her grief and her despair. He had lived with Dalton, and year after year had been the witness of a spectacle which never ceased to excite the deepest emotion, that of an innocent man, a just man, suffering wrongfully on behalf of another. His own father he had learned to regard with horror, while all the enthusiastic love of his warm young heart had fixed itself upon the man who had done all this for another. He knew for whom Dalton had suffered. It was for his mother, and for himself, and he knew that he was every day living on the sufferings and the woe of this broken-hearted friend. Gradually other motives arose. He was a witness of Dalton's profound and all-absorbing love for his daughter, and his passionate desire to save her from all knowledge of his own shame. To Reginald all this grew more and more intolerable. He now saw the worst result of all, and he felt that while his own father had thrown upon his friend his load of infamy, so he himself, the son, was throwing upon Edith Dalton all that inherited infamy.

At last his resolution was taken. He informed his mother. She had been aware of his struggles of soul for years, and did not oppose him. Indeed, she felt some relief. It was for the son's sake that she had faltered when justice demanded her action. Now that son had grown to be a calm, strong, resolute man, and he had decided.

Yes, the decision was a final one. Not one objection was disregarded. Every thing was considered, and the resolution was, at all hazards, and at every cost, to do right. That resolution involved the accusation, the trial, the condemnation, the infamy—yes, the death—of a husband and a father; but even at that cost it was the resolve of Reginald that this thing should be.

The plan of escape occupied far less time. Dalton objected at first to the whole thing, but Reginald had only to mention to him his daughter's name to induce him to concur.

After this it was given out that Freder-ick Dalton had died. This statement was received by the authorities without suspicion or examination, though the conspirators were prepared for both.

Then Frederick Dalton, under an assumed name, accompanied by Hugo, went to Sydney, where he embarked for England. No one recognized him. He had changed utterly. Grief, despair, and time had wrought this. Reginald and his mother went by another ship, a little later, and had no difficulty in taking Wilkins with them. They all reached England in safety, and met at a place agreed upon beforehand, where their future action was arranged.

On the voyage home Dalton had decided upon that policy which he afterward sought to carry out. It was, first of all, to live in the utmost seclusion, and conceal himself as far as possible from every eye. A personal encounter with some old acquaintance, who failed to recognize him, convinced him that the danger of his secret being discovered was very small. His faithful solicitor, John Wiggins, of Liverpool, would not believe that the gray-haired and venerable man who came to him was the man whom he professed to be, until Dalton and Reginald had proved it by showing the letters, and by other things. By John Wiggins's suggestion Dalton assumed the name of Wiggins, and gave himself out to be a brother of the Liverpool solicitor. No one suspected, and no questions were asked, and so Dalton went to Dalton Hall under the name of Wiggins, while Lady Dudleigh went as Mrs. Dunbar, to be housekeeper; and their domestics were only Hugo and Wilkins, whose fidelity was known to be incorruptible, and who were, of course, intimately acquainted with the secret of their master.

Here Dalton took up his abode, while John Wiggins, of Liverpool, began to set in motion the train of events which should end in the accomplishment of justice. First, it was necessary to procure from the authorities all the documentary and other evidence which had been acquired ten years before. Several things were essential, and above all the Maltese cross. But English law is slow, and these things required time.

It was the intention of Dalton to have every thing in readiness first, and then send Reginald and Lady Dudleigh to Sir Lionel to try the force of a personal appeal. If by threats or any other means they could persuade him to confess, he was to be allowed time to fly to some safe place, or take any other course which he deemed most consistent with his safety. Dalton himself was not to appear, but to preserve his secret inviolable. If Sir Lionel should prove impracticable, then the charge and arrest should take place at once; whether for forgery or murder was not decided. That should be left to Reginald's own choice. They leaned to mercy, however, and preferred the charge of forgery. Sir Lionel was mistaken in supposing Lady Dudleigh to be the only witness against him, for Reginald had been present at more than one interview between the frenzied wife and the guilty husband, and had heard his father confess the whole.

But the regular progress of affairs had been altogether interrupted by the sudden appearance of Edith. On reaching Dalton Hall Mr. Dalton had felt an uncontrollable eagerness to see her, and had written to Miss Plympton the letter already reported. He did not expect that she would come so soon. He thought that she would wait for a time; that he would get an answer, and arrange every thing for her reception. As it was, she came at once, without any announcement, accompanied by Miss Plympton and her maid.

For years Dalton had been kept alive by the force of one feeling alone—his love for his daughter. Out of the very intensity of his love for her arose also another feeling, equally intense, and that was the desire to clear his name from all stain before meeting with her. At first he had intended to refrain from seeing her, but, being in England, and so near, his desire for her was uncontrollable. Reginald had gone for a tour on the Continent. The Hall was lonely; every room brought back the memory of his lost wife, and of that little Edith who, years before, used to wander about these halls and amidst these scenes with him. He could not endure this enforced separation, and so he wrote as he did. He expected he scarcely new what. He had a vague idea that though he refused to make himself known, that she nevertheless might divine it, or else, out of some mysterious filial instinct, might love him under his assumed name as fervently as though there was no concealment.

When she came so suddenly, he was taken by surprise. He longed to see her, but was afraid to admit her companions; and so it was that his daughter, in whom his life was now bound up, was almost turned away from her father's gates.

Then followed her life at Dalton Hall. Dalton, afraid of the outside world, afraid to be discovered, after having done so much for safety, at the very time when deliverance seemed near, looked with terror upon Edith's impatience. He risked an interview. He came full of a father's holiest love, yet full of the purpose of his life to redeem the Dalton name for her sake. He met with scorn and hate. From those interviews he retired with his heart wrung by an anguish greater than any that he had ever known before.

And so it went on. It was for her own sake that he restrained her; yet he could not tell her, for he had set his heart on not revealing himself till he could do so with an un-

stained name. But he had made a mistake at the very outset from his impatient desire to see her, and he was doomed to see the results of that mistake. Miss Plympton was turned away, and forthwith appealed to Sir Lionel. The result of this was that Leon came. Leon recognized Wilkins, and could not be kept out. He did not know Dalton, but knew that he was not the man whom he professed to be, and his suspicions were aroused. On seeing Dalton he assumed a high tone toward him, which he maintained till the last. Lady Dudleigh's emotion at the sight of Leon was a sore embarrassment, and all Dalton's plans seemed about to fall into confusion. The visits of the disguised Miss Fortescue were a puzzle; and as both Dalton and Lady Dudleigh looked upon this new visitor as an emissary of Leon's, they viewed these visits as they did those of Leon. For the first time Lady Dudleigh and Dalton were of opposite views. Dalton dreaded these visits, but his sister favored them. Her mother's heart yearned over Leon; and even if he did seek Edith's affections, it did not seem an undesirable thing. That, however, was a thing from which Dalton recoiled in horror.

At that time Reginald's strong will and clear intellect were sorely needed, but he was away on his Continental tour, and knew nothing of all these occurrences till it was too late.

Thus nothing was left to Dalton but idle warnings, which Edith treated as we have seen. True, there was one other resource, and that was to tell her all; but this he hesitated to do. For years he had hoped to redeem himself. He had looked forward to the day when his name should be freed from stain, and he still looked forward to that day when he might be able to say, "Here, my beloved daughter, my name is free from stain; you can acknowledge me without shame."

But Edith's opposition, and the plans of Leon, and the absorption of Lady Dudleigh's sympathies in the interests of her son, all destroyed Dalton's chances. He could only watch, and hear from his faithful Hugo accounts of what was going on. Thus he was led into worse and worse acts, and by misunderstanding Edith at the outset, opened the way for both himself and her to many sorrows.

After the terrible events connected with the mysterious departure of Leon and the arrest of Edith, Dalton had at once written to Reginald. He had been ill in the interior of Sicily—for his testimony at the trial had been in part correct. Dalton's letter was delayed in reaching him, but he hurried back as soon as possible. Relying on his extraordinary resemblance to Leon, Dalton had urged him to personify the missing man, and this he had consented to do, with the success which has been described. His chief motive in doing this was his profound sympathy for Dalton, and for Edith also, whom he believed to have been subjected to unfair treatment. That sympathy which he had already felt for Edith was increased when he saw her face to face.

All this was not told to Edith at once, but rather in the course of several conversations. Already in that interview in the prison her father had explained to her his motives in acting as he had, and this fuller confession only made those motives more apparent. In Edith this story served only to excite fresh grief and remorse. But Dalton showed so much grief himself that Edith was forced to restrain such feelings as these in his presence. He took all the blame to himself. He would not allow her to reproach herself. He it was, he insisted, who had been alone to blame in subjecting a generous, high-spirited girl to such terrible treatment—to imprisonment and spying and coercion. So great was his own grief that Edith found herself forced from the position of penitent into that of comforter, and often had to lose sight of her own offenses in the endeavor to explain away her own sufferings.

And thus, where there was so much need of mutual forgiveness and mutual consolation, each one became less a prey to remorse.

In the joy which he felt at thus gaining at last all his daughter's love, especially after the terrible misunderstanding that had divided her from him, Dalton had no thought for those grave dangers which surrounded both her and him. But to Edith these dangers still appeared, and they were most formidable. She could not forget that she was still liable to arrest on the most appalling of accusations, and that her father also was liable to discovery and re-arrest. Reginald had tried to banish her fears and inspire her with hope; but now that he was no longer near, her position was revealed, and the full possibility of her danger could no longer be concealed.

Danger there indeed was, danger most formidable, not to her only, but to all of them. Coward Sir Lionel might be, but a coward when at bay is dangerous, since he is desperate. Sir Lionel also was powerful, since he was armed with all the force that may be given by wealth and position, and in his despair his utmost resources would undoubtedly be put forth. Those despairing efforts would be aimed at all of them—all were alike threatened: herself on the old charge, her father as an escaped convict, and Reginald as a perjurer and a conspirator against the ends of justice. As 'to Lady Dudleigh, she knew not what to think, but she was aware of Reginald's fears about her, and she shared them to the fullest extent.

In the midst of all this Edith received a letter from Miss Plympton. She was just

recovering, she said, from a severe illness, consequent on anxiety about her. She had heard the terrible tidings of her arrest, but of late had been cheered by the news of her release. The letter was most loving, and revealed all the affection of her "second mother." Yet so true was Miss Plympton to the promise which she had made to Mr. Dalton, that she did not allude to the great secret which had once been disclosed to her. Edith read the letter with varied feelings, and thought with an aching heart of her reception of that other letter. This letter, however, met with a different fate. She answered it at once, and told all about her father, concluding with the promise to go and visit her as soon as she could.

And now all her thoughts and hopes were centred upon Reginald. Where was he? Where was Lady Dudleigh? Had he found Leon? What would Sir Lionel do? Such were the thoughts that never ceased to agitate her mind.

He had been gone a whole week. She had heard nothing from him. Accustomed as she had been to see him every day for so long a time, this week seemed prolonged to the extent of a month; and as he had promised to write her under any circumstances, she could not account for his failure to keep that promise. His silence alarmed her. As day succeeded to day, and still no letter came, she became a prey to all those fearful fancies which may be raised by a vivid imagination, when one is in suspense about the fate of some dearly loved friend.

Her father, whose watchful love made him observant of every one of her varying moods, could not avoid noticing the sadness and agitation of her face and manner, and was eager to know the cause. This, however, Edith's modesty would not allow her to explain, but she frankly confessed that she was anxious. Her anxiety she attributed to her fears about their situation, and her dread lest something might be found out about the imposture of Reginald, or about her father's real character and personality. The fear was not an idle one, and Dalton, though he tried to soothe her, was himself too well aware of the danger that surrounded both of them to be very successful in his efforts.

All this time a steady improvement had been taking place in Dalton's health, and his recovery from his illness was rapid and continuous. It was Edith's love and care and sympathy which thus gave strength to him, and the joy which he felt in her presence was the best medicine for his afflictions.

Thus one day he was at last able to venture outside. It was something more than a week since Reginald had left. Edith was more anxious than ever, but strove to conceal her anxiety and to drown her own selfish cares under more assiduous attentions to that father whose whole being now seemed so to centre upon her. For this purpose she had persuaded him to leave the Hall, and come forth into the grounds; and the two were now walking in front of the Hall, around the pond, Edith supporting her father's feeble footsteps, and trying to cheer him by pointing out some improvements which ought to be made, while the old man, with his mind full of sweet peace, thought it happiness enough for him to lean on her loving arm and hear her sweet voice as she spoke those words of love which for so many years he had longed to hear.

In the midst of this they were startled by the approach of several men.

Visitors were rare at Dalton Hall. Before the recent troubles they had been prohibited, and though during Dalton's illness the prohibition had been taken off, yet there were few who cared to pass those gates. Upon this occasion the approach of visitors gave a sudden shock to Edith and her father, and when they saw that the chief one among those visitors was the sheriff, that shock was intensified.

Yes, the moment had come which they both had dreaded. All was known. The danger which they had feared was at hand, and each one trembled for the other. Edith thought that it was her father who was sought after. Dalton shuddered as he thought that his innocent daughter was once more in the grasp of the law.

The sheriff approached, followed by three others, who were evidently officers of the law. Dalton and Edith stood awaiting them, and Edith felt her father's hands clasp her arm in a closer and more tremulous embrace.

The sheriff greeted them with a mournful face and evident embarrassment. His errand was a painful one, and it was rendered doubly so by the piteous sight before him—the feeble old man thus clinging to that sad-faced young girl, the woe-worn father thus supported by the daughter whose own experience of life had been so bitter.

"My business," said the sheriff, "is a most painful one. Forgive me, Mrs. Dudleigh. Forgive me, Mr. Dalton. I did not know till now how painful it would be."

He had greeted them in silence, removing his hat respectfully, and bowing before this venerable old age and this sad-faced beauty, and then had said these words with some abruptness. And as soon as he named that name "Dalton," they both understood that he knew all.

"You have come for me?" said Dalton.

"Very well."

A shudder passed through Edith. She flung her arms about her father, and placed herself before him, as if to interpose between him and that terrible fate which still pursued its innocent victim. She turned her large mournful eyes upon the sheriff with a look of silent horror, but said not a word.

"I can not help it," said the sheriff, in still deeper embarrassment. "I feel for you, for both of you, but you must come with me."

"Oh, spare him!" cried Edith. "He is ill. He has just risen from his bed. Leave him here. He is not fit to go. Let me nurse him."

The sheriff looked at her in increasing embarrassment, with a face full of pity.

"I am deeply grieved," he said, in a low voice, "but I can not do otherwise. I must do my duty. You, Mrs. Dudleigh, must come also. I have a warrant for you too."

"What!" groaned Dalton; "for her?"

The sheriff said nothing. The old man's face had such an expression of anguish that words were useless.

"Again!" murmured Dalton. "Again! and on that false charge! She will die! she will die!"

"Oh, papa!" exclaimed Edith. "Do not think of me. I can bear it. There is no danger for me. It is for you only that I am anxious."

"My child! my darling Edith!" groaned the unhappy father, "this is my work—this is what I have wrought for you."

Edith pressed her father to her heart. She raised her pale face, and, looking upward, sighed out in her agony of soul,

"O God! Is there any justice in heaven, when this is the justice of earth!"

Nothing more was said. No one had any thing to say. This double arrest was something too terrible for words, and the darkest forebodings came to the mind of each one of these unhappy victims of the law. And thus, in silence and in fear, they were led away—to prison and to judgment.

CHAPTER LIII.

THE BROTHERS.

On leaving Dalton Hall Reginald went to the place mentioned by Miss Fortescue. It was on the railway, and was about four miles from Dudleigh Manor. Here he found Miss Fortescue.

She told him that she had tried to find Leon by making inquiries every where among his old haunts, but without any success whatever. At last she concluded that, since he was in such strict hiding, Dudleigh Manor itself would not be an unlikely place in which to find him. She had come here, and, after disguising herself with her usual skill, had made inquiries of the porter with as much adroitness as possible. All her efforts, however, were quite in vain. The porter could not be caught committing himself in any way, but professed to have seen noth-

L

ing of the missing man for months. She would have come away from this experiment in despair had it not been for one circumstance, which, though small in itself, seemed to her to have very deep meaning. It was this. While she was talking with the porter a dog came up, which at once began to fawn on her. This amazed the porter, who did not like the appearance of things, and tried to drive the dog away. But Miss Fortescue had in an instant recognized the dog of Leon, well known to herself, and once a great pet.

This casual appearance of the dog seemed to her the strongest possible proof that Leon was now in that very place. He must have been left purposely in Dalton Park for a few days, probably having been stationed at that very spot which he kept so persistently. If so, the same one who left him there must have brought him here. It was inconceivable that the dog could have found his way here alone from Dalton Park. In addition to this, the porter's uneasiness at the dog's recognition of her was of itself full of meaning. This was all that she had been able to find out, but this was enough. Fearful that Leon might suspect who she was, she had written to Reginald at once; and now that he had come, she urged him to go to Dudleigh Manor himself and find out the truth.

There was no need to urge Reginald. His anxiety about his mother was enough to make him anxious to lose no time, but the prospect of finding Leon made him now doubly anxious. It was already evening, however, and he would have to defer his visit until the following day.

At about nine o'clock the next morning Reginald Dudleigh stood at his father's gate —the gate of that home from which he had been so long an exile. The porter came out to open it, and stared at him in surprise.

"I didn't know you was out, Sir," he said.

Evidently the porter had mistaken him for Leon. This address assured him of the fact of Leon's presence. The porter was a new hand, and Reginald did not think it worth while to explain. He entered silently while the porter held the gate open, and then walked up the long avenue toward the manor-house.

The door was open. He walked in. Some servants were moving about, who seemed to think his presence a matter of course. These also evidently mistook him for Leon; and these things, slight as they were, assured him that his brother must be here. Yet in spite of the great purpose for which he had come—a purpose, as he felt, of life and death, and even more—in spite of this, he could not help pausing for a moment as he found himself within these familiar precincts, in the home of his childhood, within sight of objects so well remembered, so long lost to view.

But it was only for a few moments. The first rush of feeling passed, and then there came back the recollection of all that lay before him, of all that depended upon this visit. He walked on. He reached the great stairway. He ascended it. He came to the great hall up stairs. On one side was the drawing-room, on the other the library. The former was empty, but in the latter there was a solitary occupant. He was seated at a table, writing. So intent was this man on his occupation that he did not hear the sound of approaching footsteps, or at least did not regard them; for even as Reginald stood looking at him, he went on with his writing. His back was turned toward the door, so that Reginald could not see his face, but the outline of the figure was sufficient. Reginald stood for a moment looking at him. Then he advanced toward the writer, and laid his hand upon his shoulder.

The writer gave a sudden start, leaped from his chair, and turned round. There was fear on his face—the fear of one who is on the look-out for sudden danger—a fear without a particle of recognition. But gradually the blankness of his terrified face departed, and there came a new expression—an expression in which there was equal terror, yet at the same time a full recognition of the danger before him.

It was Leon Dudleigh.

Reginald said not one word, but looked at him with a stern, relentless face.

As these two thus stood looking at one another, each saw in the other's face the marvelous resemblance to himself, which had been already so striking to others, and so bewildering. But the expression was totally different. Aside from the general air characteristic of each, there was the look that had been called up by the present meeting. Reginald confronted his brother with a stern, menacing gaze, and a look of authority that was more than the ordinary look which might belong to an elder brother. Leon's face still kept its look of fear, and there seemed to be struggling with this fear an impulse to fly, which he was unable to obey. Reginald looked like the master, Leon like the culprit and the slave.

Leon was the first to speak.

"You—here!" he faltered.

"Where else should I be?" said Reginald, in a stern voice.

"What do you want?" asked Leon, rallying from his fear, and apparently encouraged by the sound of his own voice.

"What do I want?" repeated Reginald. "Many things. First, I want you; secondly, my mother."

"You won't get any thing out of me," said Leon, fiercely.

"In the first place, the sight of you is one of the chief things," said Reginald, with a sneer. "After having heard your sad fate, it is something to see you here in the flesh." ·

"It's that infernal porter!" cried Leon, half to himself.

"What do you mean? Do you blame him for letting me in—*me*—Reginald Dudleigh—your elder brother?"

"You're disinherited," growled Leon.

"Pooh!" said Reginald. "How can the eldest son be disinherited? But I'm not going to waste time. I have come to call you to account for what you have done, and I have that to say to you which you must hear, and, what is more, you must obey."

If Leon's face could have grown whiter than it already was, it would have become so at these words. His fear seemed swallowed up in a wild overmastering rush of fury and indignation. He started back and seized the bell-rope.

"I don't know you!" he almost yelled. "Who are you?" Saying this he pulled the bell-rope again and again. "Who are you?" he repeated over and over again, pulling the bell-rope as he spoke. "I'll have you turned out. You're an infernal impostor! Who are you? I can prove that Reginald Dudleigh is dead. I'll have you turned out. I'll have you turned out."

While he was speaking, his frantic and repeated tugs at the bell had roused the house. Outside the rush of footsteps was heard, and soon a crowd of servants poured into the room.

"You scoundrels!" roared Leon. "What do you mean by letting strangers in here in this way? Put this fellow out! Put him out! Curse you! why don't you collar him and put him out?"

As the servants entered, Reginald turned half round and faced them. Leon shouted out these words, and shook his fist toward his brother, while the servants stared in amazement at the astonishing spectacle. The two brothers stood there before them, the one calm and self-possessed, the other infuriated with excitement; but the wonderful resemblance between them held the servants spell-bound.

As soon as he could make himself heard, Reginald spoke.

"You will do nothing of the kind. Most of you are new faces, but some of you remember me. Holder," said he, as his eyes, wandering over the faces before him, rested upon one, "don't you know your young master? Have you forgotten Reginald Dudleigh?"

As he said this an old man came forth from the rear and looked at him, with his hands clasped together and his eyes full of tears.

"Lord be merciful to us all," he cried, with a trembling voice, "if it beant Master Reginald hisself come back to life again, and me mournin' over him as dead! Oh,

Master Reginald, but it's glad I am this day. And where have ye been?"

"Never mind, old man," said Reginald, kindly; "you'll know soon enough." Saying this, he shook the old man's hand, and then turned with lowering brow once more upon Leon.

"Leon," said he, "none of this foolery. You found out what I am when you were a boy. None of this hysterical excitement. *I* am master here."

But Leon made no reply. With his face now on fire with rage, he retreated a few steps and looked under the table. He called quickly to something that was there, and as he called, a huge dog came forth and stood by his side. This dog he led forward, and pointed at Reginald.

The servants looked on with pale faces at this scene, overcome with horror as they saw Leon's purpose.

"Go," said Leon, fiercely, to Reginald, "or you'll be sorry."

Reginald said nothing, but put his hand into his breast pocket and drew forth a revolver. It was not a very common weapon in England in those days, but Reginald had picked one up in his wanderings, and had brought it with him on the present occasion. Leon, however, did not seem to notice it. He was intent on one purpose, and that was to drive Reginald away.

He therefore put his hand on the dog's head, and, pointing toward his brother, shouted, "At him, Sir!" The dog hesitated for a moment. His master called again. The huge brute gathered himself up. One more cry from the now frenzied Leon, and the dog gave a tremendous leap forward full at Reginald's throat.

A cry of horror burst from the servants. They were by no means oversensitive, but this scene was too terrible.

The dog sprang.

But at that instant the loud report of Reginald's revolver rang through the house, and the fierce beast, with a sharp howl, fell back, and lay on the floor writhing in his death agony. The wound was a mortal one.

Reginald replaced his pistol in his pocket. "I'm sorry for the poor beast," said he, as he looked at the dog for a moment, "but I could not help it. And you," he continued, turning to the servants, "go down stairs. When I want you I will call for you. Holder will tell you who I am."

At this the servants all retreated, overawed by the look and manner of this new master.

The shot of the pistol seemed to have overwhelmed Leon. He shrank back, and stared by turns at Reginald and the dog, with a white face and a scowling brow.

After the servants had gone, Reginald walked up to him.

"THE FIERCE BEAST, WITH A SHARP HOWL, FELL BACK."

"I will have no more words," said he, fiercely. "I'm your master now, Leon, as I always have been. You are in my power now. You must either do as I bid you, or else go to jail. I have taken up all your notes; I have paid more than forty thousand pounds, and I now hold those notes of yours. I do not intend to let you go till you do what I wish. If you don't, I will take you from this place and put you in jail. I have warrants all ready, and in the proper hands. The officers are waiting in the neighborhood. Besides these claims, I shall have charges against you of a graver kind; you know what, so that you can not escape. Now listen. I am your only creditor now, and your only accuser. You need not hide any longer, or fly from the country. Confess; come to terms with me, and you shall be a free man; refuse, and you shall suffer the very worst that the law inflicts. If you do not come to terms with me, you are lost. I give you only this chance. You can do nothing. You can not harm Miss Dalton now, for I have found you out, and your miserable trick is of no use any longer. Come, now; decide at once. I will give you just ten minutes. If you come to terms, you are safe; if not, you go to jail."

"Who'll take me?" said Leon, in a surly voice.

"I," said Reginald—"I, with my own hands. I will take you out of this place, and hand you over to the officers who are waiting not very far away."

Saying this, Reginald looked at his watch, and then replacing it, turned once more to Leon.

"Your tricks have failed. I will produce you as you are, and Miss Dalton will be safe. You'll have to explain it all in court, so you may as well explain it to me. I don't want to be hard with you. I know you of old, and have forgiven other villainies of yours. You can't take vengeance on any one. Even your silence will be of no use. You must choose between a confession to me now, or a general confession in court. Besides, even if you could have vengeance, it wouldn't be worth so much to a man like you as what I offer you. I offer you freedom. I will give you back all your notes and bonds. You will be no longer in any danger. More, I will help you. I don't want to use harsh measures if I can help it. Don't be a fool. Do as I say, and accept my offer. If you don't, I swear, after what you've done I'll show you no more mercy than I showed your dog."

Leon was silent. His face grew more tranquil. He was evidently affected by his brother's words. He stood, in thought, with his eyes fixed on the floor. Debt was a great evil. Danger was around him. Freedom was a great blessing. Thus far he had been safe only because he had been in hiding. Besides, he was powerless now, and his knowledge of Reginald, as he had been in early life, and as he saw him now, showed him that his brother always meant what he said.

"I don't believe you have those notes and bonds."

"How could I know unless I paid them? I will tell you the names concerned in most of them, and the amounts."

And Reginald thereupon enumerated several creditors, with the amounts due to each. By this Leon was evidently convinced.

"And you've paid them?" said he.

"Yes."

"And you'll give them to me?"

"I will. I am your only creditor now. I have found out and paid every debt of yours. I did this, to force you to come to terms. That is all I want. You see that this is for your interest. More, I will give you enough to begin life on. Do you ask more than this?"

Leon hesitated for a short time longer.

"Well," said he at last, "what is it that you want me to do?"

"First of all I want you to tell me about that infernal trick of yours with—the body. Whose is it? Mind you, it's of no consequence now, so long as you are alive, and can be produced; but I wish to know."

With some hesitation Leon informed his brother. The information which he gave confirmed the suspicions of Miss Fortescue. He had determined to be avenged on Edith and her father, and after that night on which Edith had escaped he had managed to procure a body in London from some of the body-snatchers who supplied the medical schools there. He had removed the head, and dressed it in the clothes which he had last worn. He had taken it to Dalton Park and put it in the well about a week after Edith's flight. He had never gone back to his room, but had purposely left it as it was, so as to make his disappearance the more suspicious. He himself had contrived to raise those frequent rumors which had arisen and grown to such an extent that they had terminated in the search at Dalton Park. Anonymous letters to various persons had suggested to them the supposed guilt of Edith, and the probability of the remains being found in the well.

The horror which Reginald felt at this disclosure was largely mitigated by the fact that he had already imagined some such proceeding as this, for he had felt sure that it was a trick, and therefore it had only been left to account for the trick.

The next thing which Reginald had to investigate was the mock marriage. But here he did not choose to question Leon directly about Edith. He rather chose to investigate that earlier marriage with Miss Fortescue.

By this time Leon's objections to confess had vanished. The inducements which Reginald held out were of themselves attractive enough to one in his desperate position, and, what was more, he felt that there was no alternative. Having once begun, he seemed to grow accustomed to it, and spoke with greater freedom.

To Reginald's immense surprise and relief, Leon informed him that the marriage with Miss Fortescue was not a mock marriage at all. For once in his life he had been honest. The marriage had been a real one. It was only after the affair in the Dalton vaults that he had pretended that it was false. He did so in order to free himself from his real wife, and gain some control over the Dalton estate. The Rev. Mr. Porter was a bona fide clergyman, and the marriage had been conducted in a legal manner. He had found out that the Rev. Mr. Porter had gone to Scotland, and saw that he could easily deceive his wife.

"But," said Reginald, "what is the reason that your wife could never find him out? She looked over all the lists of clergymen, and wrote to all of the name of Porter. She could not find him."

"Naturally enough," said Leon, indifferently. "She supposed that he belonged to the Church, because he used the Church service; but he was a Presbyterian."

"Where is he now?"

"When last I heard about him he was at Falkirk."

"Then Miss Fortescue was regularly married, and is now your wife?"

"She is my wife," said Leon.

At this Reginald was silent for some time. The joy that filled his heart at this discovery was so great that for a time it drove away those other thoughts, deep and dread, that had taken possession of him. But these thoughts soon returned.

"One thing more," said he, in an anxious voice. "Leon, where is my mother?"

CHAPTER LIV.

"WHERE is my mother?"

Such was Reginald's last question. He asked it as though Lady Dudleigh was only *his* mother, and not the mother of Leon also. But the circumstances of his past life had made his father and his brother seem like strangers, and his mother seemed all his own.

At this question Leon stared at him with a look of surprise that was evidently unfeigned.

"Your mother?" he repeated.

"I do not say *our* mother," said Reginald. "I say *my* mother. Where is she?"

"I swear I know nothing about her," said Leon, earnestly. "I have never seen her."

"You have never seen her?" repeated Reginald, in a tremulous voice.

"Never," said Leon; "that is, not since she left this place ten years ago."

"You saw her at Dalton Hall!" cried Reginald.

"At Dalton Hall? I did not," said Leon. "Mrs. Dunbar, she called herself. You saw her often."

"Mrs. Dunbar! Good Heavens!" cried Leon, in unaffected surprise. "How was I to know that?"

Reginald looked at him gloomily and menacingly.

"Leon," said he, in a stern voice, "if you dare to deceive me about this, I will show no mercy. You must tell *all*—yes, *all!*"

"But I tell you I don't know any thing about her," said Leon; "I swear I don't. I'll tell every thing that I know. No such person has ever been here."

Reginald looked at his brother with a gloomy frown; but Leon's tone seemed sincere, and the thought came to him that his brother could have no reason for concealment. If Leon did not know, he would have to seek what he wished from another—his father. His father and his mother had gone off together; that father alone could tell.

"Where is Sir Lionel?" asked Reginald, as these thoughts came to him. He called him "Sir Lionel." He could not call him "father."

Leon looked at him with a strange expression.

"He is here," said he.

"Where shall I find him? I want to see him at once. Is he in his room?"

Leon hesitated.

"Quick!" said Reginald, impatiently. "Why don't you answer?"

"You won't get much satisfaction out of him," said Leon, in a peculiar voice.

"I'll find out what he knows. I'll tear the secret out of him," cried Reginald, fiercely. "Where is he? Come with me. Take me to him."

"You'll find it rather hard to get any thing out of him," said Leon, with a short laugh. "He's beyond even *your* reach, and your courts of law too."

"What do you mean?" cried Reginald.

"Well, you may see for yourself," said

Leon. "You won't be satisfied, I suppose, unless you do. Come along. You needn't be alarmed. I won't run. I'll stick to my part of our agreement, if you stick to yours."

With these words Leon led the way out of the library, and Reginald followed. They went up a flight of stairs and along a hall to the extreme end. Here Leon stopped at a door, and proceeded to take a key from his pocket. This action surprised Reginald. He remembered the room well. In his day it had not been used at all, except on rare occasions, and had been thus neglected on account of its gloom and dampness.

"What's the meaning of this?" he asked, gloomily, looking suspiciously at the key.

"Oh, you'll see soon enough," said Leon.

With these words he inserted the key in the lock as noiselessly as possible, and then gently turned the bolt. Having done this, he opened the door a little, and looked in with a cautious movement. These proceedings puzzled Reginald still more, and he tried in vain to conjecture what their object might be.

One cautious look satisfied Leon. He opened the door wider, and said, in a low voice, to his brother,

"Come along; he's quiet just now."

With these words he entered, and held the door for Reginald to pass through. Without a moment's hesitation Reginald went into the room. He took but one step, and then stopped, rooted to the floor by the sight that met his eyes.

The room was low, and had no furniture but an iron bed. There were two small, deep windows, over which the ivy had grown so closely that it dimmed the light, and threw an air of gloom over the scene.

Upon the iron bed was seated a strange figure, the sight of which sent a thrill of horror through Reginald's frame. It was a thin, emaciated figure, worn and bent. His hair was as white as snow; his beard and mustache were short and stubbly, as though they were the growth of but a few weeks; while his whiskers were bushy and matted together.

Over this figure a quilt was thrown in a fantastic manner, under which appeared a long night-gown, from which thin bare legs protruded, with bare, gaunt, skeleton-like feet.

As he sat there his eyes wandered about on vacancy; a silly smile was on his white, worn face; he kept muttering to himself continually some incoherent and almost inaudible sentences; and at the same time his long bony fingers kept clawing and picking at the quilt which covered him.

At first Reginald could scarce believe what he saw; but there was the fact before his eyes, and the terrible truth could not be denied that in this wretched creature before him was the wreck of that one who but

"UPON THE IRON BED WAS SEATED A STRANGE FIGURE."

a short time before had seemed to him to be a powerful and unscrupulous villain, full of the most formidable plans for inflicting fresh wrongs upon those whom he had already so foully injured. Reginald had seen him for a few moments at the trial, and had noticed that the ten eventful years for which they had been parted had made but little difference in his appearance. The casual glimpses of him which he afterward had caught showed some change, but nothing very striking; but now the change was terrible, the transformation was hideous; the strong man had become a shattered wreck; the once vigorous mind had sunk into a state of helpless imbecility and driveling idiocy.

Leon shut the door, and turning the key, stood looking on. The slight noise which he made attracted the wandering gaze of the madman. He started slightly, and stood up, wrapping the quilt carefully around him. Then, with a silly smile, he advanced a few paces.

"Well, Dr. Morton," he said, in a weak, quavering voice, "you have received my letter, I hope. Here is this person that I wrote about. Her name is Mrs. Dunbar. She is an old dependent. She is mad—ha, ha!—mad. Yes, mad, doctor. She thinks she is my wife. She calls herself Lady Dudleigh. But, doctor, her real name is Mrs. Dunbar. She is mad, doctor—mad—mad—mad. Ha, ha, ha!"

At these words a terrible suspicion came to Reginald's mind. The madman had still prominent in his thoughts the idea which he had lately been carrying out. Could there be any truth in these words, or were they mere fancies? He said not a word, but looked and listened in anxious silence. He had felt a moment's pity for this man, who, wretch though he had been, was still his father; but now his mother's image rose before him — his mother, pale, suffering, and perhaps despairing—and in his eager desire to learn her fate, all softer feelings for his father died out.

"You must keep her, Dr. Morton," said Sir Lionel, in the same tone. "You know what she wants. I will pay you well. Money is no object. You must keep her close—close — yes, close as the grave. She is incurable, doctor. She must never come out of this place with her mad fancies. For she is mad—mad—mad—mad—mad. Oh yes. Ha, ha, ha!"

Sir Lionel then smiled as before, and chuckled to himself, while a leer of cunning triumph flashed for a moment from his wandering eyes. "Trapped!" he ejaculated, softly. "Trapped! The keeper! The keeper trapped! She thought she was my keeper! And so she was. But she was trapped —yes, trapped. The keeper trapped! Ha, ha, ha! She thought it was an inn," he continued, after a brief silence, in which he chuckled to himself over the remembrance of his scheme; "and so she was trapped.

The keeper was caught herself, and found herself in a mad-house! And she'll never get out—never! She's mad. They'll all believe it. Mad! Yes, mad—and in a mad-house! Ha, ha, ha! There's Lady Dudleigh for you! But she's Mrs. Dunbar now. Ha, ha, ha!"

Reginald's eagerness to learn more was uncontrollable. In his impatience to find out, he could no longer wait for his father's stray confessions.

"What mad-house? Where?" he asked, eagerly and abruptly.

Sir Lionel did not look at him. But the question came to him none the less. It came to him as if it had been prompted by his own thoughts, and he went on upon the new idea which this question started.

"She saw me write it, too—the letter—and she saw me write the address. There it was as plain as day—the address. Dr. Morton, I wrote, Lichfield Asylum, Lichfield, Berks. But she didn't look at it. She helped me put it in the post-office. Trapped! trapped! Oh yes—the keeper trapped!" he continued. "She thought we were going to Dudleigh Manor, but we were going to Lichfield Asylum. And we stopped there. And she stopped there. And she is there now. Trapped! Ha, ha, ha! And, my good doctor, keep her close, for she's mad. Oh yes—mad—mad—mad—and very dangerous!"

The wretched man now began to totter from weakness, and finally sat down upon the floor. Here he gathered his quilt about him, and began to smile and chuckle and wag his head and pick at his fantastic dress as before. The words which he muttered were inaudible, and those which could be heard were utterly incoherent. The subject that had been presented to his mind by the entrance of Reginald was now forgotten, and his thoughts wandered at random, like the thoughts of a feverish dream, without connection and without meaning.

Reginald turned away. He could no longer endure so painful a spectacle. He had been long estranged from his father, and he had come home for the sake of obtaining justice from that father, for the sake of the innocent man who had suffered so unjustly and so terribly, and whom he loved as a second father. Yet here there was a spectacle which, if he had been a vengeful enemy, would have filled him with horror. One only feeling was present in his mind now to alleviate that horror, and this was a sense of profound relief that this terrible affliction had not been wrought by any act of his. He had no hand in it. It had come upon his father either as the gradual result of years of anxiety, or as the immediate effect of the sudden appearance of Dalton and his wife. But for these thoughts there was no leisure. His whole mind was filled with but one idea—his mother. In a few moments they were outside the room. The madman was left to himself, and Reginald questioned Leon about him.

"I have heard all this before," said Leon. "He came home very queer, and before a week was this way. I put him in there to keep him out of mischief. I feed him myself. No one else goes near him. I've had a doctor up, but he could do nothing. He has often talked in this way about trapping some one, but he never mentioned any name till to-day. He never did—I swear he never did. I swear I had no idea that he had reference to my—to Lady Dudleigh. I thought it was some crazy fancy about Mr. Dalton—some scheme of his for 'trapping' him. I did—I swear."

Such was Leon's statement, extorted from him by the fiercest of cross-questionings on the part of Reginald, accompanied by most savage threats.

Leon, however, swore that he thought it referred to a scheme of his father's to "trap" Dalton, and shut him up in a mad-house. If it was true that no names had been mentioned, Reginald saw that it was quite possible that Leon might have supposed what he said, though his knowledge of his brother did not lead him to place any particular confidence in his statement, even when accompanied by an oath.

It now remained to find out, without delay, the place which the madman had revealed. Reginald remembered it well: *Dr. Morton, Lichfield Asylum, Lichfield, Berks.* Leon also said that the same name had been always mentioned. There could not, therefore, be any mistake about this, and it only remained to find out where it was.

Leon knew both the man and the place, and told all that he knew, not because he had a particle of affection for his mother, but because he wished to satisfy Reginald, so as to gain that freedom which his brother only could give him. He had been the intimate confidant of his father, and this Dr. Morton had been connected with them previously in another affair. He was therefore able to give explicit information about the place, and the quickest manner of reaching it.

Reginald set off that very day.

"It will be better for you to stay here," said he to Leon, as he was leaving, in a significant tone.

"Oh, I'll stay," said Leon. "If you act square, that's all I want. Give me those notes and bonds, and I'll never trouble you or yours again."

Before leaving he obtained from Leon further information about his first marriage with Miss Fortescue. This he communicated to Leon's wife, whom he found waiting for him in great suspense. As soon as she heard it she set out for London to find the witness mentioned by Leon; after which she intended to go to Falkirk in search of the clergyman.

After parting with Leon's wife, Reginald left by the first train, en route for Dr. Morton's asylum at Lichfield, in accordance with Leon's directions. On the middle of the following day he reached the place.

He came there accompanied by two officers of the law, who had a warrant for the arrest of Dr. Morton on a charge of conspiracy and illegal imprisonment. That distinguished physician came down to see his visitors, under the impression that one of them was a patient, and was very much surprised when he found himself under arrest. Still more surprised was he when Reginald asked him, fiercely, after Lady Dudleigh.

In a few moments the door of Lady Dudleigh's room was flung open, and the almost despairing inmate found herself in the arms of her son. She looked feeble and emaciated, though not so much so as Reginald had feared. She had known too much of the sorrows of life to yield altogether to this new calamity. Her chief grief had been about others, the fear that they might have become the prey of the villain who had shut her in here; but in spite of her terrible suspense, she struggled against the gloom of her situation, and tried to hope for release. It had come at last, and with it came also the news that there was no longer any need for her or for Reginald to take any proceedings against the guilty husband and father, since he had been struck down by a more powerful arm.

When they went away, Dr. Morton was taken away also. In due time he was tried on the charge above mentioned. He showed, however, that Lady Dudleigh had been put under his care by Sir Lionel himself, and in the usual way; that Sir Lionel had specified the nature of her insanity to consist in the belief that she was his wife, and that so long as she maintained that belief he thought her actually insane. He showed that, apart from that confinement which he had deemed requisite, she had been treated with no unnecessary cruelty. Many other things he contrived also showed, by means of which he contrived to obtain an acquittal. Still, so much came out in the course of the trial, and so very narrow was his escape, and so strong was his fear of being re-arrested on other charges, that he concluded to emigrate to another country, and this he did without delay.

But Reginald returned at once with his mother to Dudleigh Manor. Here Lady Dudleigh for a few days sank under the effects of the accumulated troubles through which she had passed, and when at length she was able to move about, Sir Lionel was the first one of whom she thought, and she at once devoted herself to him. But the wretched man was already beyond the reach of her care. His strength was failing rapidly; he refused all nourishment; his mind was a hopeless wreck; he recognized no one; and all that was now left to the wife to do was to watch over him and nurse him as patiently as possible until the end, which she knew must be near.

In the excitement consequent upon his first return, his interviews with Leon and Sir Lionel, his rescue of Lady Dudleigh, and his deep anxiety about her after her release, Reginald had sent no word to Edith of any kind. This arose neither from neglect nor forgetfulness, but because his surroundings were too sad, and he had not the heart to write to her until some brighter prospect should appear. His mother's short illness at first alarmed him; but this passed away, and on her recovery he felt sufficiently cheerful to send to Edith an account of all that had occurred.

Ten days had passed since he parted with her. On the day after he wrote to her he received a letter from her. It was the first communication that he had received.

That letter conveyed to him awful intelligence. It informed him of the arrest of Edith and Frederick Dalton.

CHAPTER LV.
CONCLUSION.

THIS intelligence was so terrible and so unexpected that for some time he felt overwhelmed with utter horror. Then a dark suspicion came to him that this was the work of Leon, who, enraged at his baffled schemes, had dealt this last blow upon those whom he had already so deeply wronged. This suspicion roused the utmost fury of Reginald's nature, and he hurried forth at once to seek his brother.

He found him sauntering up and down in front of the house. Leon had remained here ever since his interview with Reginald, in accordance with his promise. As he now saw his brother approach, he started, and looked at him with an expression of astonishment not unmingled with terror.

Without any preliminaries, Reginald at once assailed him with the most vehement denunciations, and in a few burning words, full of abhorrence and wrath, he accused him of this new piece of villainy.

"You're wrong—you're wrong—you're altogether wrong!" cried Leon, eagerly. "I have done nothing—I swear I've done nothing! I've never left the place."

"You've sent word!" cried Reginald, furiously.

"I have not—I swear I haven't!" said Leon. "I haven't written a line to any one. I've had no communication whatever with a single soul."

"It's your work, and yours only!" cried

Reginald; "and, by Heaven, you shall suffer for it! You've broken the agreement between us, and now I'll show you no mercy!"

"I haven't broken it! I swear by all that's most holy!" cried Leon, earnestly. "I see how it is. This is merely the result of the old rumors—the old work going on. I swear it is! Besides, what danger can happen to Miss Dalton? I need only show myself. I'll go there with you at once. Can I do more than that? When I am seen alive, there is no more danger for her. Do you think I'd be such an infernal fool as to work out such a piece of spite, which I would know to be utterly useless? No. I only want to wind up the whole affair, and get my freedom. I'll go there with you or without you, and make it all right so far as she is concerned. There. Can I do any thing more?"

These words mollified Reginald in some degree, since they showed that, after all, this new trouble might, as Leon said, have arisen from old machinations, as their natural result, and did not necessarily involve any new action on Leon's part.

"I'll go," said Reginald, "and you shall go with me; but if I find that you have played me false this time, by Heaven, I'll crush you!"

Reginald, accompanied by Leon, hurried off at once to the succor of Edith, and arrived there on the following day. It was the fifth day of their imprisonment, but, to Reginald's immense relief, this new misfortune did not seem to have affected either of them so painfully as he had feared. For to Edith imprisonment was familiar now, and this time she had the discovery of Miss Fortescue to console her. Besides, she had her father to think of and to care for. The kindness of the authorities had allowed the two to be together as much as possible; and Edith, in the endeavor to console her father, had forced herself to look on the brighter side of things, and to hope for the best.

Dalton, too, had borne this arrest with equanimity. After the first shock was past he thought over all that was most favorable to escape rather than the gloomier surroundings of a situation like his. For himself he cared nothing. To be brought once more before a court of law was desirable rather than otherwise. His arrangements for his own vindication were all complete, and he knew that the court could only acquit him with honor. But about Edith he felt an anxiety which was deeper than he cared to show, for he did not know how the evidence against her would be received.

The arrival of Reginald, however, drove away every fear. He brought the missing man himself. All was now explained. The news ran through the community like wildfire, and public opinion, which had so se-

verely prejudged Edith, now turned around with a flood of universal sympathy in her favor. Some formalities had to be undergone, and then she was free.

The circumstances that had brought to light Edith's innocence served also to make known the innocence, the wrongs, and the sufferings of the father. The whole story of Dalton was made public through the exertions of Reginald, and society, which had once condemned him, now sought to vindicate him. But the work of vindication had to be done elsewhere, and in a more formal manner. Until then Dalton had to wait; yet this much of benefit he received from public sympathy, that he was allowed to go free and live at Dalton Hall until the law should finally decide his fate.

Long before that decision Sir Lionel passed away from the judgment of man to answer for his crimes at a higher tribunal. He passed away in his madness, unconscious of the presence of that wife whom he had doomed to exile, and who now, his only attendant, sought to soothe the madman's last moments. But the measures that were taken to vindicate Dalton were successful. Lady Dudleigh and Reginald could give their evidence in his favor without the fear of dealing out death to one so near as Sir Lionel. Death had already come to him, sent by a mightier power, and Dalton's vindication involved no new anguish. So it was that Frederick Dalton was at length cleared of that guilt that had so long clung to him; and if any thing could atone for his past sufferings, it was the restoration of his name to its ancient honor, the public expression of sympathy from the court and from the world, and the deep joy of Edith over such a termination to his sorrows.

But this was a work of time. Before this Reginald and Edith were married. They lived at Dudleigh Manor, for the associations of Dalton Hall were too painful, and Edith did not care to make a home in her old prison-house. To her father, too, the Hall was distasteful as a residence, and he made his abode with his daughter, who was now the only one on earth in whom he took any interest. But Dalton Hall was not untenanted. Lady Dudleigh lived there in the old home of her childhood, and passed her time in works of charity. She made an effort to reclaim Leon, and succeeded in keeping him with her for a few weeks; but the quiet life soon proved intolerable, and he wandered away at length to other scenes.

Reginald had dealt faithfully and even generously by him. After all his crimes and villainies, he could not forget that he was his brother, and he had done all in his power to renew his life for him. He had given him all the claims which he had collected, and thus had freed him from debt. He had also given him money enough to enable him to start afresh in life. But the money was soon gone, and the habits which Leon had formed made any change for the better impossible. He wandered away into his former associations and became a miserable vagabond, constantly sinking down deep into misery, to be saved for a time by his mother's assistance, but only to sink once more.

Mention must be made of two others before this story closes.

One of these is Leon's wife. She went away from Dudleigh Manor to Scotland in search of the clergyman who had married her. She succeeded in finding him, and in obtaining from him a formal certificate of her marriage. This, however, was not for the purpose of acquiring any hold whatever upon Leon, but rather for the sake of her own honor, and also out of regard for Edith,

whom she wished to free from the last shadow of that evil which her own deceit had thrown upon the innocent girl. After this she was satisfied. She did not seek Leon again, nor did she ever again see him. She retired from the world altogether, and joining a sisterhood of mercy, devoted the remainder of her life to acts of charity and humanity.

Last of all remains Miss Plympton, with whom this story began, and with whom it may end. That good lady recovered from the illness into which she had fallen on account of her anxiety about Edith, and was able to visit her not long after her release from her last imprisonment. She had given up her school; and as she had no home, she yielded to Edith's affectionate entreaties, and found a new home with her, where she passed the remainder of her days.

THE END.

www.ingramcontent.com/pod-product-compliance
Lightning Source LLC
Chambersburg PA
CBHW020547270326
41927CB00006B/749